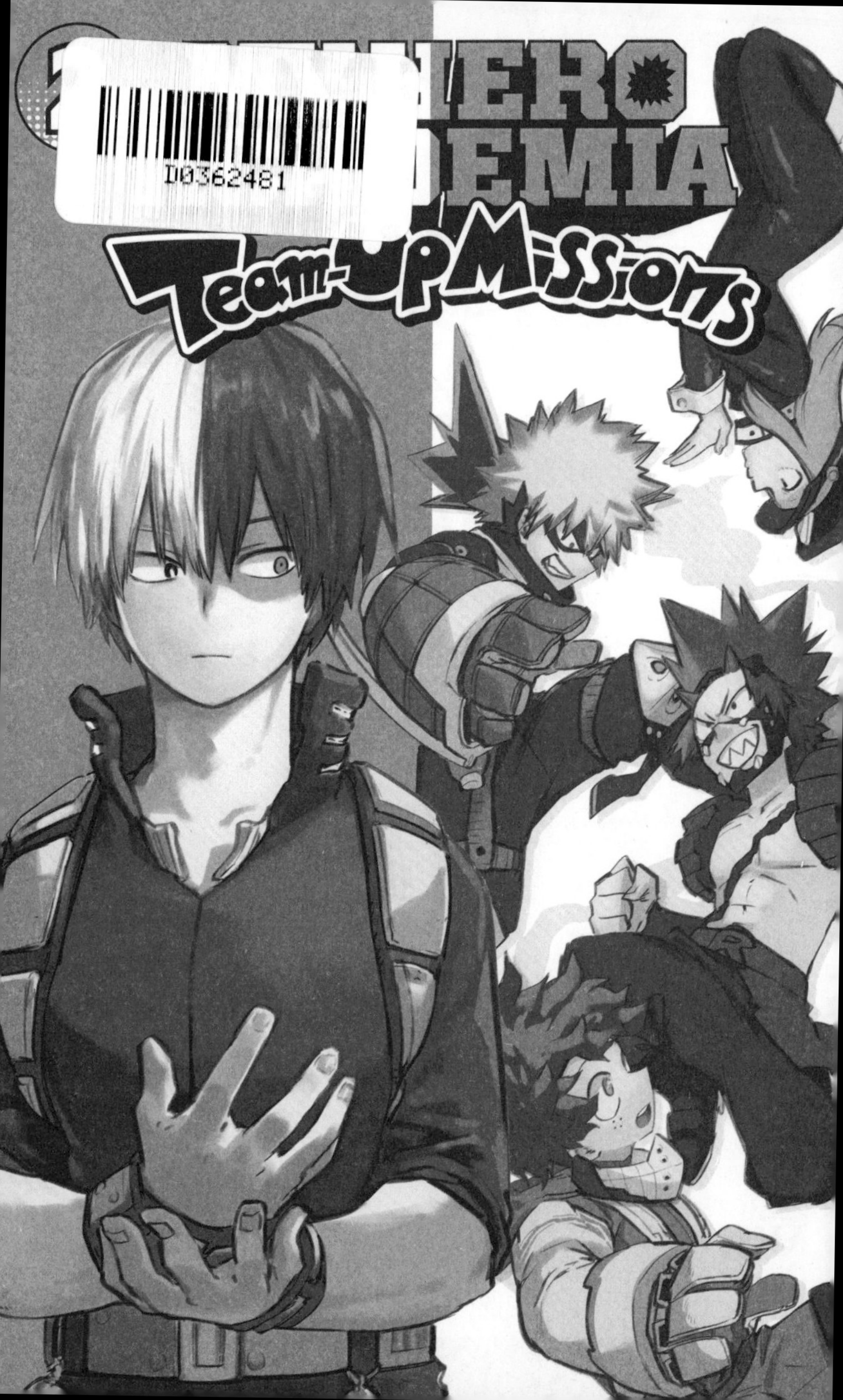
HERO
EMIA
Team-Up Missions

SHONEN JUMP Manga Edition

STORY & ART BY
YOKO AKIYAMA

ORIGINAL CONCEPT BY
KOHEI HORIKOSHI

TRANSLATION **Caleb Cook**
TOUCH-UP ART & LETTERING **John Hunt**
DESIGNER **Julian [JR] Robinson**
EDITOR **Hope Donovan**

BOKU NO HERO ACADEMIA TEAM UP MISSION © 2019
by Kohei Horikoshi, Yoko Akiyama
All rights reserved.
First published in Japan in 2019 by SHUEISHA Inc., Tokyo.
English translation rights arranged by SHUEISHA Inc.

The stories, characters, and incidents mentioned in this
publication are entirely fictional.

Printed in Italy

Published by VIZ Media, LLC
P.O. Box 77010
San Francisco, CA 94107

10 9 8 7 6 5 4 3 2
First printing, January 2022
Second printing, January 2022

PARENTAL ADVISORY
MY HERO ACADEMIA: TEAM-UP MISSIONS
is rated T for Teen and is recommended
for ages 13 and up. This volume contains
fantasy violence.

MY HERO ACADEMIA Team-Up Missions 2

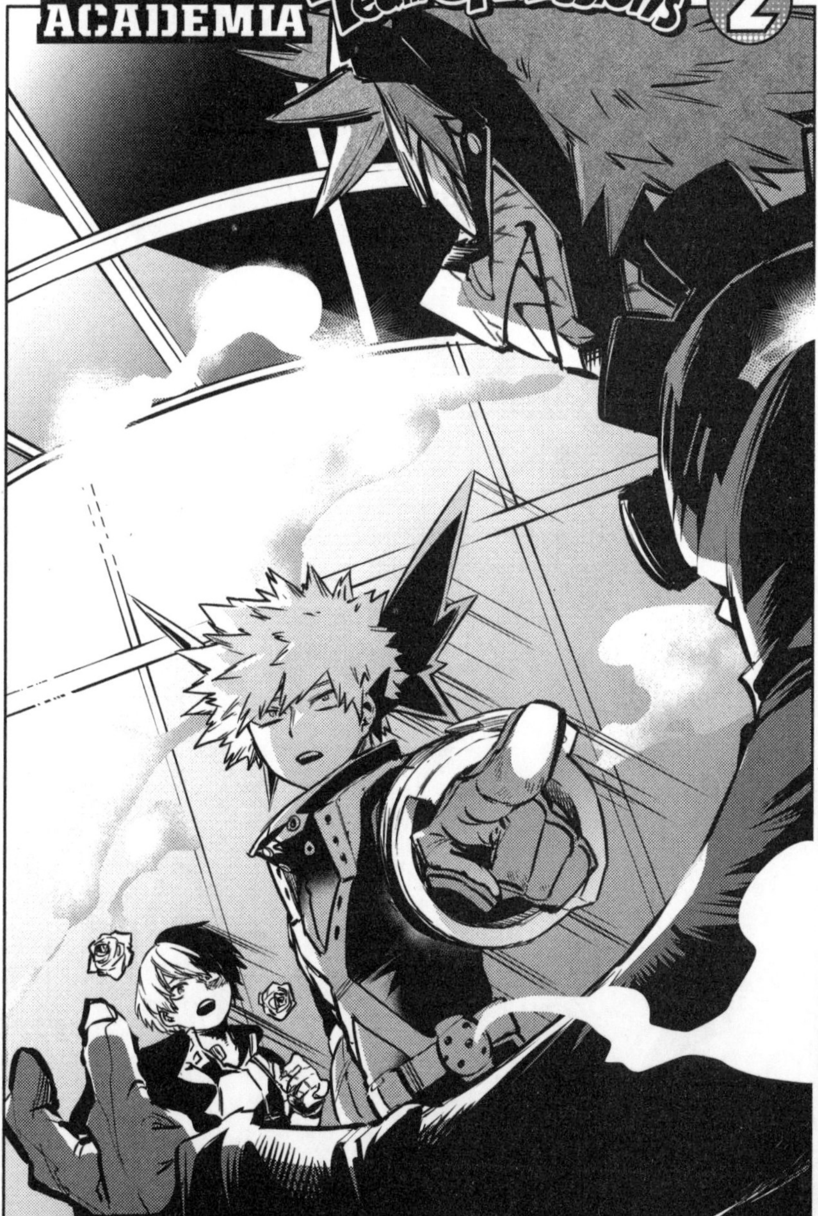
Todoroki

STORY & ART BY
YOKO AKIYAMA

ORIGINAL CONCEPT BY
KOHEI HORIKOSHI

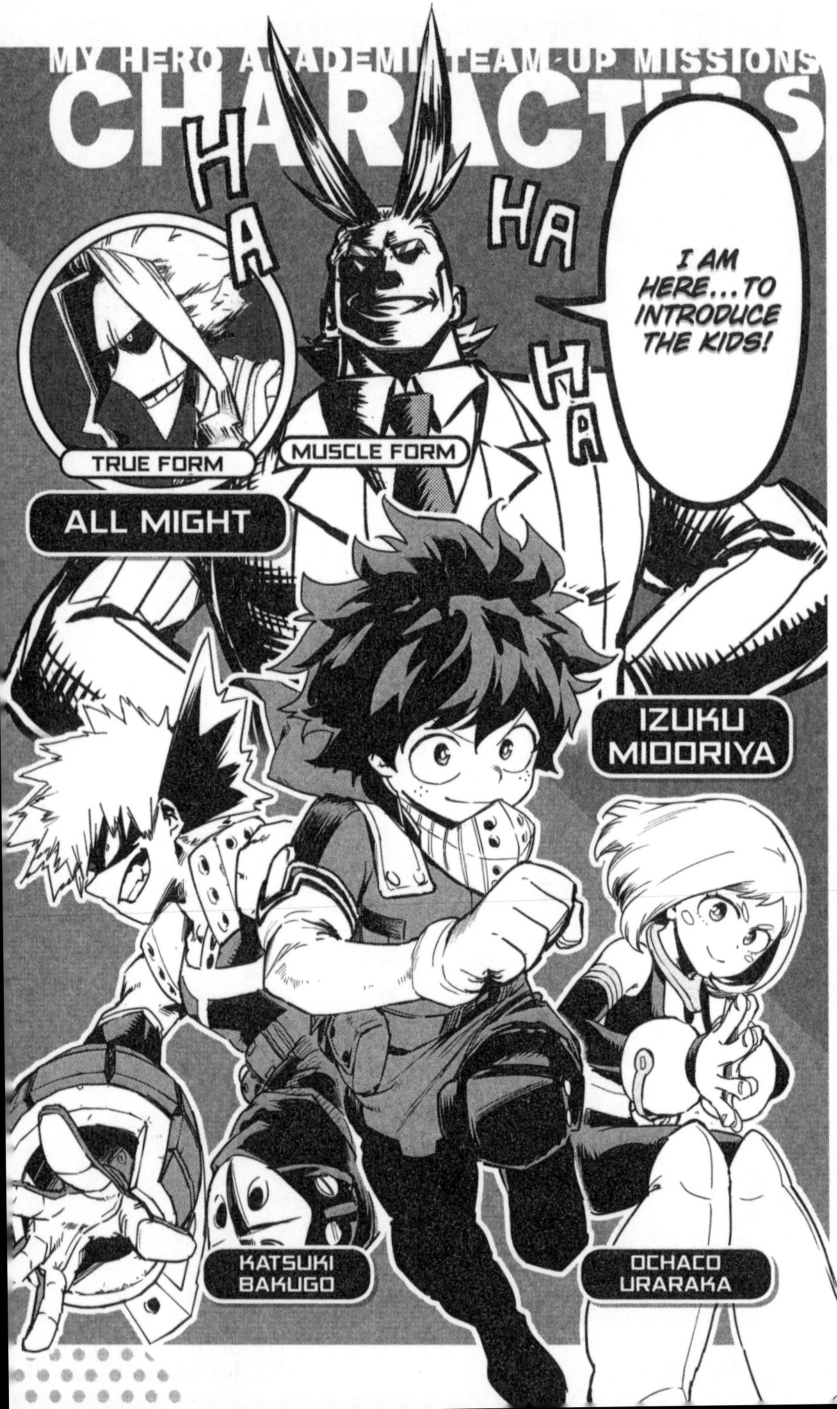
MY HERO ACADEMIA TEAM-UP MISSIONS
CHARACTERS
I AM HERE...TO INTRODUCE THE KIDS!
HA HA HA HA
MUSCLE FORM
TRUE FORM
ALL MIGHT
IZUKU MIDORIYA
OCHACO URARAKA
KATSUKI BAKUGO

STORY

MY HERO ACADEMIA

One day, people began manifesting special abilities that came to be known as "Quirks," and before long, the world was full of superpowered humans. The world then saw an uptick in crime, perpetrated by villains armed with new abilities. Heroes emerged to protect society and are now officially authorized to fight crime in the name of peace.

WHAT'S A TEAM-UP MISSION?

For many years, All Might was known as "the Symbol of Peace," and his mere presence was enough to deter crime. With his retirement from public duty, people are clamoring for the next generation of heroes to rise up, which has led to the creation of a new program—centered around hero students—called Team-Up Missions. By pairing schools all over the country with pro heroes, these heroes in training get a chance to improve their teamwork!

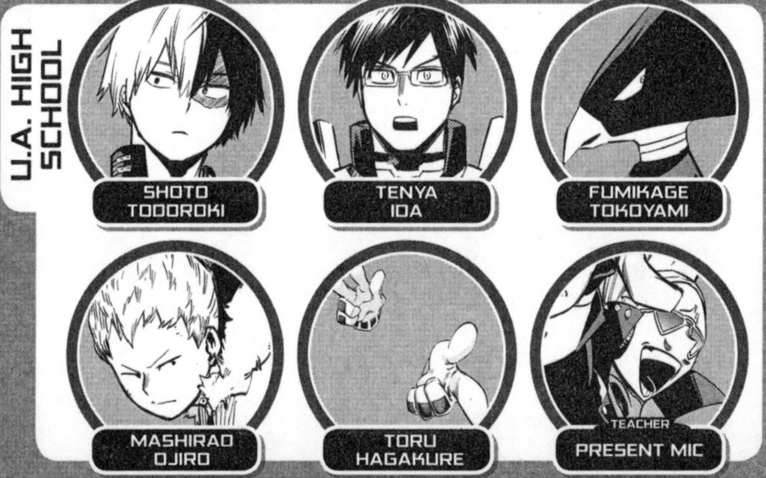
U.A. HIGH SCHOOL
SHOTO TODOROKI
TENYA IDA
FUMIKAGE TOKOYAMI
MASHIRAO OJIRO
TORU HAGAKURE
TEACHER
PRESENT MIC

AND MANY MORE!

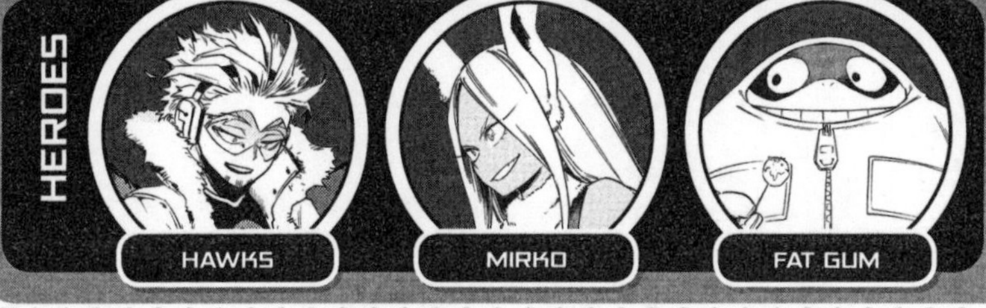
HEROES
HAWKS
MIRKO
FAT GUM

MY HERO ACADEMIA 2
Team-Up Missions

CONTENTS

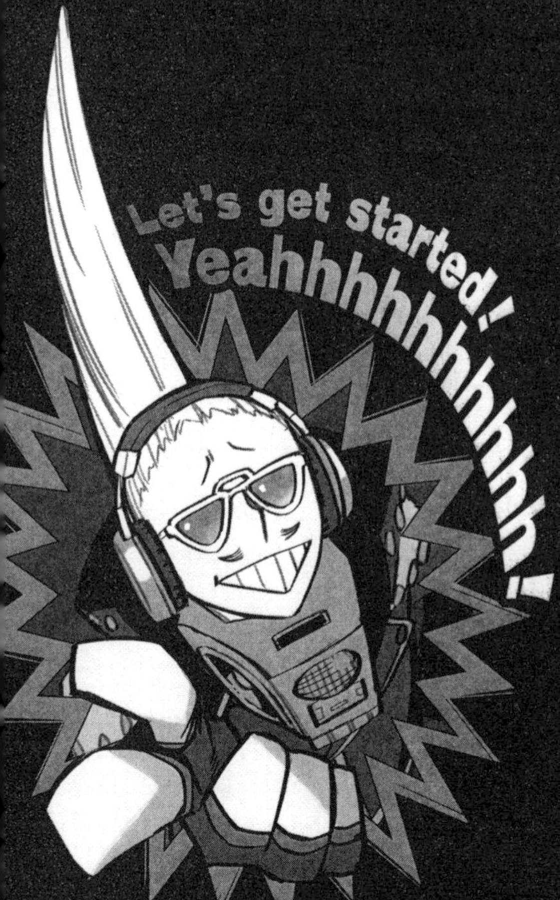
Let's get started! Yeahhhhhhhhhh!

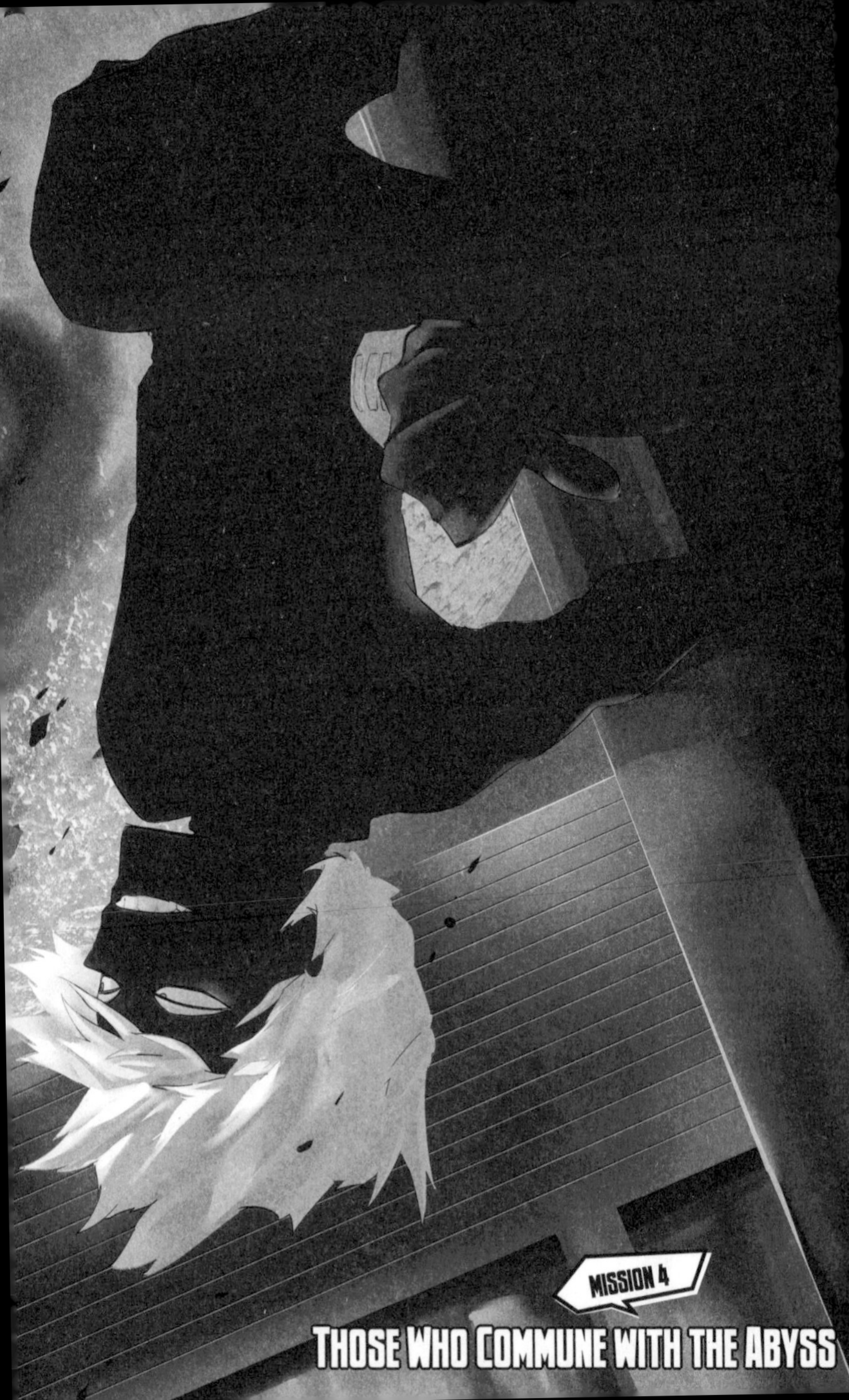
MISSION 4
THOSE WHO COMMUNE WITH THE ABYSS

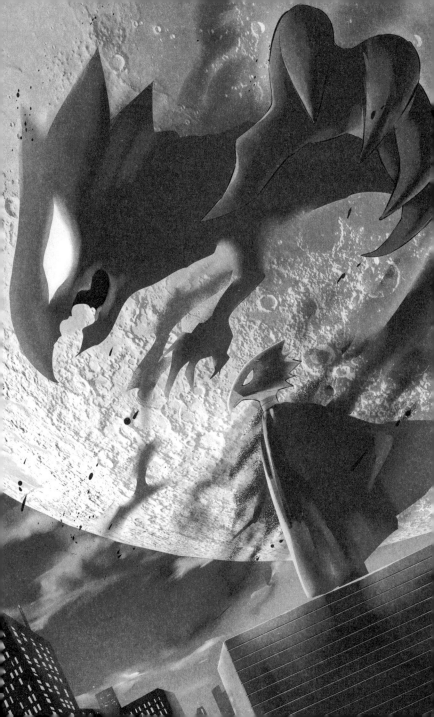

MY HERO ACADEMIA
Team-Up Missions

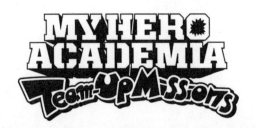

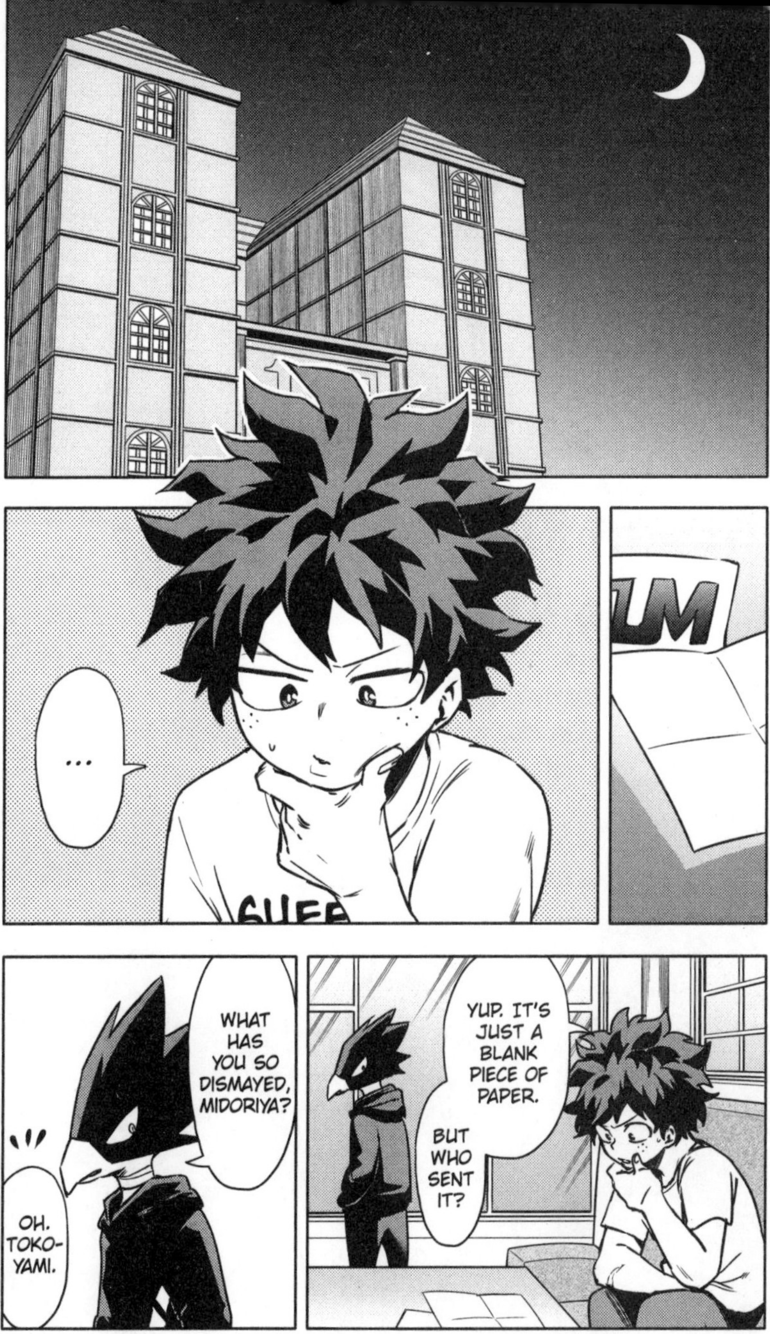
...
YUP. IT'S JUST A BLANK PIECE OF PAPER.
BUT WHO SENT IT?
WHAT HAS YOU SO DISMAYED, MIDORIYA?
OH. TOKO-YAMI.

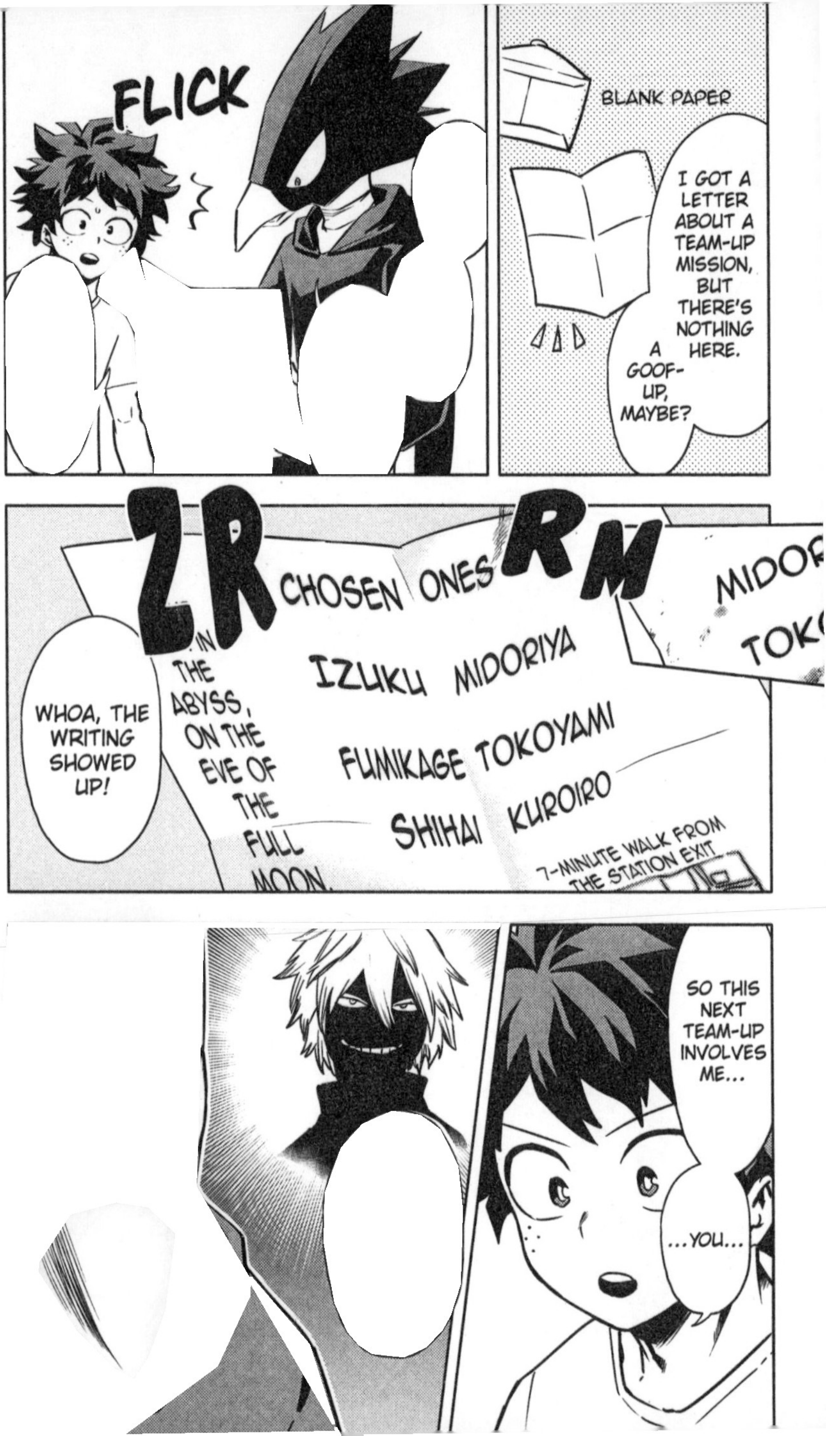
BLANK PAPER
I GOT A LETTER ABOUT A TEAM-UP MISSION, BUT THERE'S NOTHING HERE.
A GOOF-UP, MAYBE?
FLICK
ZRRM
CHOSEN ONES
IN THE ABYSS, ON THE EVE OF THE FULL MOON,
IZUKU MIDORIYA
FUMIKAGE TOKOYAMI
SHIHAI KUROIRO
7-MINUTE WALK FROM THE STATION EXIT
WHOA, THE WRITING SHOWED UP!
SO THIS NEXT TEAM-UP INVOLVES ME...
...YOU...

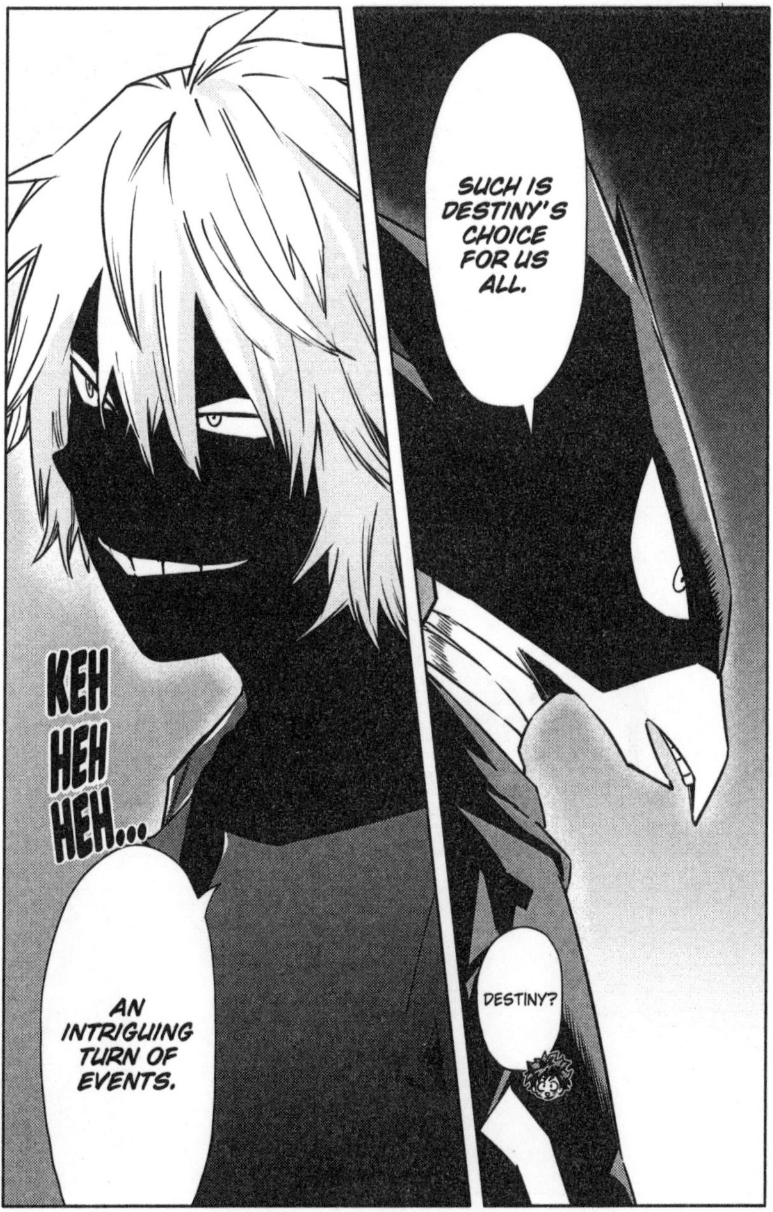
SUCH IS DESTINY'S CHOICE FOR US ALL.
DESTINY?
KEH HEH HEH...
AN INTRIGUING TURN OF EVENTS.

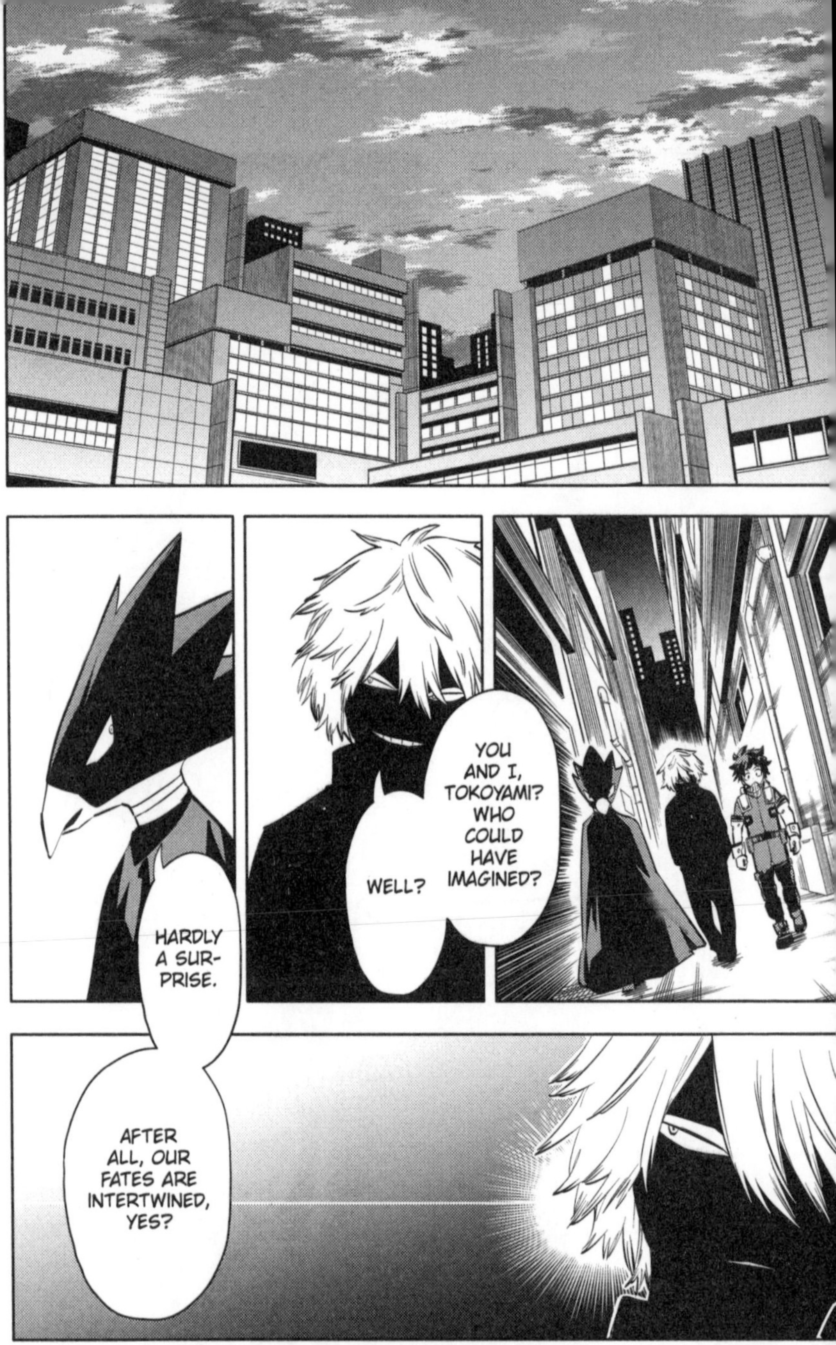
YOU AND I, TOKOYAMI? WHO COULD HAVE IMAGINED?
WELL?
HARDLY A SUR-PRISE.
AFTER ALL, OUR FATES ARE INTERTWINED, YES?

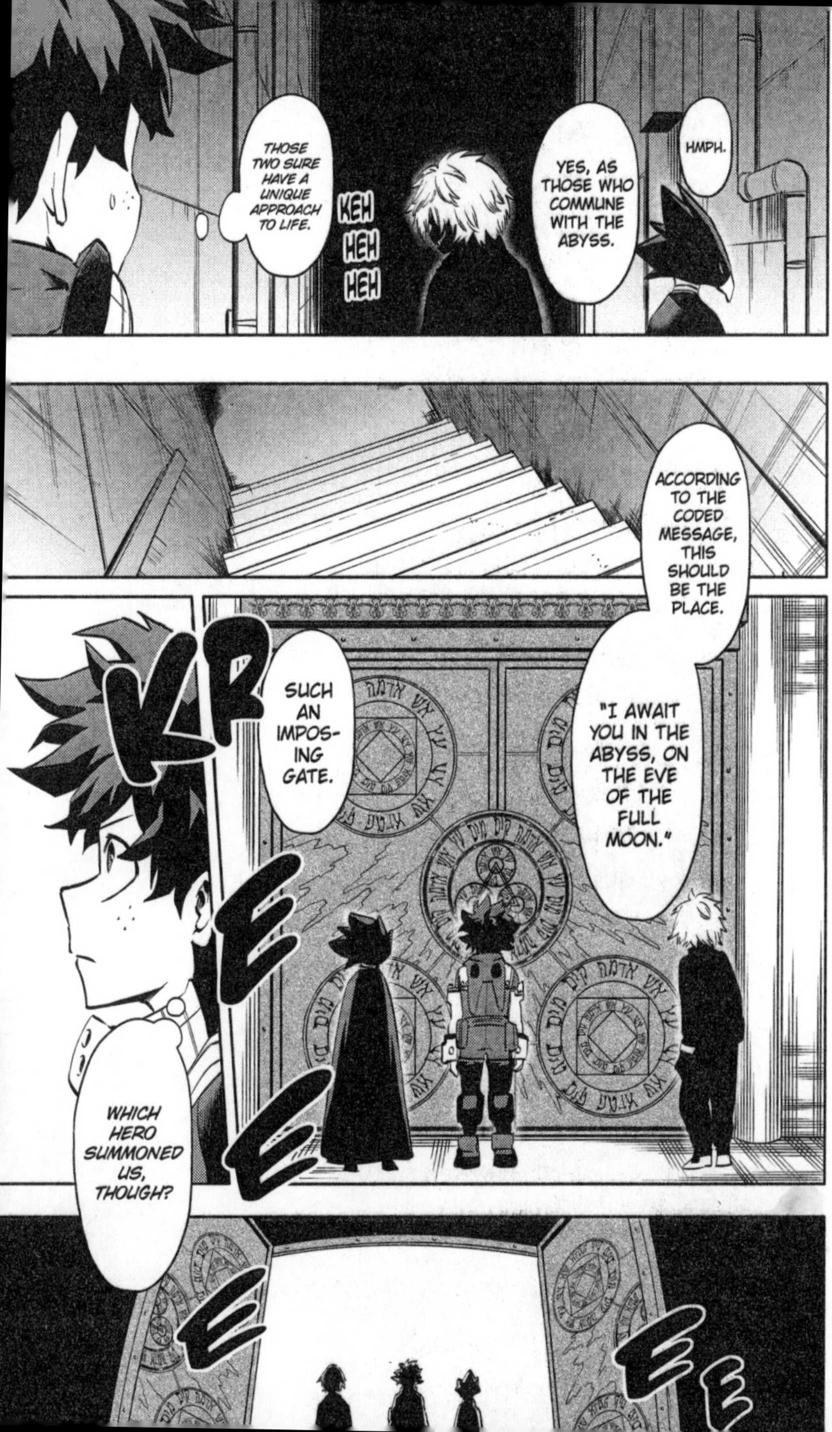
HMPH.
YES, AS THOSE WHO COMMUNE WITH THE ABYSS.
KEH HEH HEH
THOSE TWO SURE HAVE A UNIQUE APPROACH TO LIFE.
ACCORDING TO THE CODED MESSAGE, THIS SHOULD BE THE PLACE.
"I AWAIT YOU IN THE ABYSS, ON THE EVE OF THE FULL MOON."
SUCH AN IMPOSING GATE.
WHICH HERO SUMMONED US, THOUGH?
KREEEEE

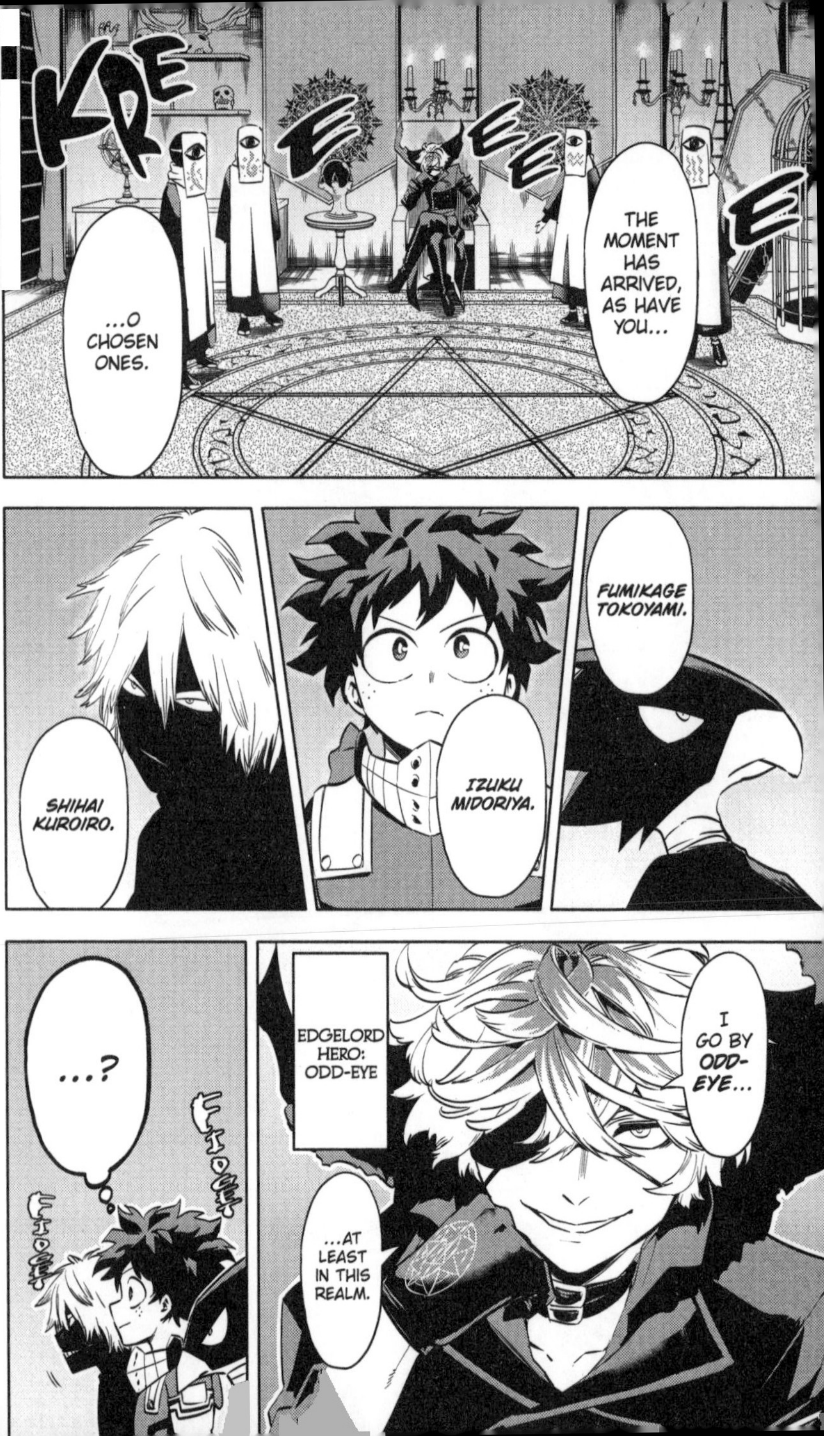
KREEEEEE
THE MOMENT HAS ARRIVED, AS HAVE YOU...
...O CHOSEN ONES.
FUMIKAGE TOKOYAMI.
IZUKU MIDORIYA.
SHIHAI KUROIRO.
I GO BY ODD-EYE...
EDGELORD HERO: ODD-EYE
...AT LEAST IN THIS REALM.
...?

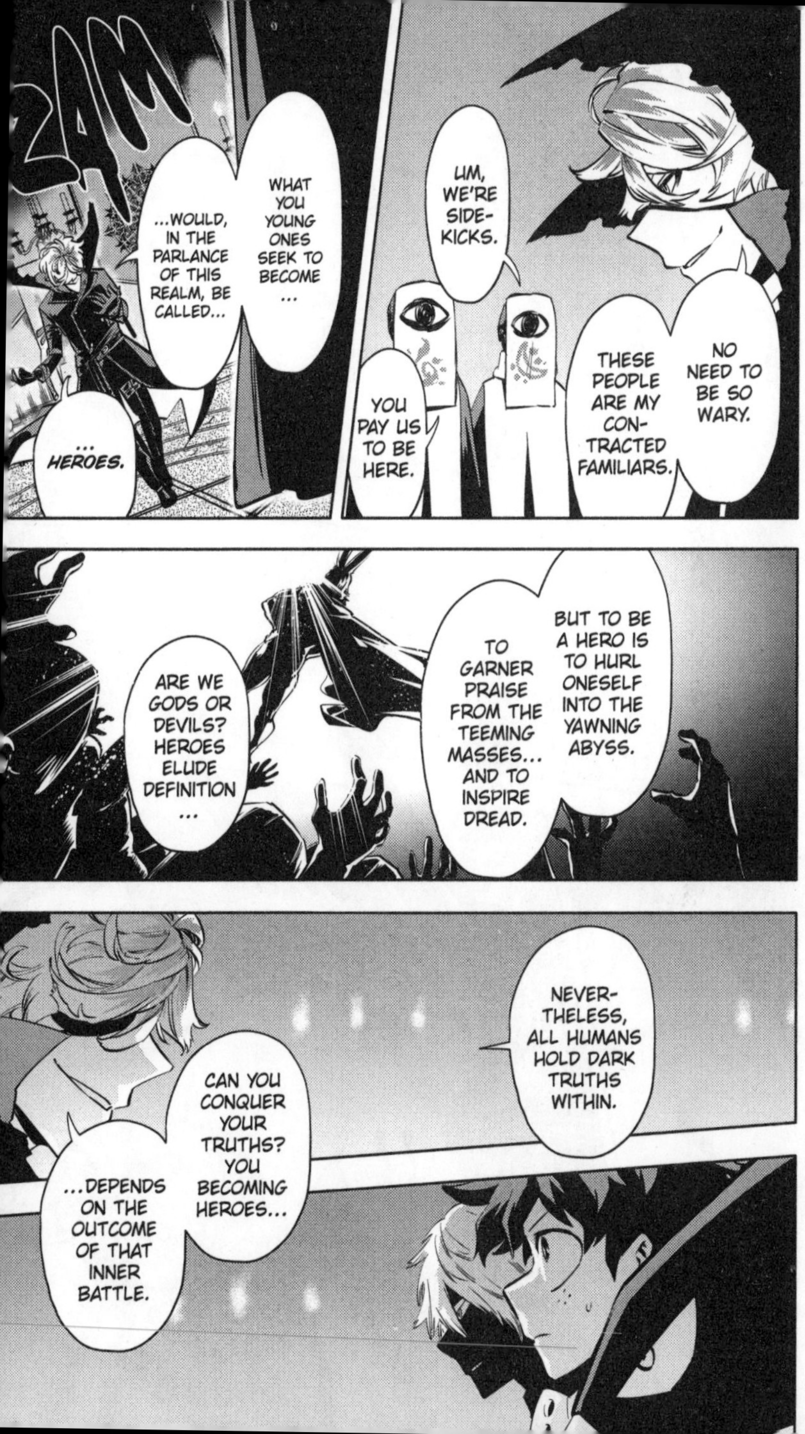
NO NEED TO BE SO WARY.
THESE PEOPLE ARE MY CONTRACTED FAMILIARS.
UM, WE'RE SIDEKICKS.
YOU PAY US TO BE HERE.
ZAM
WHAT YOU YOUNG ONES SEEK TO BECOME ...
...WOULD, IN THE PARLANCE OF THIS REALM, BE CALLED...
... HEROES.
BUT TO BE A HERO IS TO HURL ONESELF INTO THE YAWNING ABYSS.
TO GARNER PRAISE FROM THE TEEMING MASSES... AND TO INSPIRE DREAD.
ARE WE GODS OR DEVILS? HEROES ELUDE DEFINITION ...
NEVERTHELESS, ALL HUMANS HOLD DARK TRUTHS WITHIN.
CAN YOU CONQUER YOUR TRUTHS? YOU BECOMING HEROES...
...DEPENDS ON THE OUTCOME OF THAT INNER BATTLE.

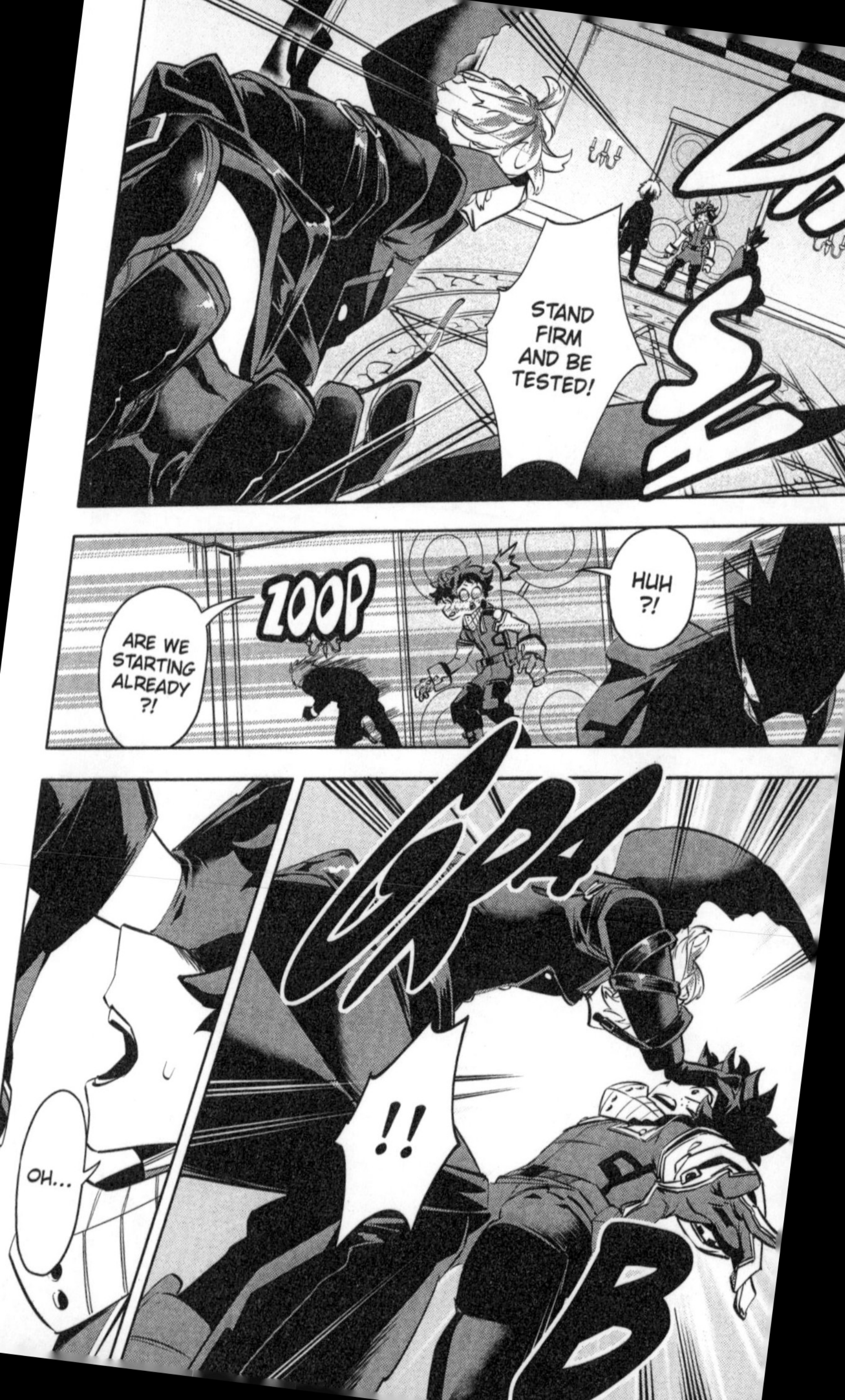
STAND FIRM AND BE TESTED!
HUH ?!
ZOOP
ARE WE STARTING ALREADY ?!
!!
OH...

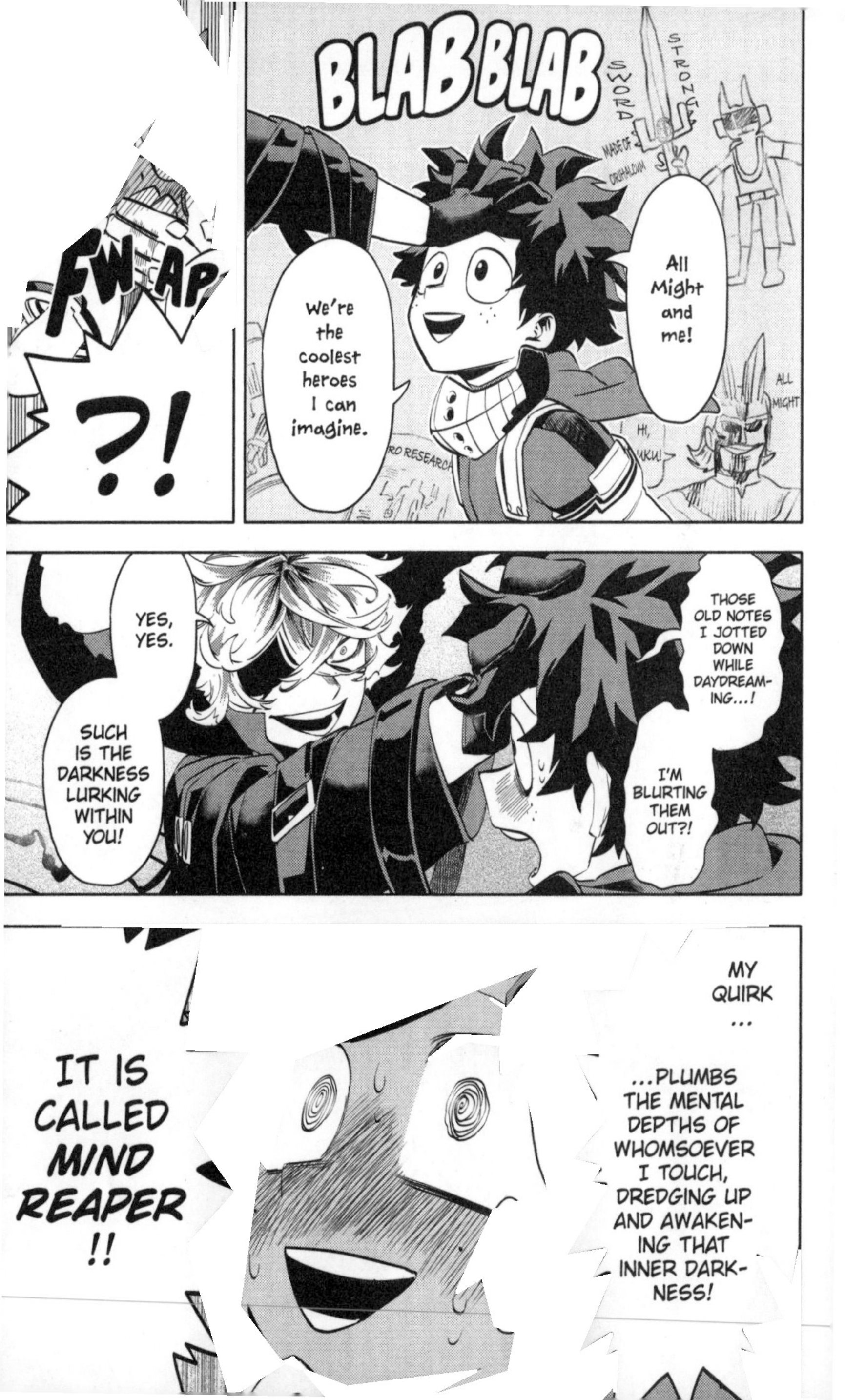
BLAB BLAB
STRONG
SWORD
ALL MIGHT
All Might and me!
We're the coolest heroes I can imagine.
FWAP
?!
THOSE OLD NOTES I JOTTED DOWN WHILE DAYDREAM-ING...!
I'M BLURTING THEM OUT?!
YES, YES.
SUCH IS THE DARKNESS LURKING WITHIN YOU!
MY QUIRK...
...PLUMBS THE MENTAL DEPTHS OF WHOMSOEVER I TOUCH, DREDGING UP AND AWAKEN-ING THAT INNER DARK-NESS!
IT IS CALLED *MIND REAPER*!!

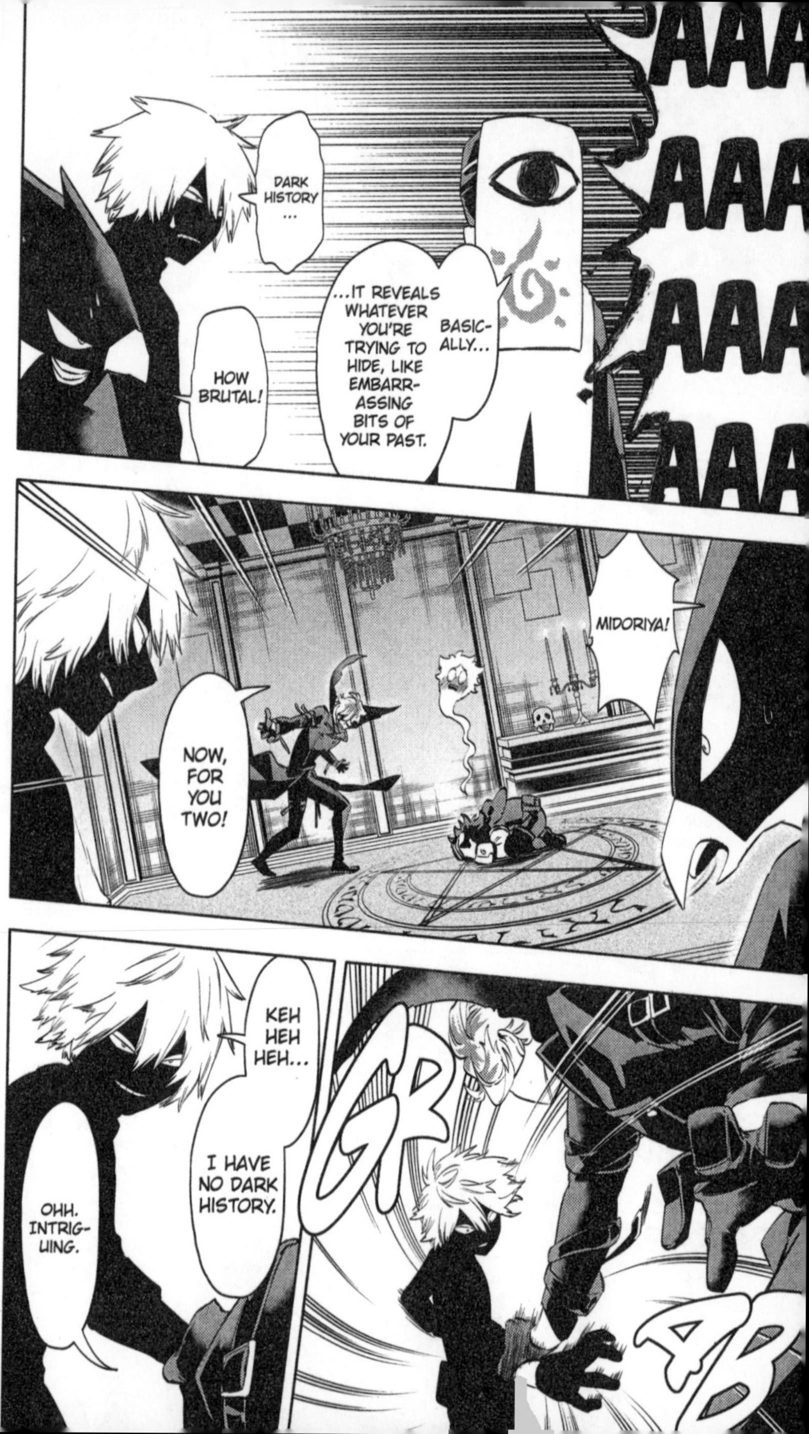
AAA
AAA
AAA
AAA
BASIC-ALLY...
...IT REVEALS WHATEVER YOU'RE TRYING TO HIDE, LIKE EMBARR-ASSING BITS OF YOUR PAST.
DARK HISTORY ...
HOW BRUTAL!
MIDORIYA!
NOW, FOR YOU TWO!
KEH HEH HEH...
I HAVE NO DARK HISTORY.
GR
OHH. INTRIG-UING.

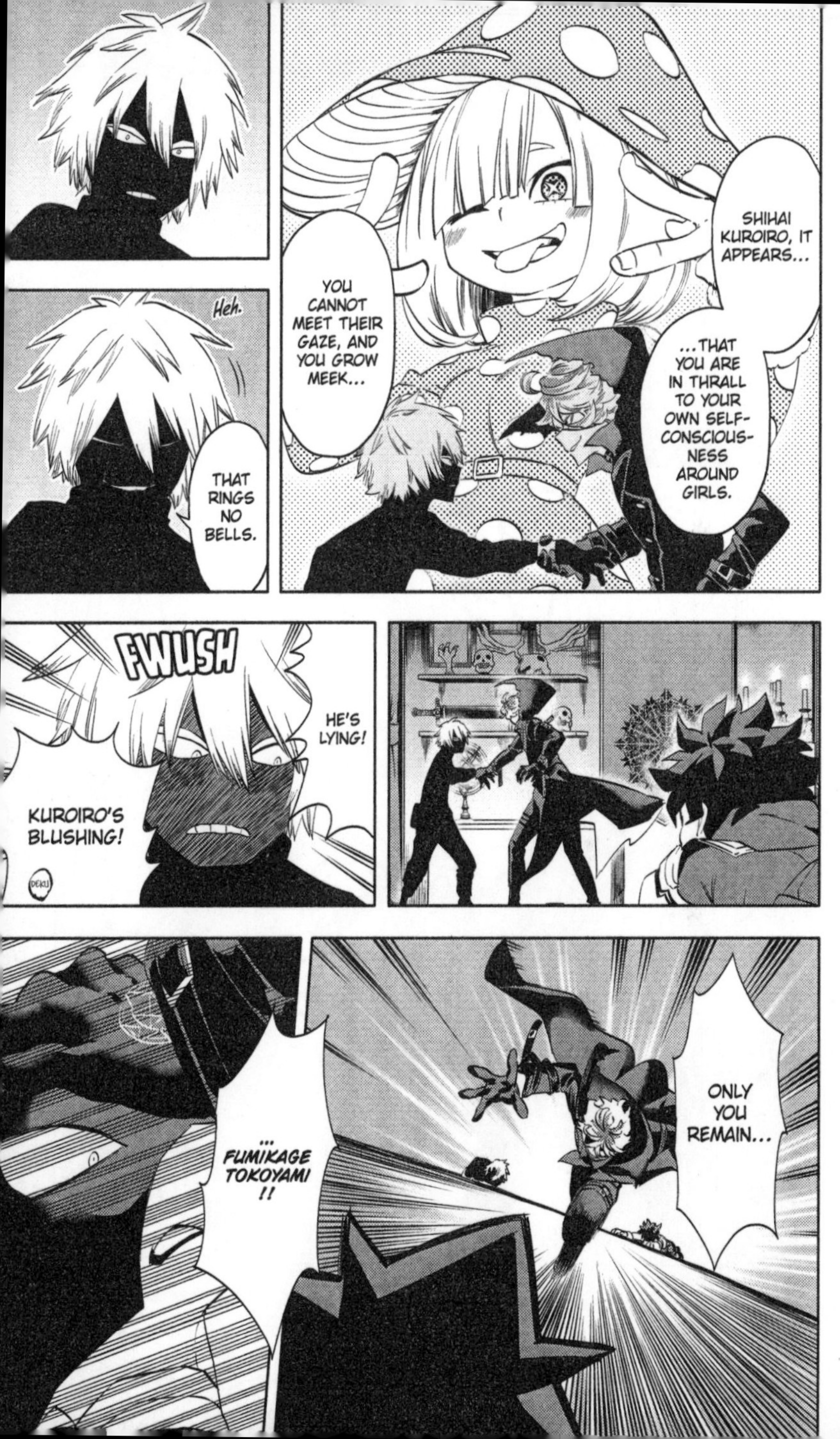
SHIHAI KUROIRO, IT APPEARS...
...THAT YOU ARE IN THRALL TO YOUR OWN SELF-CONSCIOUSNESS AROUND GIRLS.
YOU CANNOT MEET THEIR GAZE, AND YOU GROW MEEK...
Heh.
THAT RINGS NO BELLS.
FWUSH
HE'S LYING!
KUROIRO'S BLUSHING!
DEKU
ONLY YOU REMAIN...
...FUMIKAGE TOKOYAMI!!

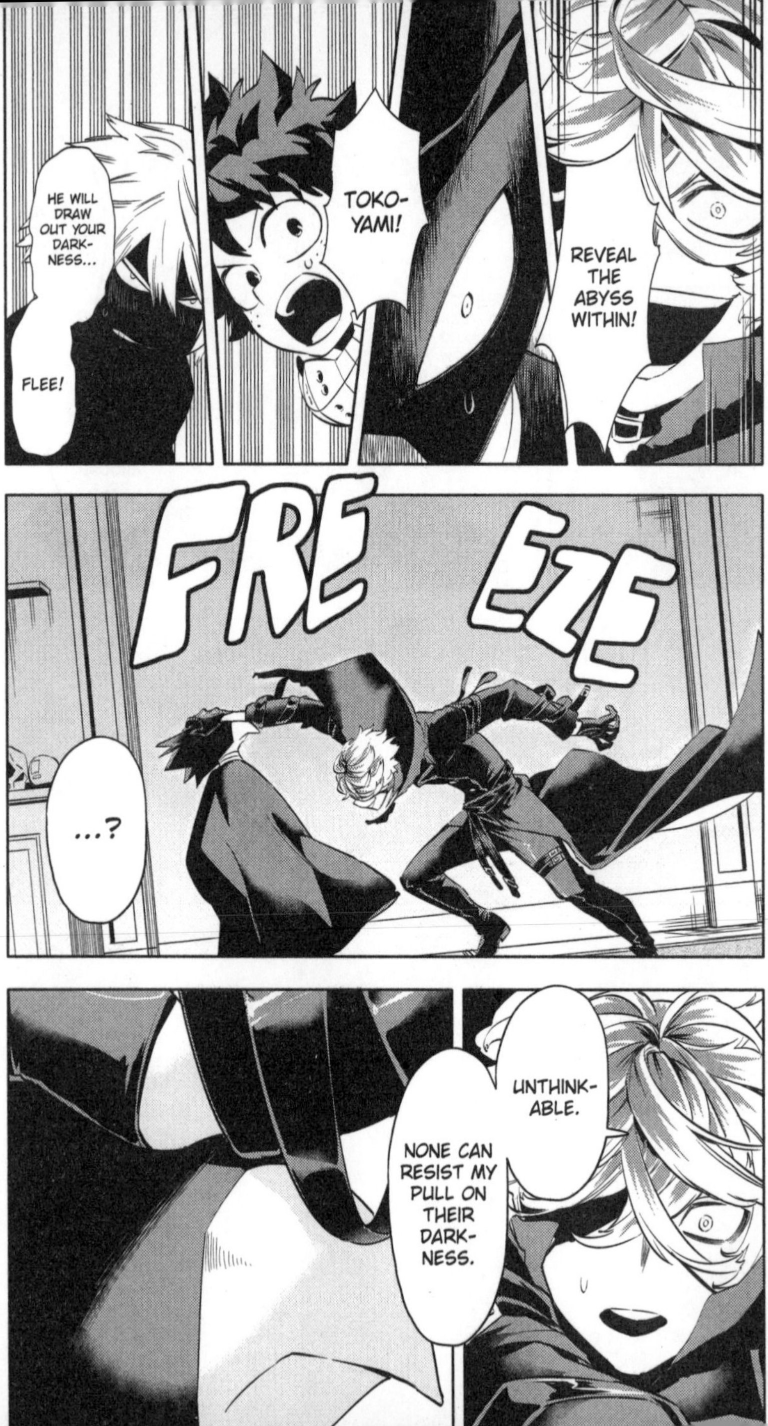
REVEAL THE ABYSS WITHIN!
TOKO-YAMI!
HE WILL DRAW OUT YOUR DARK-NESS...
FLEE!
FRE EZE
...?
UNTHINK-ABLE.
NONE CAN RESIST MY PULL ON THEIR DARK-NESS.

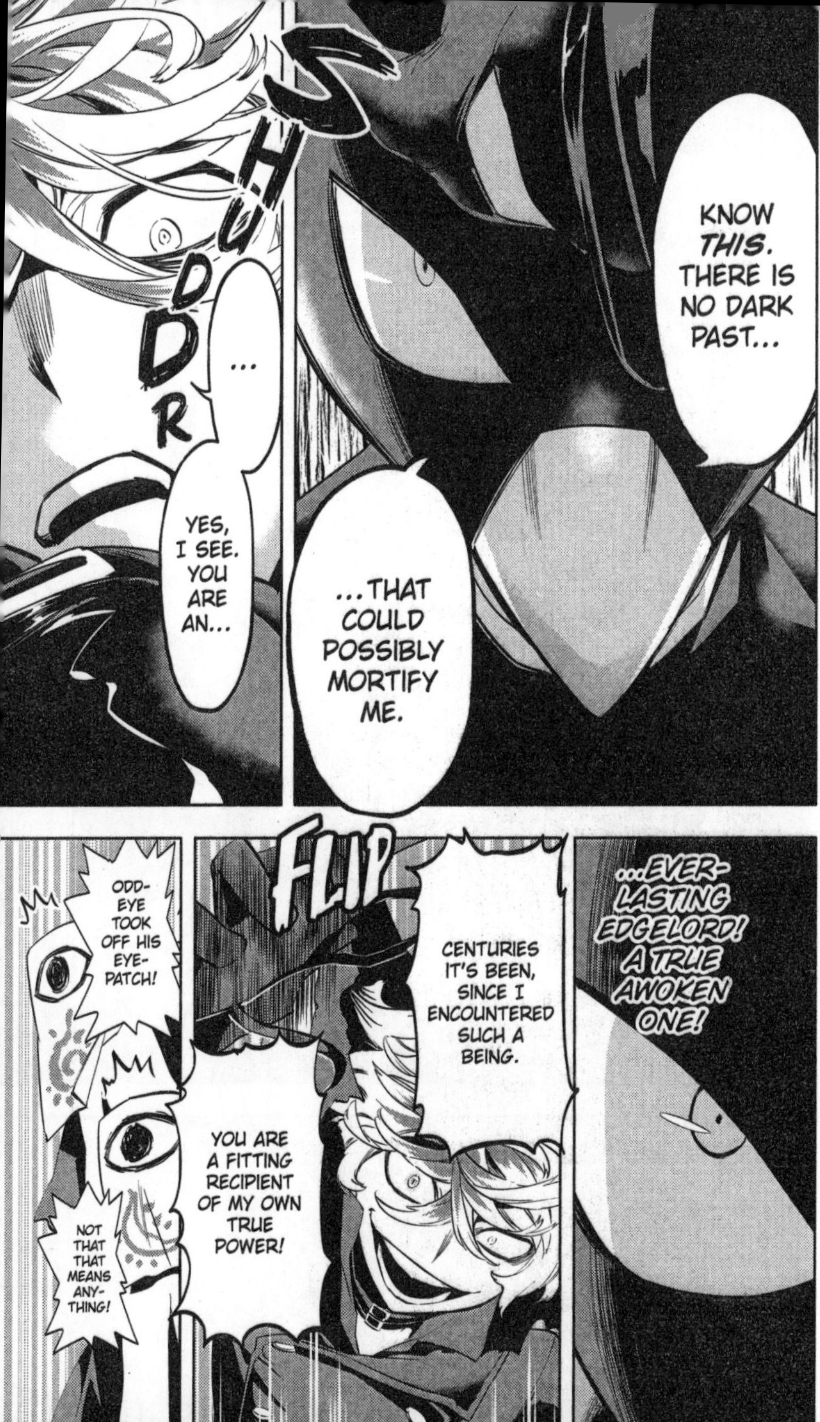
KNOW THIS. THERE IS NO DARK PAST...
...THAT COULD POSSIBLY MORTIFY ME.
SHUDDR
...
YES, I SEE. YOU ARE AN...
...EVER-LASTING EDGELORD! A TRUE AWOKEN ONE!
FLIP
CENTURIES IT'S BEEN, SINCE I ENCOUNTERED SUCH A BEING.
YOU ARE A FITTING RECIPIENT OF MY OWN TRUE POWER!
ODD-EYE TOOK OFF HIS EYE-PATCH!
NOT THAT THAT MEANS ANY-THING!

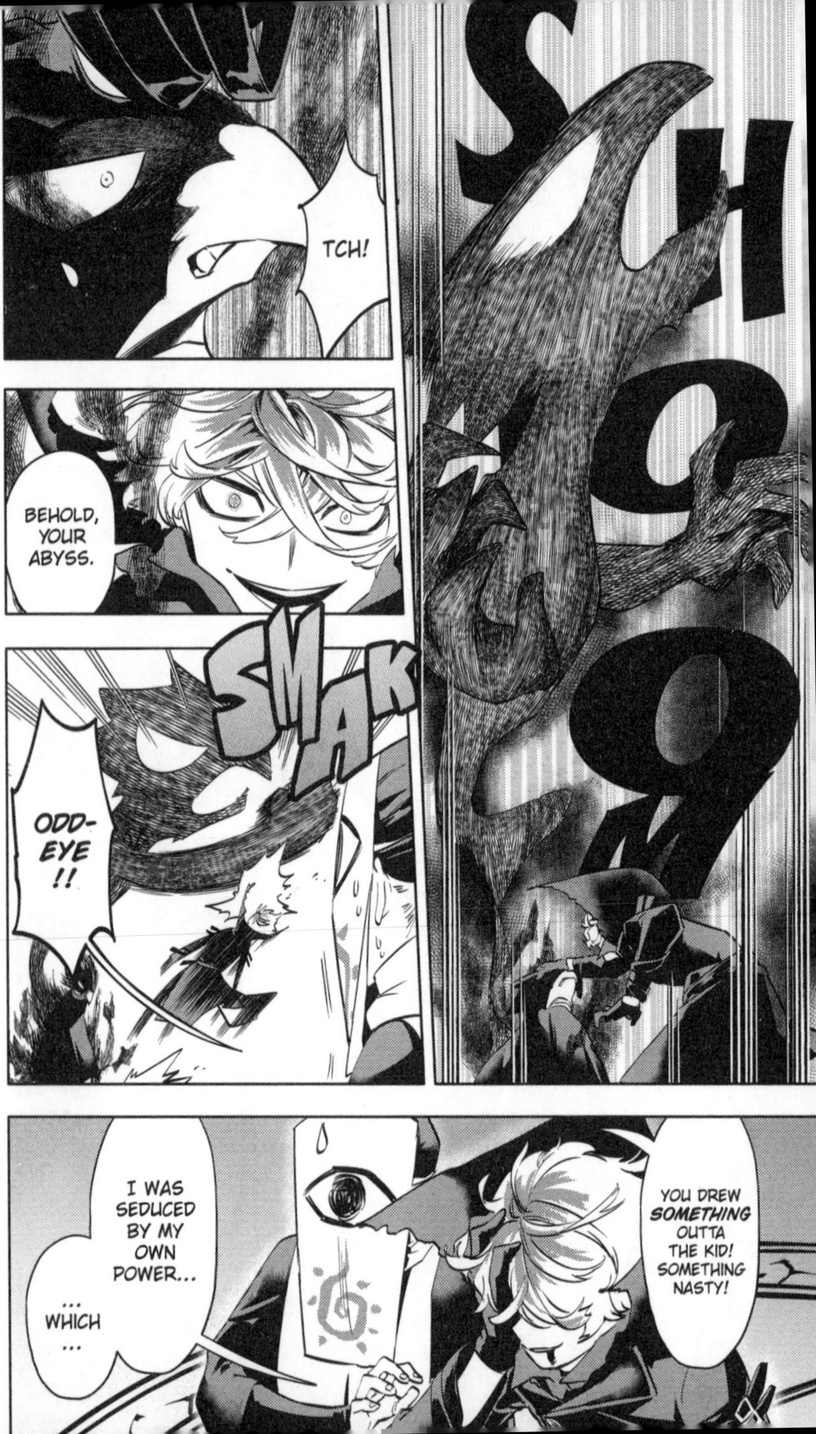
TCH!
BEHOLD, YOUR ABYSS.
SMAK
ODD-EYE!!
YOU DREW *SOMETHING* OUTTA THE KID! SOMETHING NASTY!
I WAS SEDUCED BY MY OWN POWER...
...WHICH...

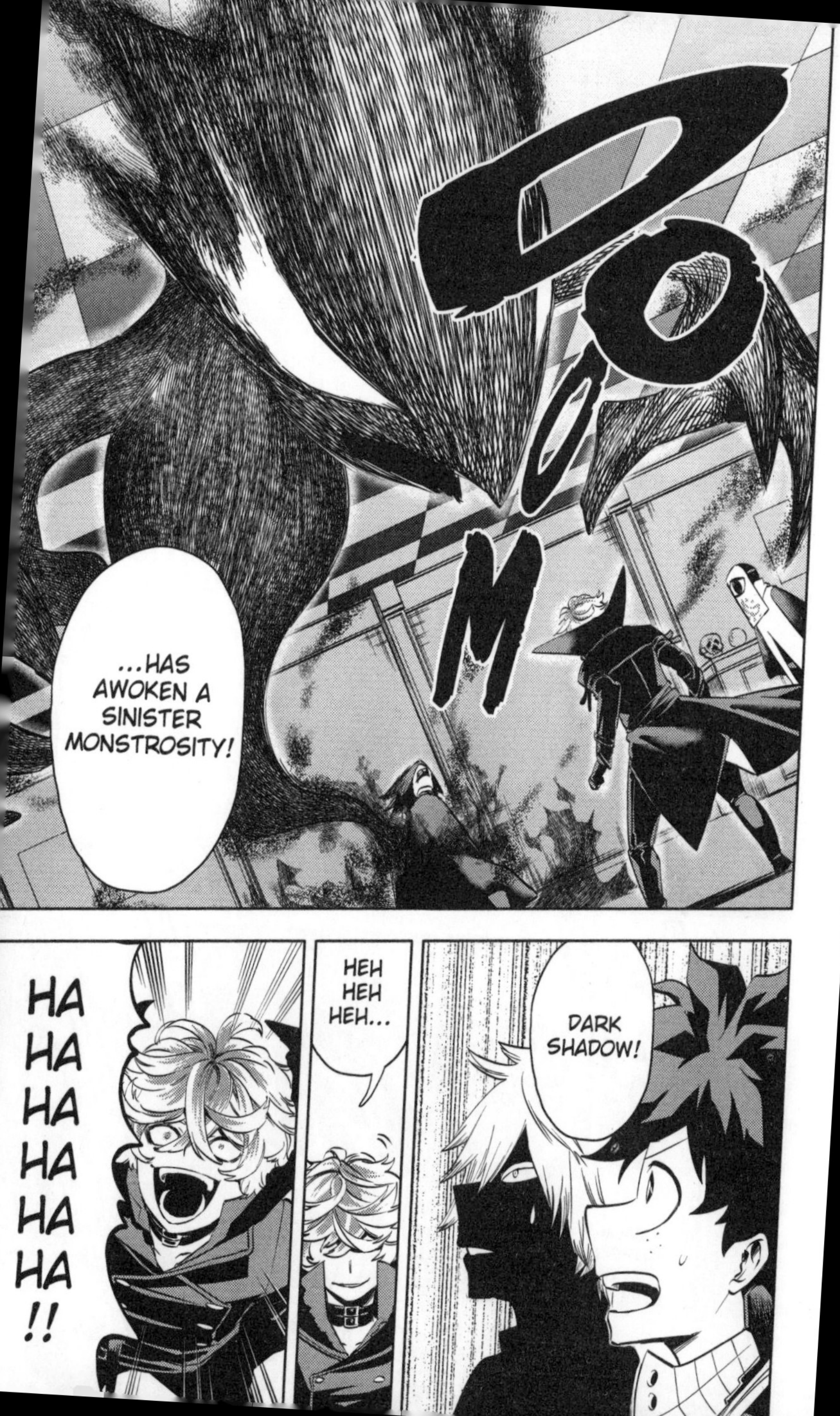
DOOOM
...HAS AWOKEN A SINISTER MONSTROSITY!
DARK SHADOW!
HEH HEH HEH...
HA HA HA HA HA HA!!

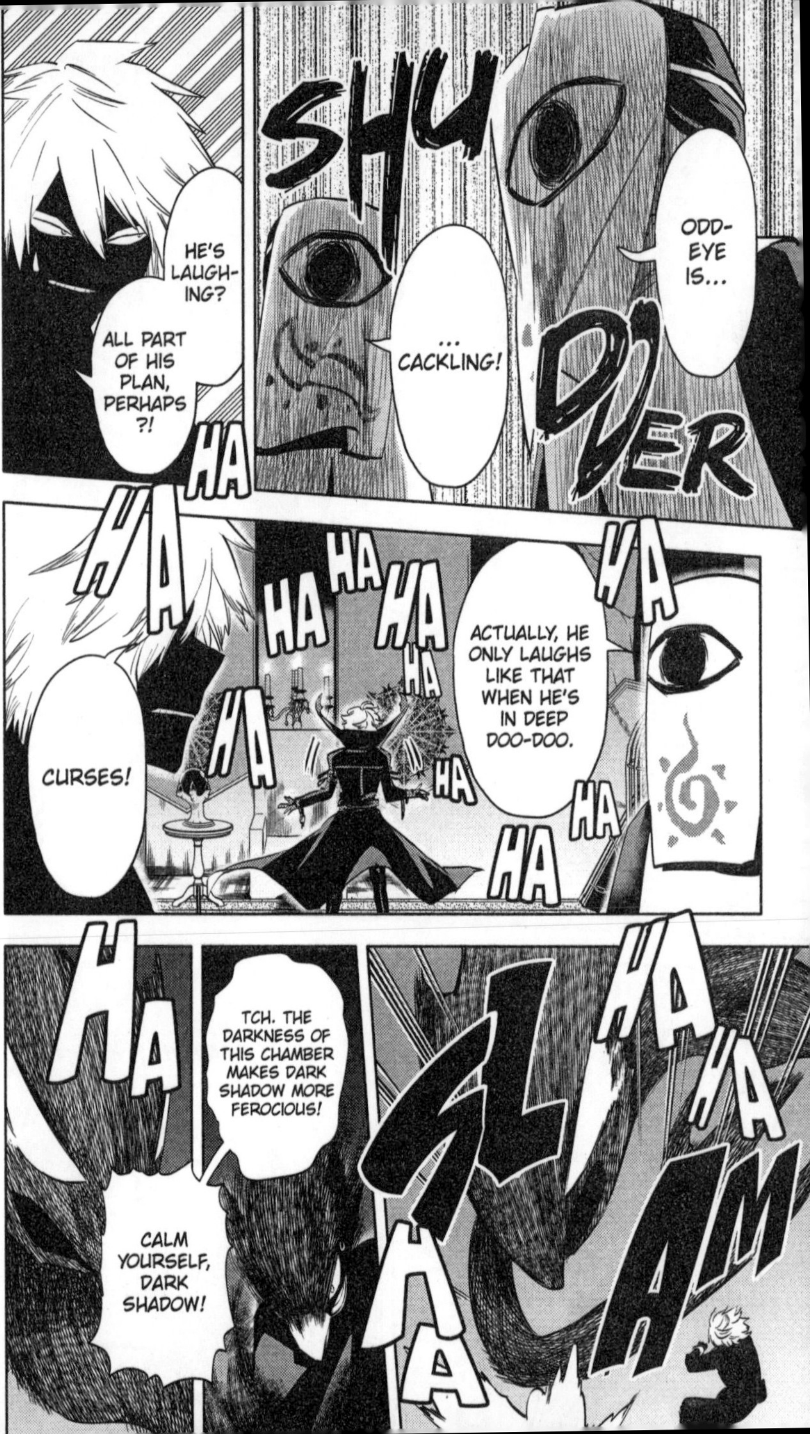
ODD-EYE IS...
...CACKLING!
SHUDDER
HE'S LAUGHING?
ALL PART OF HIS PLAN, PERHAPS?!
HA HA
HA HA
ACTUALLY, HE ONLY LAUGHS LIKE THAT WHEN HE'S IN DEEP DOO-DOO.
HA HA HA HA HA HA HA HA HA
CURSES!
HA HA
HA HA HA
SLAM
HA HA
TCH. THE DARKNESS OF THIS CHAMBER MAKES DARK SHADOW MORE FEROCIOUS!
CALM YOURSELF, DARK SHADOW!
HA HA

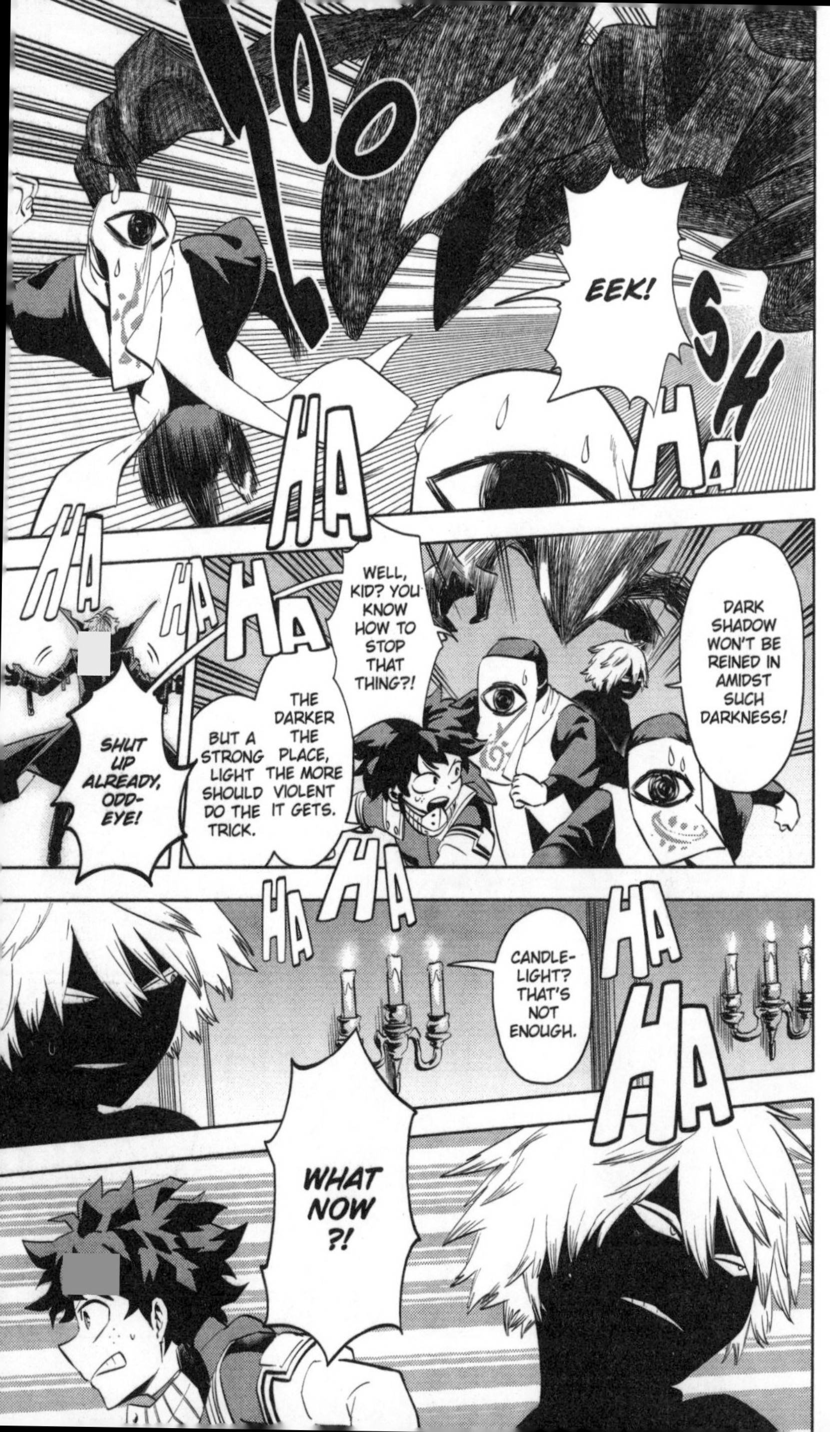
EEK!
HA HA
HA HA
DARK SHADOW WON'T BE REINED IN AMIDST SUCH DARKNESS!
WELL, KID? YOU KNOW HOW TO STOP THAT THING?!
THE DARKER THE PLACE, THE MORE VIOLENT IT GETS.
BUT A STRONG LIGHT SHOULD DO THE TRICK.
HA HA HA
SHUT UP ALREADY, ODD-EYE!
HA HA
CANDLE-LIGHT? THAT'S NOT ENOUGH.
HA HA HA
WHAT NOW?!

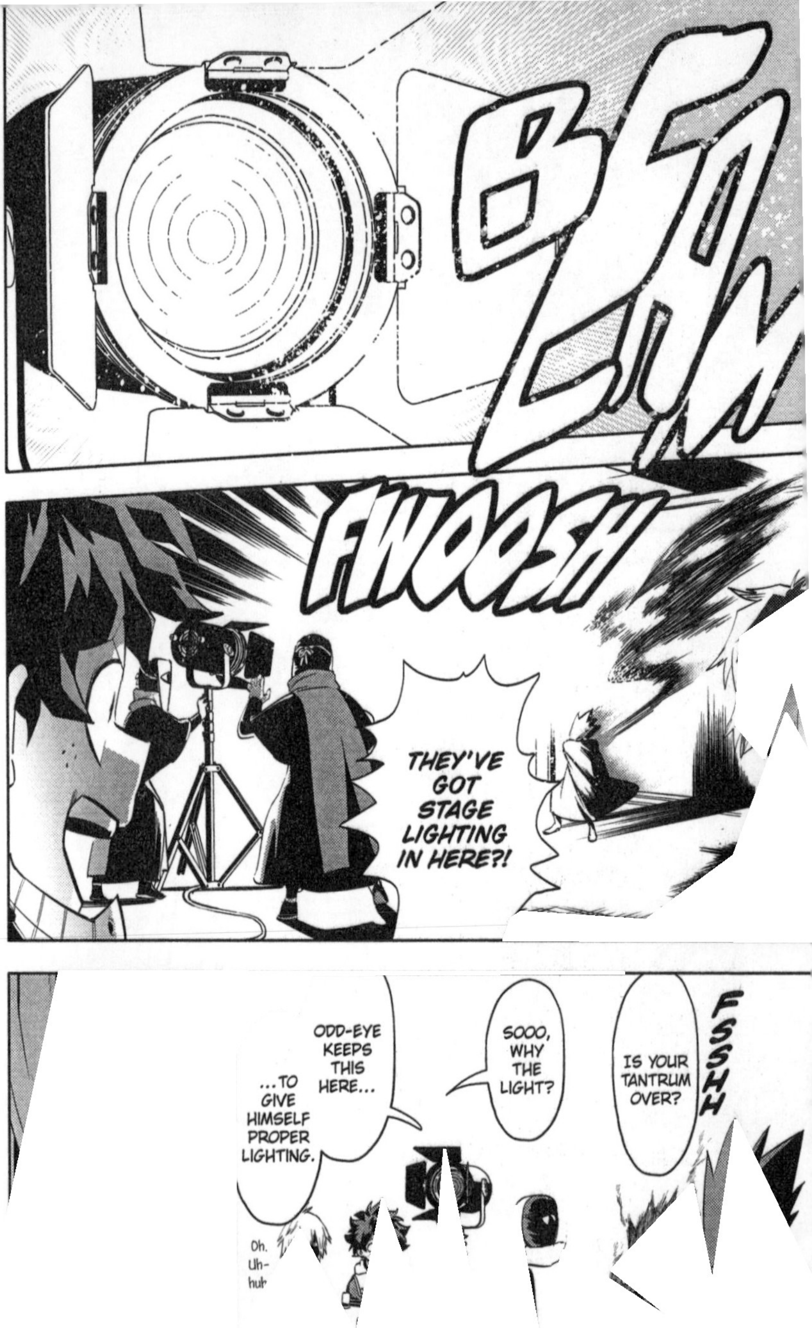
FWOOSH
THEY'VE GOT STAGE LIGHTING IN HERE?!
FSSHH
IS YOUR TANTRUM OVER?
SOOO, WHY THE LIGHT?
ODD-EYE KEEPS THIS HERE...
...TO GIVE HIMSELF PROPER LIGHTING.
Oh. Uh-huh

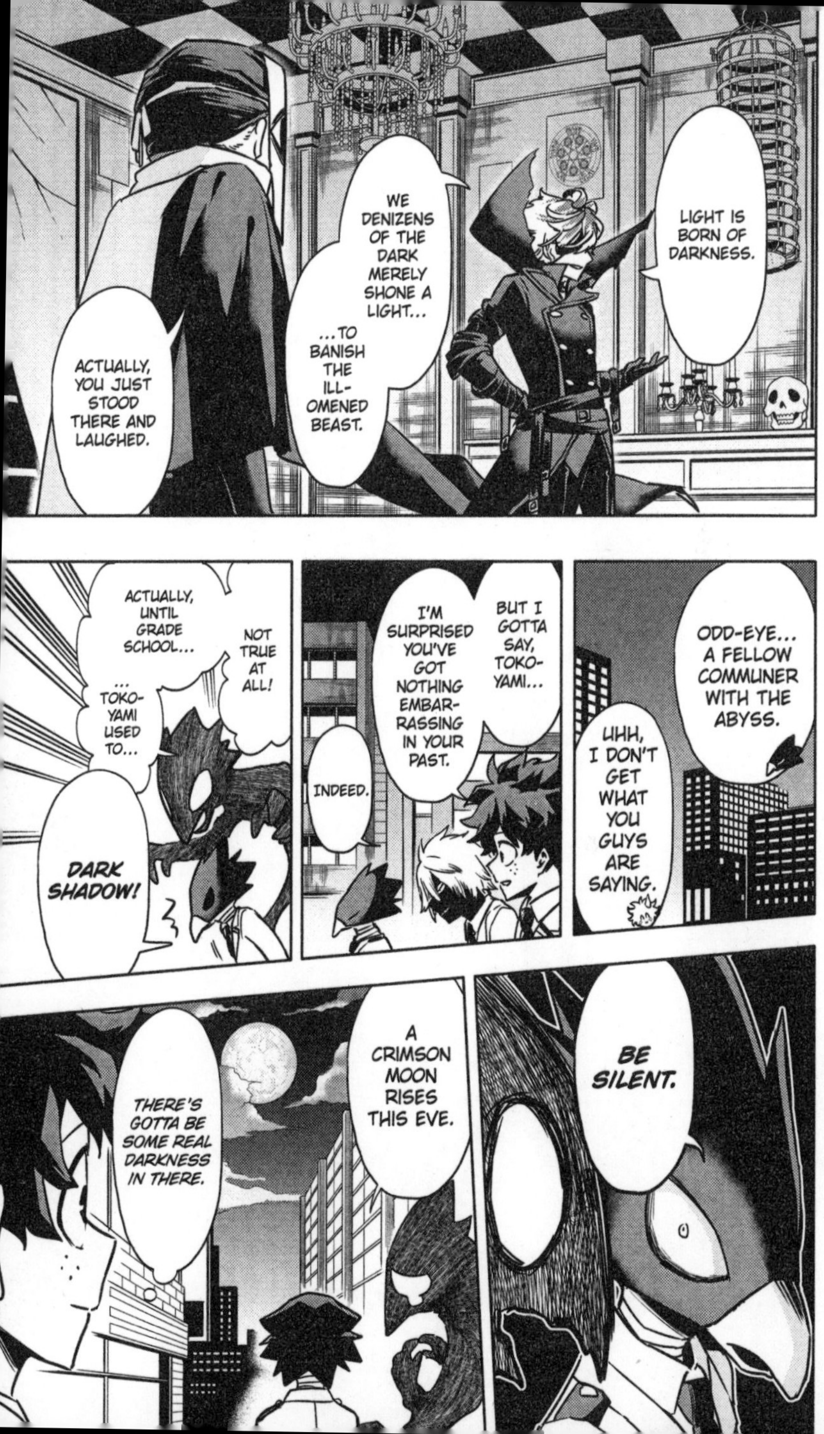
LIGHT IS BORN OF DARKNESS.
WE DENIZENS OF THE DARK MERELY SHONE A LIGHT...
...TO BANISH THE ILL-OMENED BEAST.
ACTUALLY, YOU JUST STOOD THERE AND LAUGHED.
ODD-EYE... A FELLOW COMMUNER WITH THE ABYSS.
UHH, I DON'T GET WHAT YOU GUYS ARE SAYING.
BUT I GOTTA SAY, TOKO-YAMI...
I'M SURPRISED YOU'VE GOT NOTHING EMBAR-RASSING IN YOUR PAST.
INDEED.
ACTUALLY, UNTIL GRADE SCHOOL...
... TOKO-YAMI USED TO...
NOT TRUE AT ALL!
DARK SHADOW!
BE SILENT.
A CRIMSON MOON RISES THIS EVE.
THERE'S GOTTA BE SOME REAL DARKNESS IN THERE.

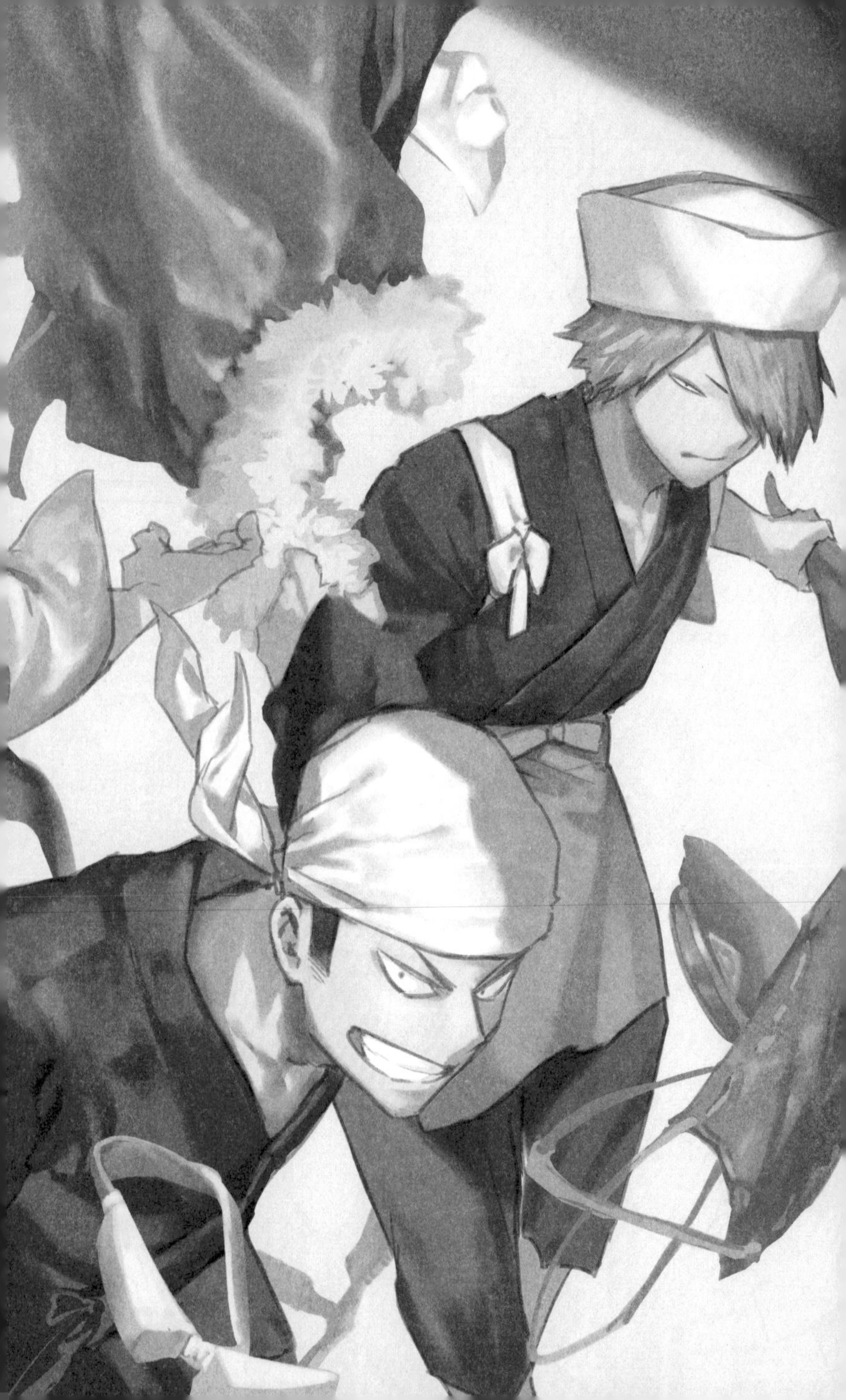

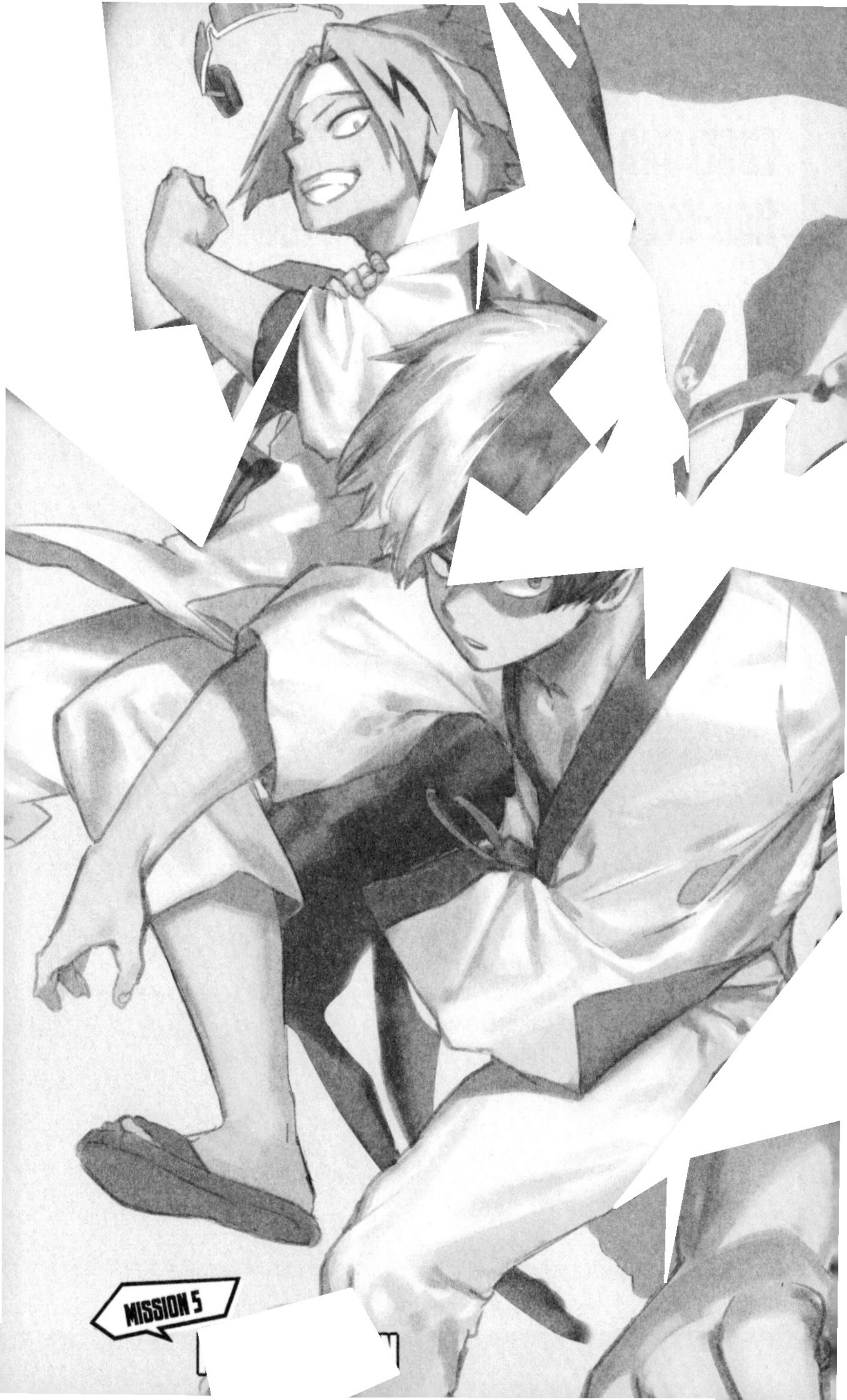
MISSION 5

EDGELORD HERO: ODD-EYE (AGE: NOT PUBLIC KNOWLEDGE)

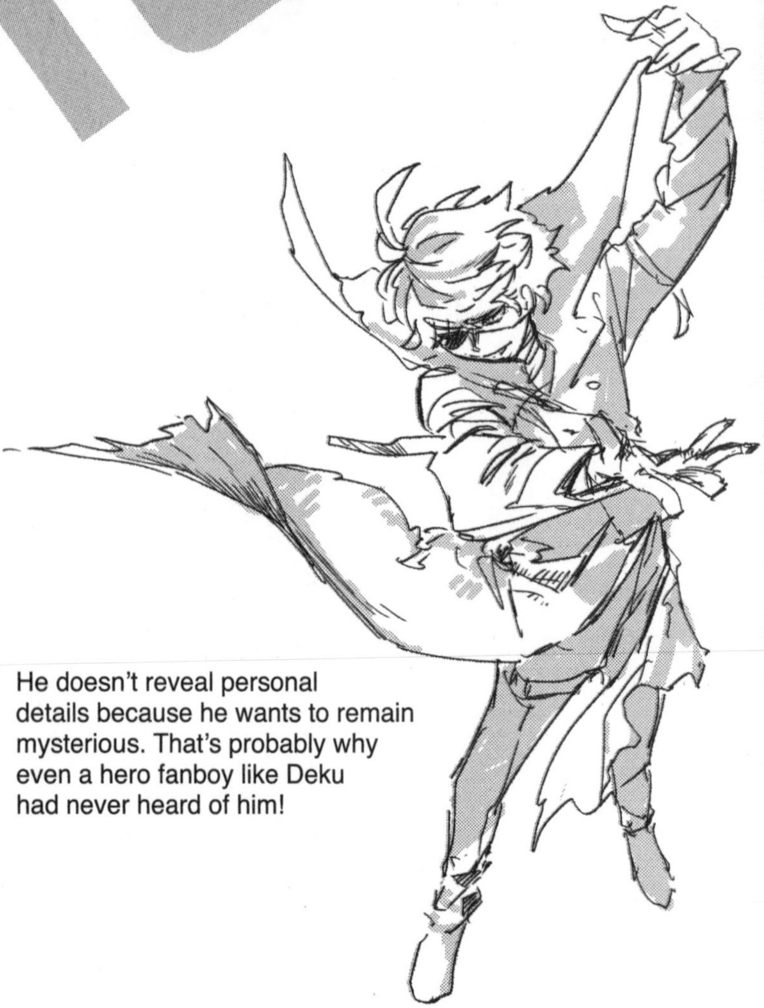

He doesn't reveal personal details because he wants to remain mysterious. That's probably why even a hero fanboy like Deku had never heard of him!

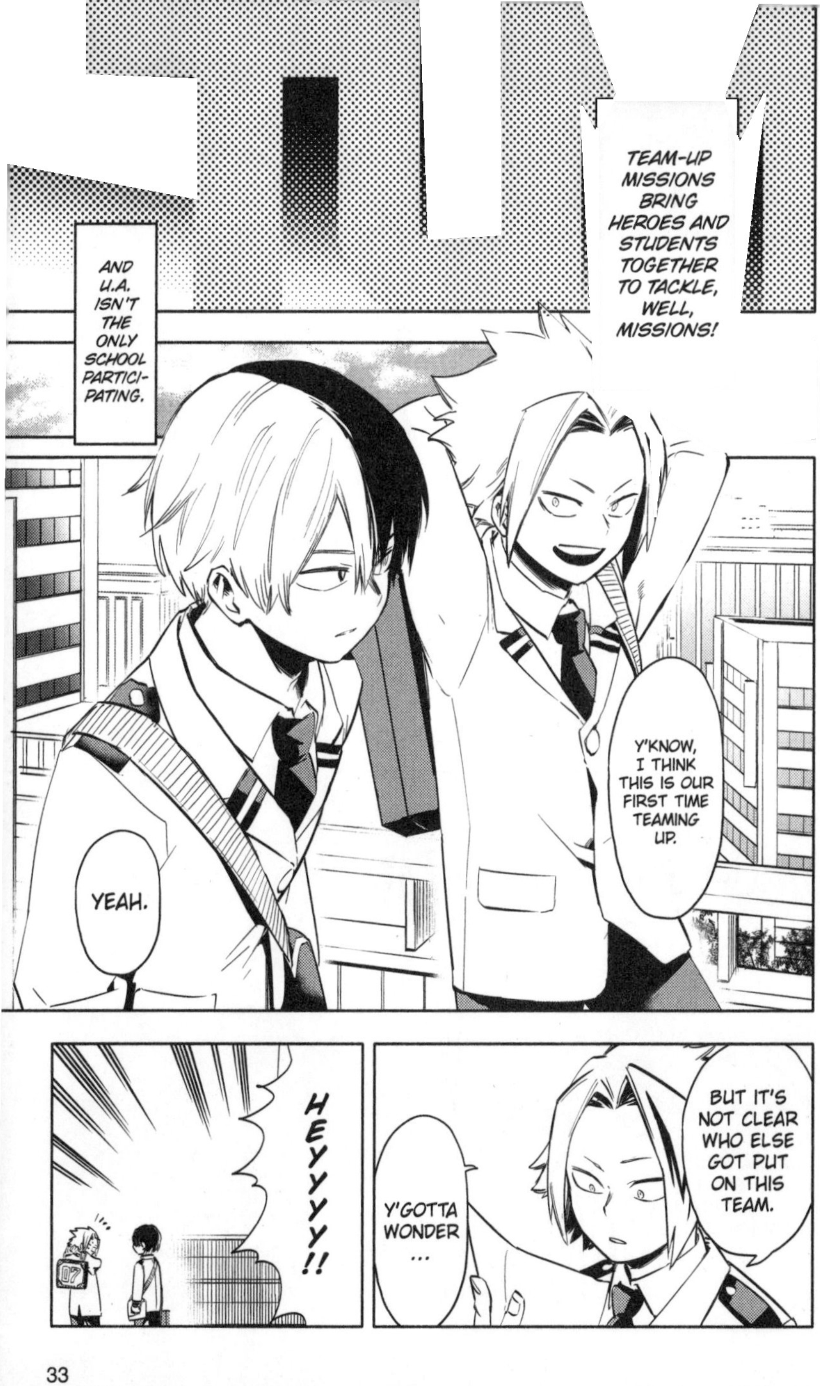
TEAM-UP MISSIONS BRING HEROES AND STUDENTS TOGETHER TO TACKLE, WELL, MISSIONS!
AND U.A. ISN'T THE ONLY SCHOOL PARTICI-PATING.
Y'KNOW, I THINK THIS IS OUR FIRST TIME TEAMING UP.
YEAH.
BUT IT'S NOT CLEAR WHO ELSE GOT PUT ON THIS TEAM.
Y'GOTTA WONDER ...
HEYYYY!!

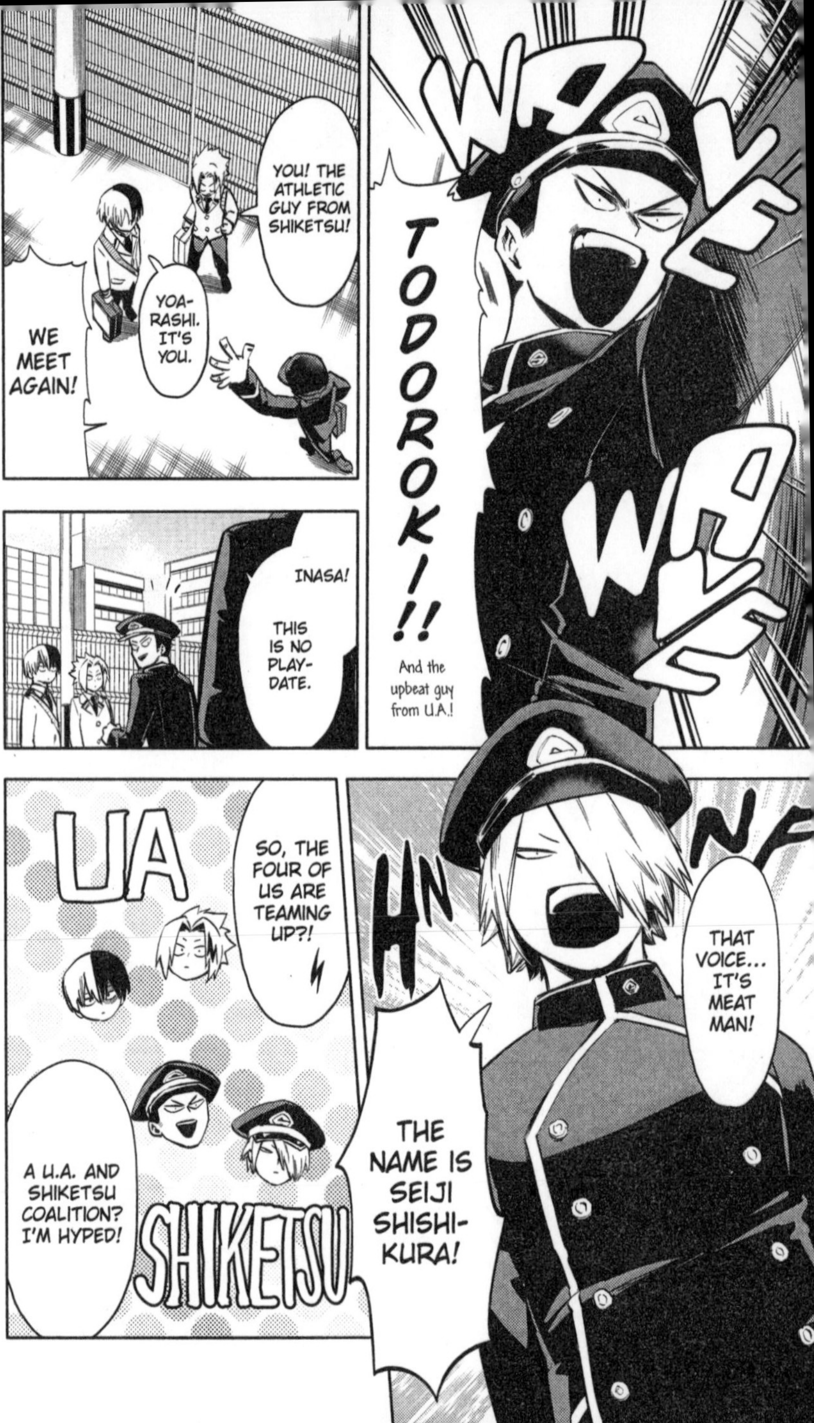
TODOROKI!!
And the upbeat guy from U.A.!
YOU! THE ATHLETIC GUY FROM SHIKETSU!
YOA-RASHI. IT'S YOU.
WE MEET AGAIN!
INASA!
THIS IS NO PLAY-DATE.
THAT VOICE... IT'S MEAT MAN!
THE NAME IS SEIJI SHISHI-KURA!
UA
SO, THE FOUR OF US ARE TEAMING UP?!
A U.A. AND SHIKETSU COALITION? I'M HYPED!
SHIKETSU

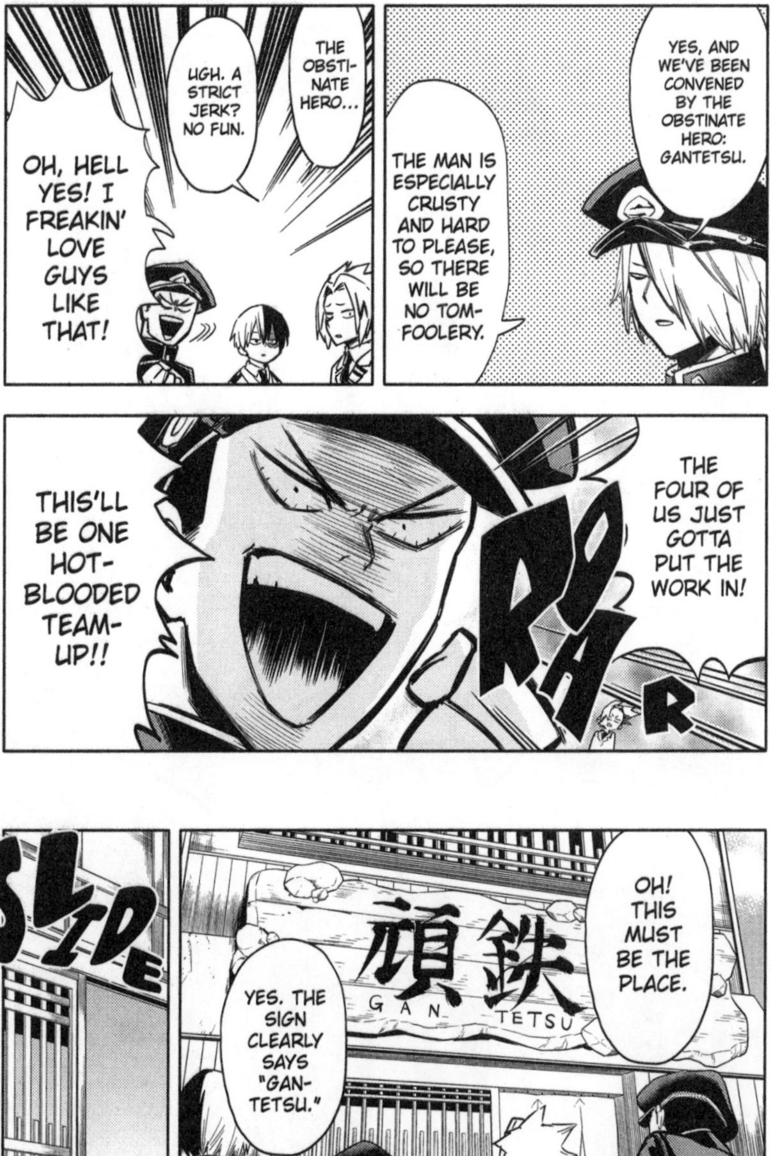
YES, AND WE'VE BEEN CONVENED BY THE OBSTINATE HERO: GANTETSU.
THE MAN IS ESPECIALLY CRUSTY AND HARD TO PLEASE, SO THERE WILL BE NO TOMFOOLERY.
THE OBSTINATE HERO...
UGH. A STRICT JERK? NO FUN.
OH, HELL YES! I FREAKIN' LOVE GUYS LIKE THAT!
THE FOUR OF US JUST GOTTA PUT THE WORK IN!
RAAR
THIS'LL BE ONE HOT-BLOODED TEAM-UP!!
OH! THIS MUST BE THE PLACE.
頑鉄
GAN TETSU
YES. THE SIGN CLEARLY SAYS "GANTETSU."
SLIDE

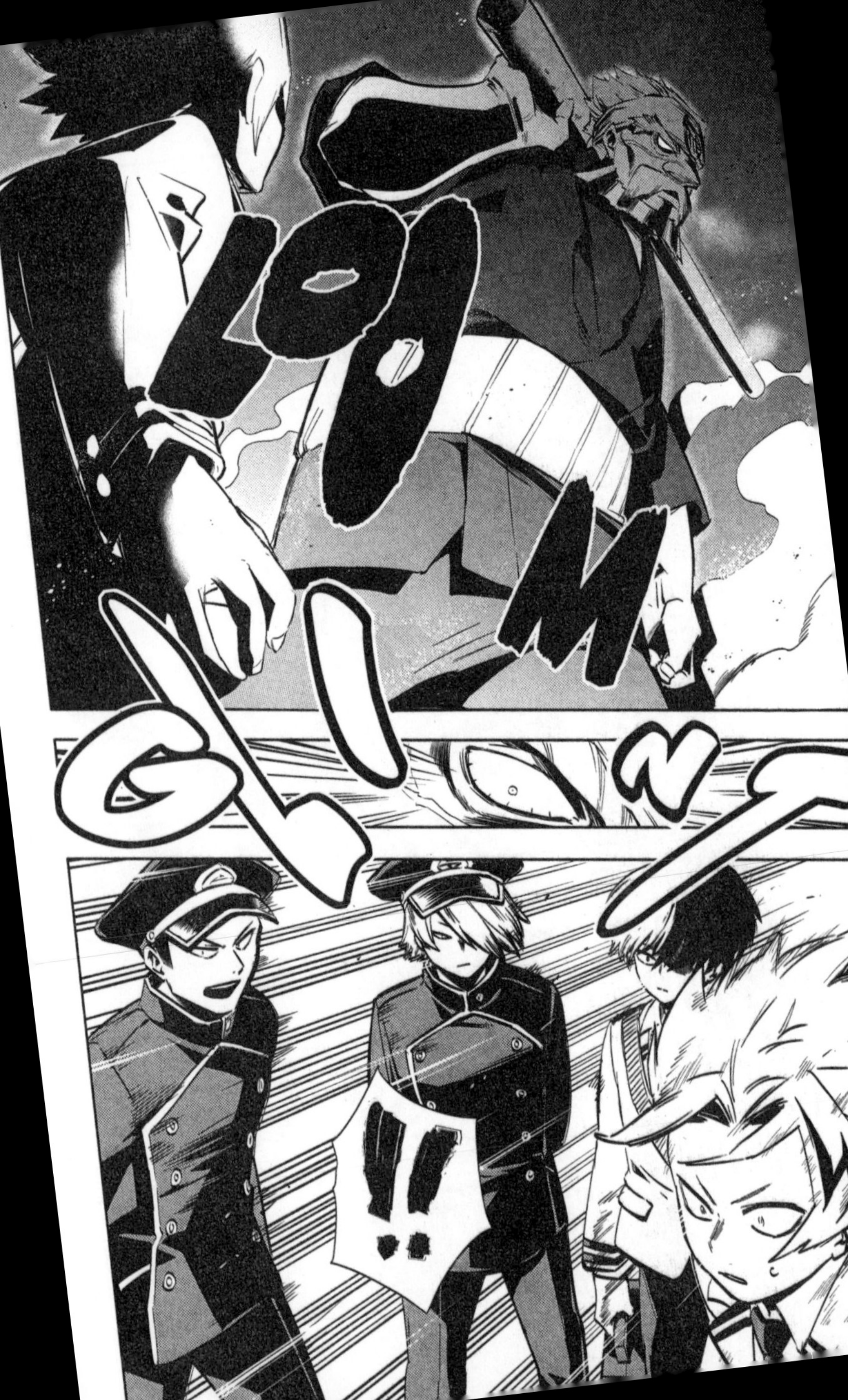
BOOM
GLINT
!!

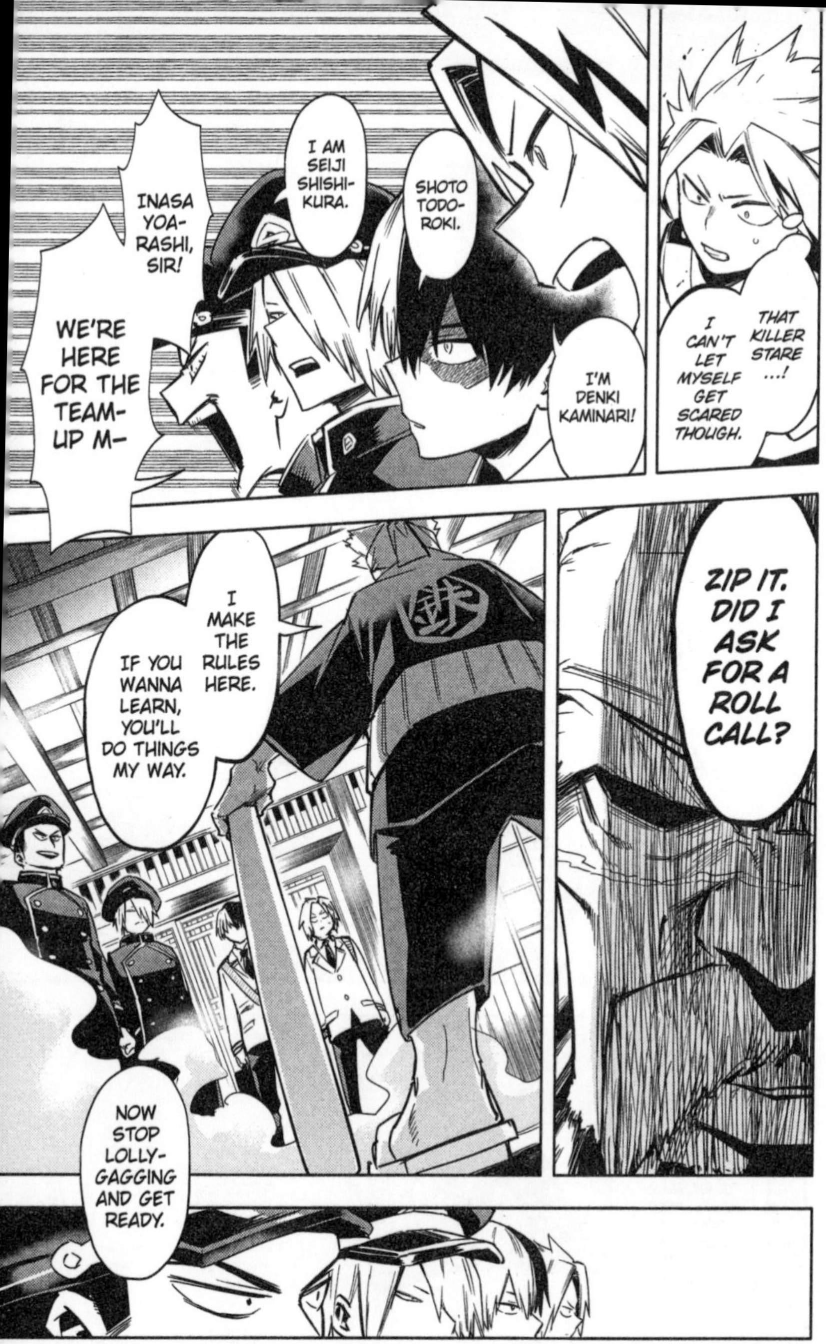
THAT KILLER STARE ...!
I CAN'T LET MYSELF GET SCARED THOUGH.
I'M DENKI KAMINARI!
SHOTO TODOROKI.
I AM SEIJI SHISHIKURA.
INASA YOARASHI, SIR!
WE'RE HERE FOR THE TEAM-UP M—
ZIP IT. DID I ASK FOR A ROLL CALL?
I MAKE THE RULES HERE.
IF YOU WANNA LEARN, YOU'LL DO THINGS MY WAY.
NOW STOP LOLLYGAGGING AND GET READY.

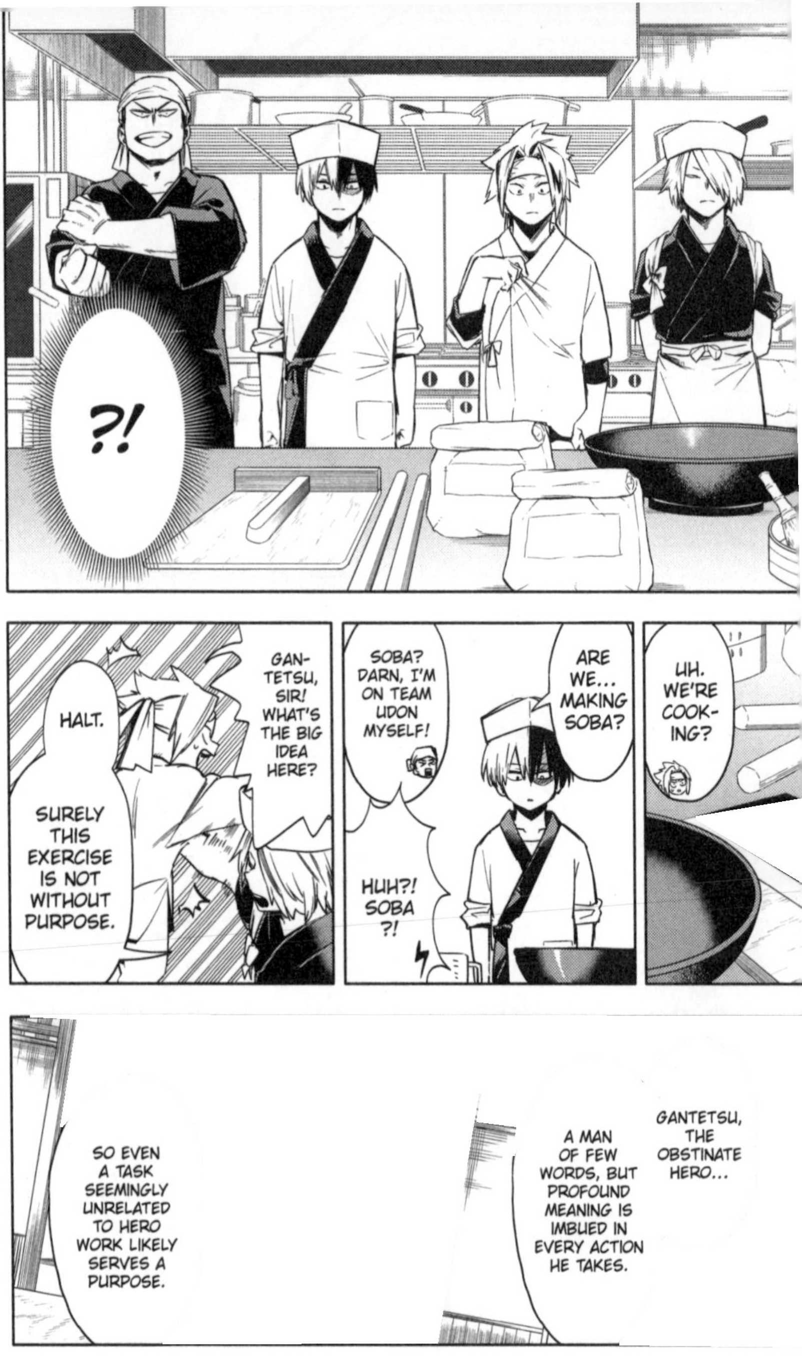
?!
UH. WE'RE COOK-ING?
ARE WE... MAKING SOBA?
SOBA? DARN, I'M ON TEAM UDON MYSELF!
HUH?! SOBA ?!
GAN-TETSU, SIR! WHAT'S THE BIG IDEA HERE?
HALT.
SURELY THIS EXERCISE IS NOT WITHOUT PURPOSE.
GANTETSU, THE OBSTINATE HERO...
A MAN OF FEW WORDS, BUT PROFOUND MEANING IS IMBUED IN EVERY ACTION HE TAKES.
SO EVEN A TASK SEEMINGLY UNRELATED TO HERO WORK LIKELY SERVES A PURPOSE.

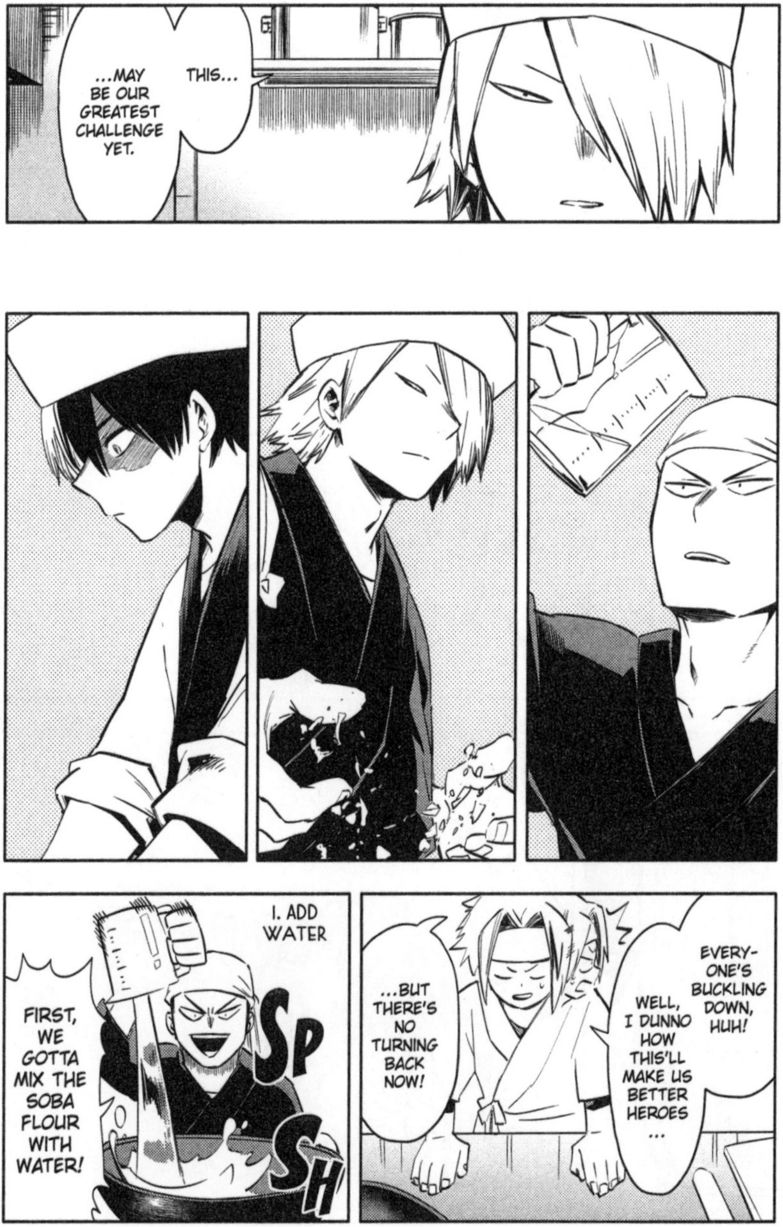
THIS...
...MAY BE OUR GREATEST CHALLENGE YET.
EVERY-ONE'S BUCKLING DOWN, HUH!
WELL, I DUNNO HOW THIS'LL MAKE US BETTER HEROES...
...BUT THERE'S NO TURNING BACK NOW!
1. ADD WATER
FIRST, WE GOTTA MIX THE SOBA FLOUR WITH WATER!
SPSH

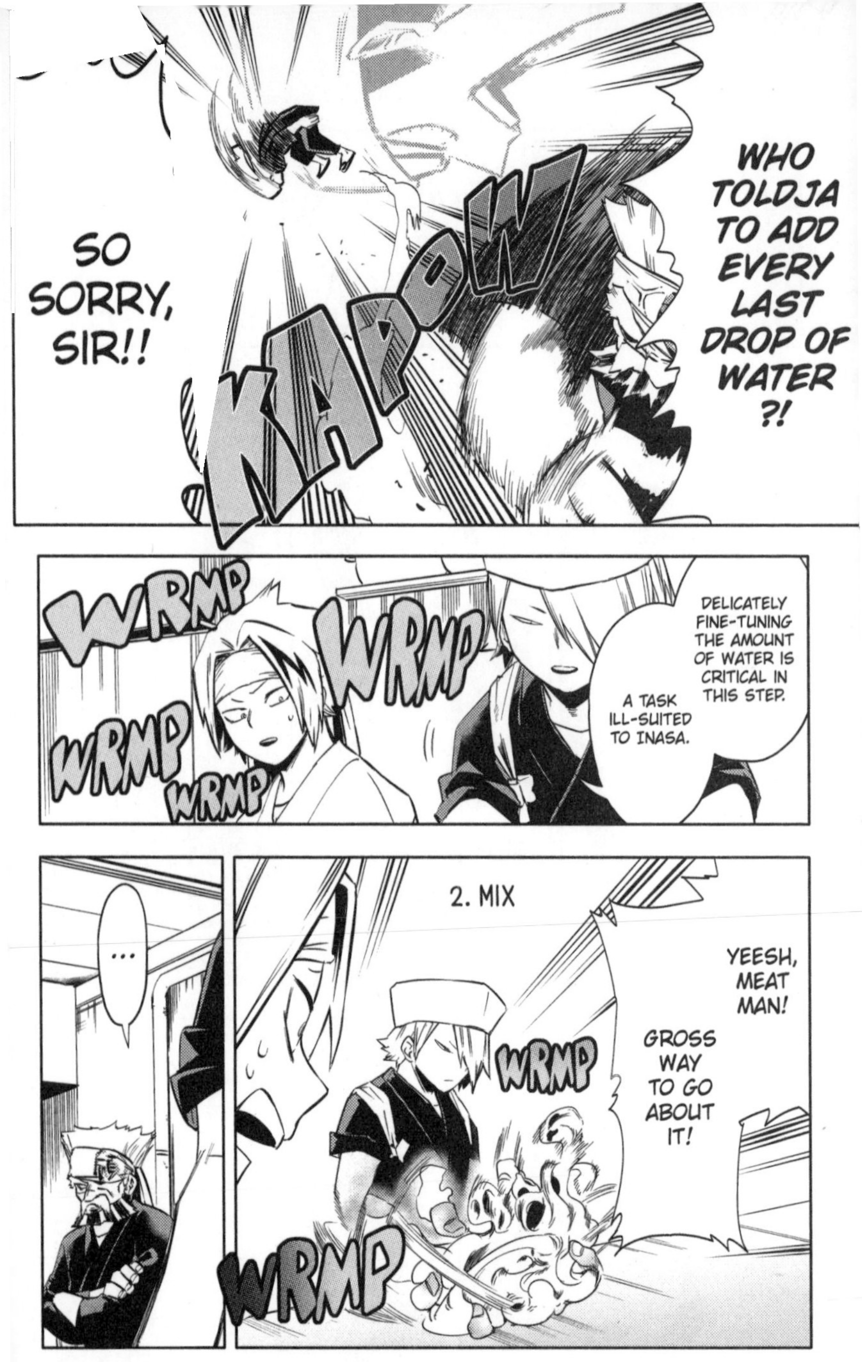
WHO TOLDJA TO ADD EVERY LAST DROP OF WATER ?!
KAPOW
SO SORRY, SIR!!
DELICATELY FINE-TUNING THE AMOUNT OF WATER IS CRITICAL IN THIS STEP.
A TASK ILL-SUITED TO INASA.
WRMP
WRMP
WRMP
WRMP
2. MIX
YEESH, MEAT MAN!
GROSS WAY TO GO ABOUT IT!
WRMP
WRMP
...

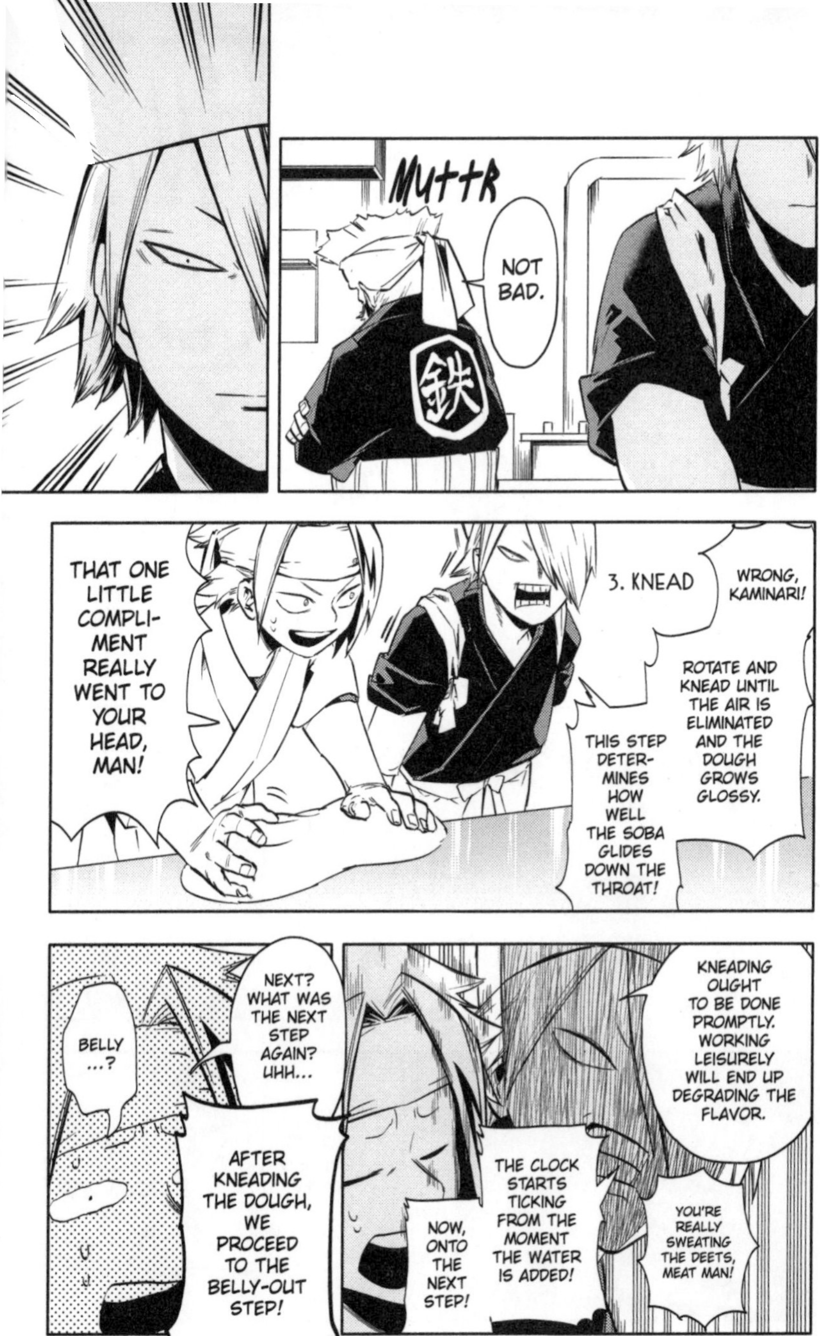
MUTTR
NOT BAD.
WRONG, KAMINARI!
3. KNEAD
ROTATE AND KNEAD UNTIL THE AIR IS ELIMINATED AND THE DOUGH GROWS GLOSSY.
THIS STEP DETERMINES HOW WELL THE SOBA GLIDES DOWN THE THROAT!
THAT ONE LITTLE COMPLIMENT REALLY WENT TO YOUR HEAD, MAN!
KNEADING OUGHT TO BE DONE PROMPTLY. WORKING LEISURELY WILL END UP DEGRADING THE FLAVOR.
THE CLOCK STARTS TICKING FROM THE MOMENT THE WATER IS ADDED!
NOW, ONTO THE NEXT STEP!
YOU'RE REALLY SWEATING THE DEETS, MEAT MAN!
NEXT? WHAT WAS THE NEXT STEP AGAIN? UHH...
BELLY ...?
AFTER KNEADING THE DOUGH, WE PROCEED TO THE BELLY-OUT STEP!

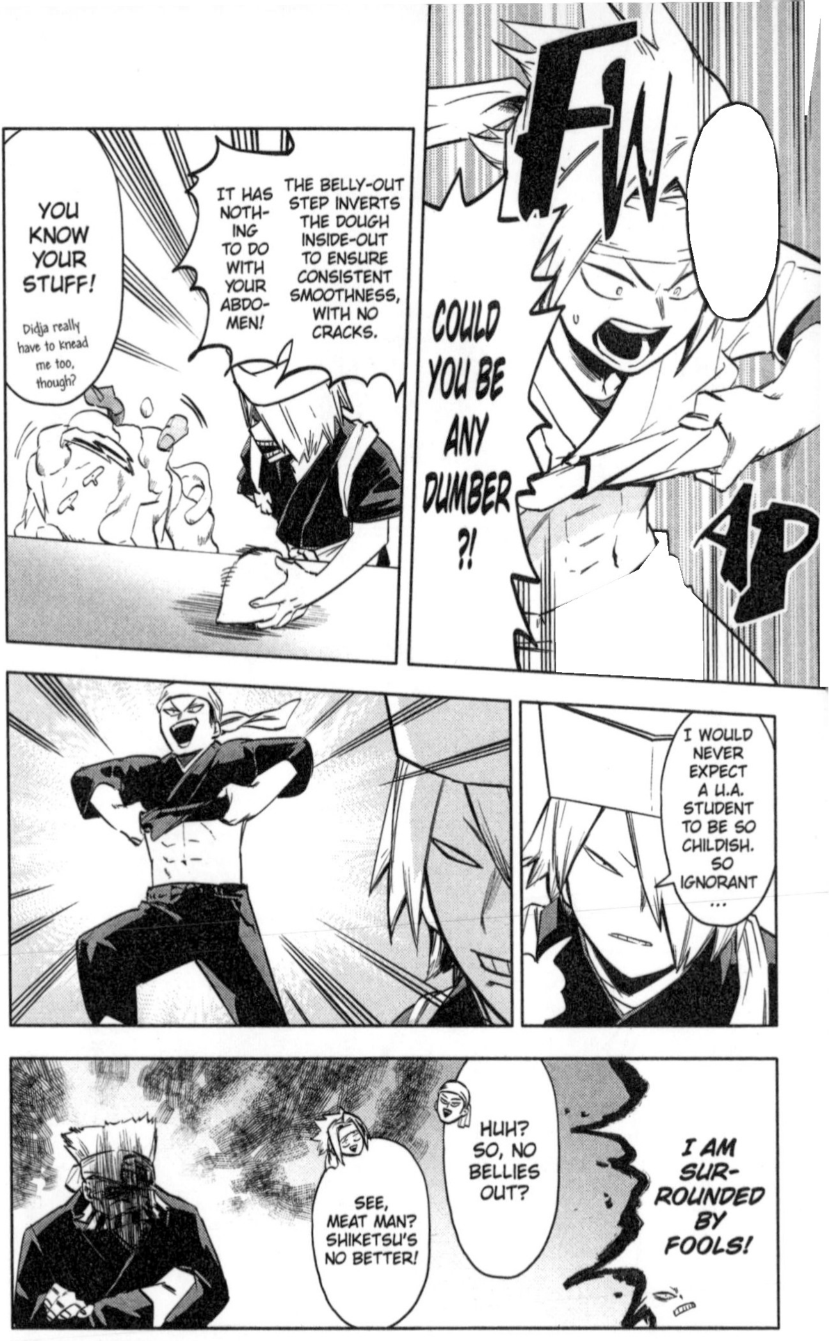

FW
COULD YOU BE ANY DUMBER?!
AP
THE BELLY-OUT STEP INVERTS THE DOUGH INSIDE-OUT TO ENSURE CONSISTENT SMOOTHNESS, WITH NO CRACKS.
IT HAS NOTHING TO DO WITH YOUR ABDOMEN!
YOU KNOW YOUR STUFF!
Didja really have to knead me too, though?
I WOULD NEVER EXPECT A U.A. STUDENT TO BE SO CHILDISH. SO IGNORANT...
I AM SURROUNDED BY FOOLS!
HUH? SO, NO BELLIES OUT?
SEE, MEAT MAN? SHIKETSU'S NO BETTER!

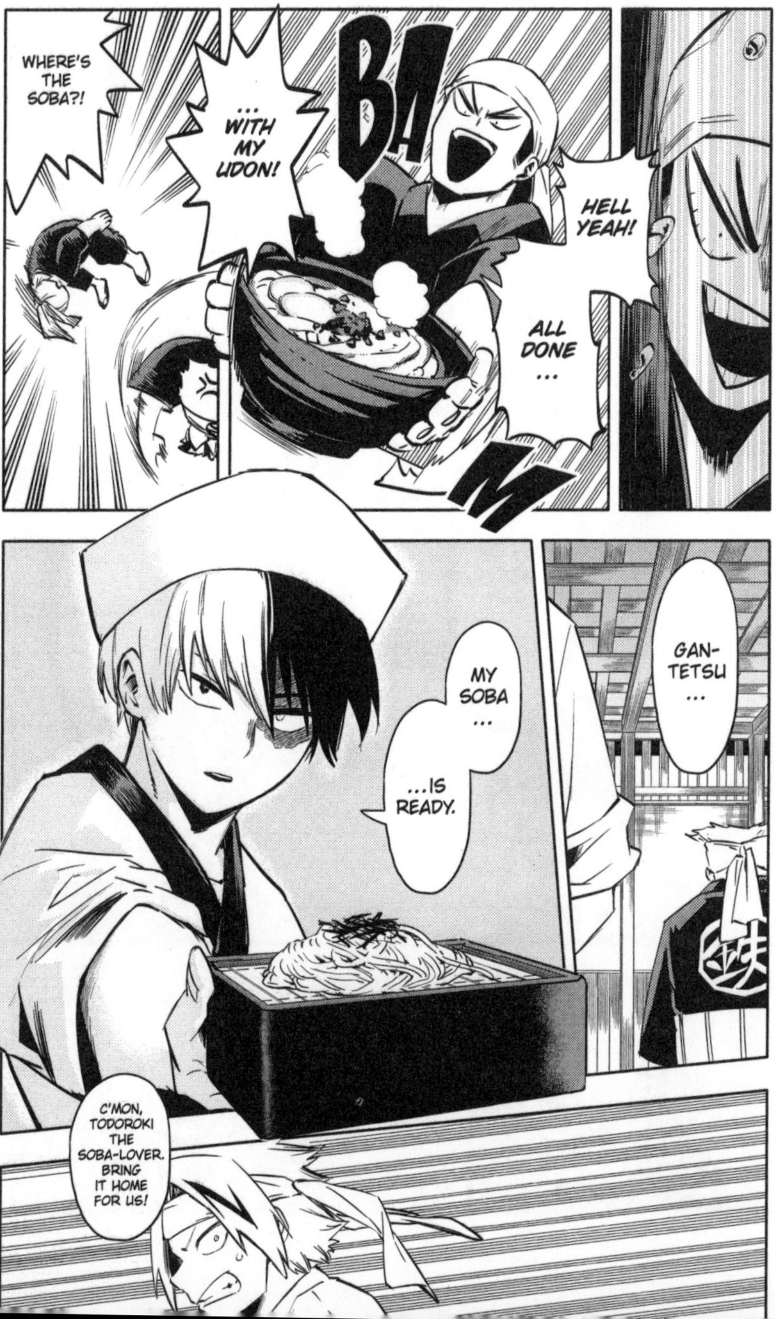
HELL YEAH!
ALL DONE...
...WITH MY UDON!
BAM
WHERE'S THE SOBA?!
GAN-TETSU...
MY SOBA...
...IS READY.
C'MON, TODOROKI THE SOBA-LOVER. BRING IT HOME FOR US!

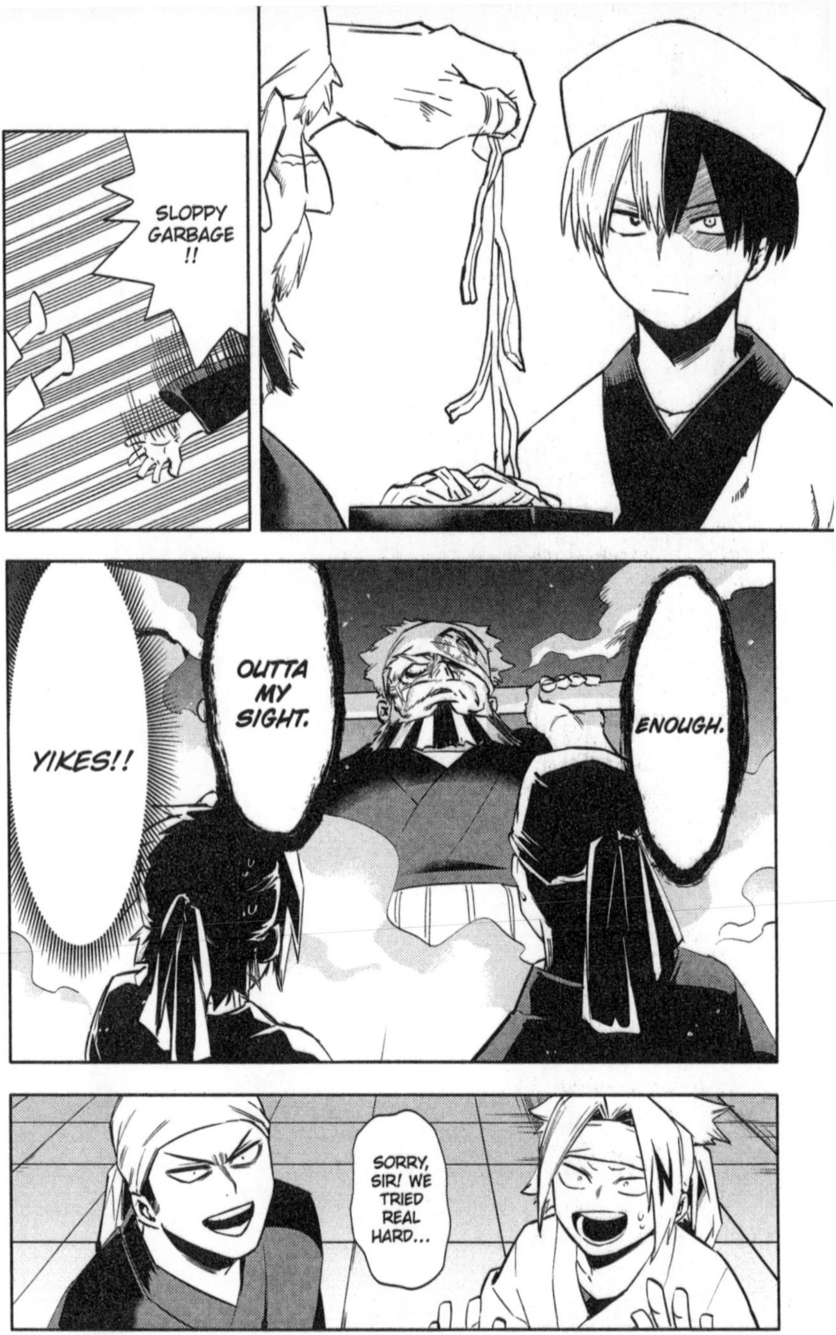
SLOPPY GARBAGE !!
ENOUGH.
OUTTA MY SIGHT.
YIKES!!
SORRY, SIR! WE TRIED REAL HARD...

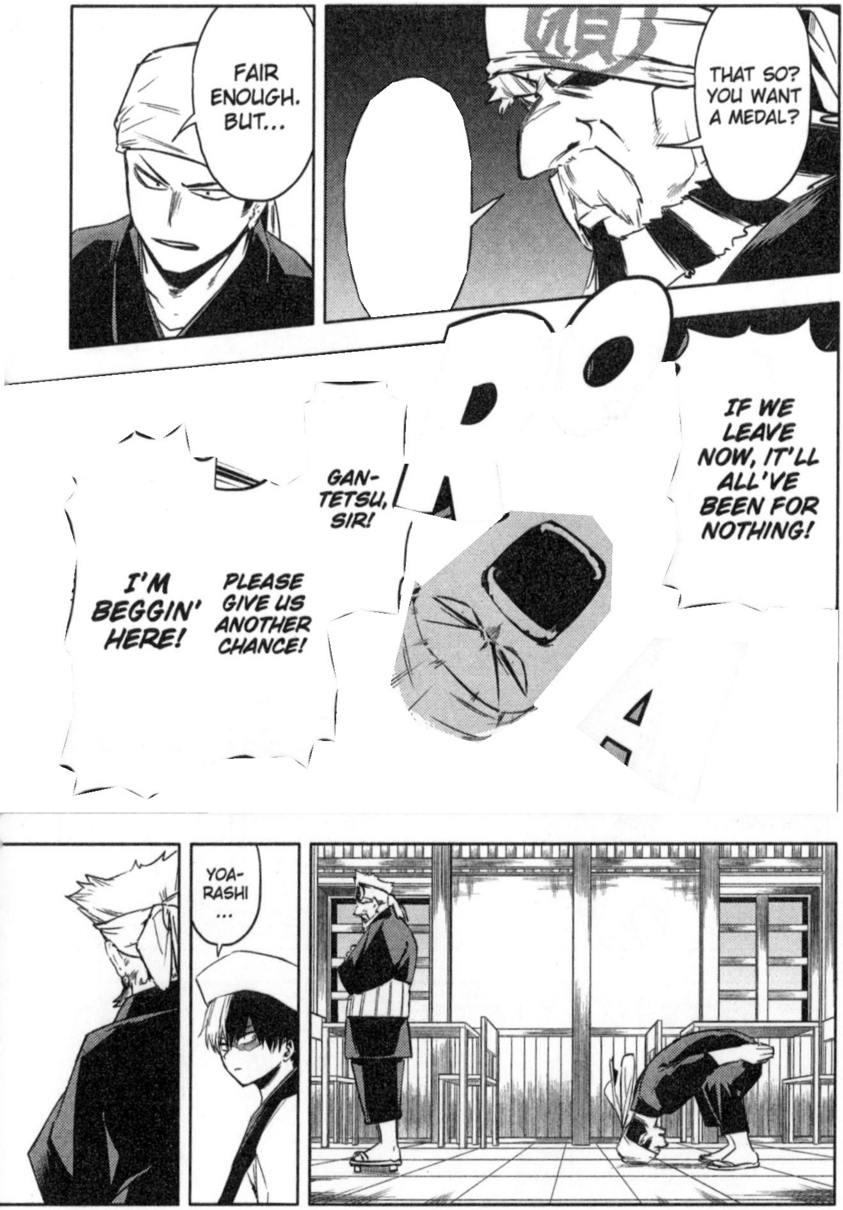
THAT SO? YOU WANT A MEDAL?
FAIR ENOUGH. BUT...
IF WE LEAVE NOW, IT'LL ALL'VE BEEN FOR NOTHING!
GAN-TETSU, SIR!
PLEASE GIVE US ANOTHER CHANCE!
I'M BEGGIN' HERE!
YOA-RASHI ...

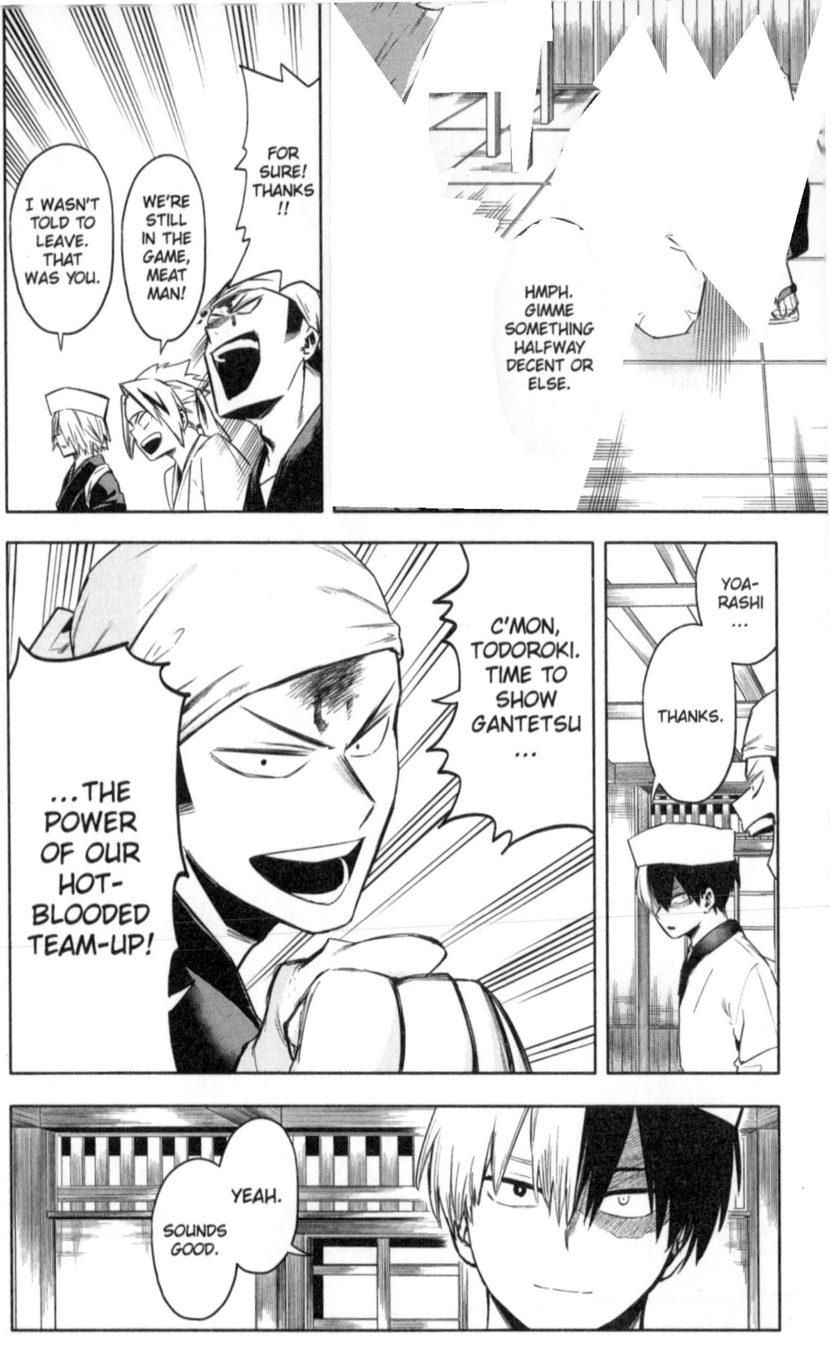
HMPH. GIMME SOMETHING HALFWAY DECENT OR ELSE.
FOR SURE! THANKS!!
WE'RE STILL IN THE GAME, MEAT MAN!
I WASN'T TOLD TO LEAVE. THAT WAS YOU.
YOA-RASHI...
THANKS.
C'MON, TODOROKI. TIME TO SHOW GANTETSU...
...THE POWER OF OUR HOT-BLOODED TEAM-UP!
YEAH.
SOUNDS GOOD.

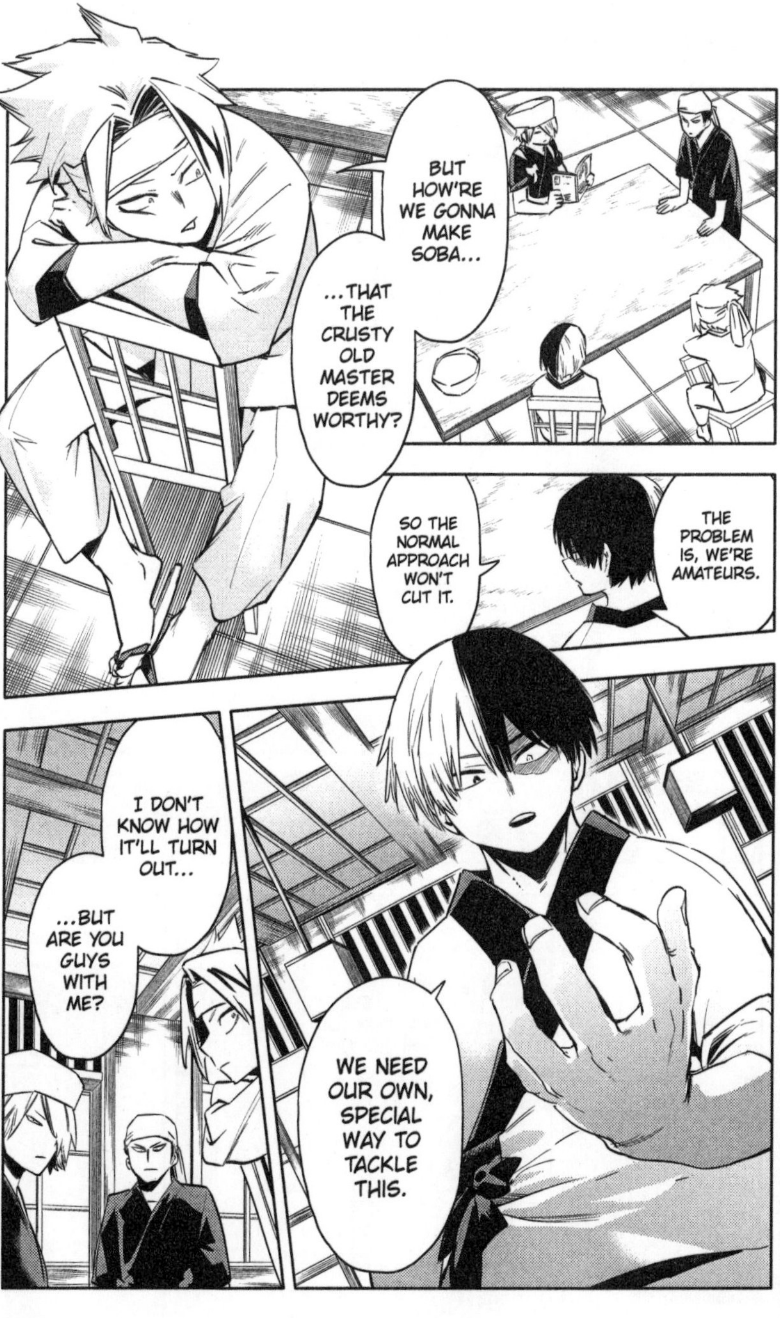
BUT HOW'RE WE GONNA MAKE SOBA...
...THAT THE CRUSTY OLD MASTER DEEMS WORTHY?
THE PROBLEM IS, WE'RE AMATEURS.
SO THE NORMAL APPROACH WON'T CUT IT.
WE NEED OUR OWN, SPECIAL WAY TO TACKLE THIS.
I DON'T KNOW HOW IT'LL TURN OUT...
...BUT ARE YOU GUYS WITH ME?

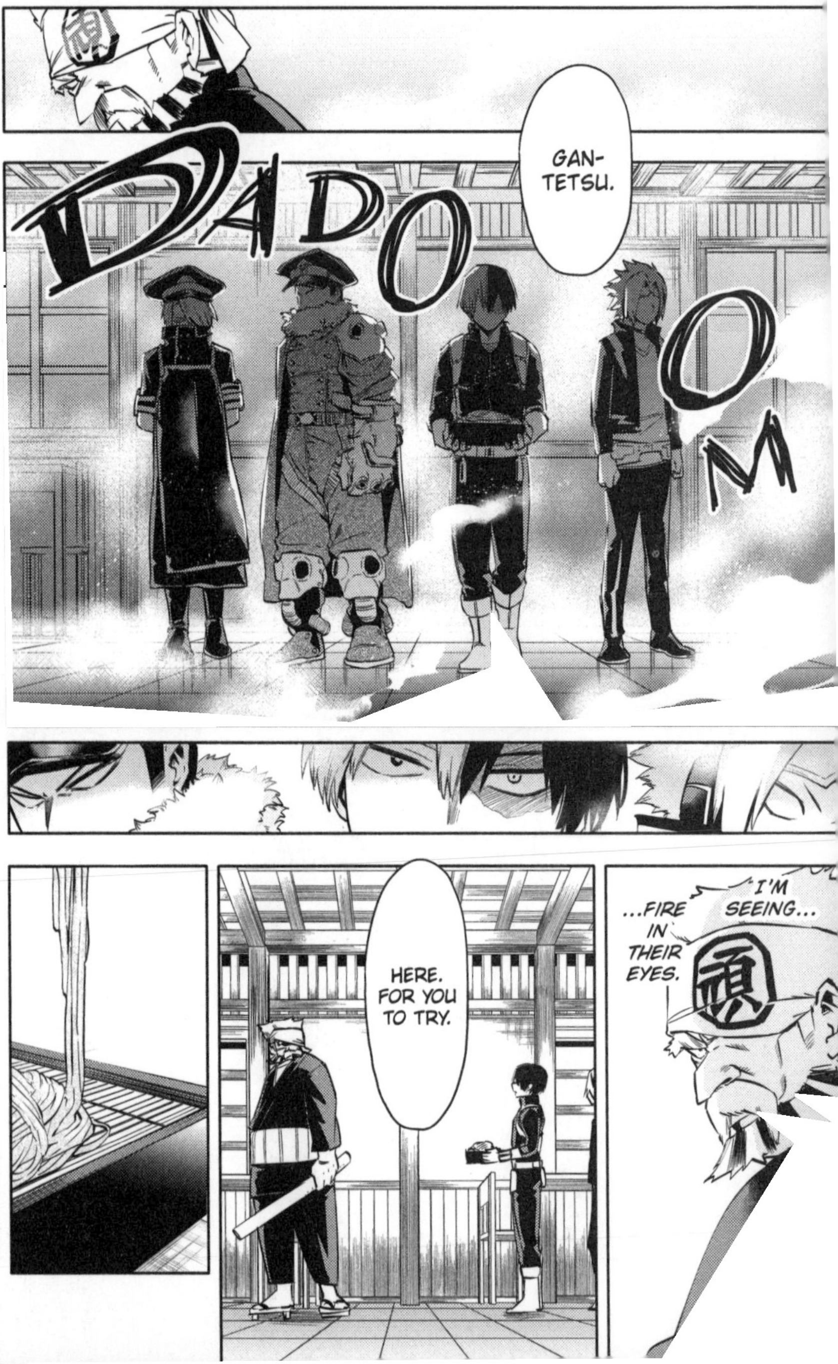
GAN-TETSU.
DADOOOM
I'M SEEING...
...FIRE IN THEIR EYES.
HERE. FOR YOU TO TRY.

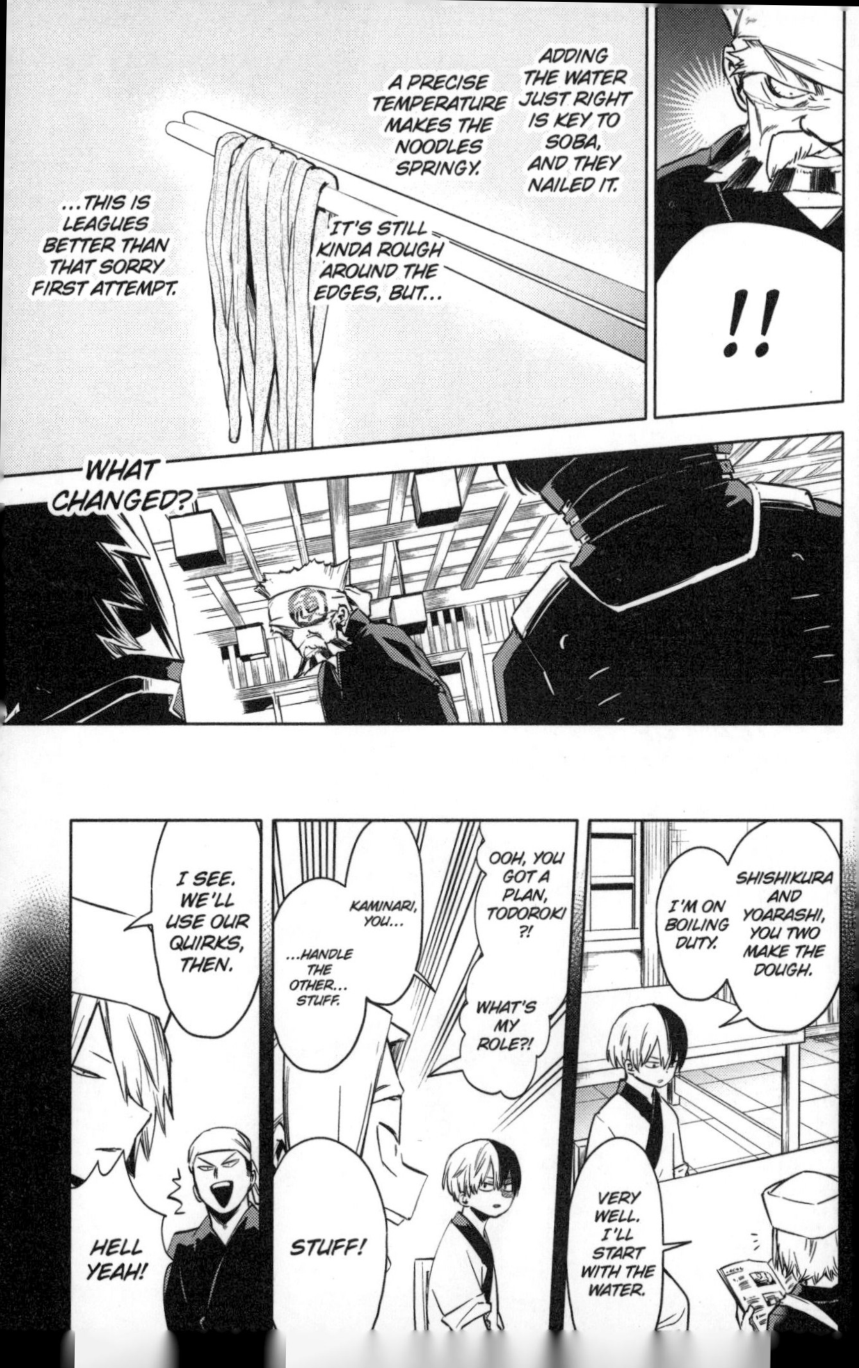
!!
ADDING THE WATER JUST RIGHT IS KEY TO SOBA, AND THEY NAILED IT.
A PRECISE TEMPERATURE MAKES THE NOODLES SPRINGY.
IT'S STILL KINDA ROUGH AROUND THE EDGES, BUT...
...THIS IS LEAGUES BETTER THAN THAT SORRY FIRST ATTEMPT.
WHAT CHANGED?
SHISHIKURA AND YOARASHI, YOU TWO MAKE THE DOUGH.
I'M ON BOILING DUTY.
VERY WELL. I'LL START WITH THE WATER.
OOH, YOU GOT A PLAN, TODOROKI?!
WHAT'S MY ROLE?!
KAMINARI, YOU...
...HANDLE THE OTHER... STUFF.
STUFF!
I SEE. WE'LL USE OUR QUIRKS, THEN.
HELL YEAH!

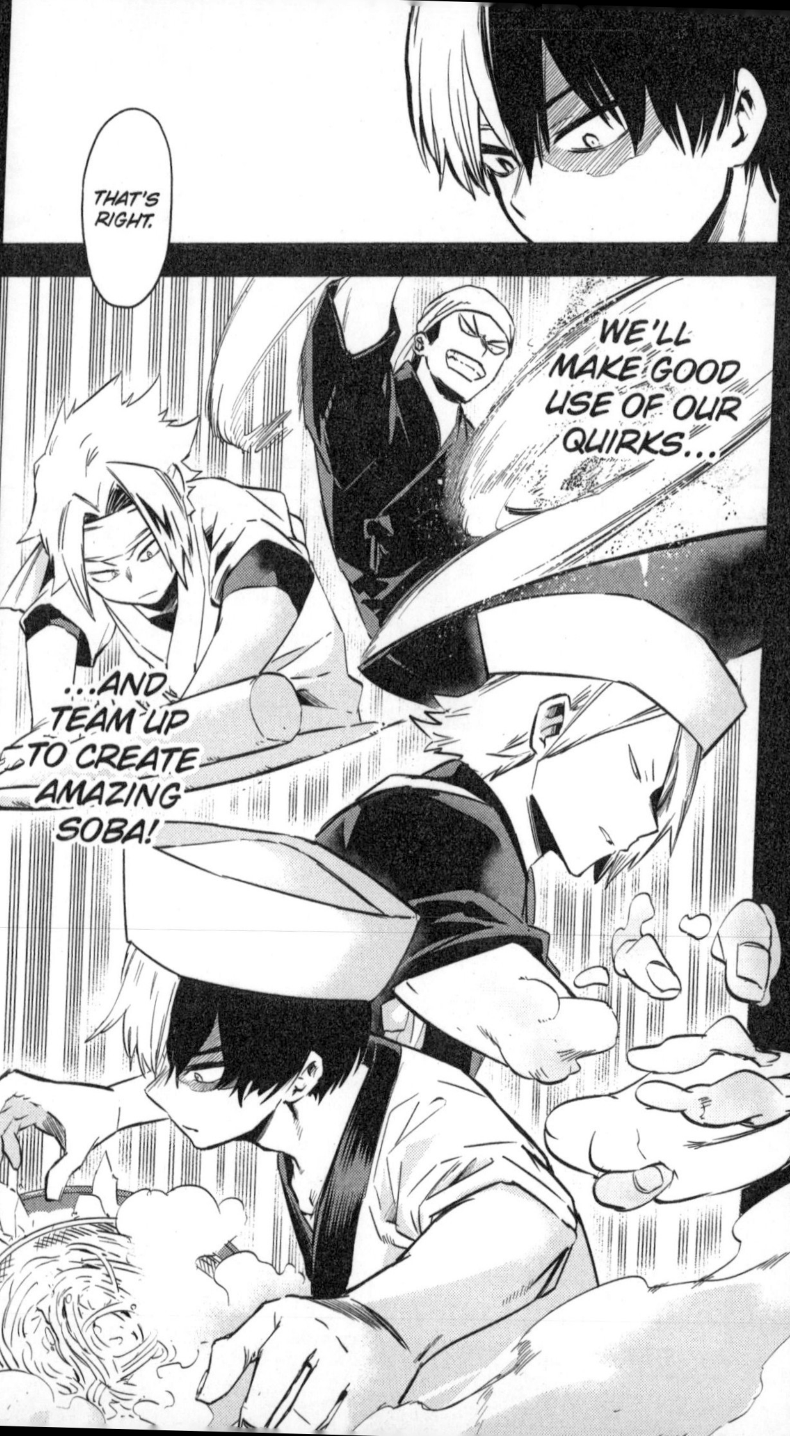
THAT'S RIGHT.
WE'LL MAKE GOOD USE OF OUR QUIRKS...
...AND TEAM UP TO CREATE AMAZING SOBA!

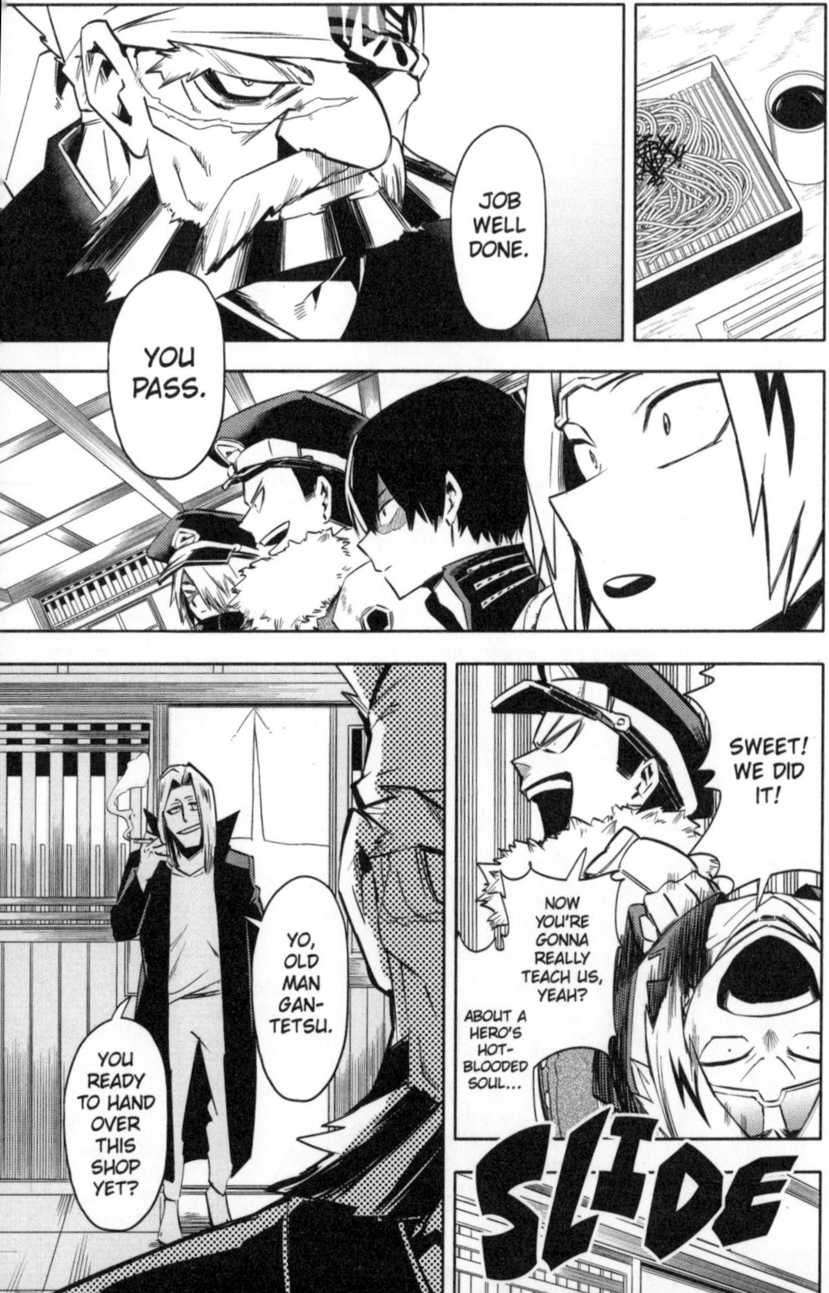
JOB WELL DONE.
YOU PASS.
SWEET! WE DID IT!
NOW YOU'RE GONNA REALLY TEACH US, YEAH?
ABOUT A HERO'S HOT-BLOODED SOUL...
SLIDE
YO, OLD MAN GAN-TETSU.
YOU READY TO HAND OVER THIS SHOP YET?

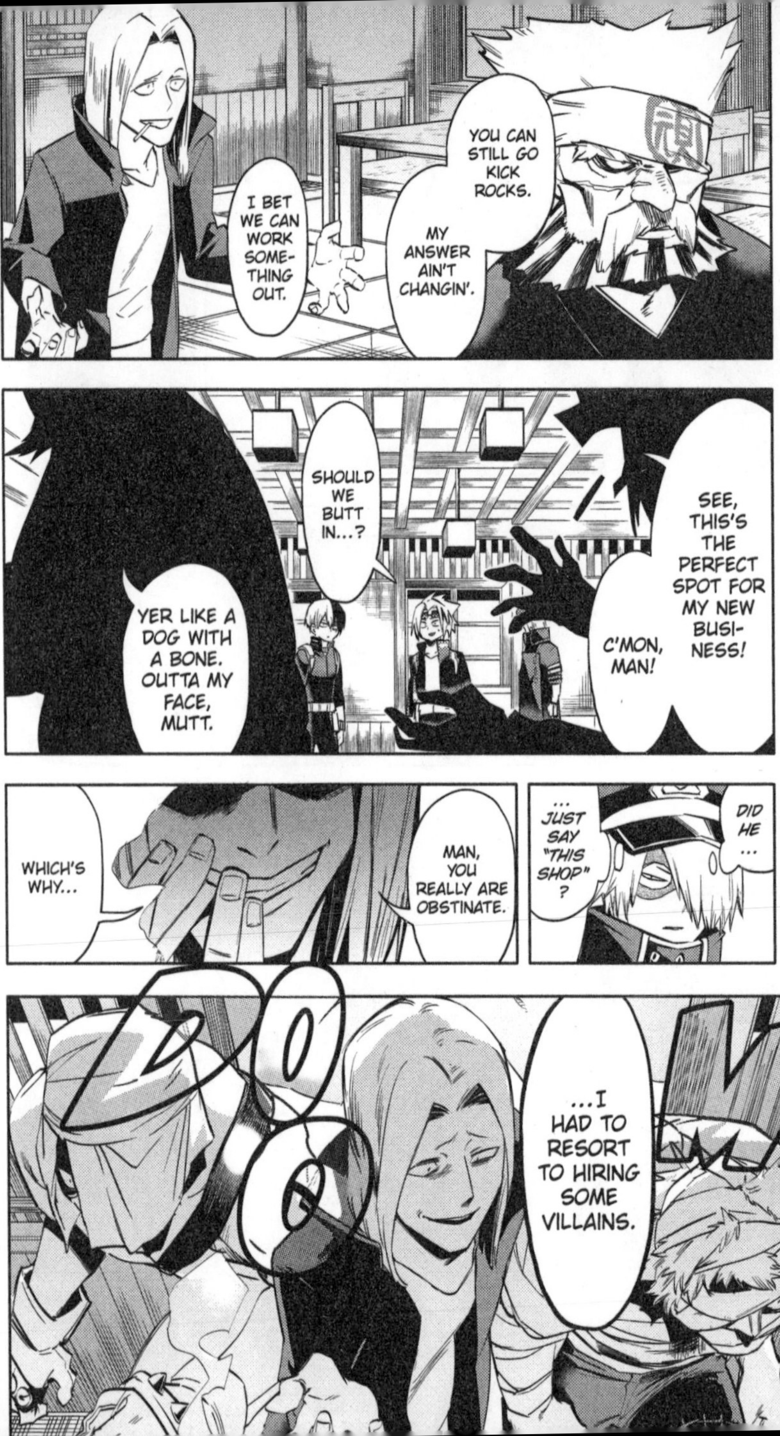
YOU CAN STILL GO KICK ROCKS.
MY ANSWER AIN'T CHANGIN'.
I BET WE CAN WORK SOME-THING OUT.
SEE, THIS'S THE PERFECT SPOT FOR MY NEW BUSI-NESS!
C'MON, MAN!
SHOULD WE BUTT IN...?
YER LIKE A DOG WITH A BONE. OUTTA MY FACE, MUTT.
DID HE...
...JUST SAY "THIS SHOP"?
MAN, YOU REALLY ARE OBSTINATE.
WHICH'S WHY...
...I HAD TO RESORT TO HIRING SOME VILLAINS.
DOOM

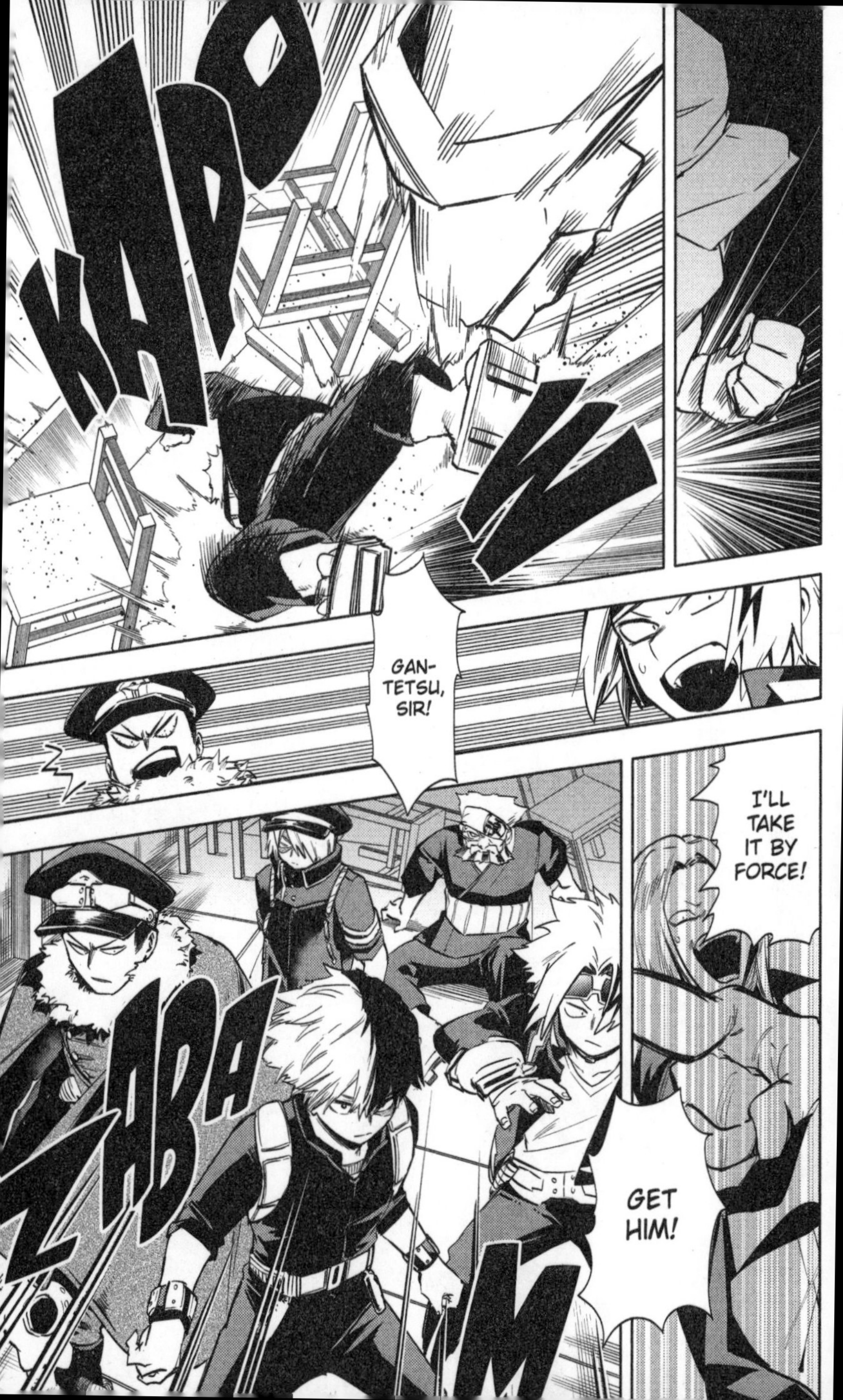
GAN-TETSU, SIR!
I'LL TAKE IT BY FORCE!
GET HIM!

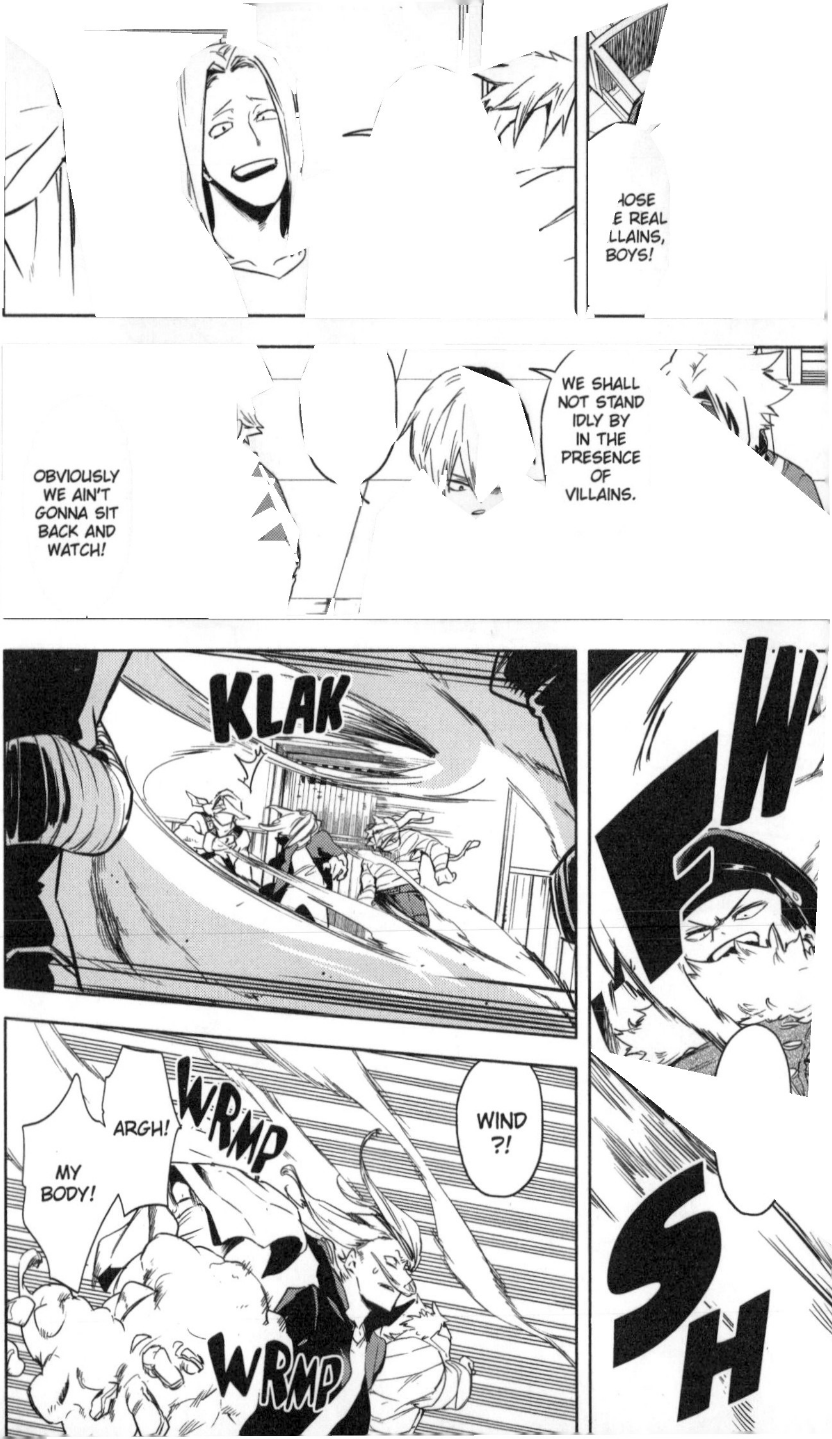
HOSE
E REAL
LLAINS,
BOYS!
WE SHALL NOT STAND IDLY BY IN THE PRESENCE OF VILLAINS.
OBVIOUSLY WE AIN'T GONNA SIT BACK AND WATCH!
SH
KLAK
WIND ?!
WRMP
ARGH!
MY BODY!
WRMP

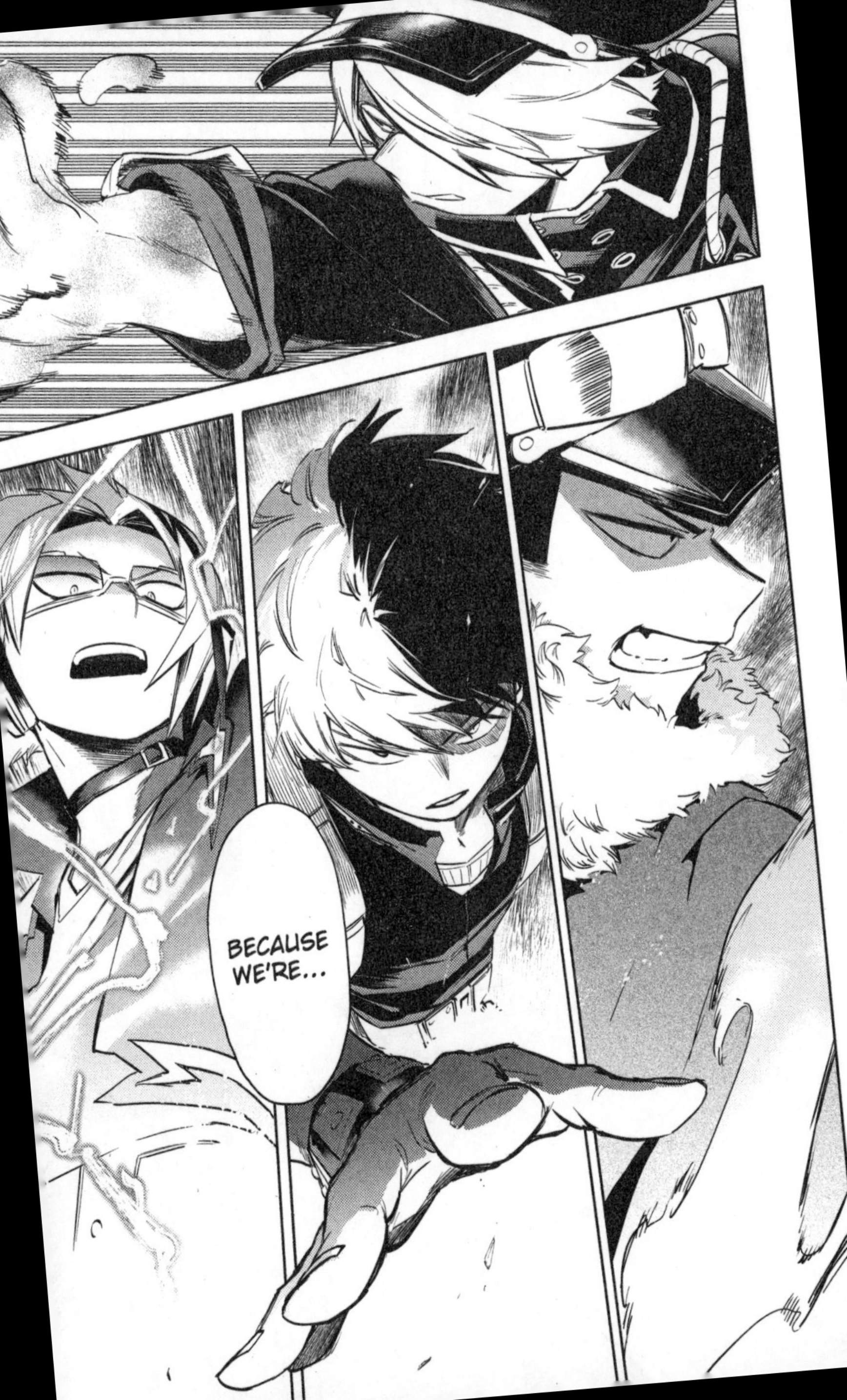
BECAUSE WE'RE...

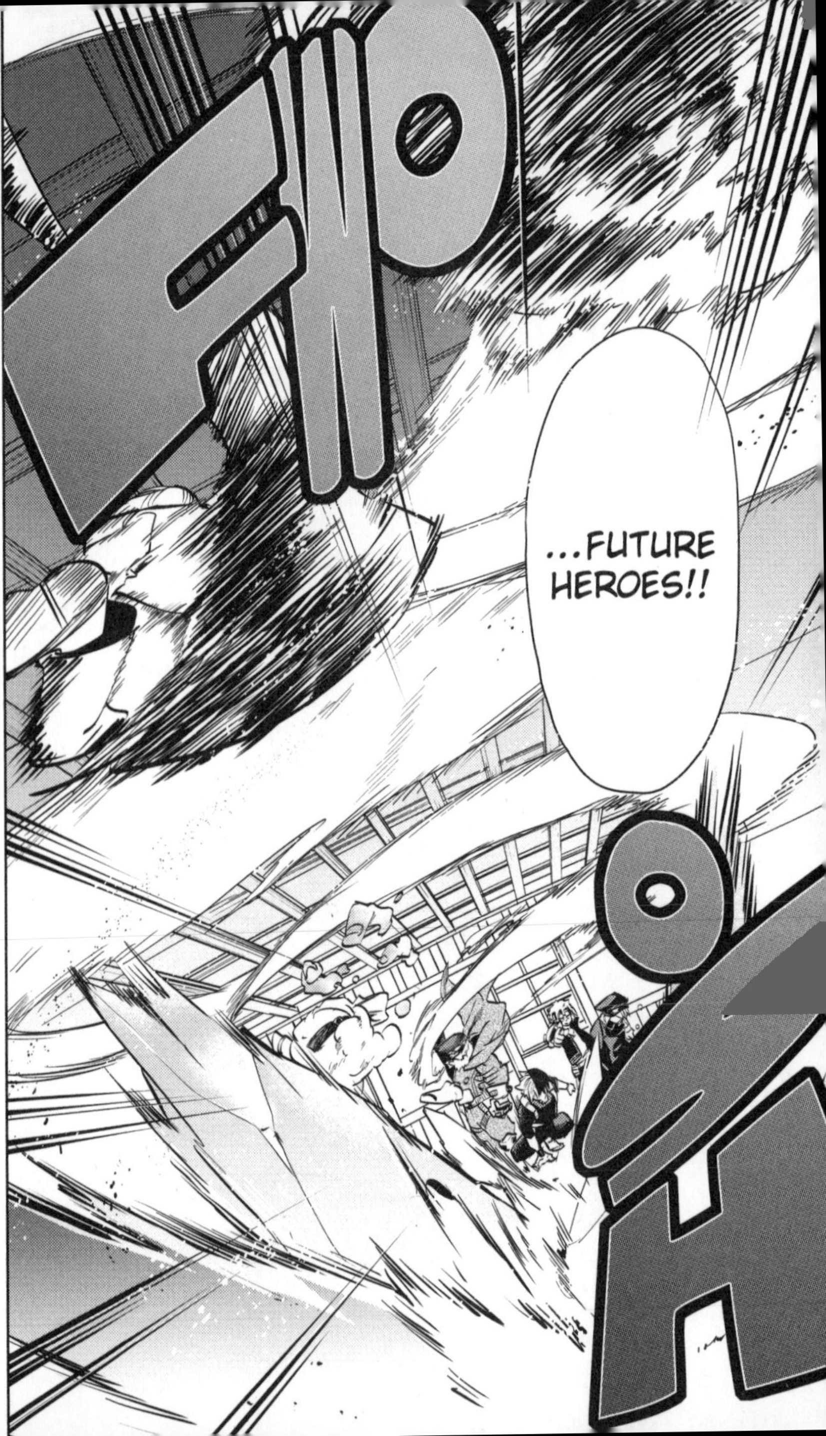
...FUTURE HEROES!!

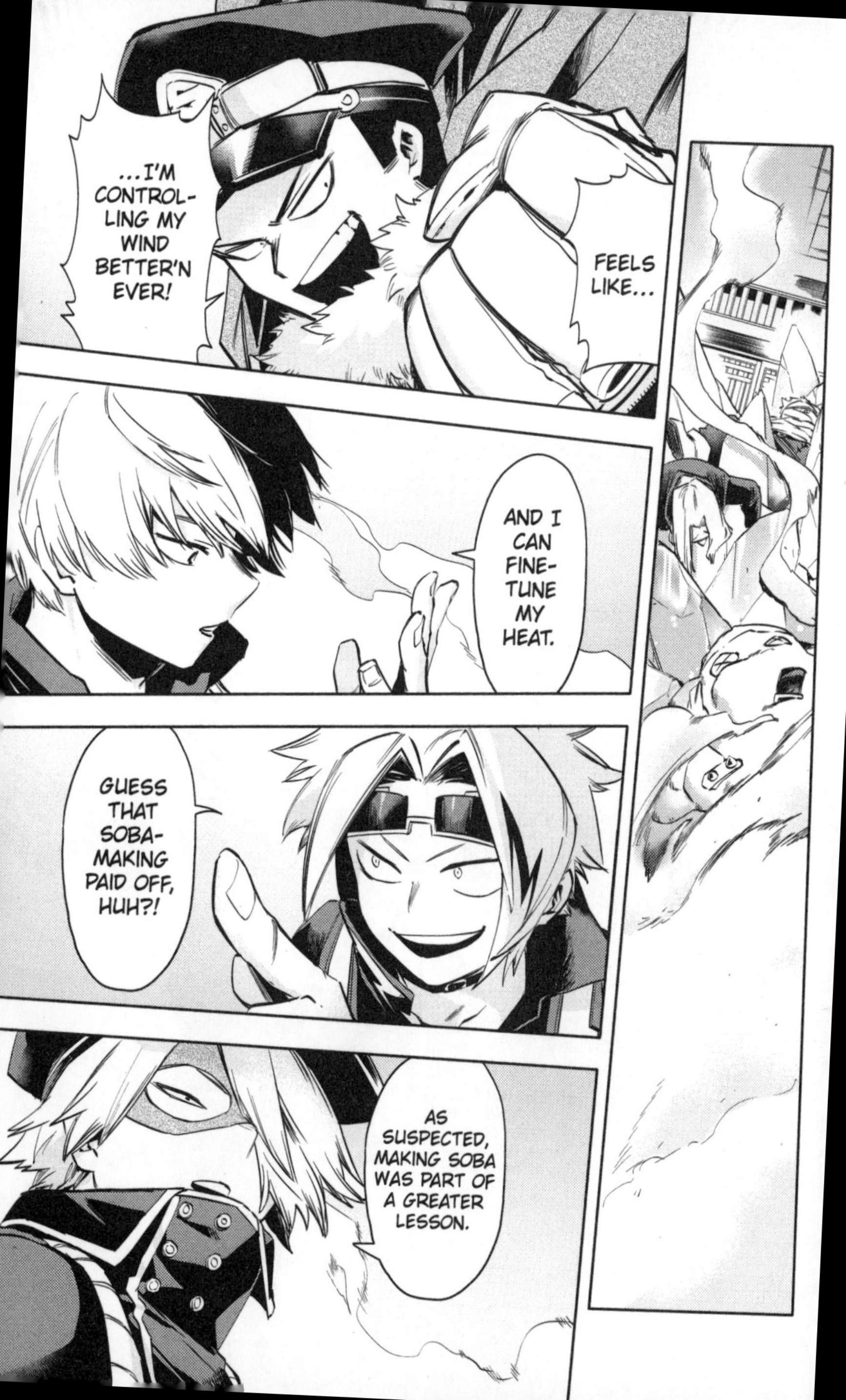
FEELS LIKE...
...I'M CONTROLLING MY WIND BETTER'N EVER!
AND I CAN FINE-TUNE MY HEAT.
GUESS THAT SOBA-MAKING PAID OFF, HUH?!
AS SUSPECTED, MAKING SOBA WAS PART OF A GREATER LESSON.

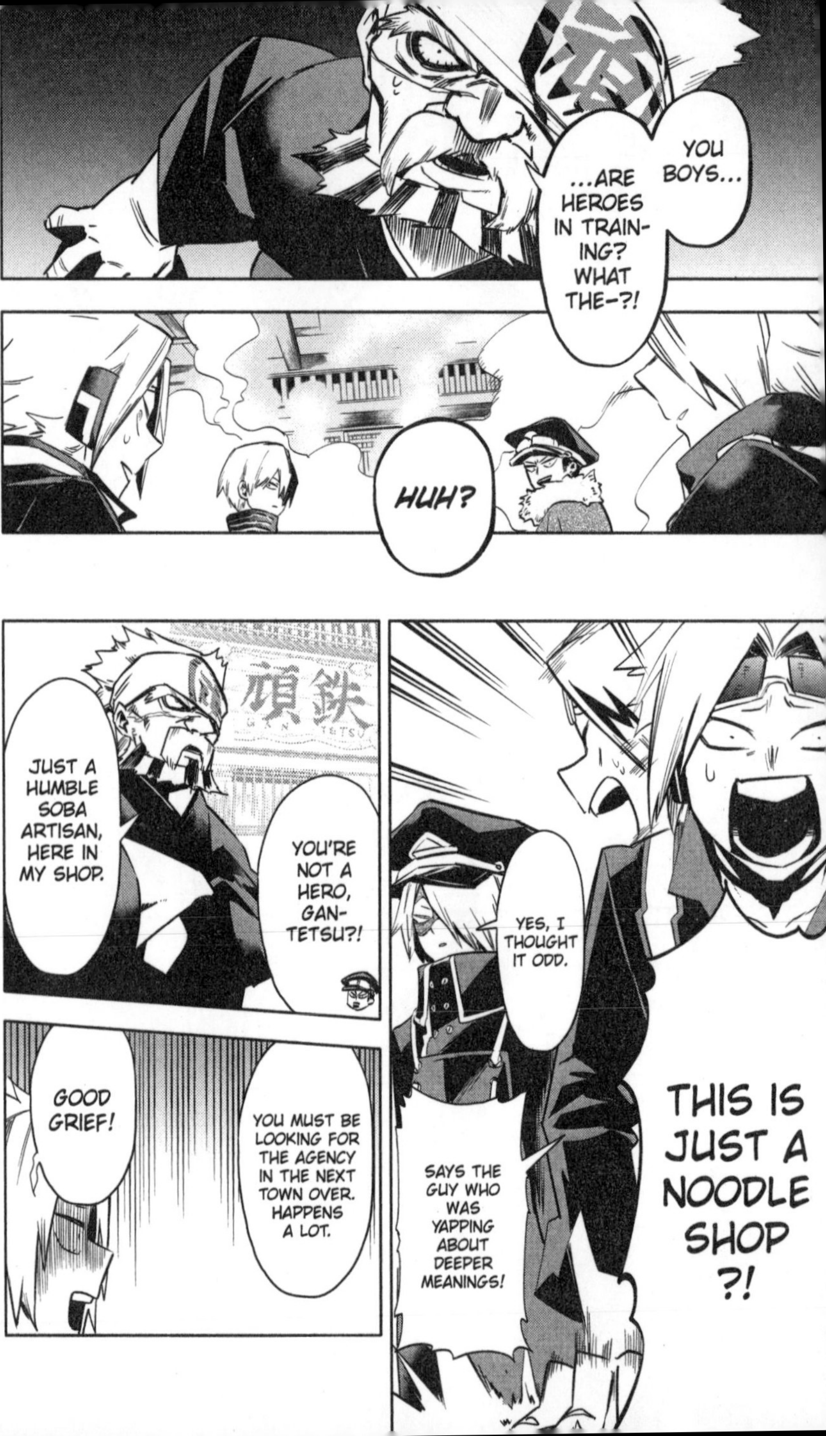
YOU BOYS...
...ARE HEROES IN TRAIN-ING? WHAT THE-?!
HUH?
THIS IS JUST A NOODLE SHOP ?!
YES, I THOUGHT IT ODD.
SAYS THE GUY WHO WAS YAPPING ABOUT DEEPER MEANINGS!
YOU'RE NOT A HERO, GAN-TETSU?!
JUST A HUMBLE SOBA ARTISAN, HERE IN MY SHOP.
頑鉄
GAN TETSU
YOU MUST BE LOOKING FOR THE AGENCY IN THE NEXT TOWN OVER. HAPPENS A LOT.
GOOD GRIEF!

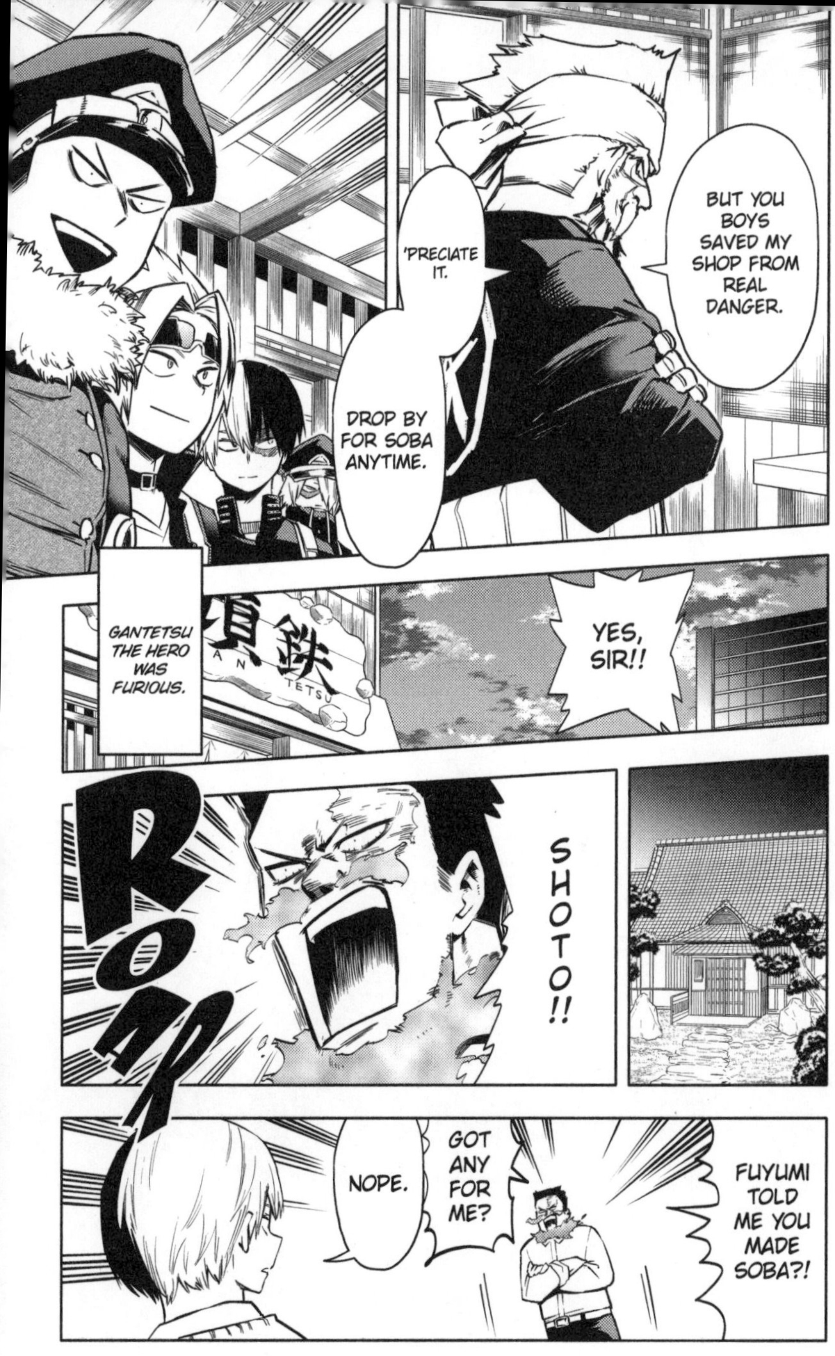
BUT YOU BOYS SAVED MY SHOP FROM REAL DANGER.
'PRECIATE IT.
DROP BY FOR SOBA ANYTIME.
YES, SIR!!
GANTETSU THE HERO WAS FURIOUS.
SHOTO!!
ROAR
FUYUMI TOLD ME YOU MADE SOBA?!
GOT ANY FOR ME?
NOPE.

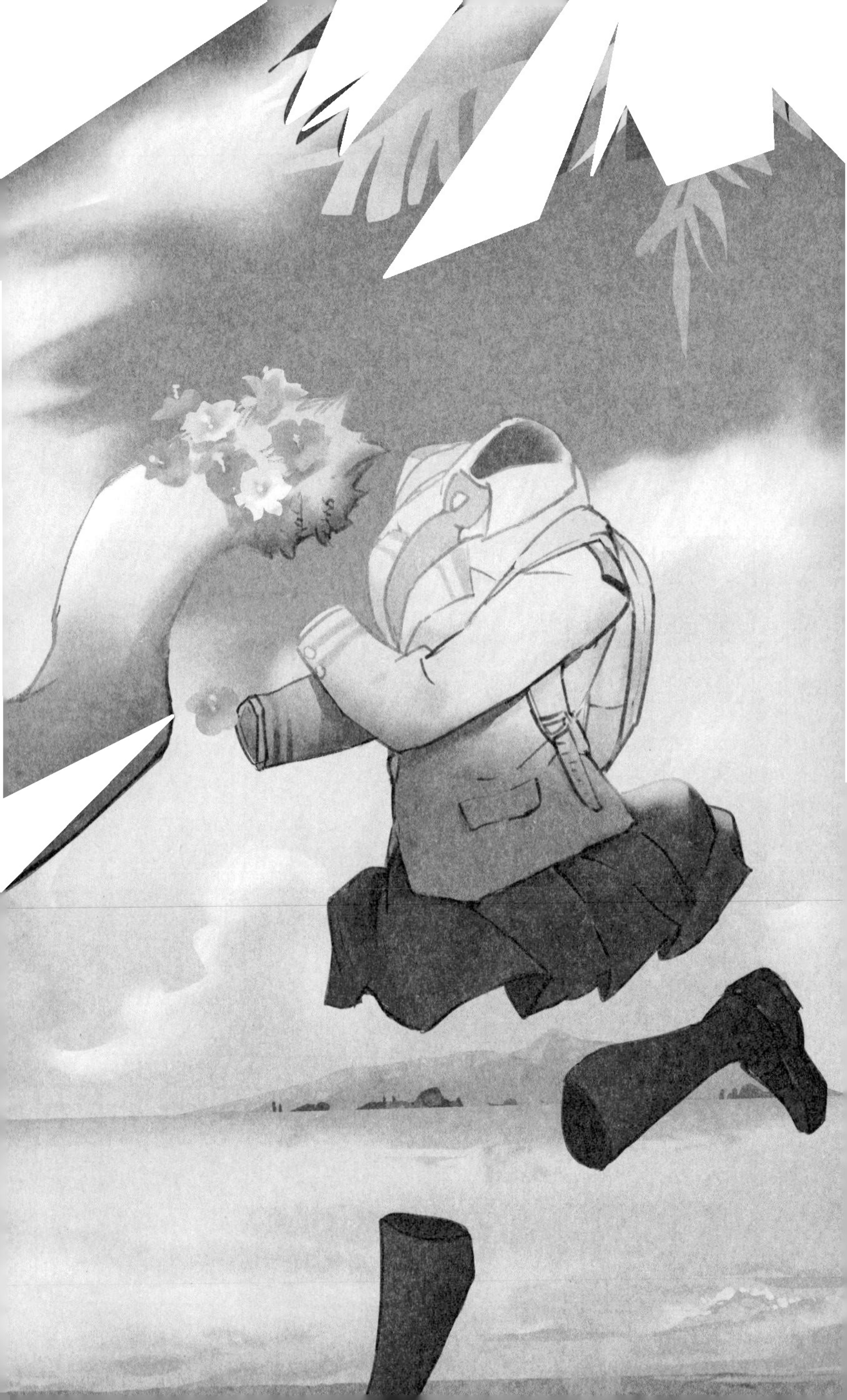

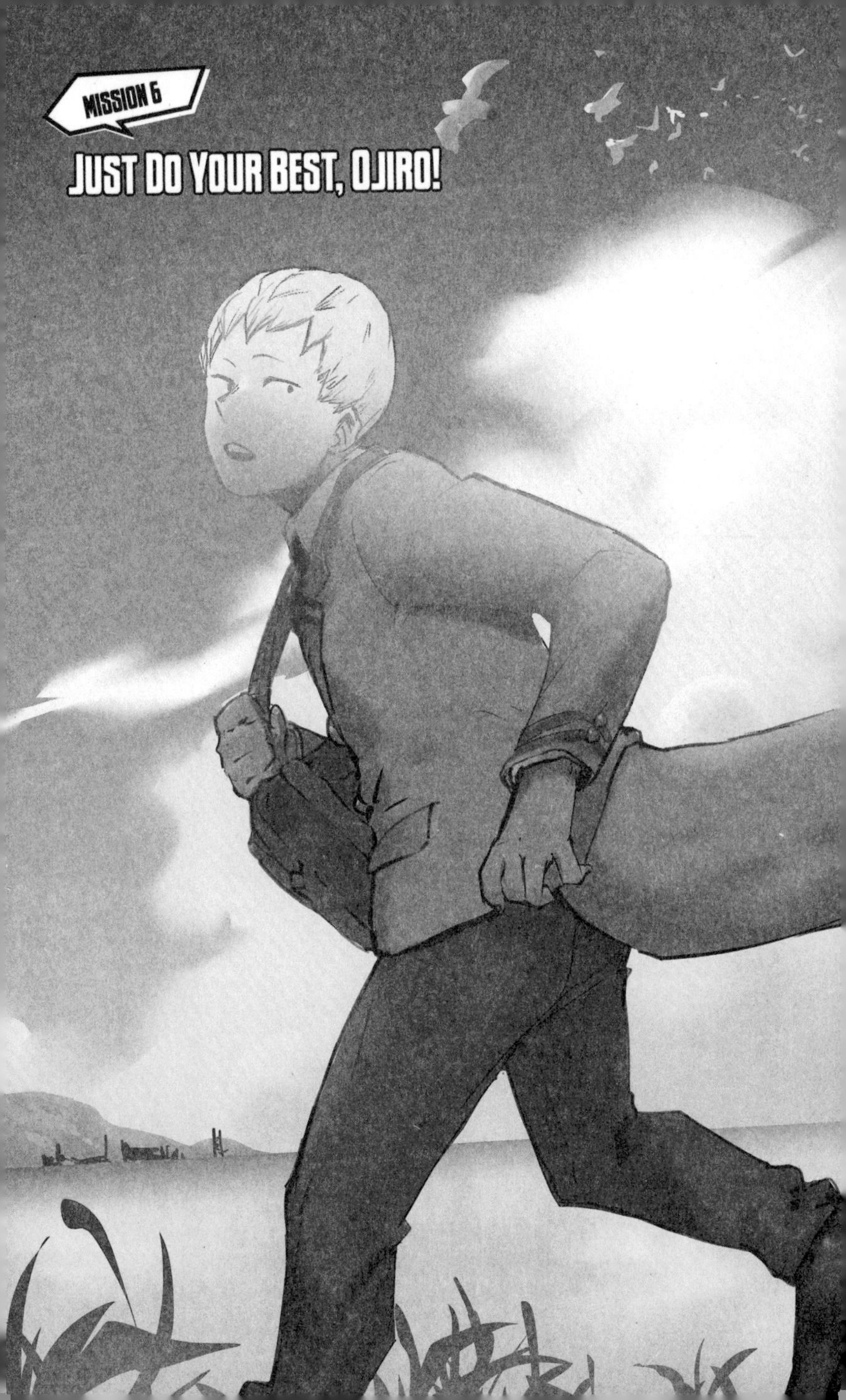
MISSION 6
JUST DO YOUR BEST, OJIRO!

MY HERO ACADEMIA
Team-Up Missions

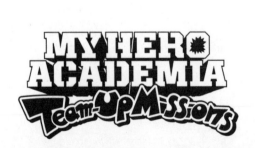

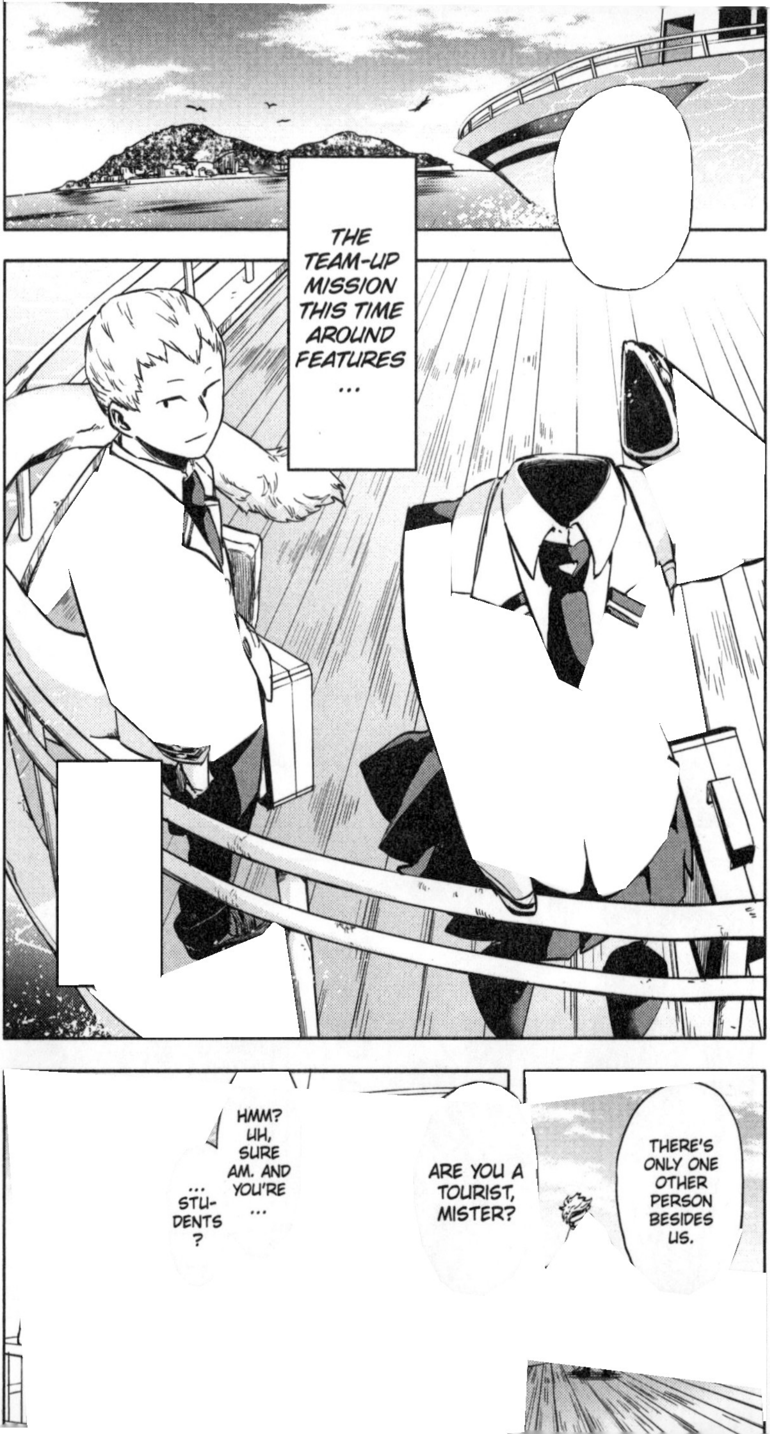
THE TEAM-UP MISSION THIS TIME AROUND FEATURES ...
THERE'S ONLY ONE OTHER PERSON BESIDES US.
ARE YOU A TOURIST, MISTER?
HMM? UH, SURE AM. AND YOU'RE ...
... STU-DENTS ?

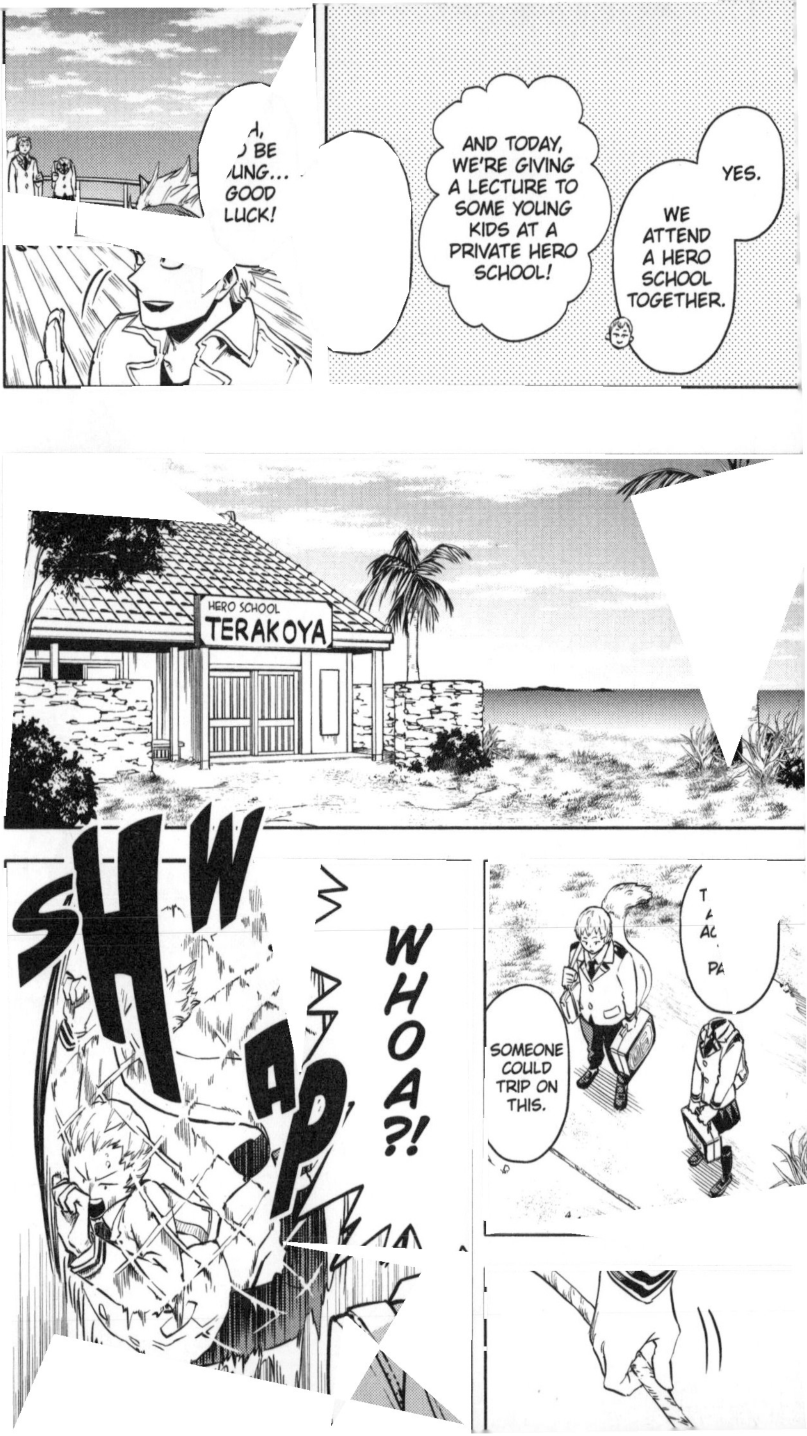
YES.
WE ATTEND A HERO SCHOOL TOGETHER.
AND TODAY, WE'RE GIVING A LECTURE TO SOME YOUNG KIDS AT A PRIVATE HERO SCHOOL!
GOOD LUCK!
HERO SCHOOL
TERAKOYA
SOMEONE COULD TRIP ON THIS.
WHOA?!
SHWAP

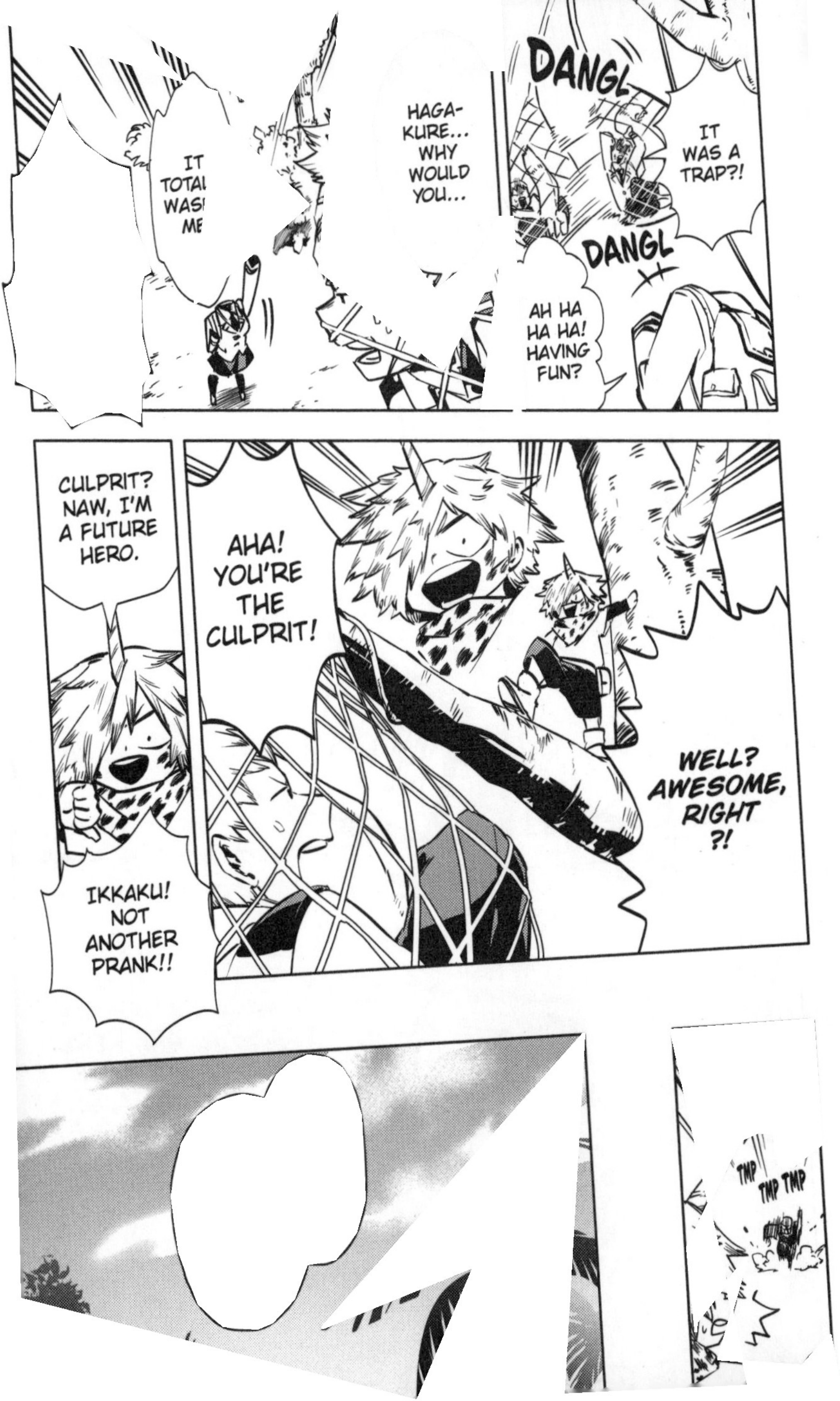
DANGL
IT WAS A TRAP?!
DANGL
AH HA HA HA! HAVING FUN?
HAGA-KURE... WHY WOULD YOU...
IT TOTAL WAS ME
AHA! YOU'RE THE CULPRIT!
WELL? AWESOME, RIGHT ?!
CULPRIT? NAW, I'M A FUTURE HERO.
IKKAKU! NOT ANOTHER PRANK!!
TMP TMP TMP

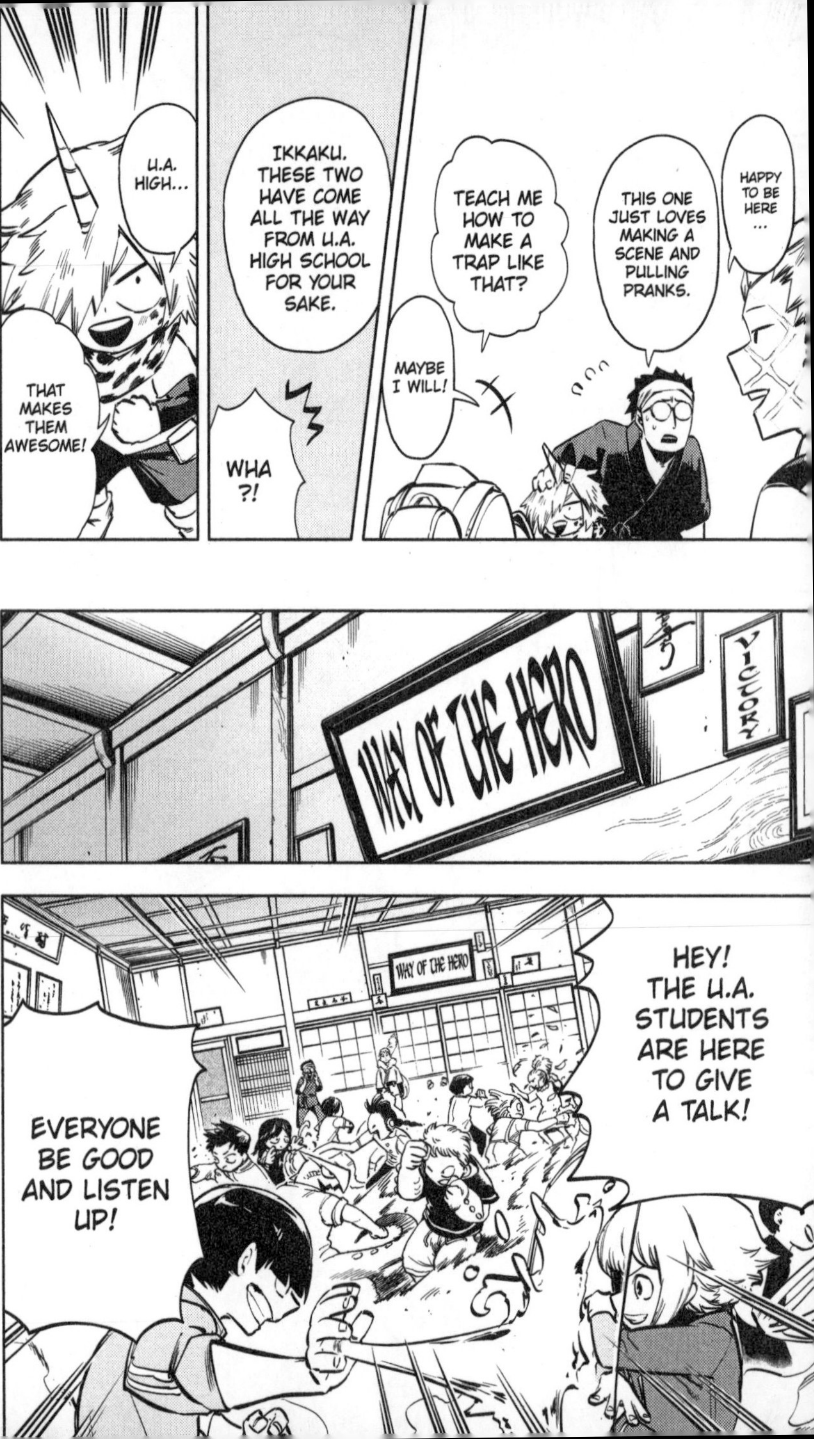

HAPPY TO BE HERE...
THIS ONE JUST LOVES MAKING A SCENE AND PULLING PRANKS.
TEACH ME HOW TO MAKE A TRAP LIKE THAT?
MAYBE I WILL!
IKKAKU. THESE TWO HAVE COME ALL THE WAY FROM U.A. HIGH SCHOOL FOR YOUR SAKE.
WHA?!
U.A. HIGH...
THAT MAKES THEM AWESOME!
VICTORY
WAY OF THE HERO
HEY! THE U.A. STUDENTS ARE HERE TO GIVE A TALK!
WAY OF THE HERO
EVERYONE BE GOOD AND LISTEN UP!

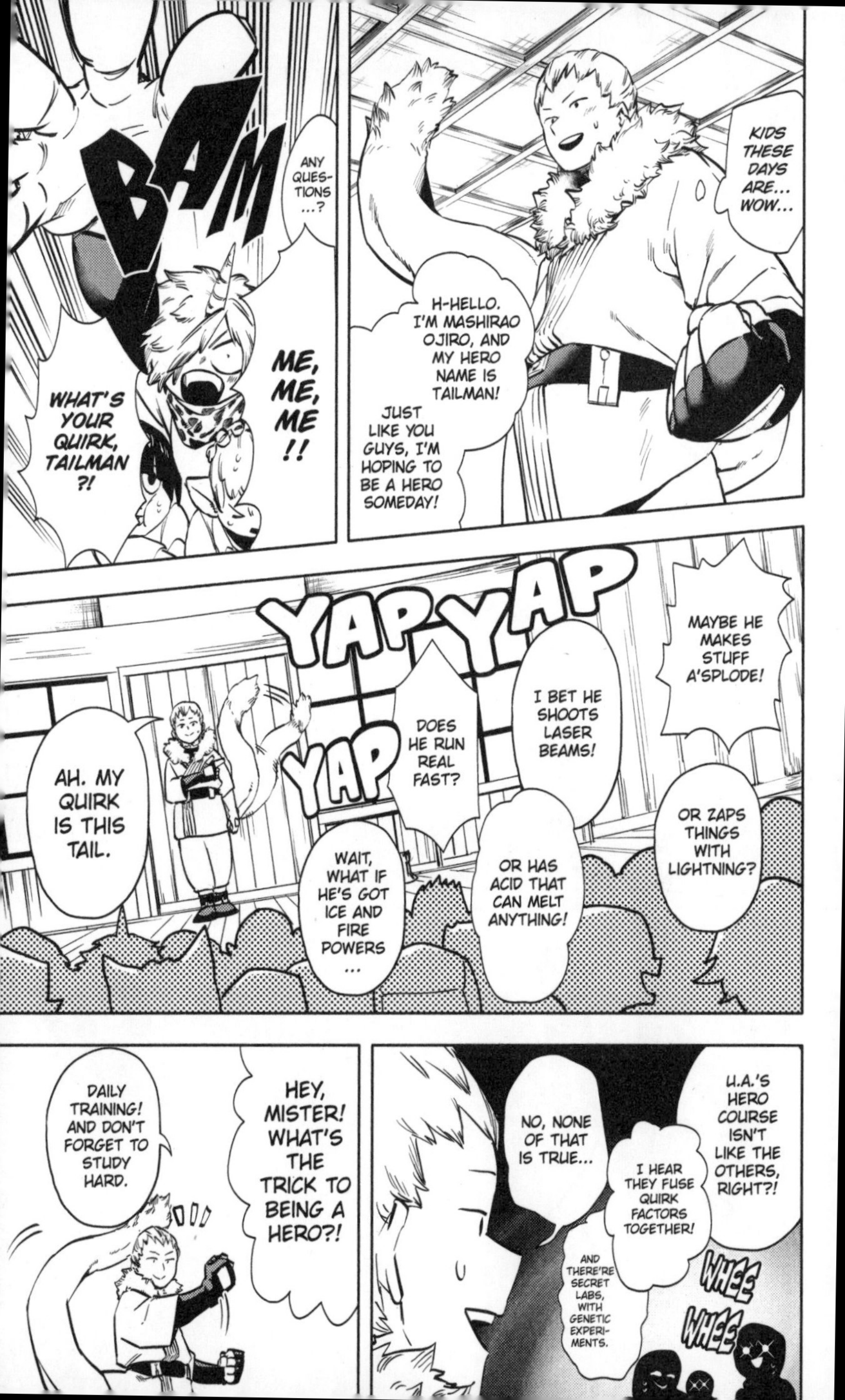
KIDS THESE DAYS ARE... WOW...
H-HELLO. I'M MASHIRAO OJIRO, AND MY HERO NAME IS TAILMAN!
JUST LIKE YOU GUYS, I'M HOPING TO BE A HERO SOMEDAY!
ANY QUESTIONS ...?
BAM
ME, ME, ME!!
WHAT'S YOUR QUIRK, TAILMAN?!
YAP YAP
MAYBE HE MAKES STUFF A'SPLODE!
I BET HE SHOOTS LASER BEAMS!
DOES HE RUN REAL FAST?
YAP
OR ZAPS THINGS WITH LIGHTNING?
OR HAS ACID THAT CAN MELT ANYTHING!
WAIT, WHAT IF HE'S GOT ICE AND FIRE POWERS ...
AH. MY QUIRK IS THIS TAIL.
U.A.'S HERO COURSE ISN'T LIKE THE OTHERS, RIGHT?!
I HEAR THEY FUSE QUIRK FACTORS TOGETHER!
NO, NONE OF THAT IS TRUE...
AND THERE'RE SECRET LABS, WITH GENETIC EXPERIMENTS.
WHEE
WHEE
HEY, MISTER! WHAT'S THE TRICK TO BEING A HERO?!
DAILY TRAINING! AND DON'T FORGET TO STUDY HARD.

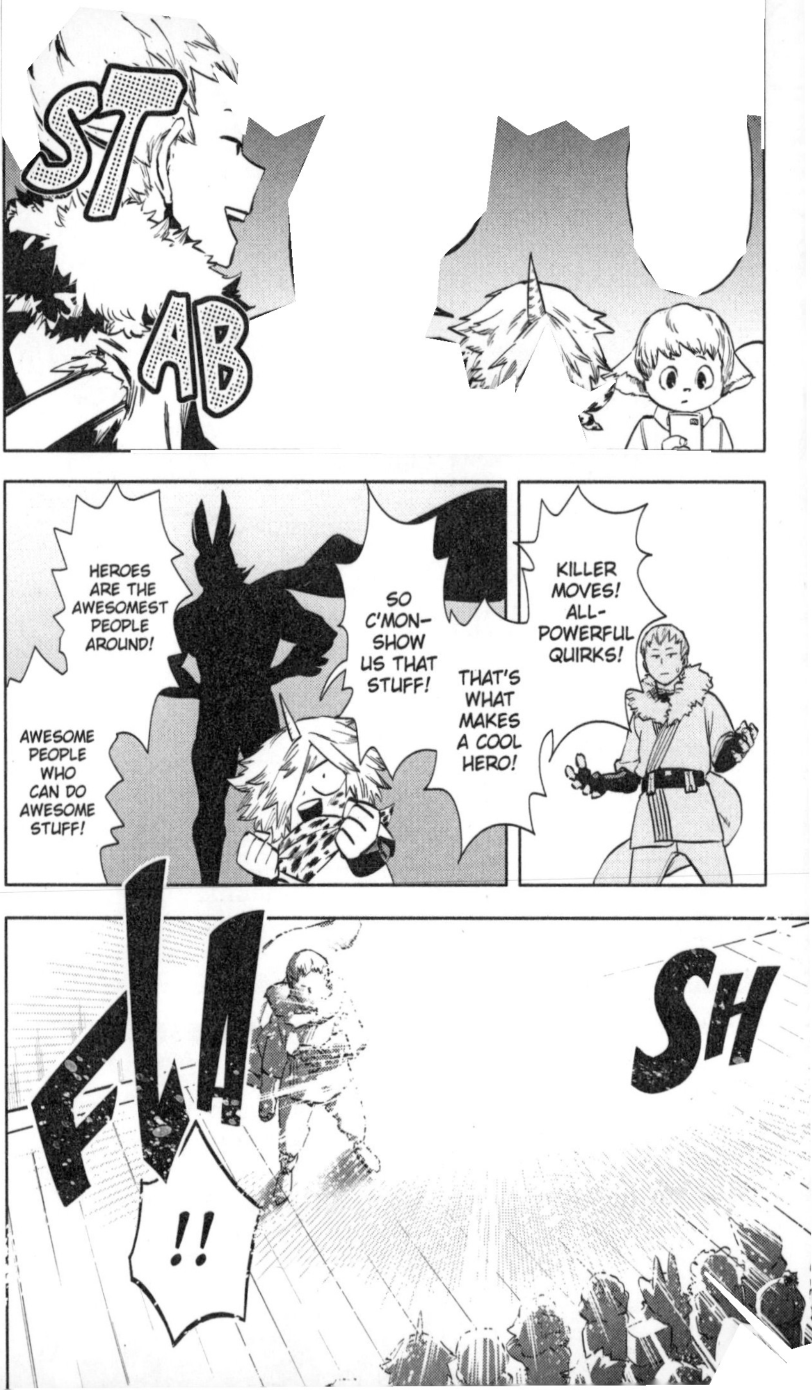
STAB
KILLER MOVES! ALL-POWERFUL QUIRKS!
THAT'S WHAT MAKES A COOL HERO!
SO C'MON-SHOW US THAT STUFF!
HEROES ARE THE AWESOMEST PEOPLE AROUND!
AWESOME PEOPLE WHO CAN DO AWESOME STUFF!
FLA
SH
!!

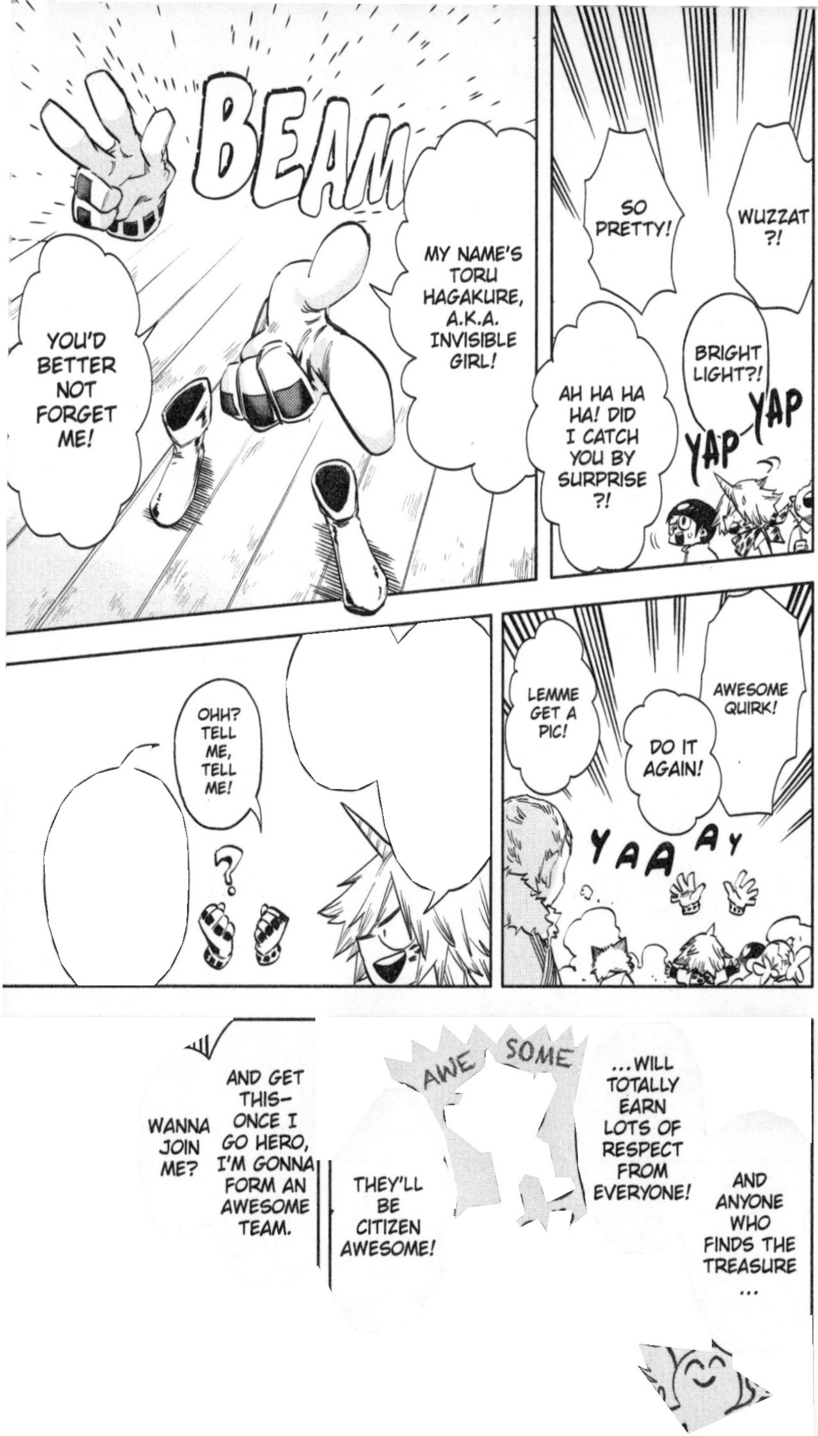
WUZZAT?!
SO PRETTY!
BRIGHT LIGHT?!
YAP YAP
AH HA HA HA! DID I CATCH YOU BY SURPRISE?!
BEAM
MY NAME'S TORU HAGAKURE, A.K.A. INVISIBLE GIRL!
YOU'D BETTER NOT FORGET ME!
AWESOME QUIRK!
LEMME GET A PIC!
DO IT AGAIN!
YAAAY
OHH? TELL ME, TELL ME!
?
AND ANYONE WHO FINDS THE TREASURE...
...WILL TOTALLY EARN LOTS OF RESPECT FROM EVERYONE!
AWESOME
THEY'LL BE CITIZEN AWESOME!
AND GET THIS— ONCE I GO HERO, I'M GONNA FORM AN AWESOME TEAM.
WANNA JOIN ME?

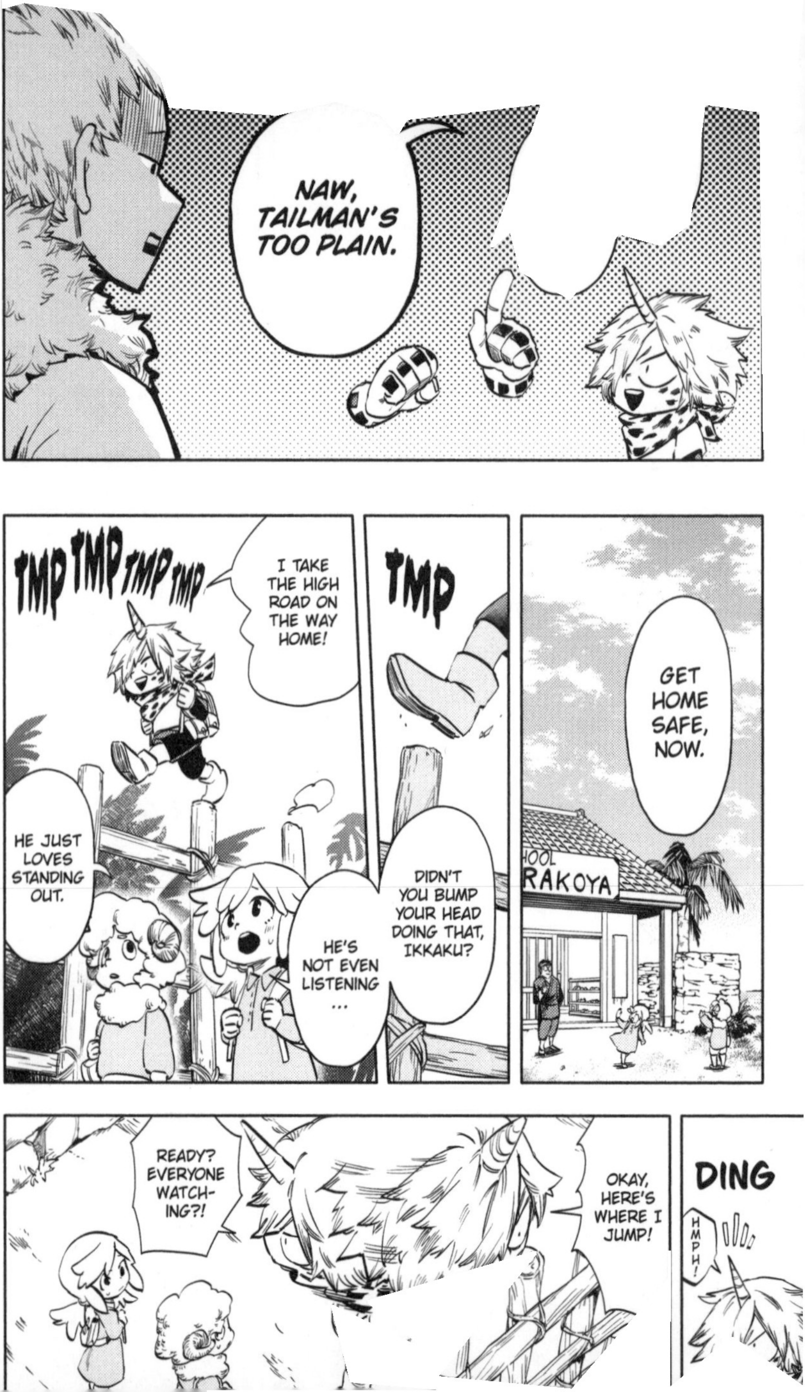
NAW, TAILMAN'S TOO PLAIN.
GET HOME SAFE, NOW.
TMP
DIDN'T YOU BUMP YOUR HEAD DOING THAT, IKKAKU?
TMP TMP TMP TMP
I TAKE THE HIGH ROAD ON THE WAY HOME!
HE'S NOT EVEN LISTENING ...
HE JUST LOVES STANDING OUT.
DING
HMPH!
OKAY, HERE'S WHERE I JUMP!
READY? EVERYONE WATCHING?!

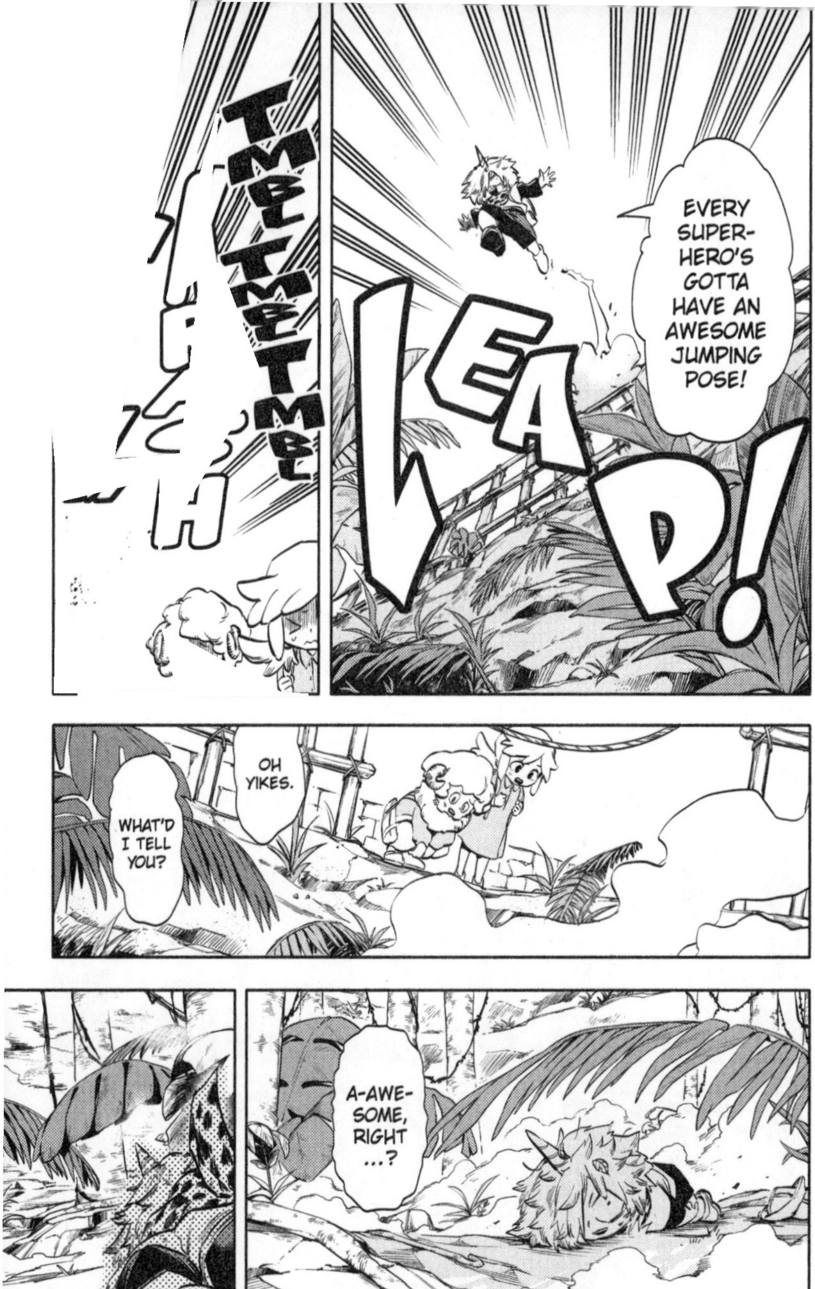
EVERY SUPER-HERO'S GOTTA HAVE AN AWESOME JUMPING POSE!
LEAP!
TMBL TMBL TMBL
OH YIKES.
WHAT'D I TELL YOU?
A-AWE-SOME, RIGHT ...?

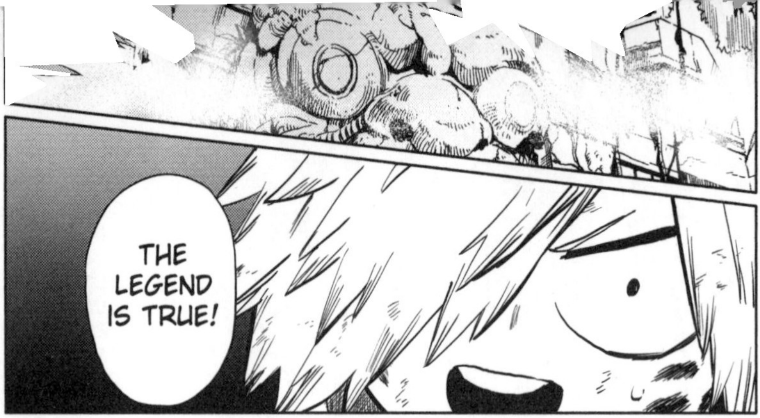
THE LEGEND IS TRUE!

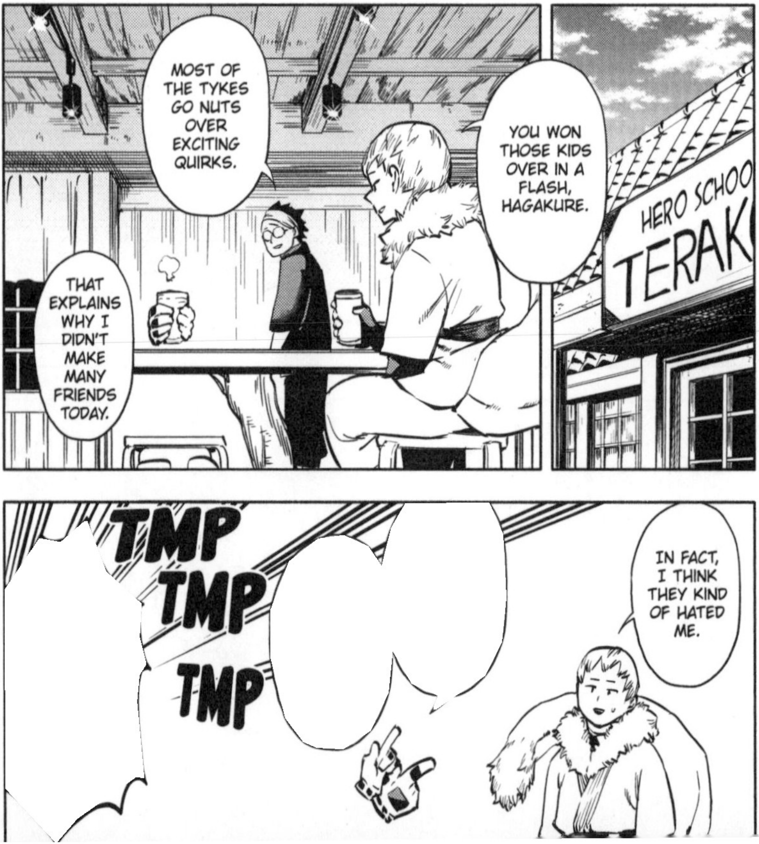
HERO SCHOO
TERAK
YOU WON THOSE KIDS OVER IN A FLASH, HAGAKURE.
MOST OF THE TYKES GO NUTS OVER EXCITING QUIRKS.
THAT EXPLAINS WHY I DIDN'T MAKE MANY FRIENDS TODAY.
IN FACT, I THINK THEY KIND OF HATED ME.
TMP
TMP
TMP

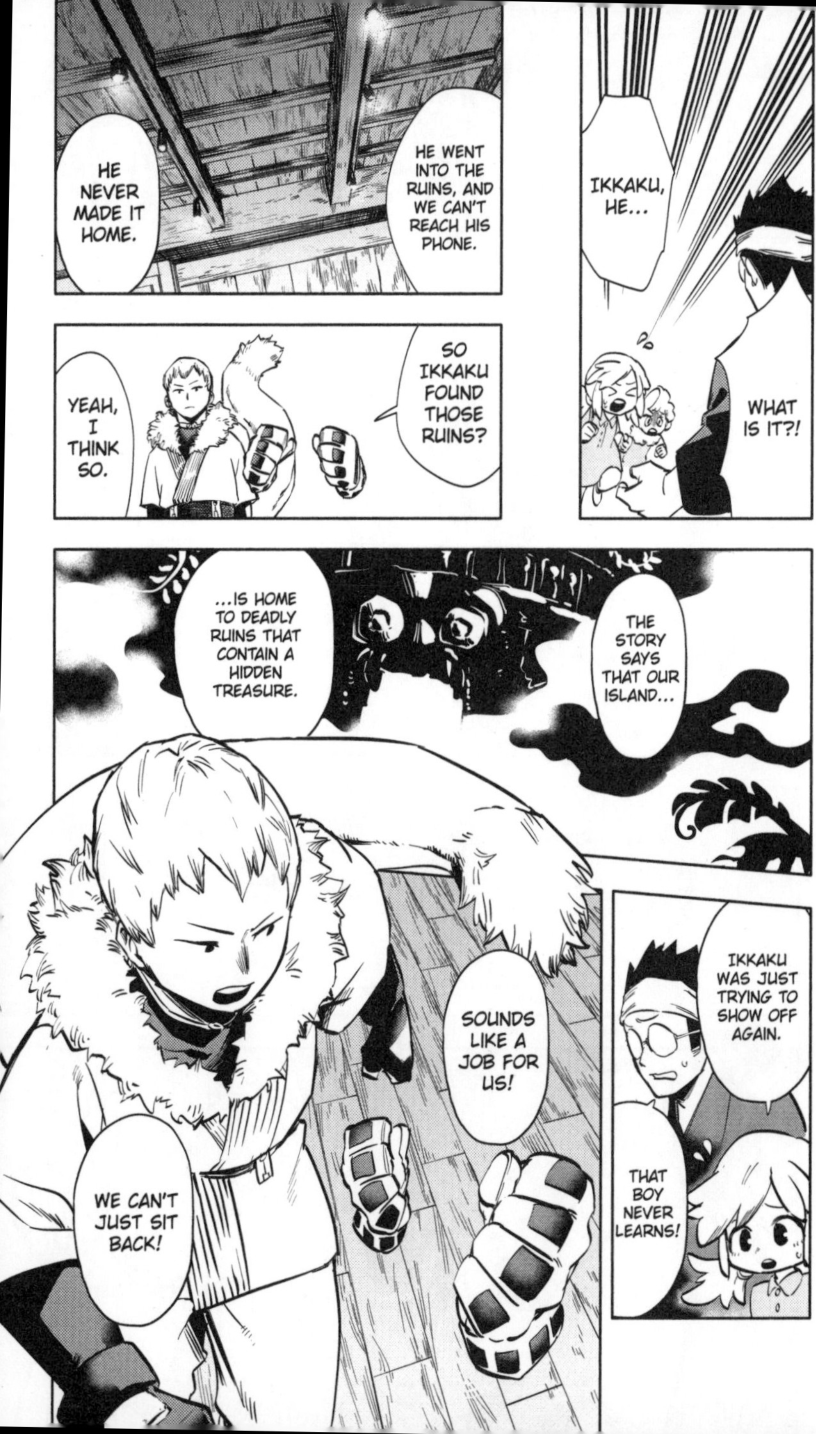
IKKAKU, HE...
WHAT IS IT?!
HE WENT INTO THE RUINS, AND WE CAN'T REACH HIS PHONE.
HE NEVER MADE IT HOME.
SO IKKAKU FOUND THOSE RUINS?
YEAH, I THINK SO.
THE STORY SAYS THAT OUR ISLAND...
...IS HOME TO DEADLY RUINS THAT CONTAIN A HIDDEN TREASURE.
IKKAKU WAS JUST TRYING TO SHOW OFF AGAIN.
THAT BOY NEVER LEARNS!
SOUNDS LIKE A JOB FOR US!
WE CAN'T JUST SIT BACK!

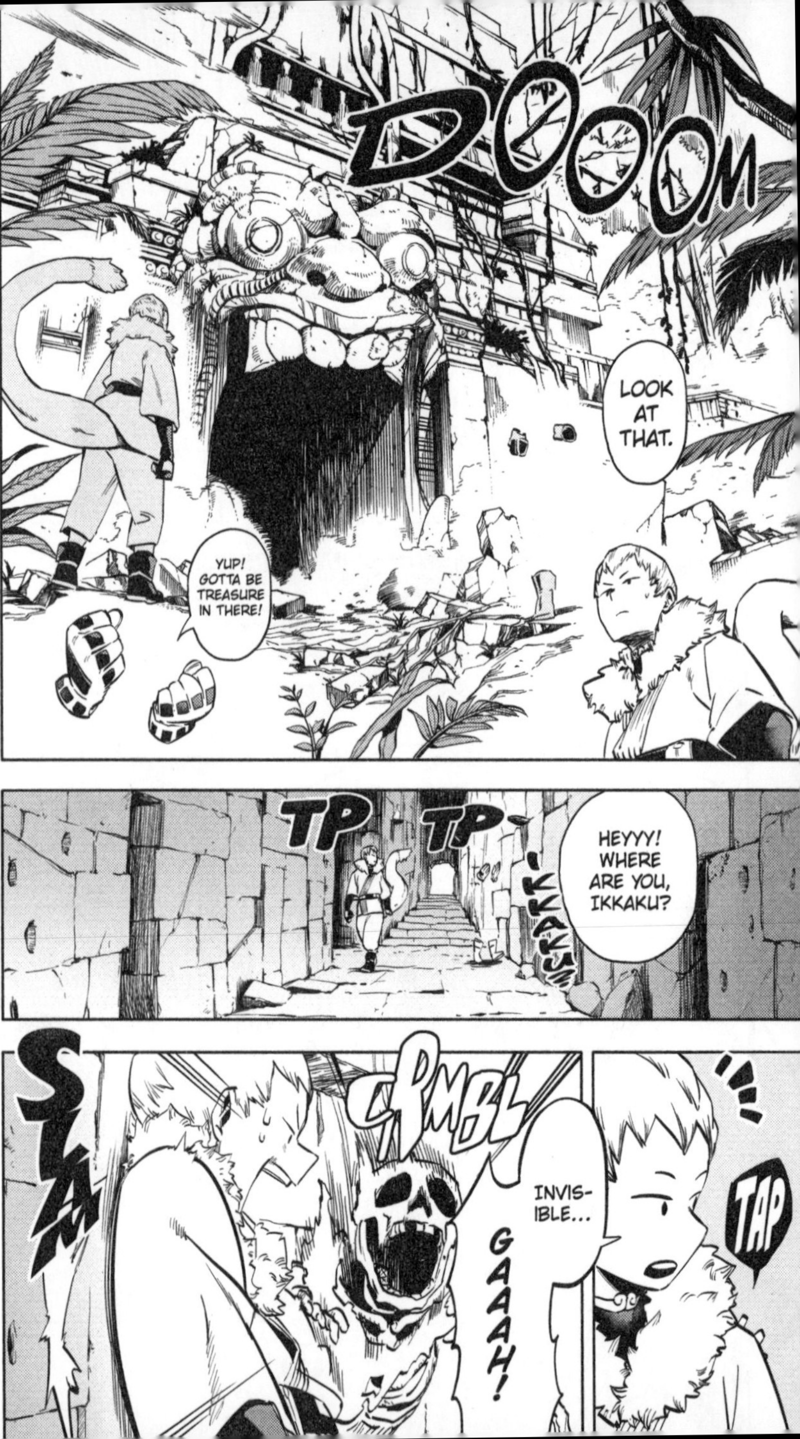
DOOOM
LOOK AT THAT.
YUP! GOTTA BE TREASURE IN THERE!
HEYYY! WHERE ARE YOU, IKKAKU?
IKKAKU
TP TP
INVISIBLE...
TAP
CRMBL
GAAAH!

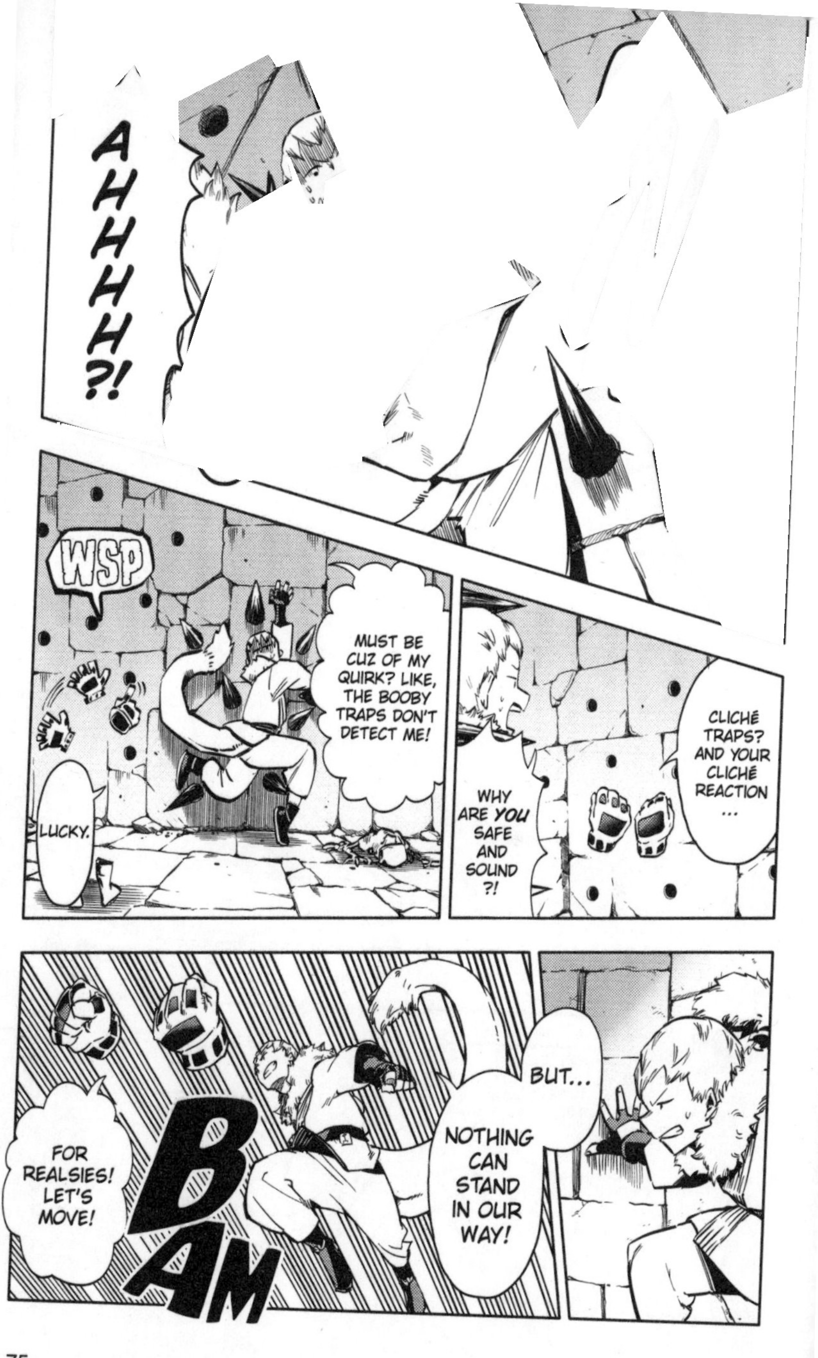
AHHHHH?!
CLICHÉ TRAPS? AND YOUR CLICHÉ REACTION ...
WHY ARE *YOU* SAFE AND SOUND ?!
MUST BE CUZ OF MY QUIRK? LIKE, THE BOOBY TRAPS DON'T DETECT ME!
WSP
LUCKY.
BUT...
NOTHING CAN STAND IN OUR WAY!
BAM
FOR REALSIES! LET'S MOVE!

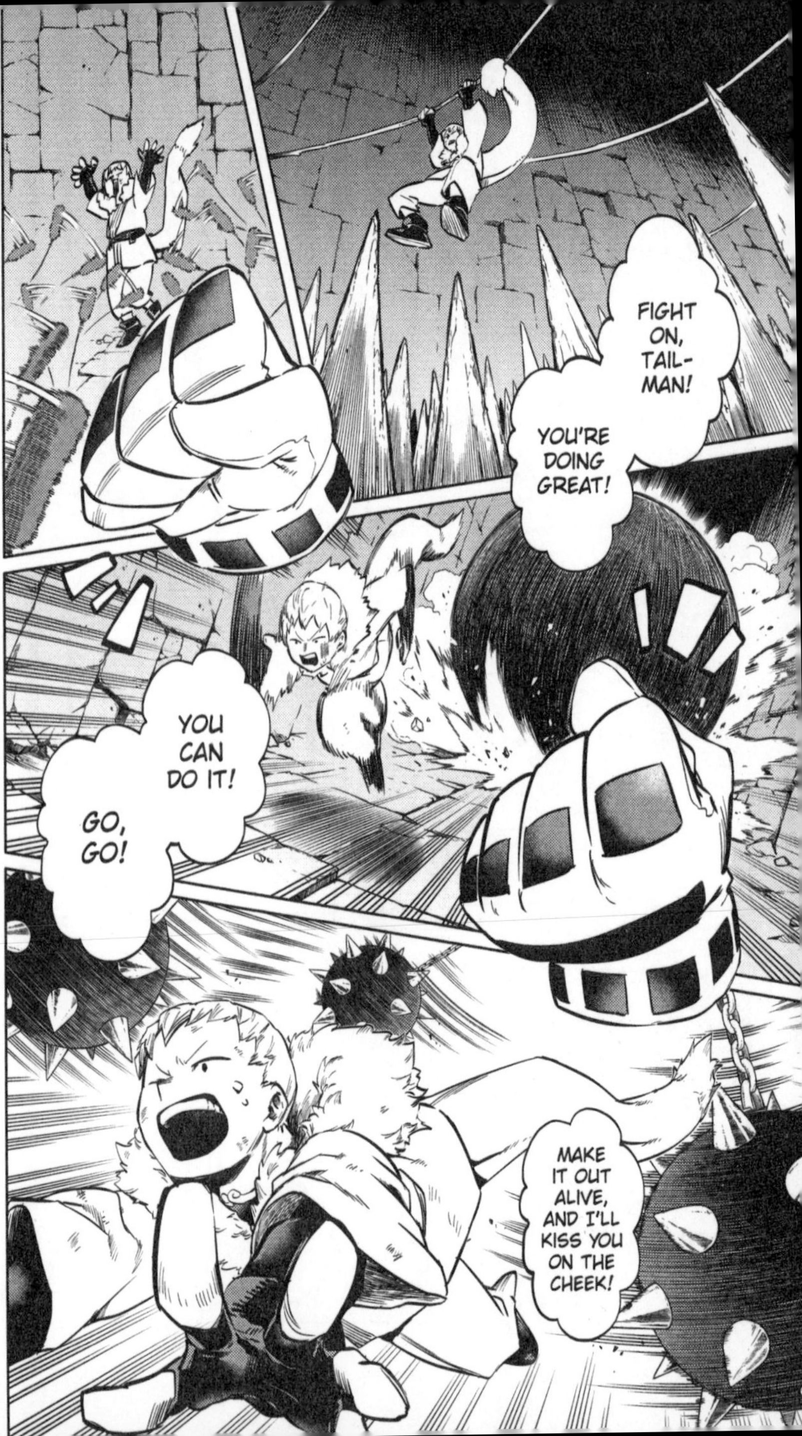
FIGHT ON, TAIL-MAN!
YOU'RE DOING GREAT!
YOU CAN DO IT!
GO, GO!
MAKE IT OUT ALIVE, AND I'LL KISS YOU ON THE CHEEK!

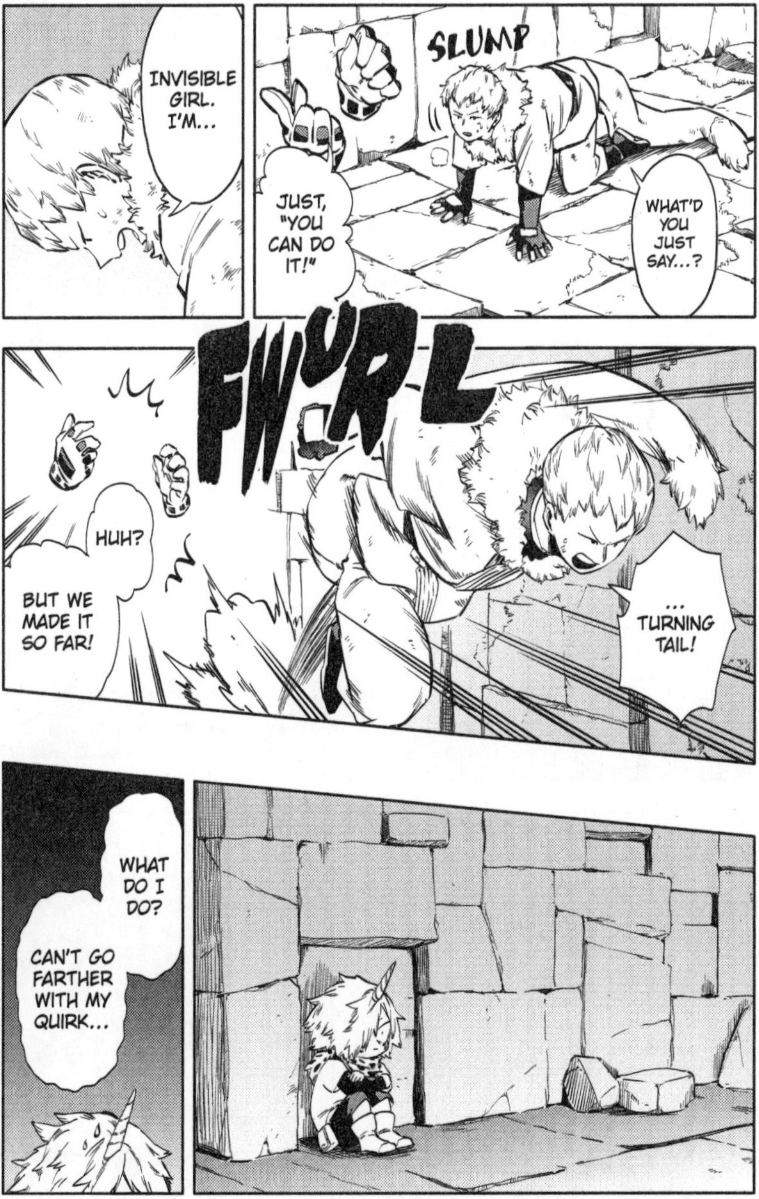
SLUMP
WHAT'D YOU JUST SAY...?
JUST, "YOU CAN DO IT!"
INVISIBLE GIRL. I'M...
FWURL
...TURNING TAIL!
HUH?
BUT WE MADE IT SO FAR!
WHAT DO I DO?
CAN'T GO FARTHER WITH MY QUIRK...

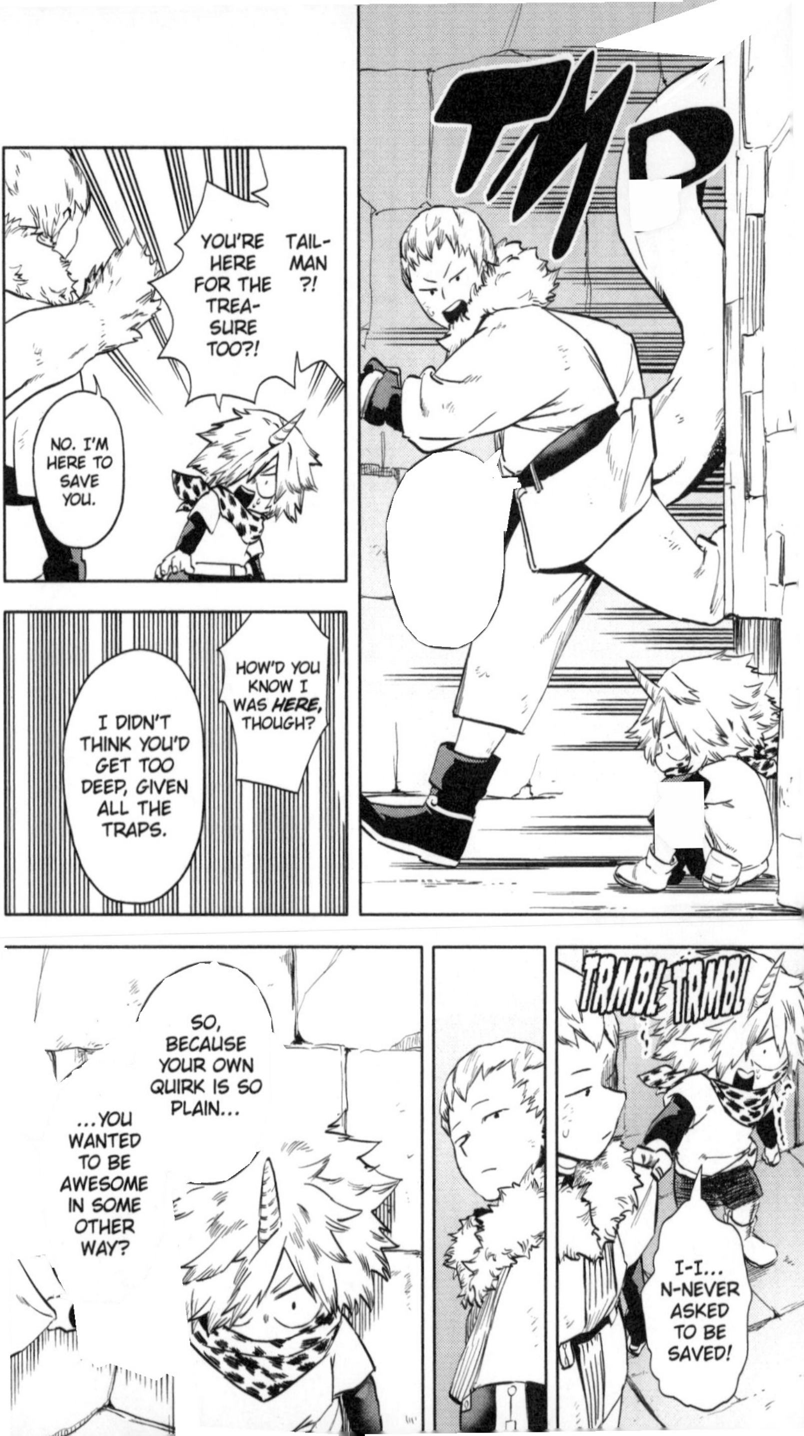
TMP
TAIL-MAN?!
YOU'RE HERE FOR THE TREASURE TOO?!
NO. I'M HERE TO SAVE YOU.
HOW'D YOU KNOW I WAS *HERE,* THOUGH?
I DIDN'T THINK YOU'D GET TOO DEEP, GIVEN ALL THE TRAPS.
TRMBL TRMBL
I-I... N-NEVER ASKED TO BE SAVED!
SO, BECAUSE YOUR OWN QUIRK IS SO PLAIN...
...YOU WANTED TO BE AWESOME IN SOME OTHER WAY?

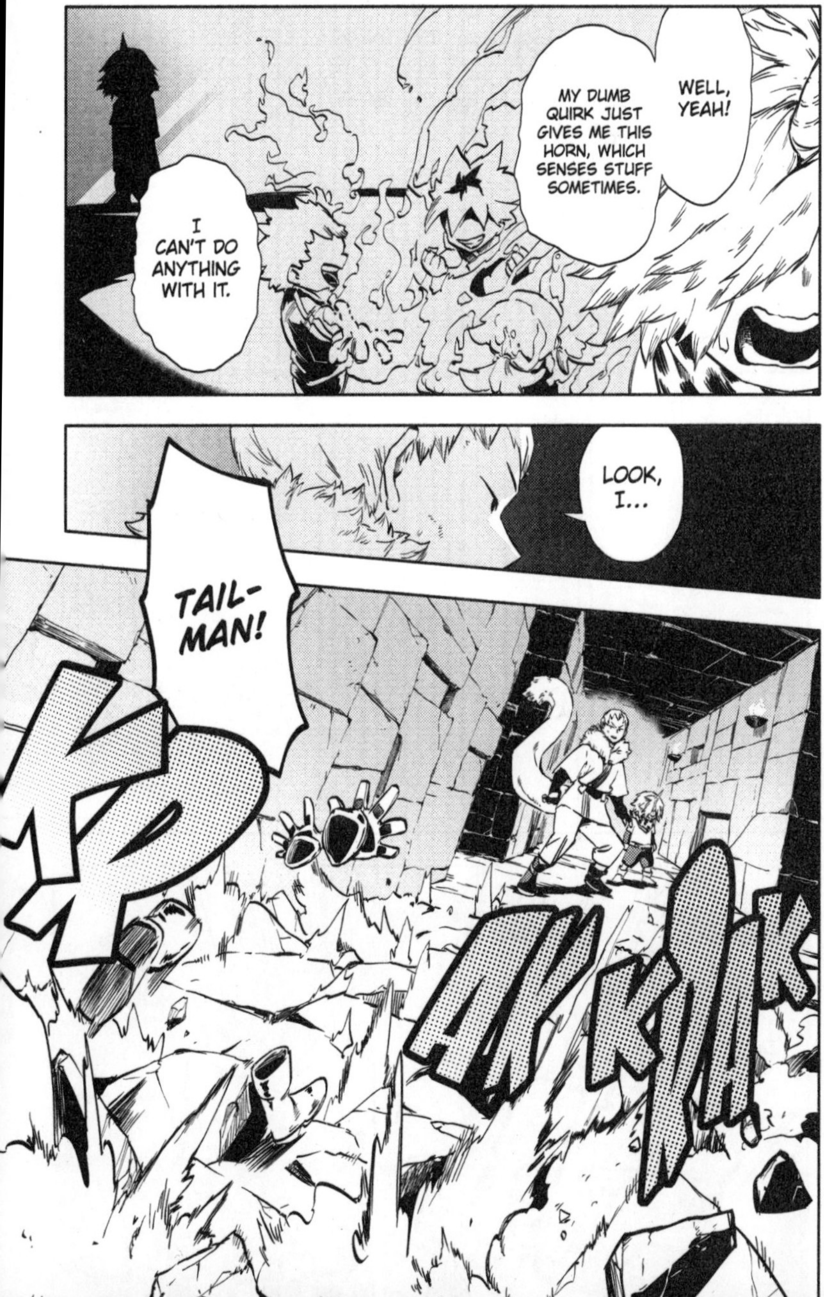
WELL, YEAH!
MY DUMB QUIRK JUST GIVES ME THIS HORN, WHICH SENSES STUFF SOMETIMES.
I CAN'T DO ANYTHING WITH IT.
LOOK, I...
TAIL-MAN!

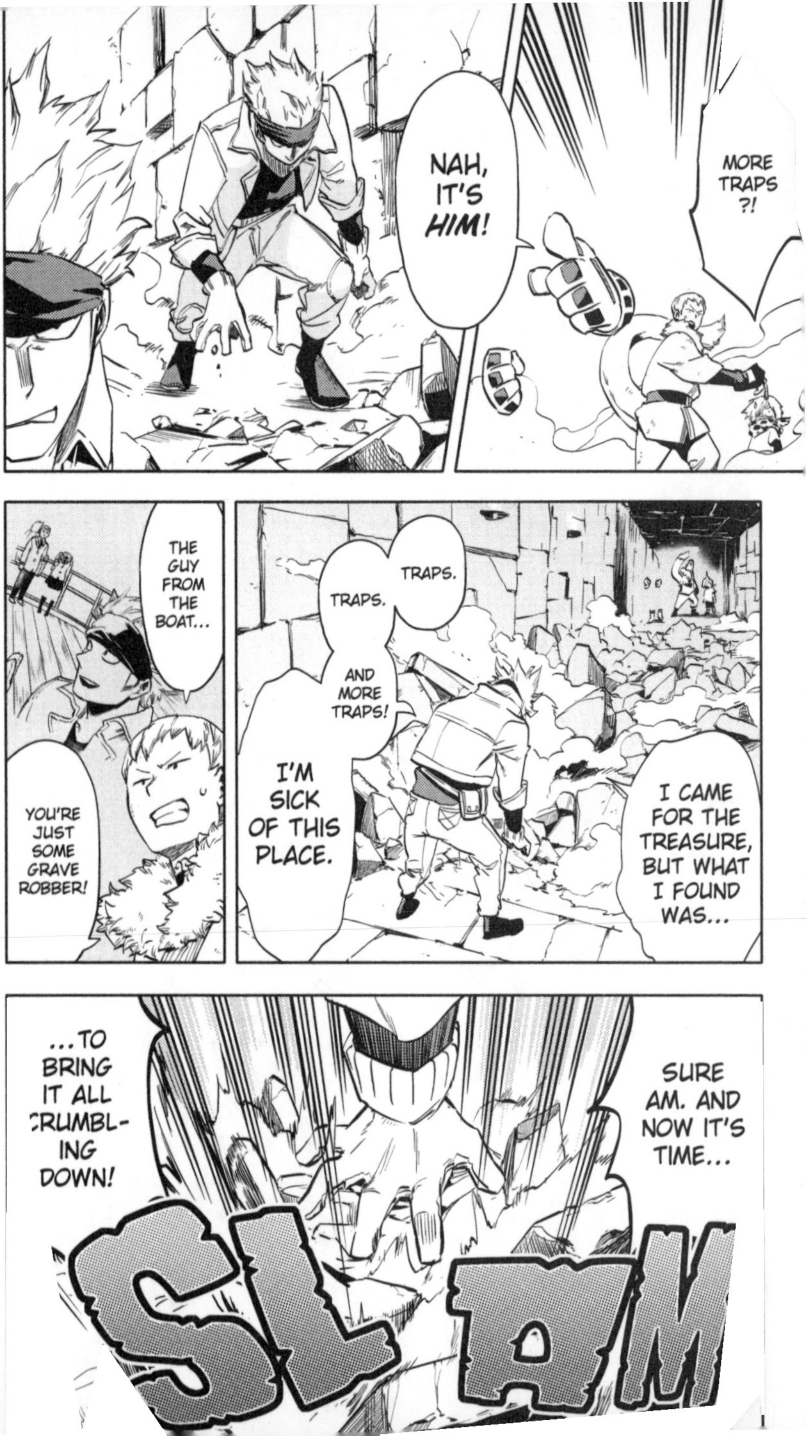
MORE TRAPS ?!
NAH, IT'S HIM!
I CAME FOR THE TREASURE, BUT WHAT I FOUND WAS...
TRAPS.
TRAPS.
AND MORE TRAPS!
I'M SICK OF THIS PLACE.
THE GUY FROM THE BOAT...
YOU'RE JUST SOME GRAVE ROBBER!
SURE AM. AND NOW IT'S TIME...
...TO BRING IT ALL CRUMBL-ING DOWN!
SLAM

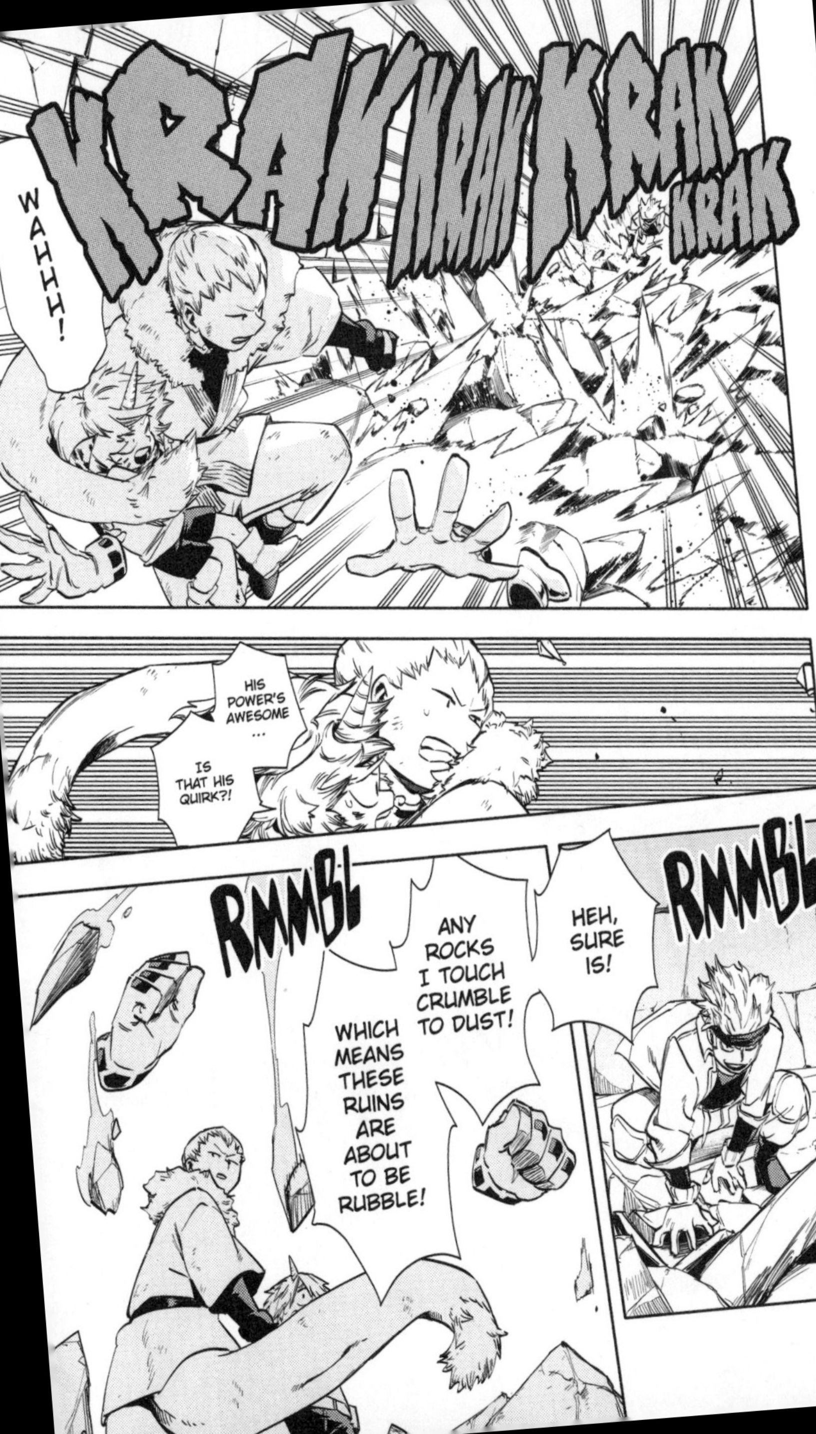
KRAK KRAK KRAK KRAK
WAHHH!
HIS POWER'S AWESOME...
IS THAT HIS QUIRK?!
RMMBL
HEH, SURE IS!
ANY ROCKS I TOUCH CRUMBLE TO DUST!
WHICH MEANS THESE RUINS ARE ABOUT TO BE RUBBLE!
RMMBL

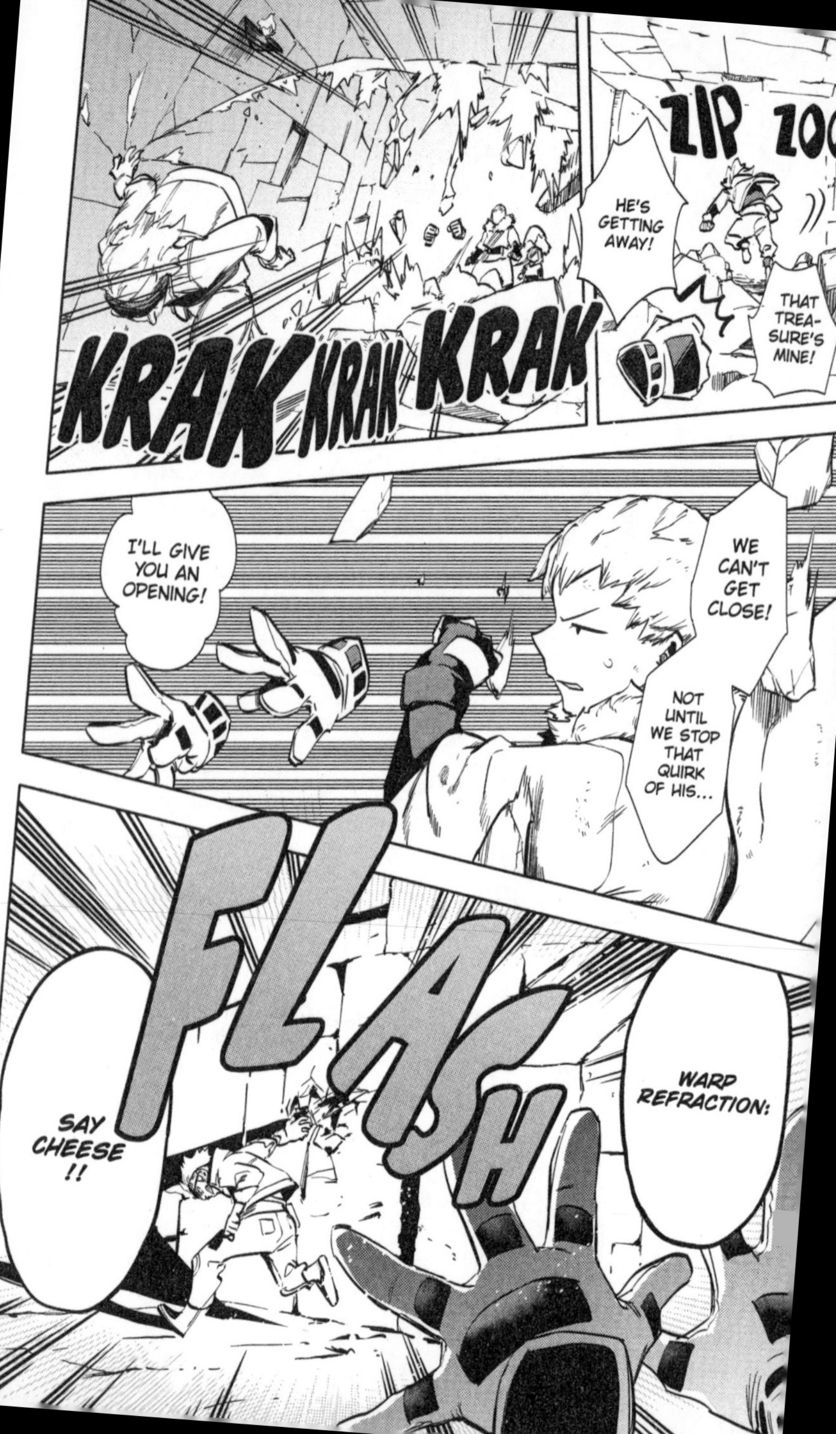
ZIP ZOO
THAT TREA-SURE'S MINE!
HE'S GETTING AWAY!
KRAK KRAK KRAK
WE CAN'T GET CLOSE!
NOT UNTIL WE STOP THAT QUIRK OF HIS...
I'LL GIVE YOU AN OPENING!
WARP REFRACTION:
FLASH
SAY CHEESE!!

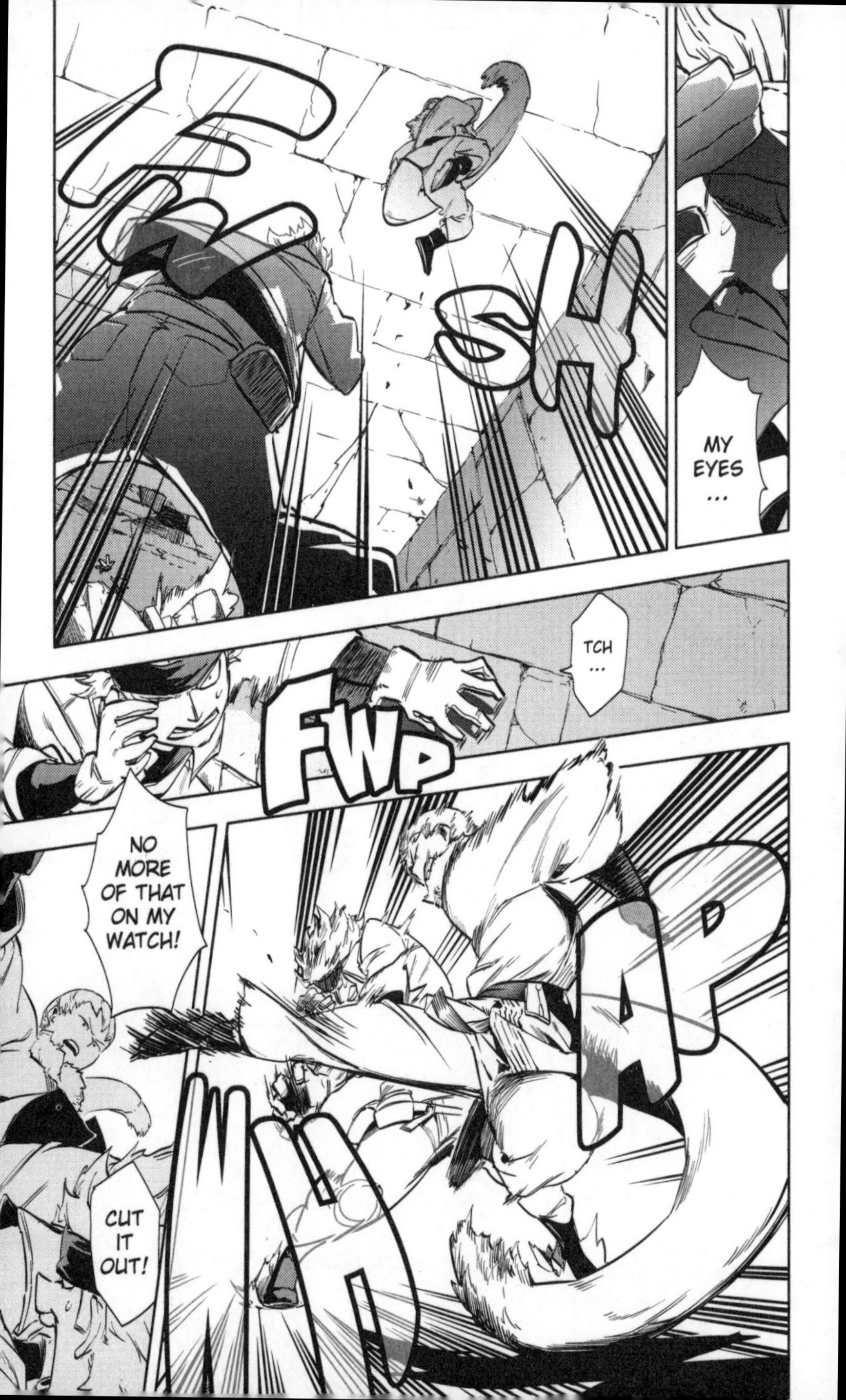
MY EYES ...
FWSH
TCH ...
FWP
NO MORE OF THAT ON MY WATCH!
CUT IT OUT!

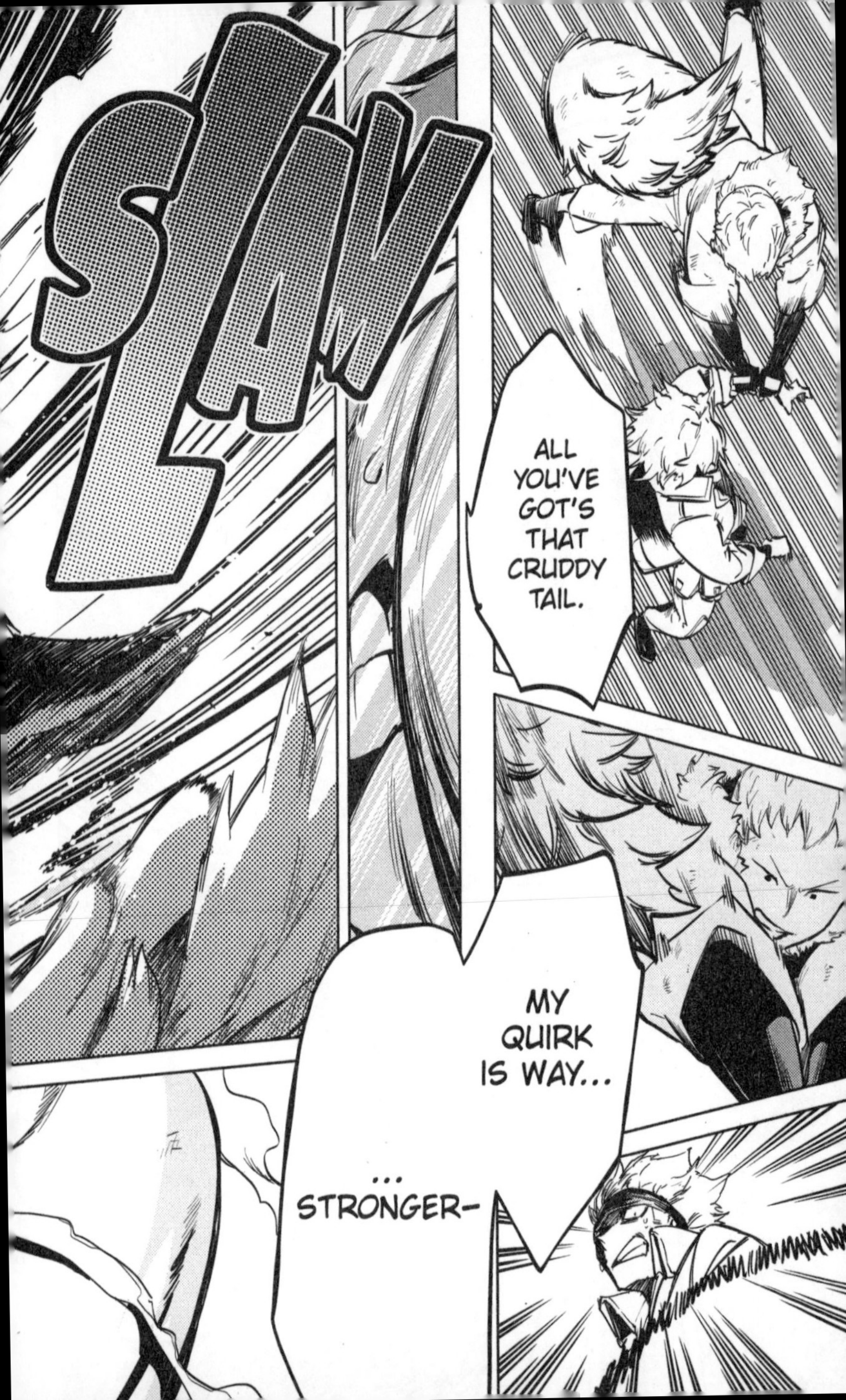
SLAM
ALL YOU'VE GOT'S THAT CRUDDY TAIL.
MY QUIRK IS WAY...
...STRONGER-

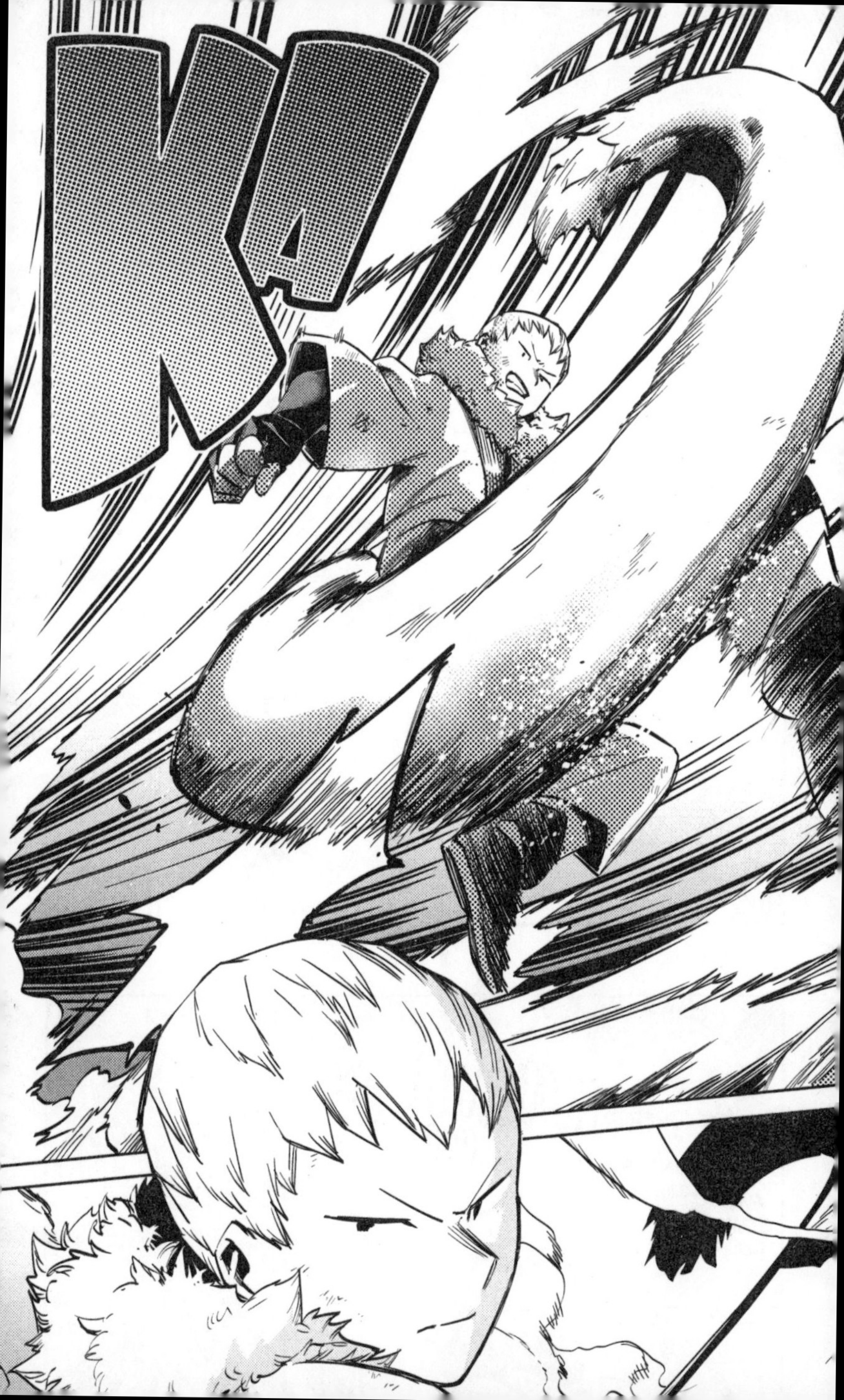

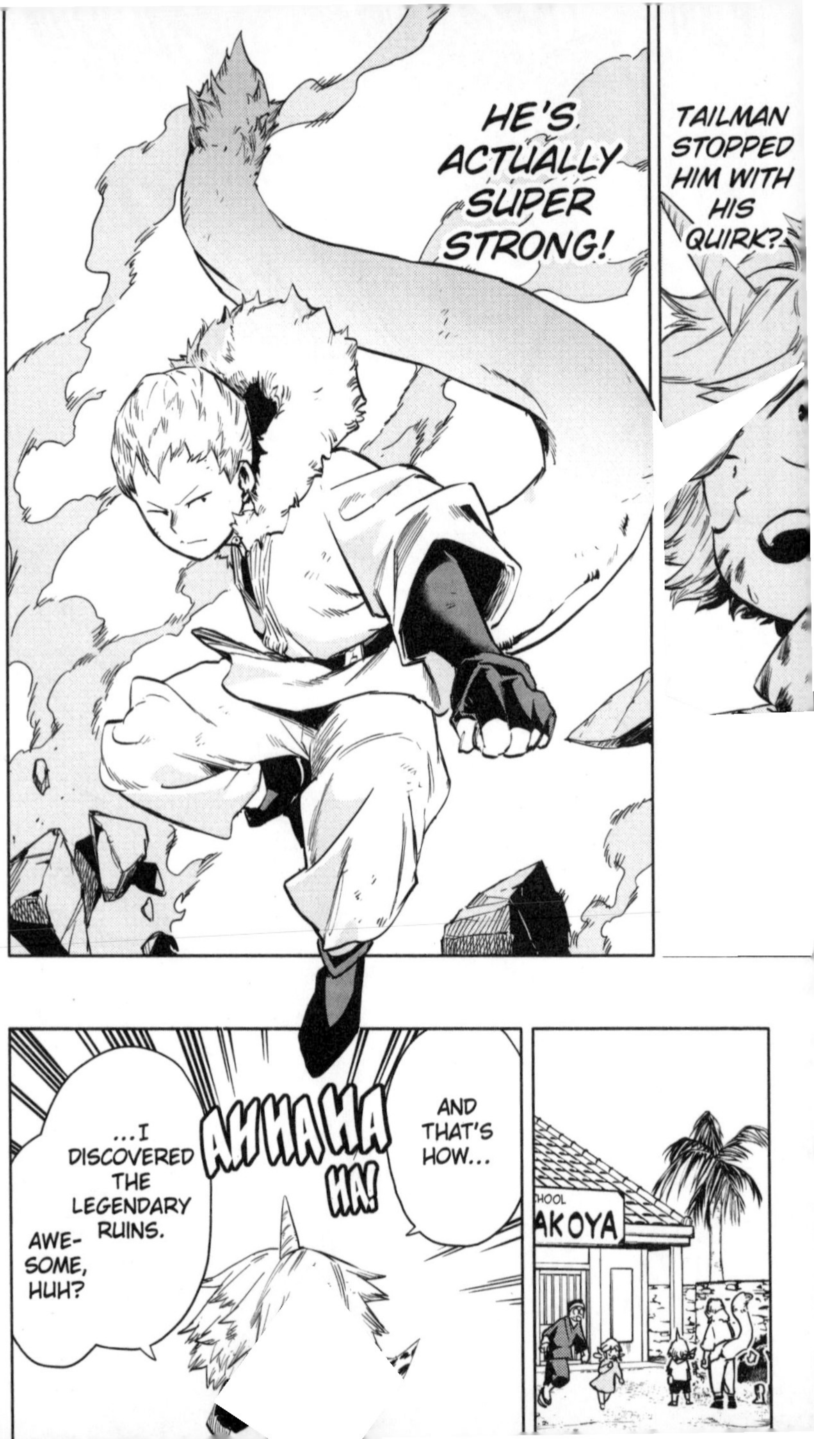
TAILMAN STOPPED HIM WITH HIS QUIRK?
HE'S ACTUALLY SUPER STRONG!
AKOYA
AND THAT'S HOW...
AHHAHAHA HA!
...I DISCOVERED THE LEGENDARY RUINS.
AWE-SOME, HUH?

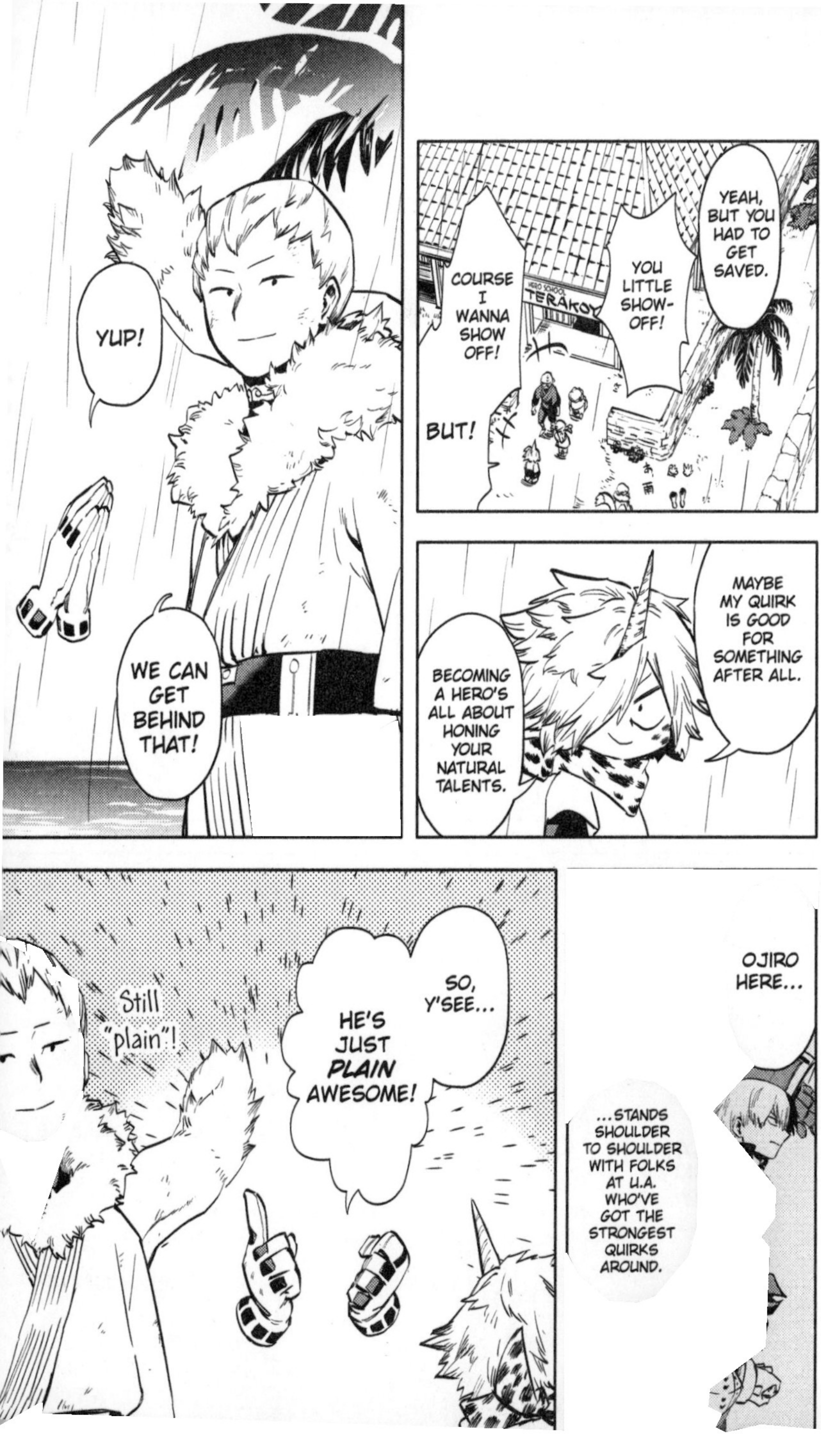
YEAH, BUT YOU HAD TO GET SAVED.
YOU LITTLE SHOW-OFF!
HERO SCHOOL
TERAKOY
COURSE I WANNA SHOW OFF!
BUT!
MAYBE MY QUIRK IS GOOD FOR SOMETHING AFTER ALL.
BECOMING A HERO'S ALL ABOUT HONING YOUR NATURAL TALENTS.
YUP!
WE CAN GET BEHIND THAT!
OJIRO HERE...
...STANDS SHOULDER TO SHOULDER WITH FOLKS AT U.A. WHO'VE GOT THE STRONGEST QUIRKS AROUND.
SO, Y'SEE...
HE'S JUST *PLAIN* AWESOME!
Still "plain"!

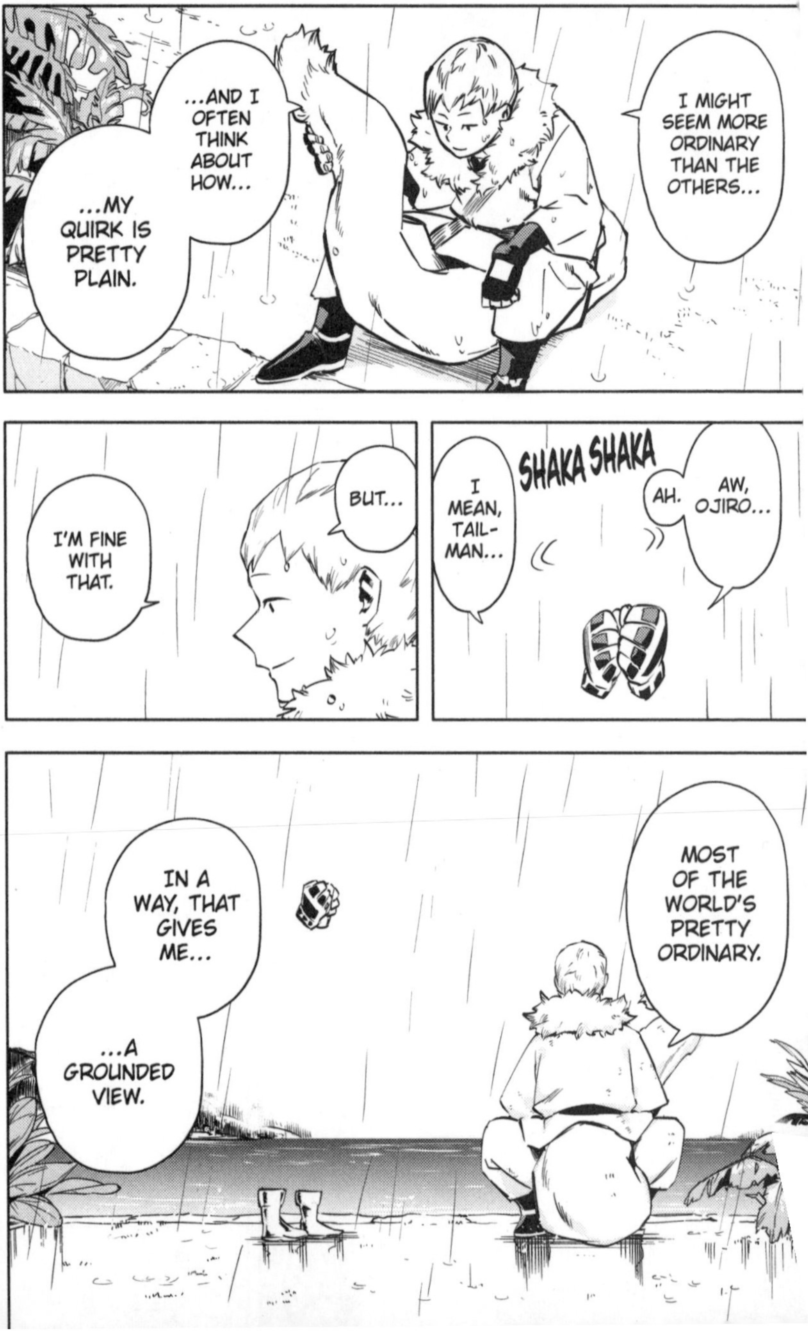
I MIGHT SEEM MORE ORDINARY THAN THE OTHERS...
...AND I OFTEN THINK ABOUT HOW...
...MY QUIRK IS PRETTY PLAIN.
AW, OJIRO...
AH.
SHAKA SHAKA
I MEAN, TAIL-MAN...
BUT...
I'M FINE WITH THAT.
MOST OF THE WORLD'S PRETTY ORDINARY.
IN A WAY, THAT GIVES ME...
...A GROUNDED VIEW.

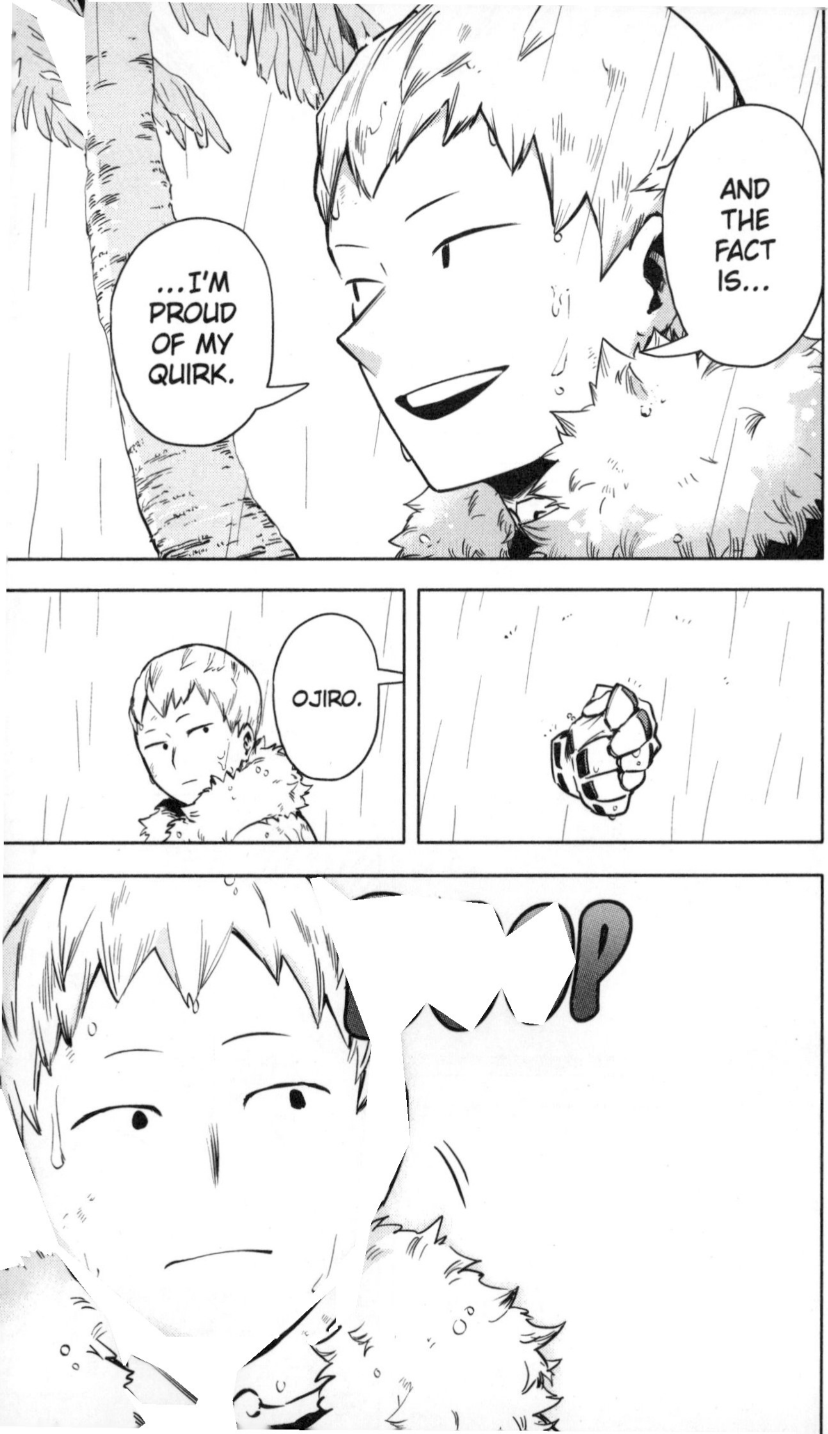
AND THE FACT IS...
...I'M PROUD OF MY QUIRK.
OJIRO.

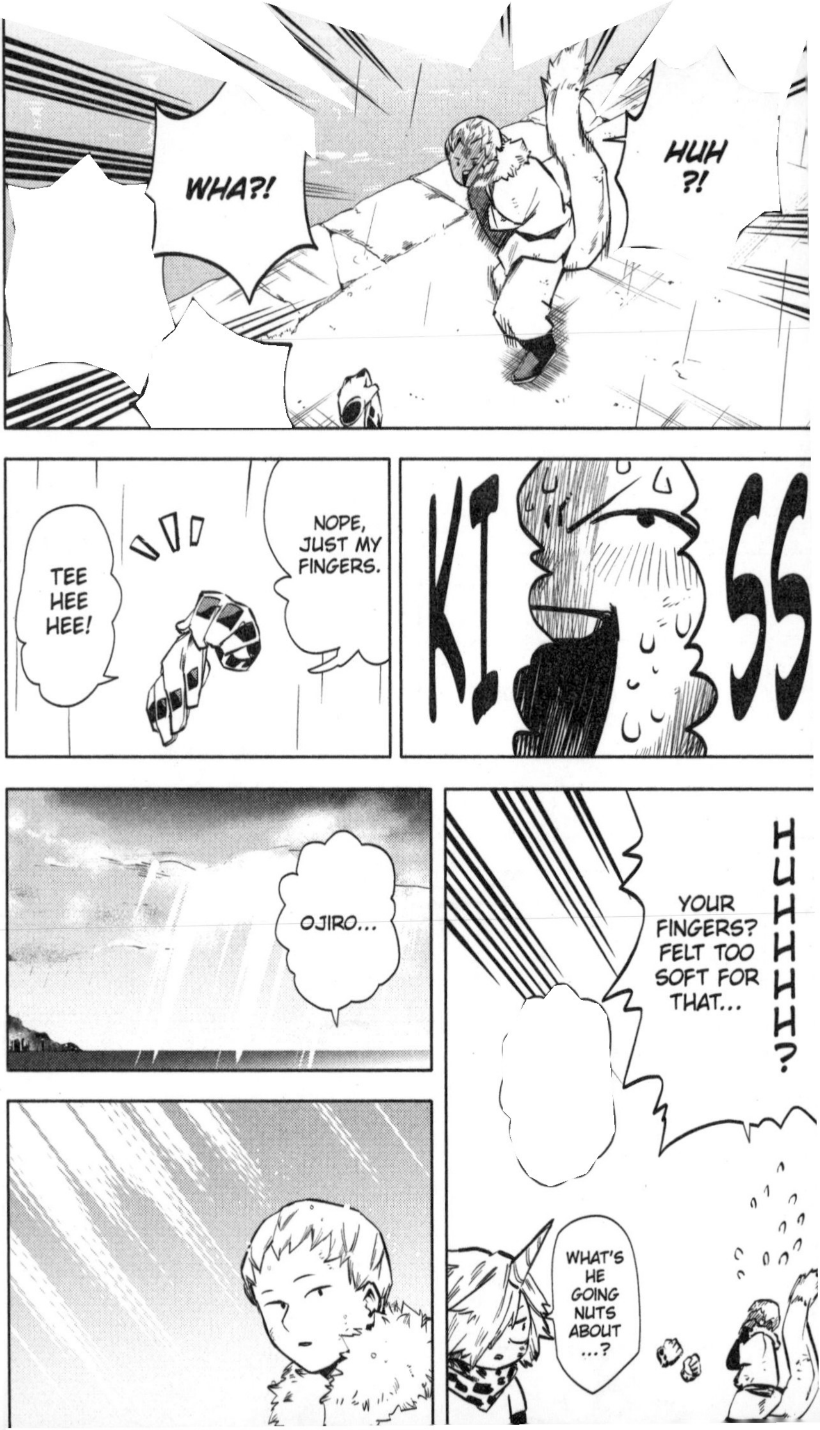
HUH ?!
WHA?!
KISS
NOPE, JUST MY FINGERS.
TEE HEE HEE!
HUHHHHH?
YOUR FINGERS? FELT TOO SOFT FOR THAT...
WHAT'S HE GOING NUTS ABOUT ...?
OJIRO...

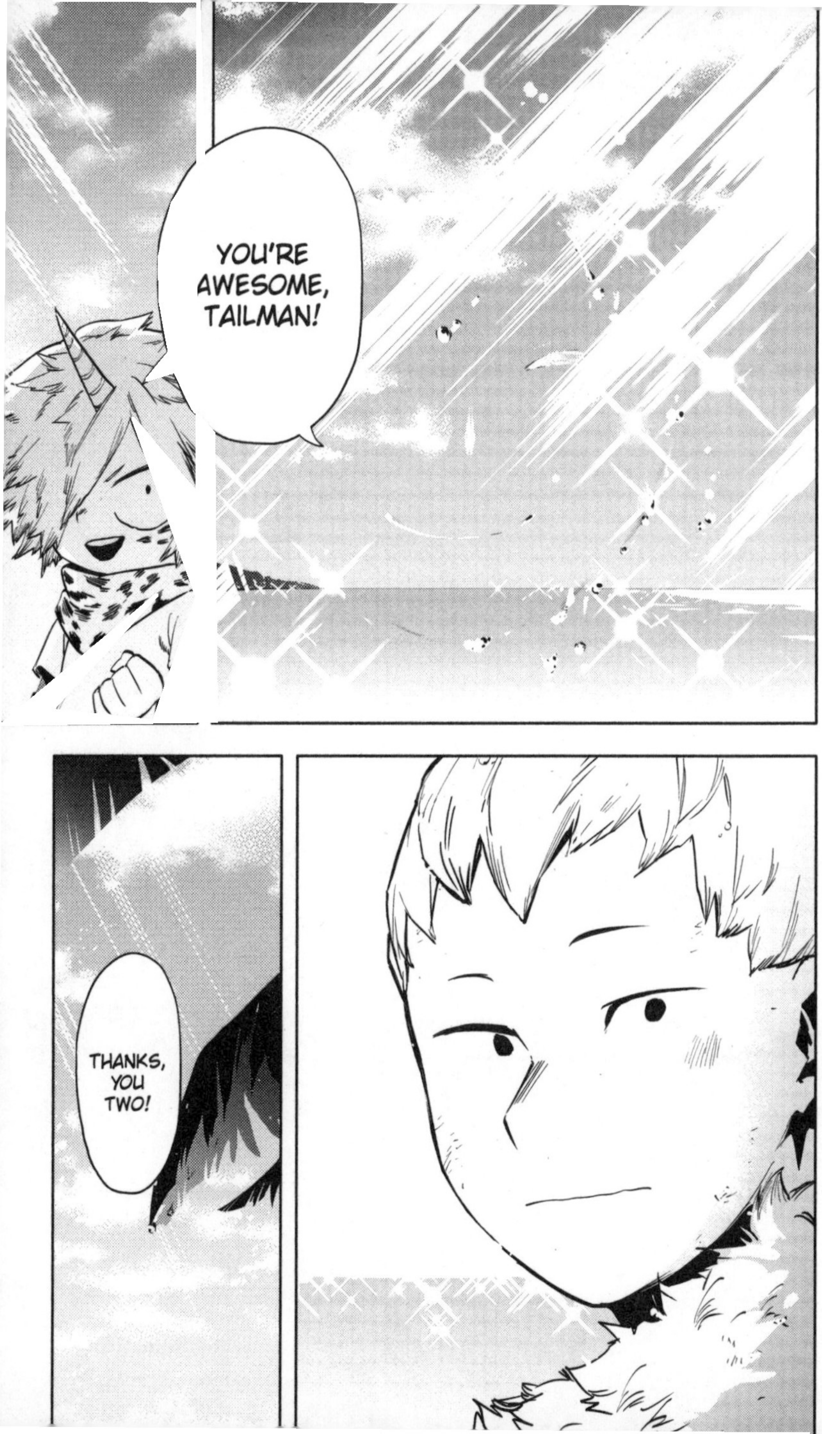
YOU'RE AWESOME, TAILMAN!
THANKS, YOU TWO!

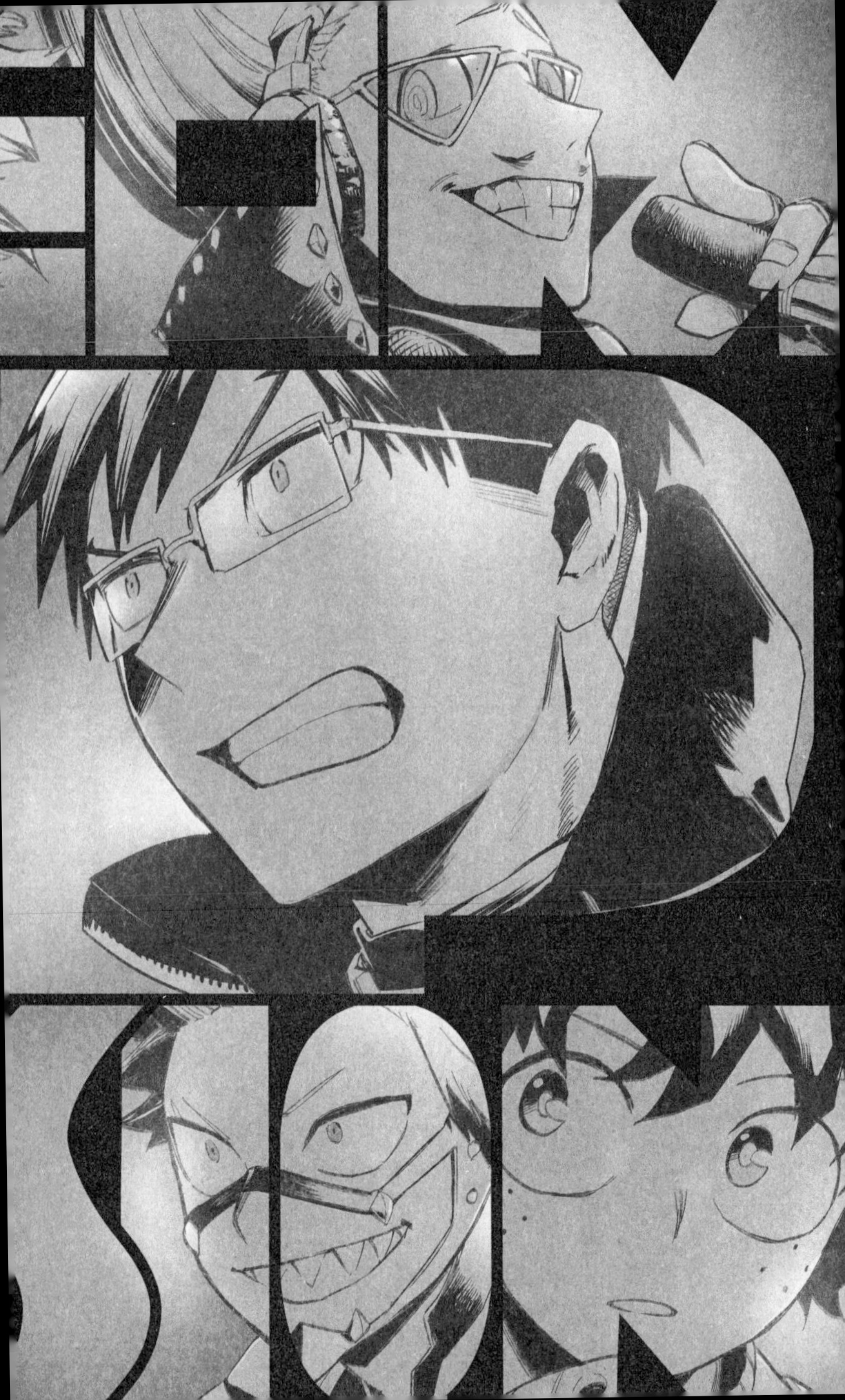

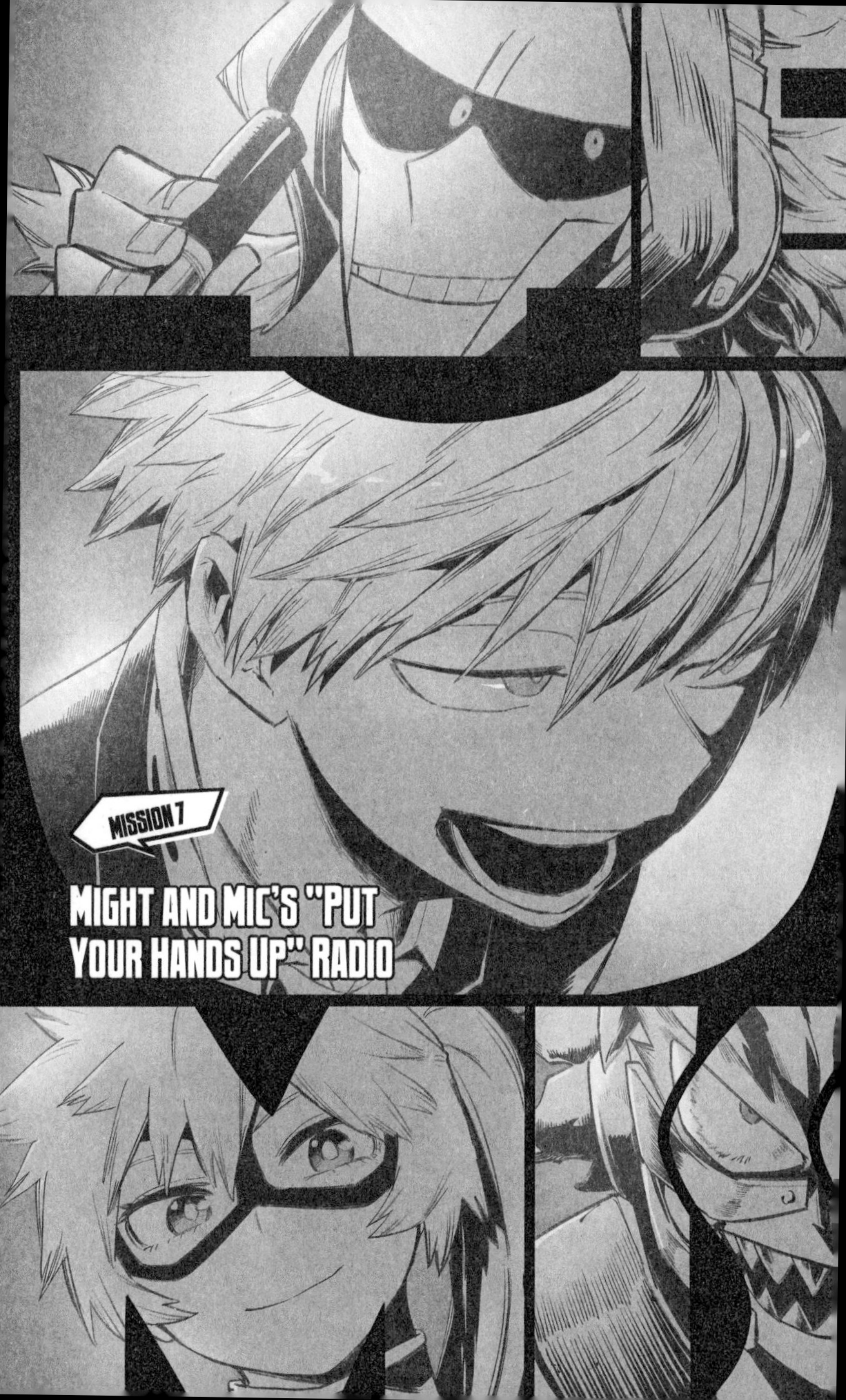
MISSION 7
MIGHT AND MIC'S "PUT YOUR HANDS UP" RADIO

MY HERO ACADEMIA
Team-Up Missions

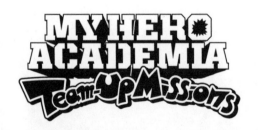

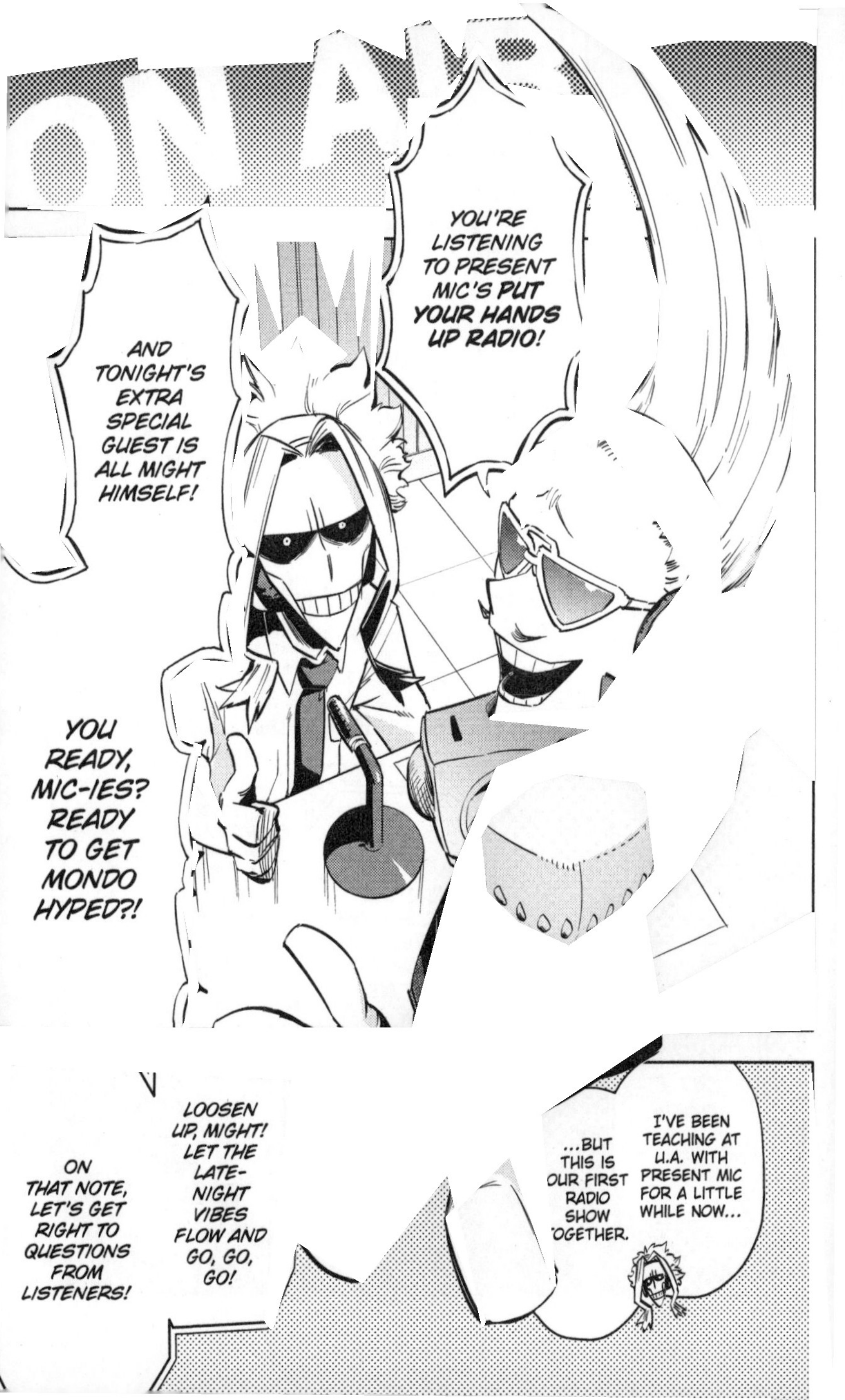
ON AIR
YOU'RE LISTENING TO PRESENT MIC'S PUT YOUR HANDS UP RADIO!
AND TONIGHT'S EXTRA SPECIAL GUEST IS ALL MIGHT HIMSELF!
YOU READY, MIC-IES? READY TO GET MONDO HYPED?!
I'VE BEEN TEACHING AT U.A. WITH PRESENT MIC FOR A LITTLE WHILE NOW...
...BUT THIS IS OUR FIRST RADIO SHOW TOGETHER.
LOOSEN UP, MIGHT! LET THE LATE-NIGHT VIBES FLOW AND GO, GO, GO!
ON THAT NOTE, LET'S GET RIGHT TO QUESTIONS FROM LISTENERS!

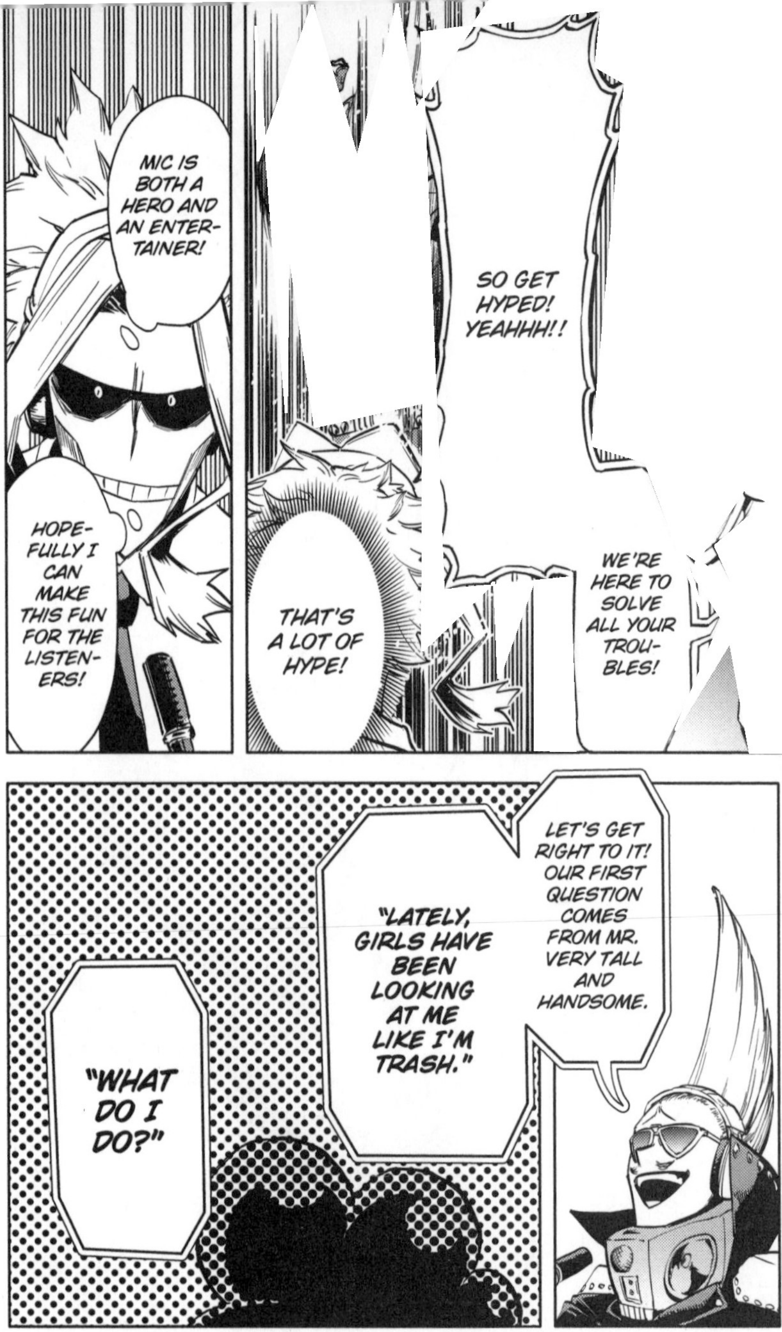
SO GET HYPED! YEAHHH!!
WE'RE HERE TO SOLVE ALL YOUR TROUBLES!
THAT'S A LOT OF HYPE!
MIC IS BOTH A HERO AND AN ENTERTAINER!
HOPEFULLY I CAN MAKE THIS FUN FOR THE LISTENERS!
LET'S GET RIGHT TO IT! OUR FIRST QUESTION COMES FROM MR. VERY TALL AND HANDSOME.
"LATELY, GIRLS HAVE BEEN LOOKING AT ME LIKE I'M TRASH."
"WHAT DO I DO?"

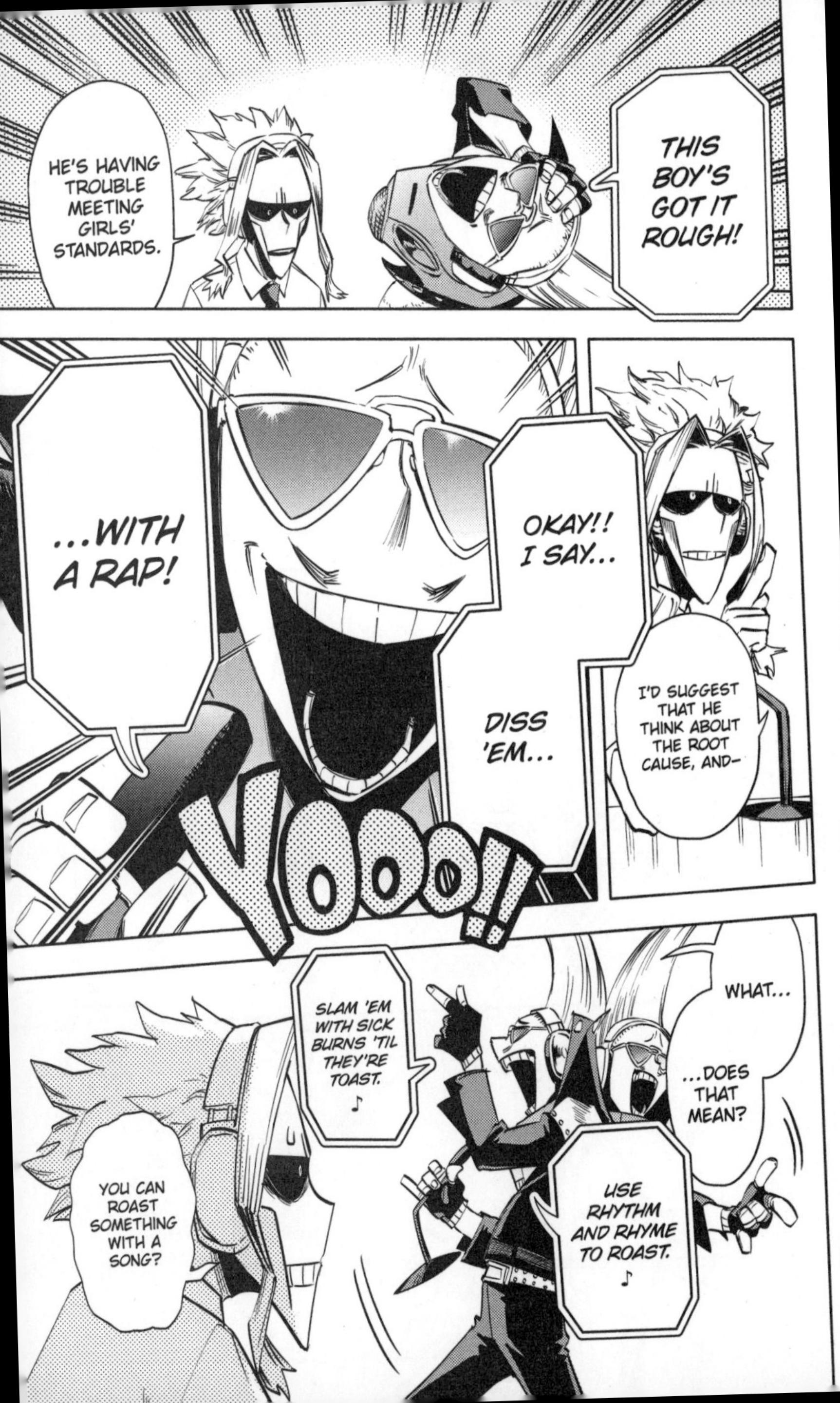
THIS BOY'S GOT IT ROUGH!
HE'S HAVING TROUBLE MEETING GIRLS' STANDARDS.
I'D SUGGEST THAT HE THINK ABOUT THE ROOT CAUSE, AND–
OKAY!! I SAY...
DISS 'EM...
...WITH A RAP!
YOOOO!!
WHAT...
...DOES THAT MEAN?
SLAM 'EM WITH SICK BURNS 'TIL THEY'RE TOAST. ♪
USE RHYTHM AND RHYME TO ROAST. ♪
YOU CAN ROAST SOMETHING WITH A SONG?

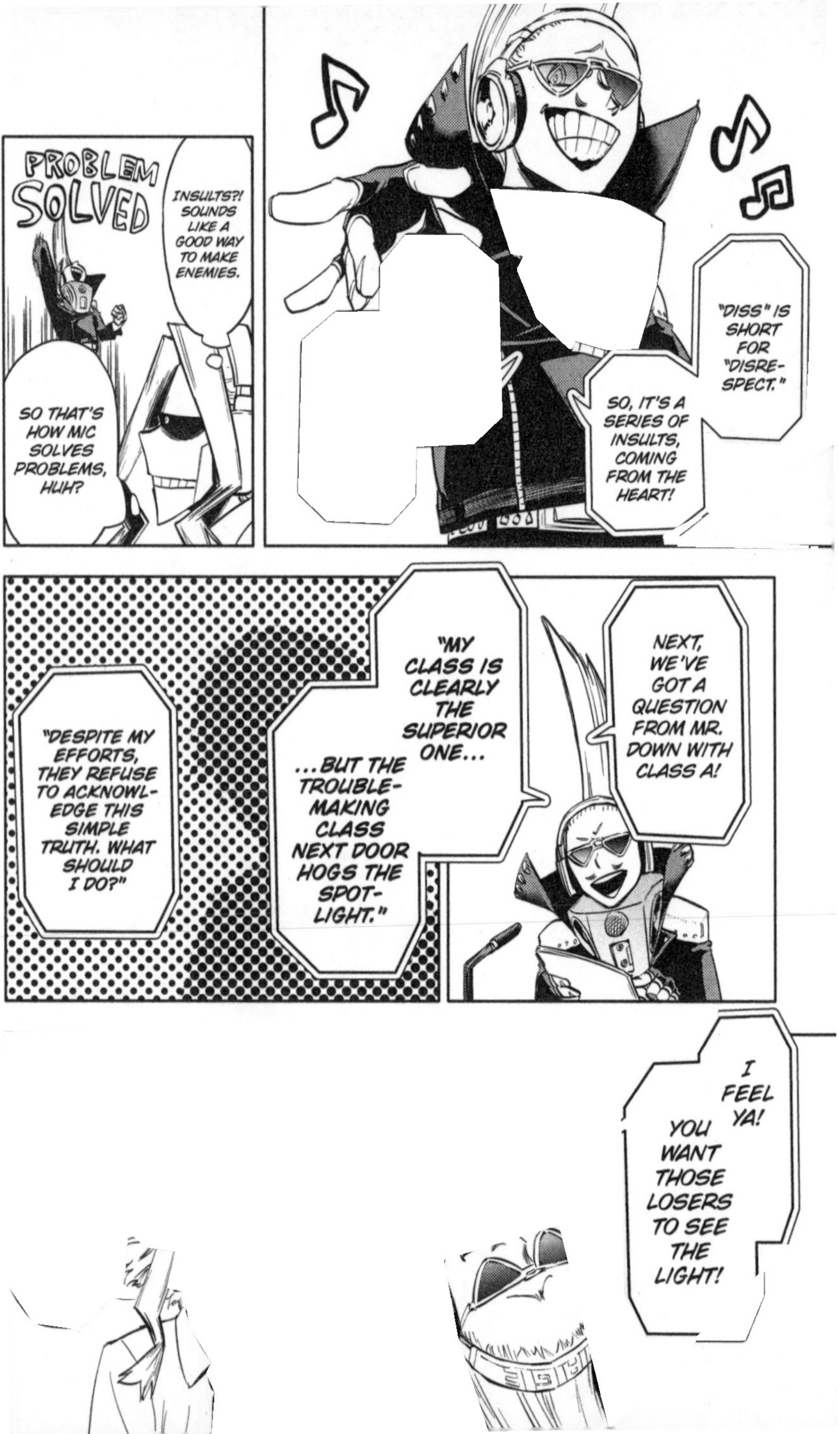
"DISS" IS SHORT FOR "DISRESPECT."
SO, IT'S A SERIES OF INSULTS, COMING FROM THE HEART!
INSULTS?! SOUNDS LIKE A GOOD WAY TO MAKE ENEMIES.
PROBLEM SOLVED
SO THAT'S HOW MIC SOLVES PROBLEMS, HUH?
NEXT, WE'VE GOT A QUESTION FROM MR. DOWN WITH CLASS A!
"MY CLASS IS CLEARLY THE SUPERIOR ONE...
...BUT THE TROUBLE-MAKING CLASS NEXT DOOR HOGS THE SPOTLIGHT."
"DESPITE MY EFFORTS, THEY REFUSE TO ACKNOWLEDGE THIS SIMPLE TRUTH. WHAT SHOULD I DO?"
I FEEL YA!
YOU WANT THOSE LOSERS TO SEE THE LIGHT!

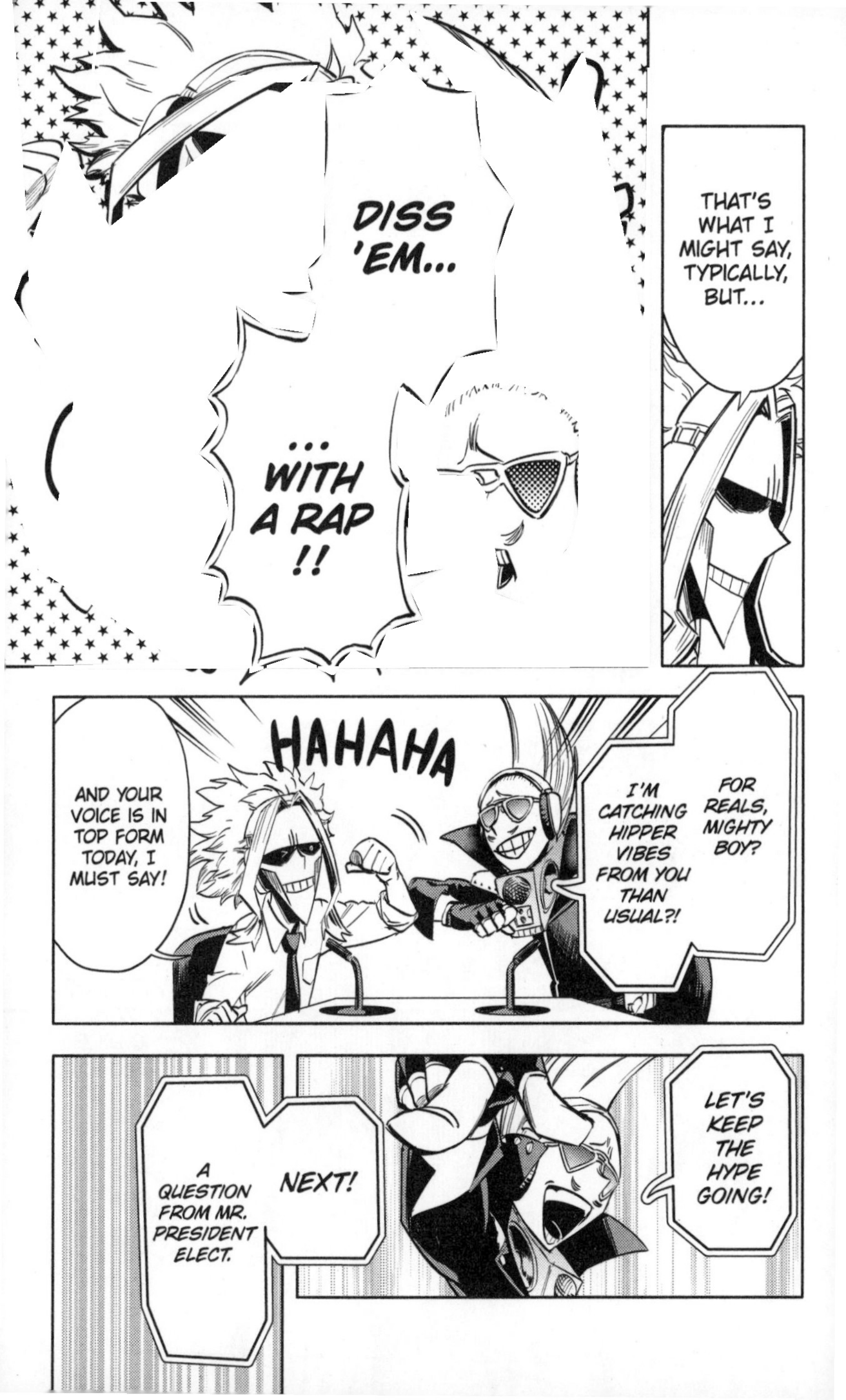

THAT'S WHAT I MIGHT SAY, TYPICALLY, BUT...
DISS 'EM...
...WITH A RAP!!
FOR REALS, MIGHTY BOY?
I'M CATCHING HIPPER VIBES FROM YOU THAN USUAL?!
HAHAHA
AND YOUR VOICE IS IN TOP FORM TODAY, I MUST SAY!
LET'S KEEP THE HYPE GOING!
NEXT!
A QUESTION FROM MR. PRESIDENT ELECT.

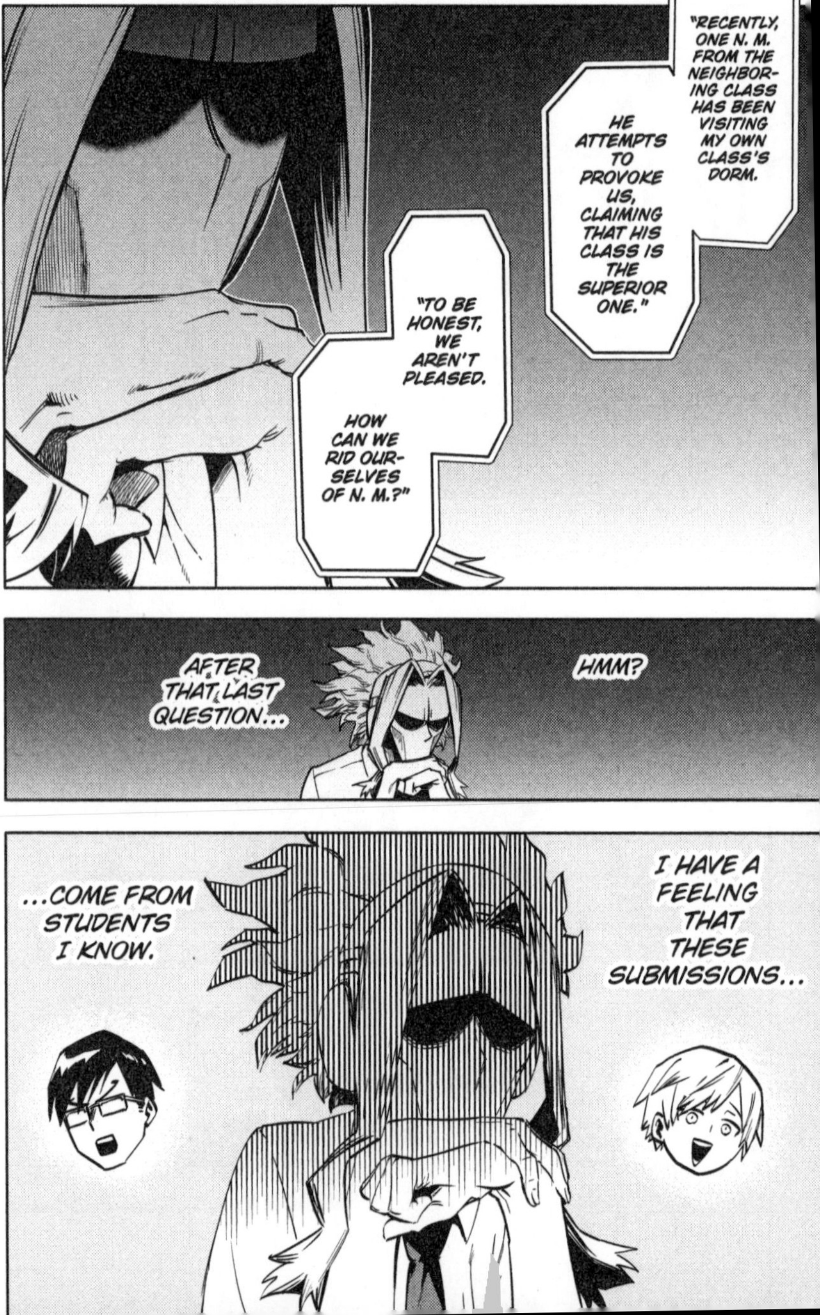
"RECENTLY, ONE N. M. FROM THE NEIGHBORING CLASS HAS BEEN VISITING MY OWN CLASS'S DORM.
HE ATTEMPTS TO PROVOKE US, CLAIMING THAT HIS CLASS IS THE SUPERIOR ONE."
"TO BE HONEST, WE AREN'T PLEASED.
HOW CAN WE RID OURSELVES OF N. M.?"
HMM?
AFTER THAT LAST QUESTION...
I HAVE A FEELING THAT THESE SUBMISSIONS...
...COME FROM STUDENTS I KNOW.

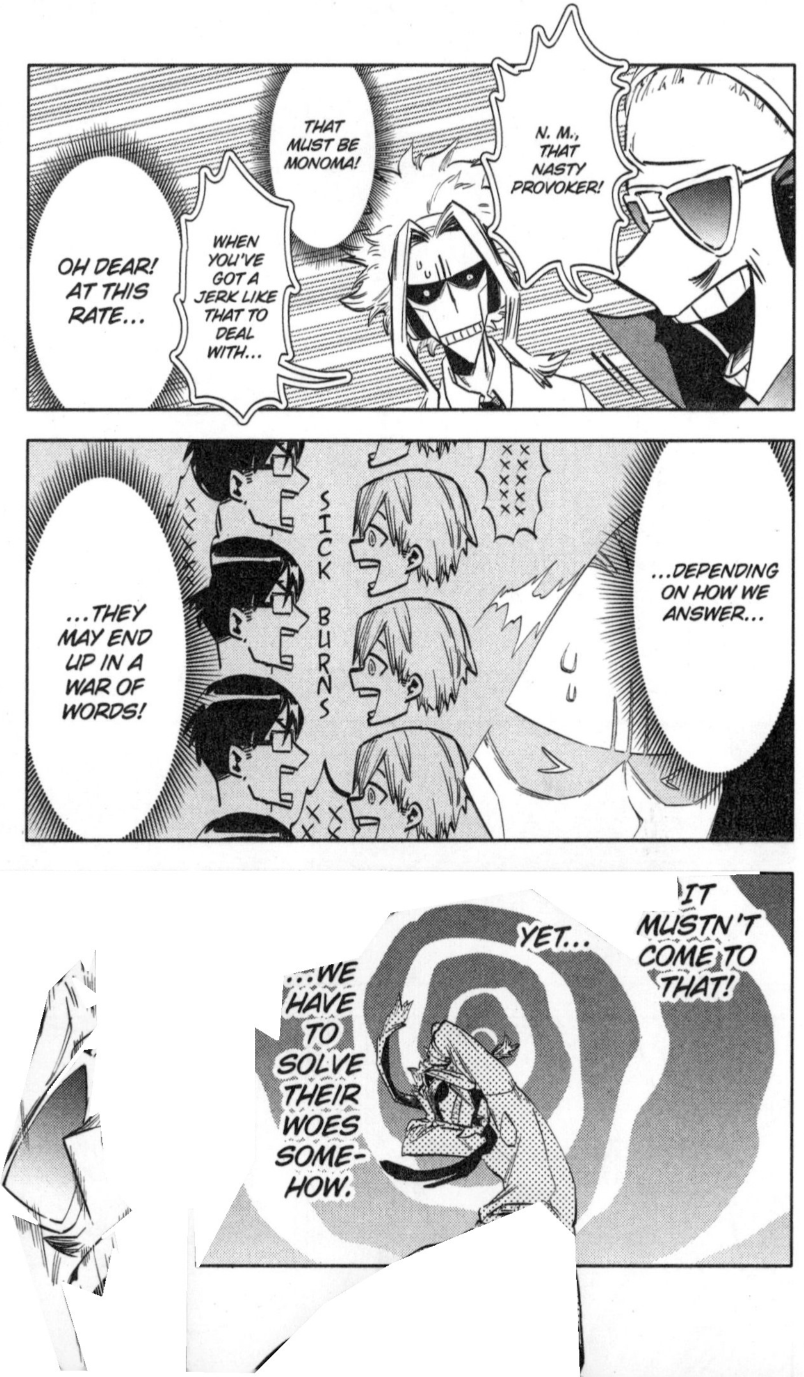
N. M., THAT NASTY PROVOKER!
THAT MUST BE MONOMA!
WHEN YOU'VE GOT A JERK LIKE THAT TO DEAL WITH...
OH DEAR! AT THIS RATE...
...DEPENDING ON HOW WE ANSWER...
SICK BURNS
...THEY MAY END UP IN A WAR OF WORDS!
IT MUSTN'T COME TO THAT!
YET...
...WE HAVE TO SOLVE THEIR WOES SOME-HOW.

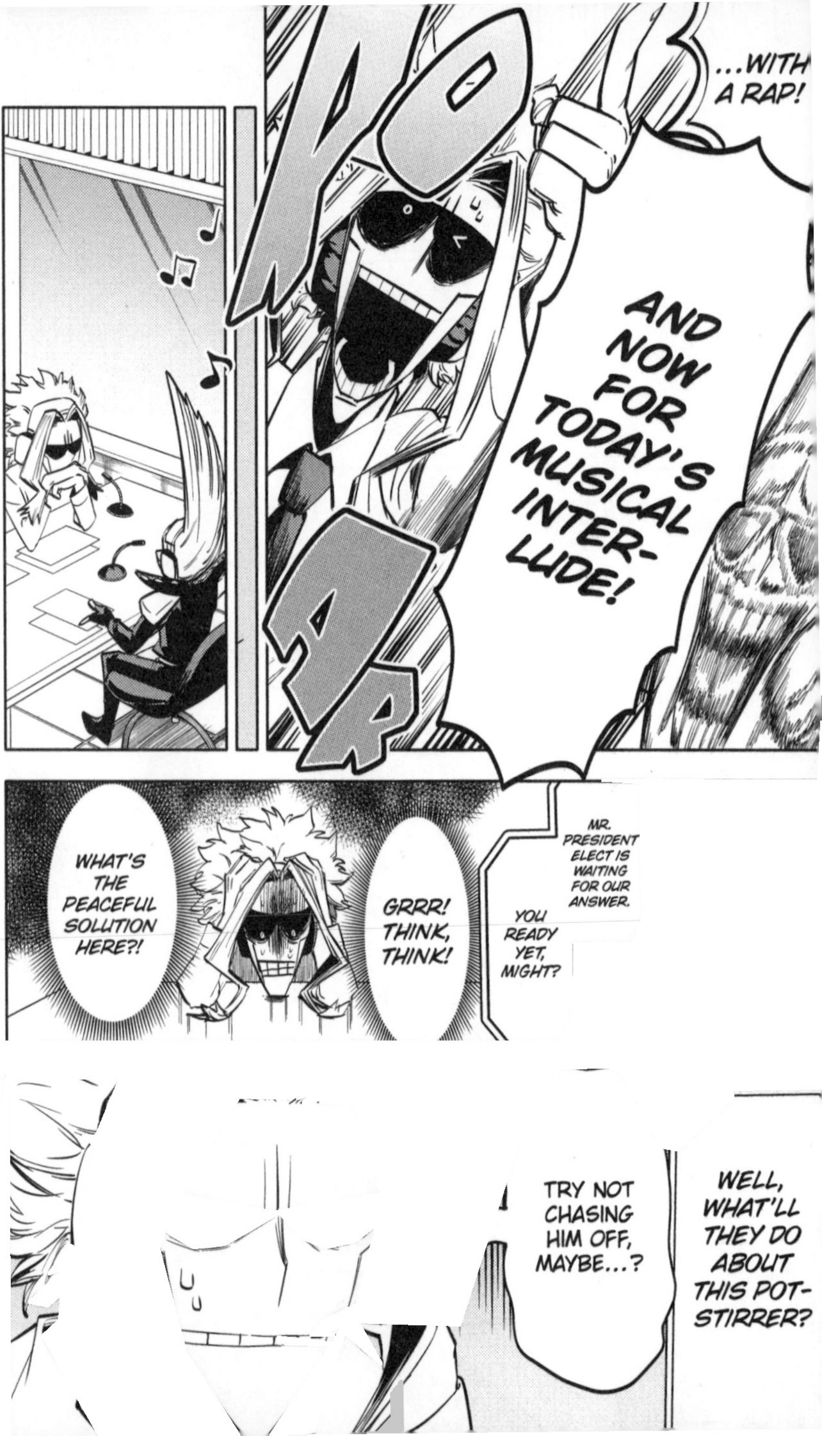
AND NOW FOR TODAY'S MUSICAL INTER-LUDE!
...WITH A RAP!
MR. PRESIDENT ELECT IS WAITING FOR OUR ANSWER.
YOU READY YET, MIGHT?
GRRR! THINK, THINK!
WHAT'S THE PEACEFUL SOLUTION HERE?!
WELL, WHAT'LL THEY DO ABOUT THIS POT-STIRRER?
TRY NOT CHASING HIM OFF, MAYBE...?

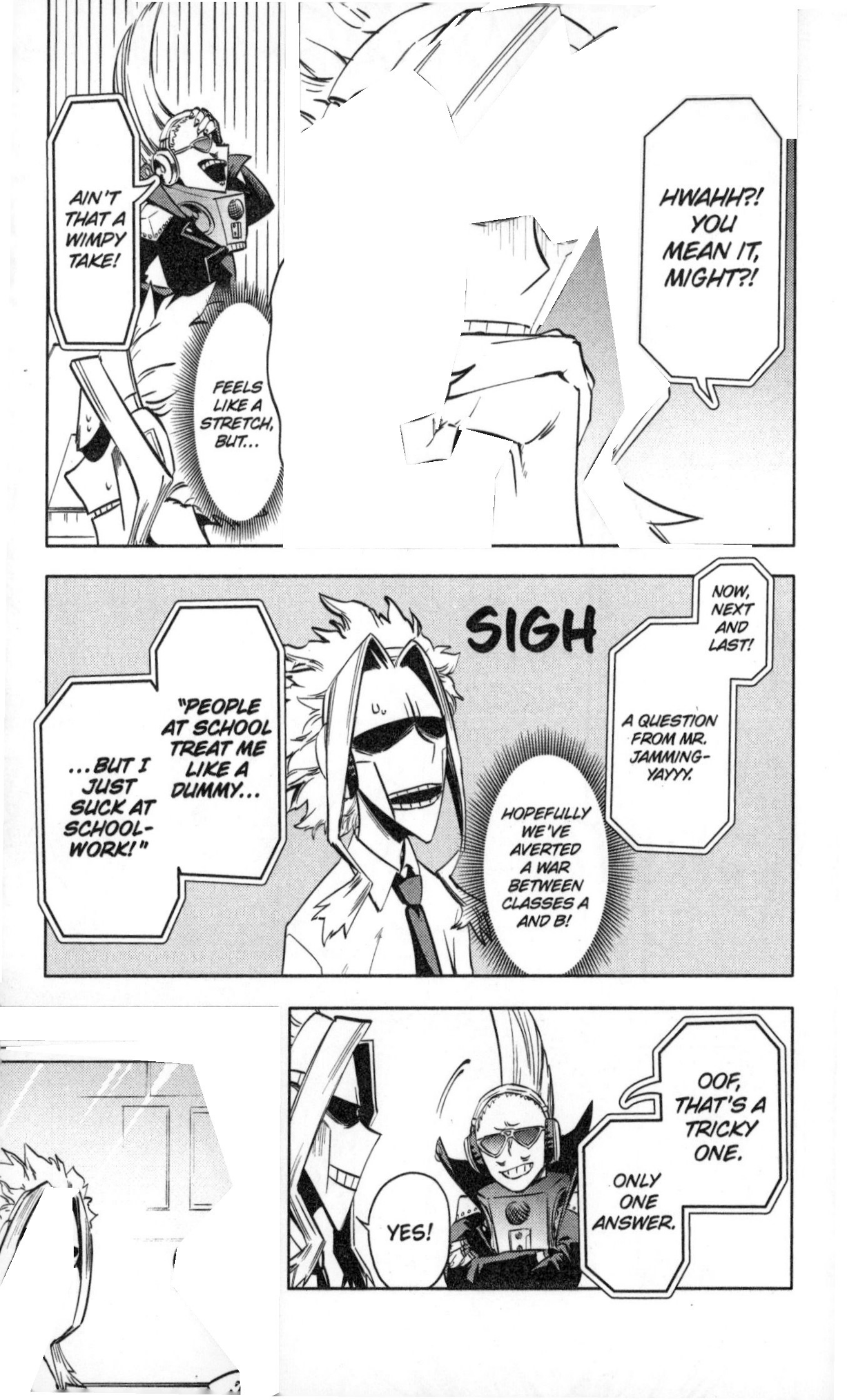
HWAHH?! YOU MEAN IT, MIGHT?!
AIN'T THAT A WIMPY TAKE!
FEELS LIKE A STRETCH, BUT...
NOW, NEXT AND LAST!
A QUESTION FROM MR. JAMMING-YAYYY.
SIGH
HOPEFULLY WE'VE AVERTED A WAR BETWEEN CLASSES A AND B!
"PEOPLE AT SCHOOL TREAT ME LIKE A DUMMY...
...BUT I JUST SUCK AT SCHOOL-WORK!"
OOF, THAT'S A TRICKY ONE.
ONLY ONE ANSWER.
YES!

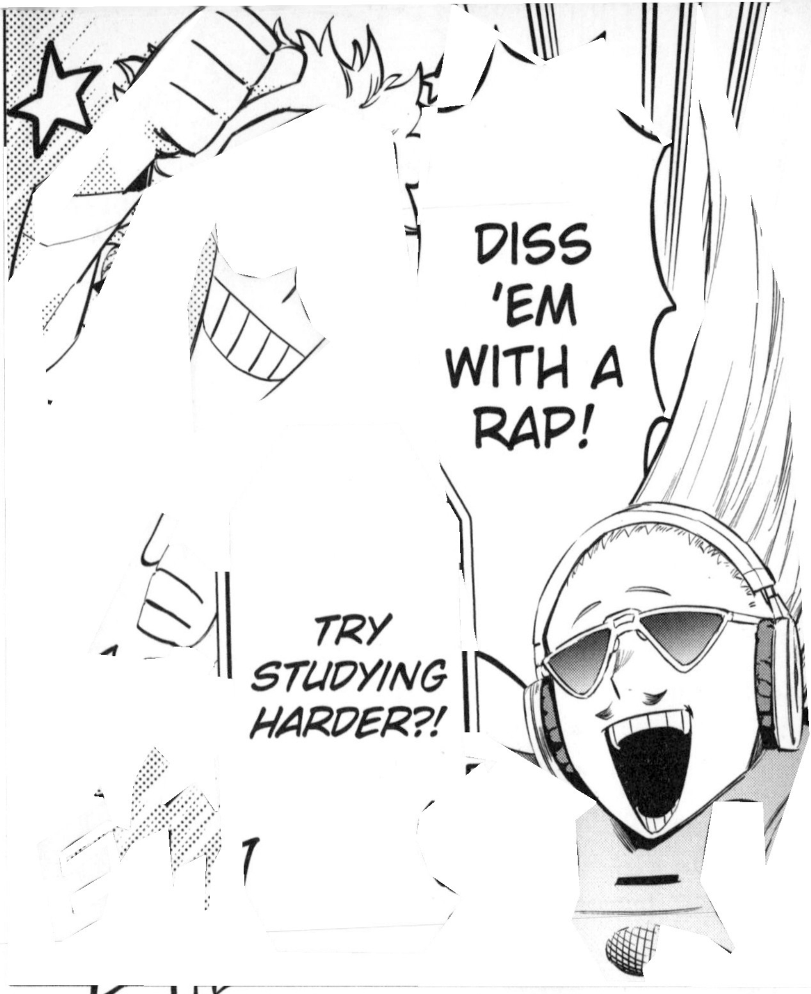
DISS 'EM WITH A RAP!
TRY STUDYING HARDER?!

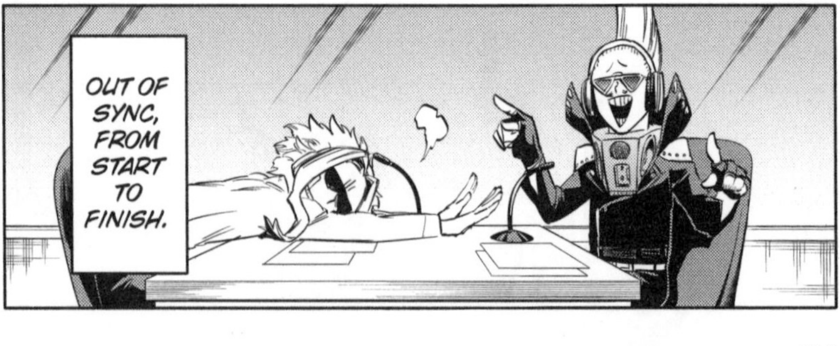
OUT OF SYNC, FROM START TO FINISH.

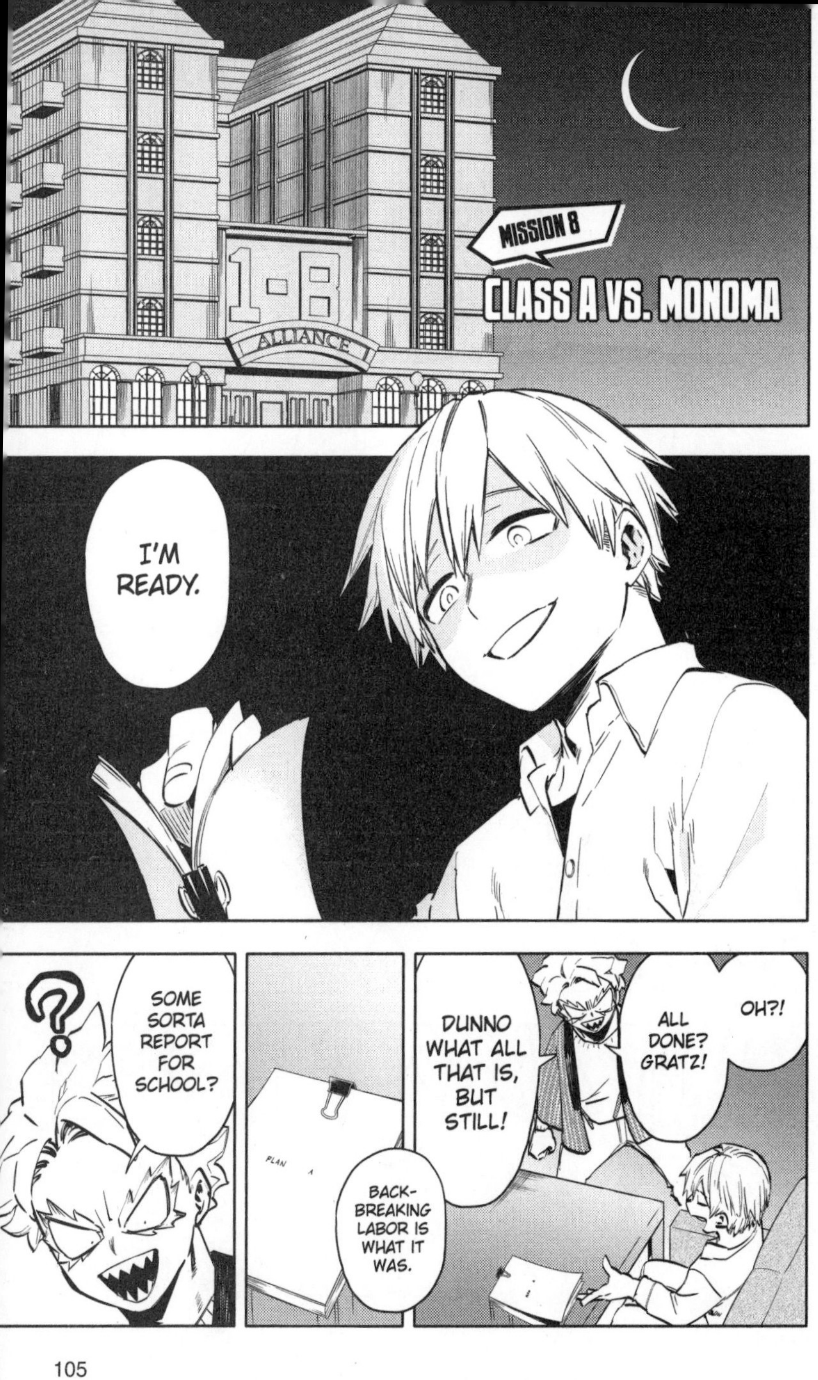
MISSION 8
CLASS A VS. MONOMA
1-B
ALLIANCE
I'M READY.
OH?!
ALL DONE? GRATZ!
DUNNO WHAT ALL THAT IS, BUT STILL!
BACK-BREAKING LABOR IS WHAT IT WAS.
PLAN A
SOME SORTA REPORT FOR SCHOOL?

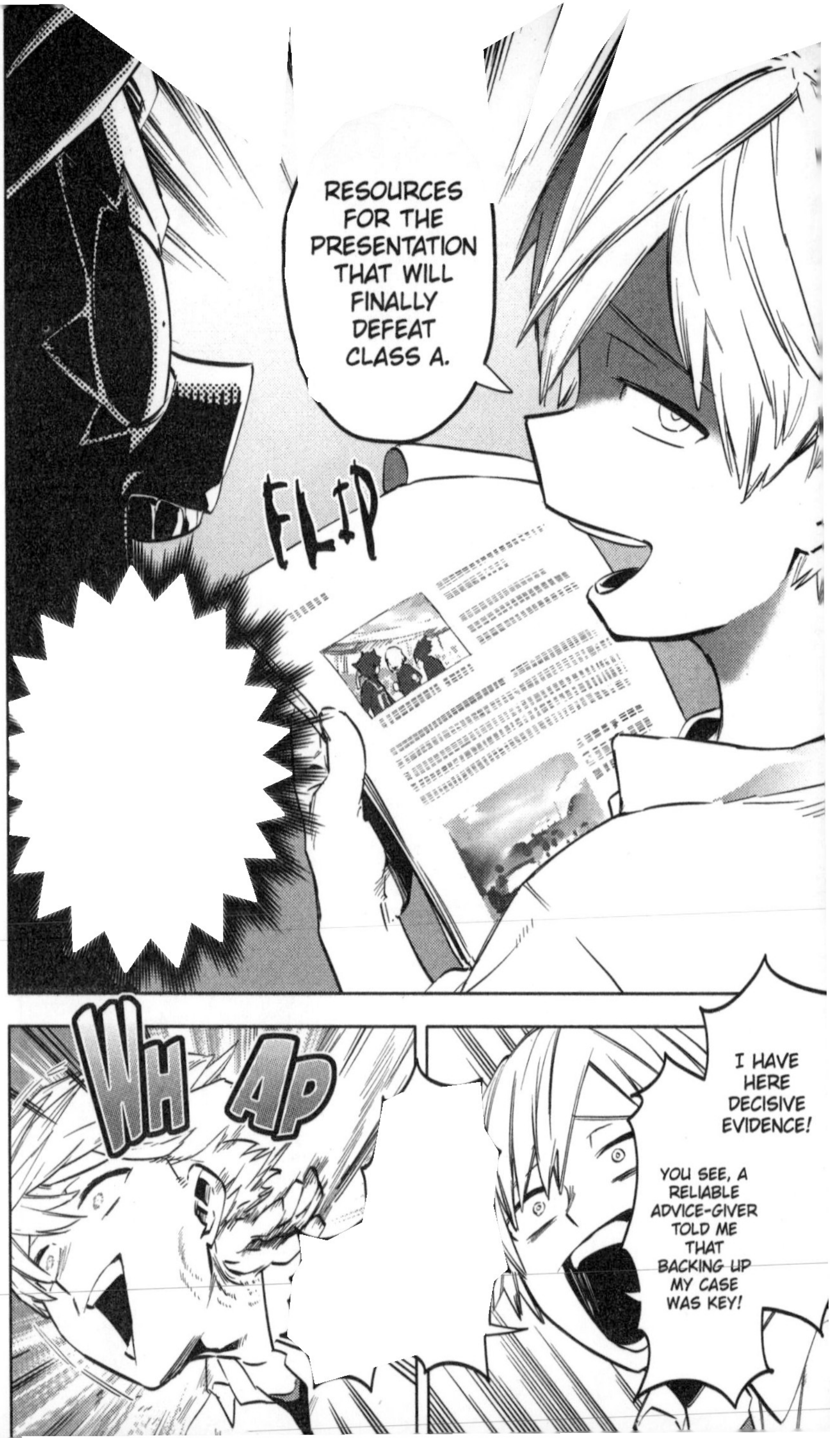
RESOURCES FOR THE PRESENTATION THAT WILL FINALLY DEFEAT CLASS A.
FLIP
I HAVE HERE DECISIVE EVIDENCE!
YOU SEE, A RELIABLE ADVICE-GIVER TOLD ME THAT BACKING UP MY CASE WAS KEY!
WHAP

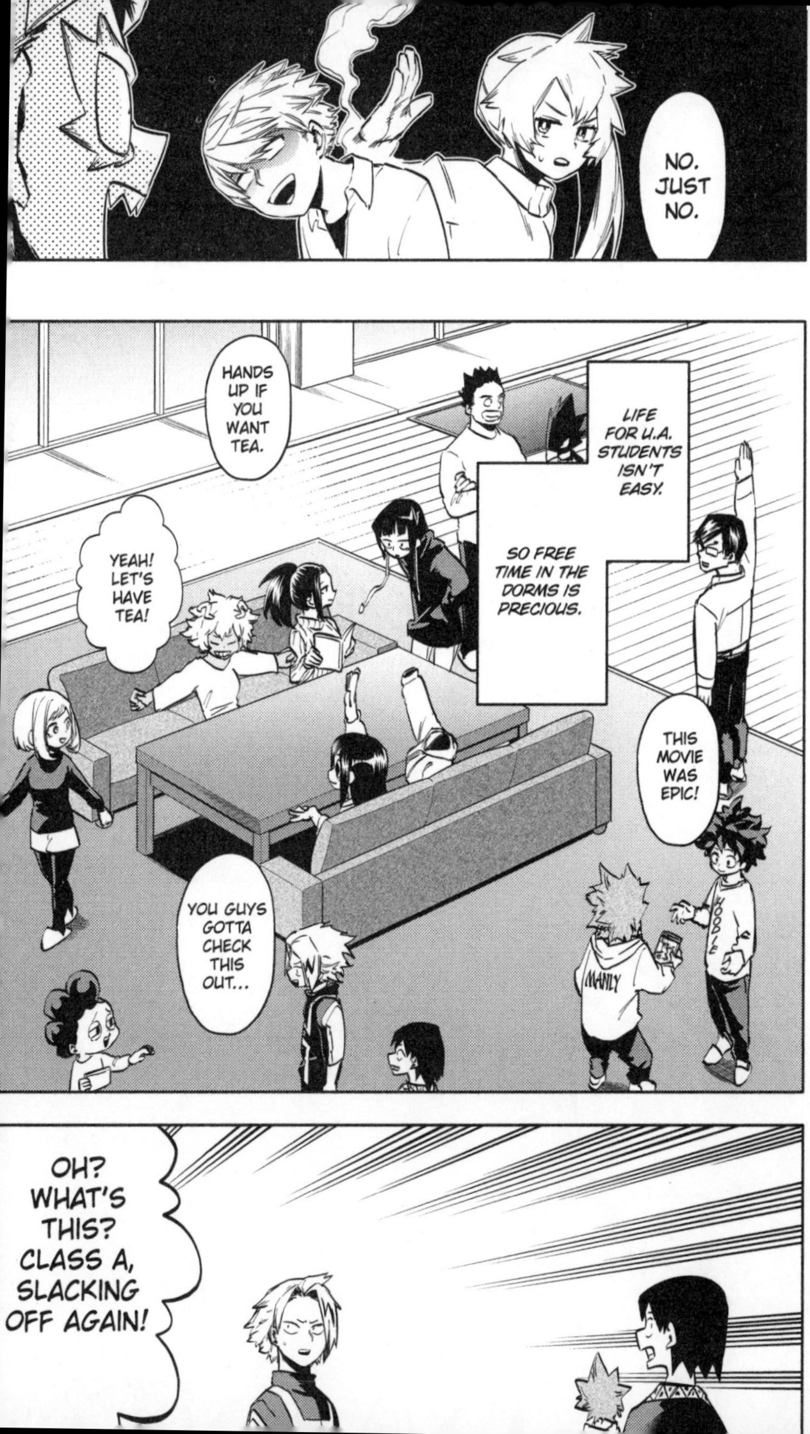
NO. JUST NO.
LIFE FOR U.A. STUDENTS ISN'T EASY.
SO FREE TIME IN THE DORMS IS PRECIOUS.
HANDS UP IF YOU WANT TEA.
THIS MOVIE WAS EPIC!
YEAH! LET'S HAVE TEA!
HOODIE
MANLY
YOU GUYS GOTTA CHECK THIS OUT...
OH? WHAT'S THIS? CLASS A, SLACKING OFF AGAIN!

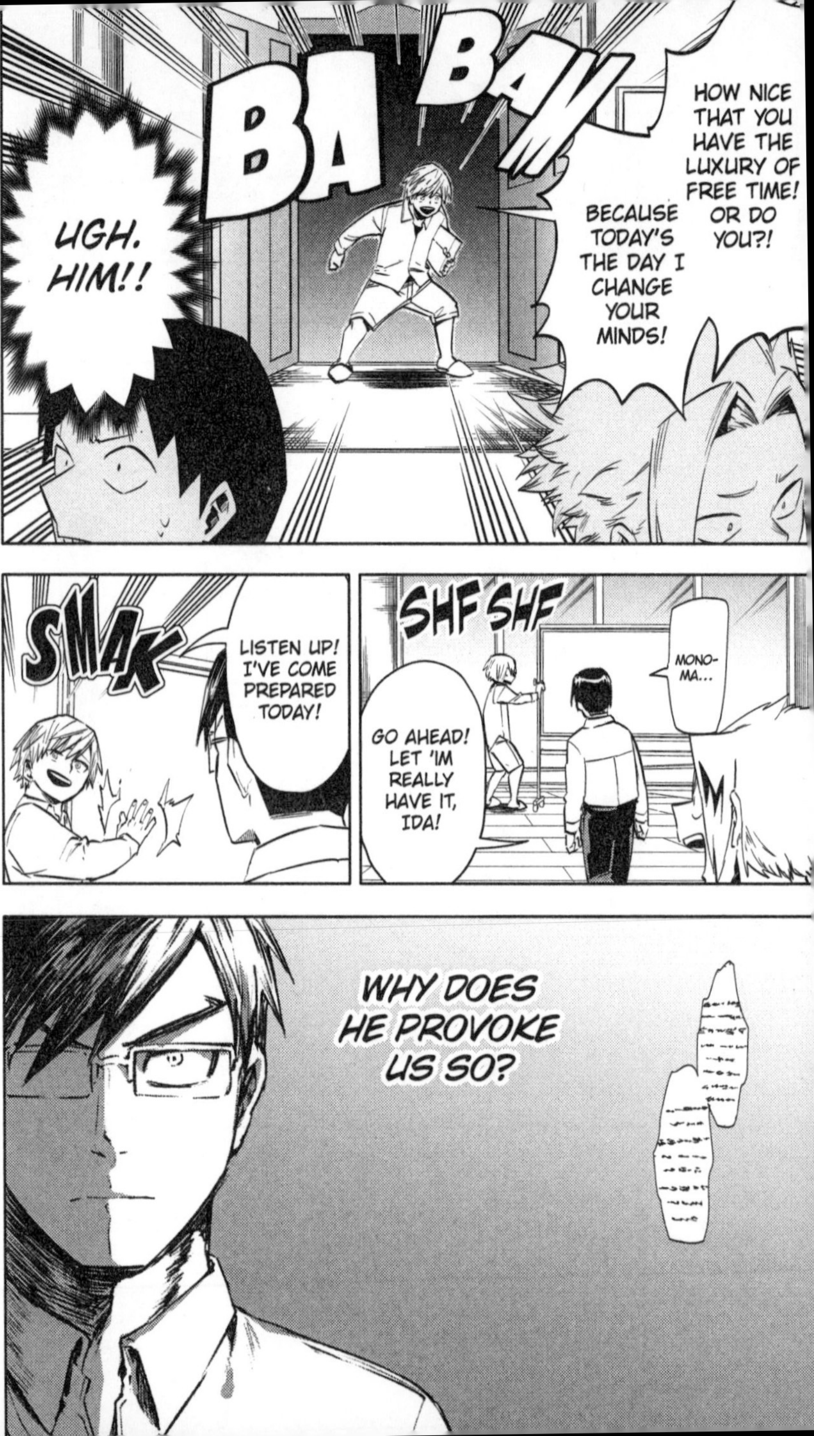
HOW NICE THAT YOU HAVE THE LUXURY OF FREE TIME! OR DO YOU?!
BECAUSE TODAY'S THE DAY I CHANGE YOUR MINDS!
BA BAM
UGH. HIM!!
MONO-MA...
SHF SHF
GO AHEAD! LET 'IM REALLY HAVE IT, IDA!
LISTEN UP! I'VE COME PREPARED TODAY!
SMAK
WHY DOES HE PROVOKE US SO?

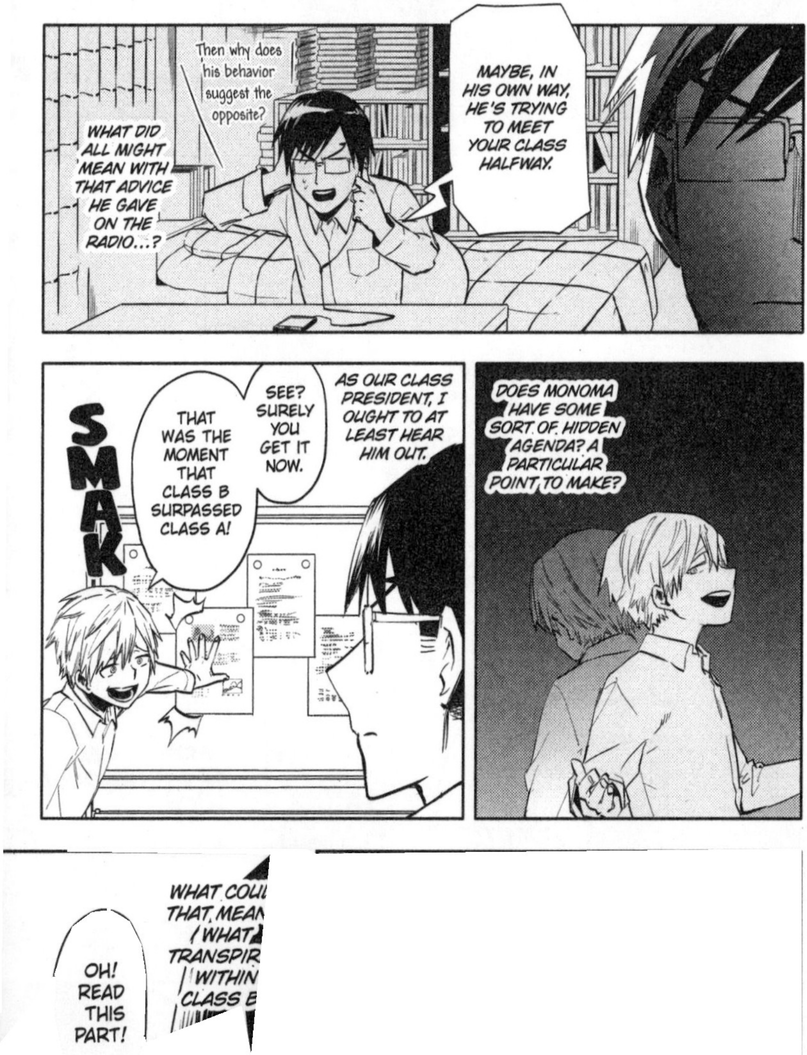
MAYBE, IN HIS OWN WAY, HE'S TRYING TO MEET YOUR CLASS HALFWAY.
Then why does his behavior suggest the opposite?
WHAT DID ALL MIGHT MEAN WITH THAT ADVICE HE GAVE ON THE RADIO...?
DOES MONOMA HAVE SOME SORT OF HIDDEN AGENDA? A PARTICULAR POINT TO MAKE?
AS OUR CLASS PRESIDENT, I OUGHT TO AT LEAST HEAR HIM OUT.
SEE? SURELY YOU GET IT NOW.
THAT WAS THE MOMENT THAT CLASS B SURPASSED CLASS A!
SMAK
WHAT COU
THAT MEAN
/ WHAT
TRANSPIR
WITHIN
CLASS B
OH! READ THIS PART!

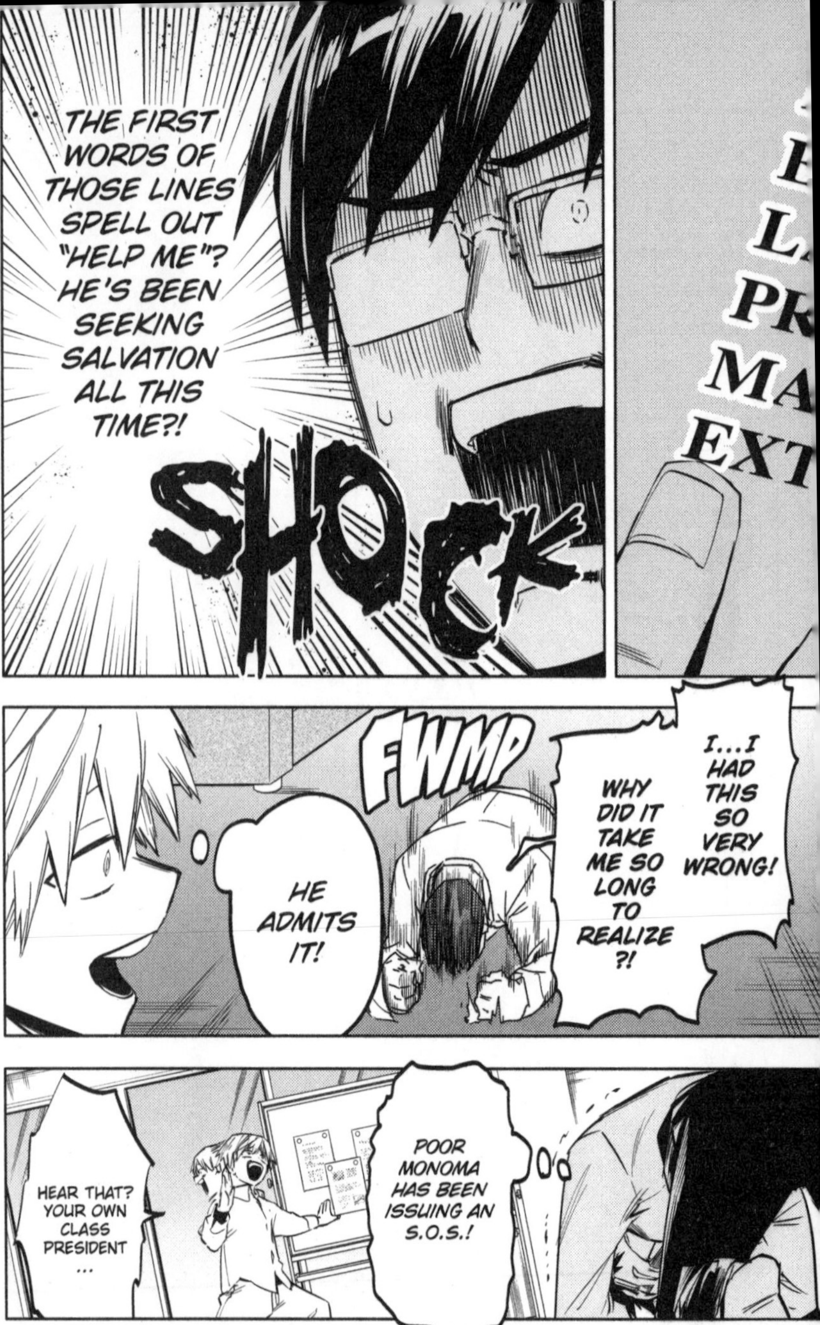
THE FIRST WORDS OF THOSE LINES SPELL OUT "HELP ME"? HE'S BEEN SEEKING SALVATION ALL THIS TIME?!
SHOCK
I...I HAD THIS SO VERY WRONG!
WHY DID IT TAKE ME SO LONG TO REALIZE?!
FWIMP
HE ADMITS IT!
POOR MONOMA HAS BEEN ISSUING AN S.O.S.!
HEAR THAT? YOUR OWN CLASS PRESIDENT ...

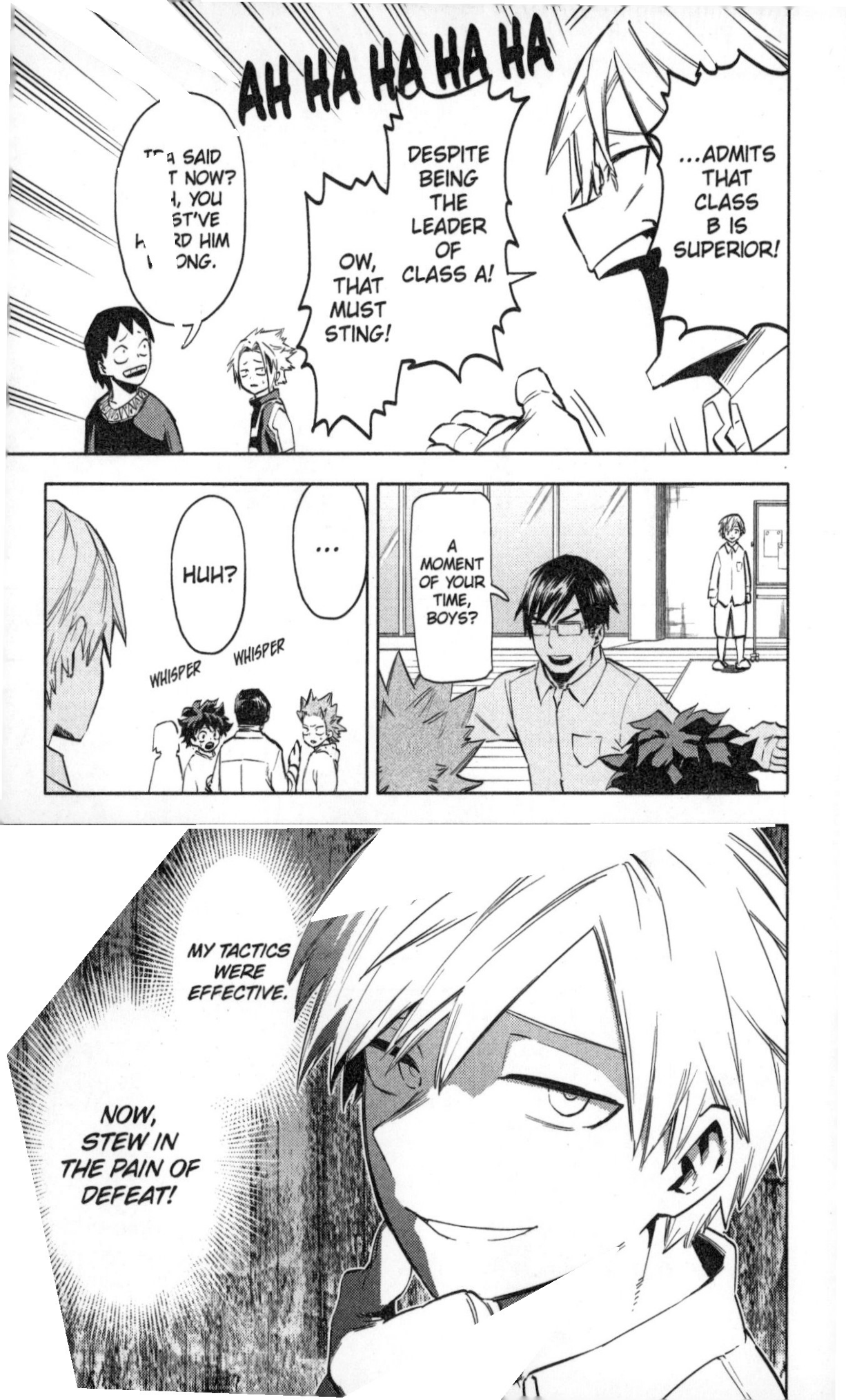
AH HA HA HA HA
...ADMITS THAT CLASS B IS SUPERIOR!
DESPITE BEING THE LEADER OF CLASS A!
OW, THAT MUST STING!
SAID NOW? YOU ST'VE RD HIM ONG.
A MOMENT OF YOUR TIME, BOYS?
...
HUH?
WHISPER
WHISPER
MY TACTICS WERE EFFECTIVE.
NOW, STEW IN THE PAIN OF DEFEAT!

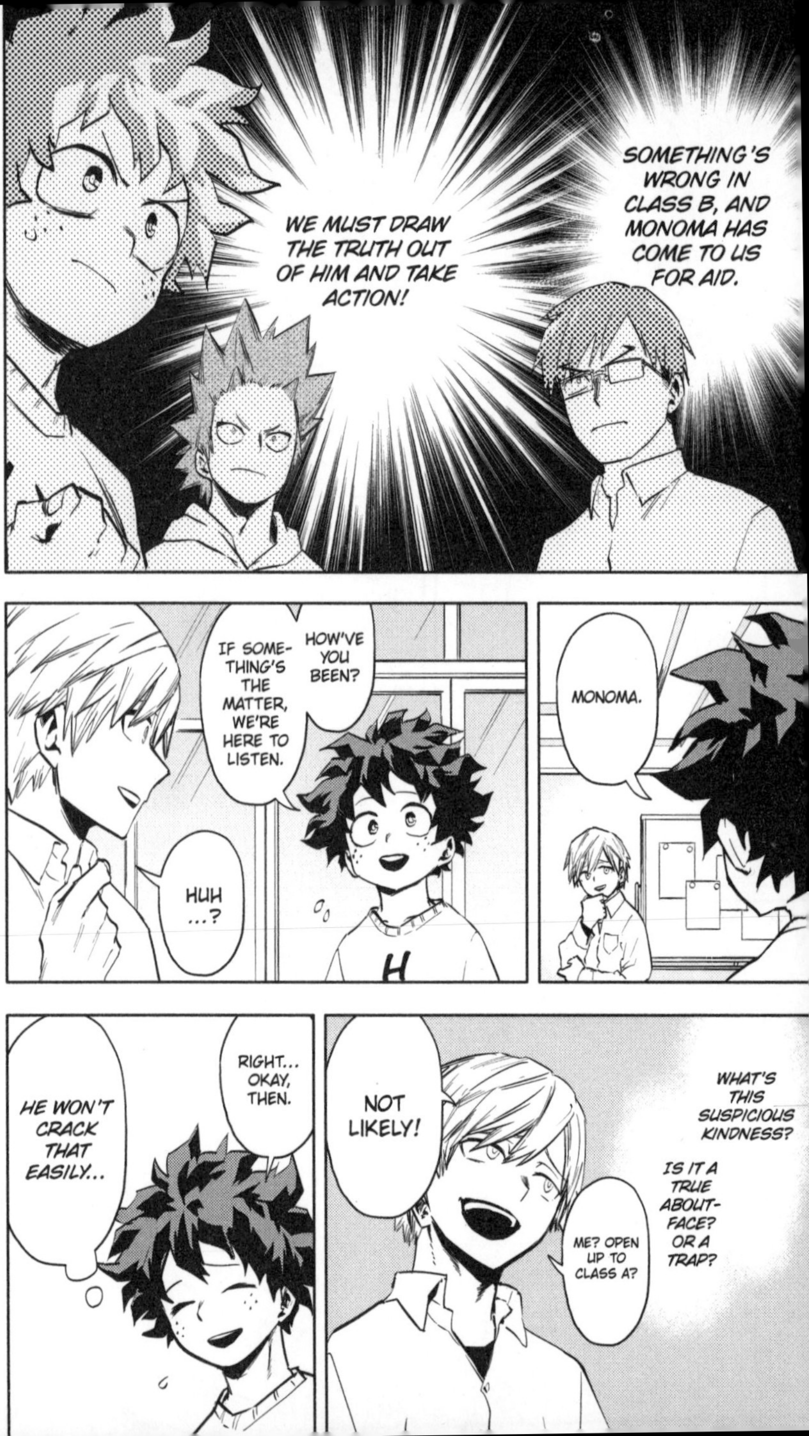
SOMETHING'S WRONG IN CLASS B, AND MONOMA HAS COME TO US FOR AID.
WE MUST DRAW THE TRUTH OUT OF HIM AND TAKE ACTION!
MONOMA.
HOW'VE YOU BEEN?
IF SOME-THING'S THE MATTER, WE'RE HERE TO LISTEN.
HUH...?
WHAT'S THIS SUSPICIOUS KINDNESS?
IS IT A TRUE ABOUT-FACE? OR A TRAP?
ME? OPEN UP TO CLASS A?
NOT LIKELY!
RIGHT... OKAY, THEN.
HE WON'T CRACK THAT EASILY...

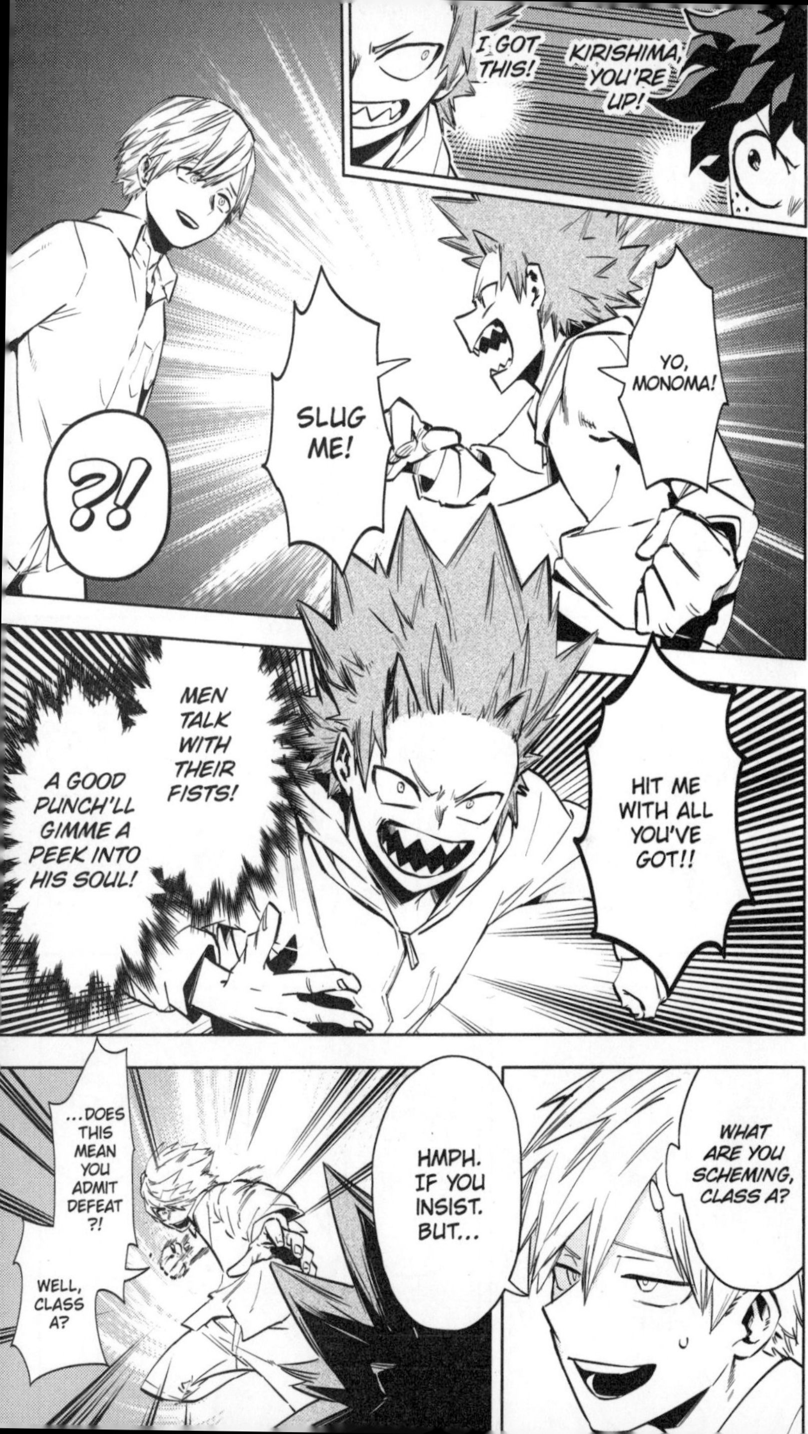
KIRISHIMA, YOU'RE UP!
I GOT THIS!
YO, MONOMA!
SLUG ME!
?!
HIT ME WITH ALL YOU'VE GOT!!
MEN TALK WITH THEIR FISTS!
A GOOD PUNCH'LL GIMME A PEEK INTO HIS SOUL!
WHAT ARE YOU SCHEMING, CLASS A?
HMPH. IF YOU INSIST. BUT...
...DOES THIS MEAN YOU ADMIT DEFEAT?!
WELL, CLASS A?

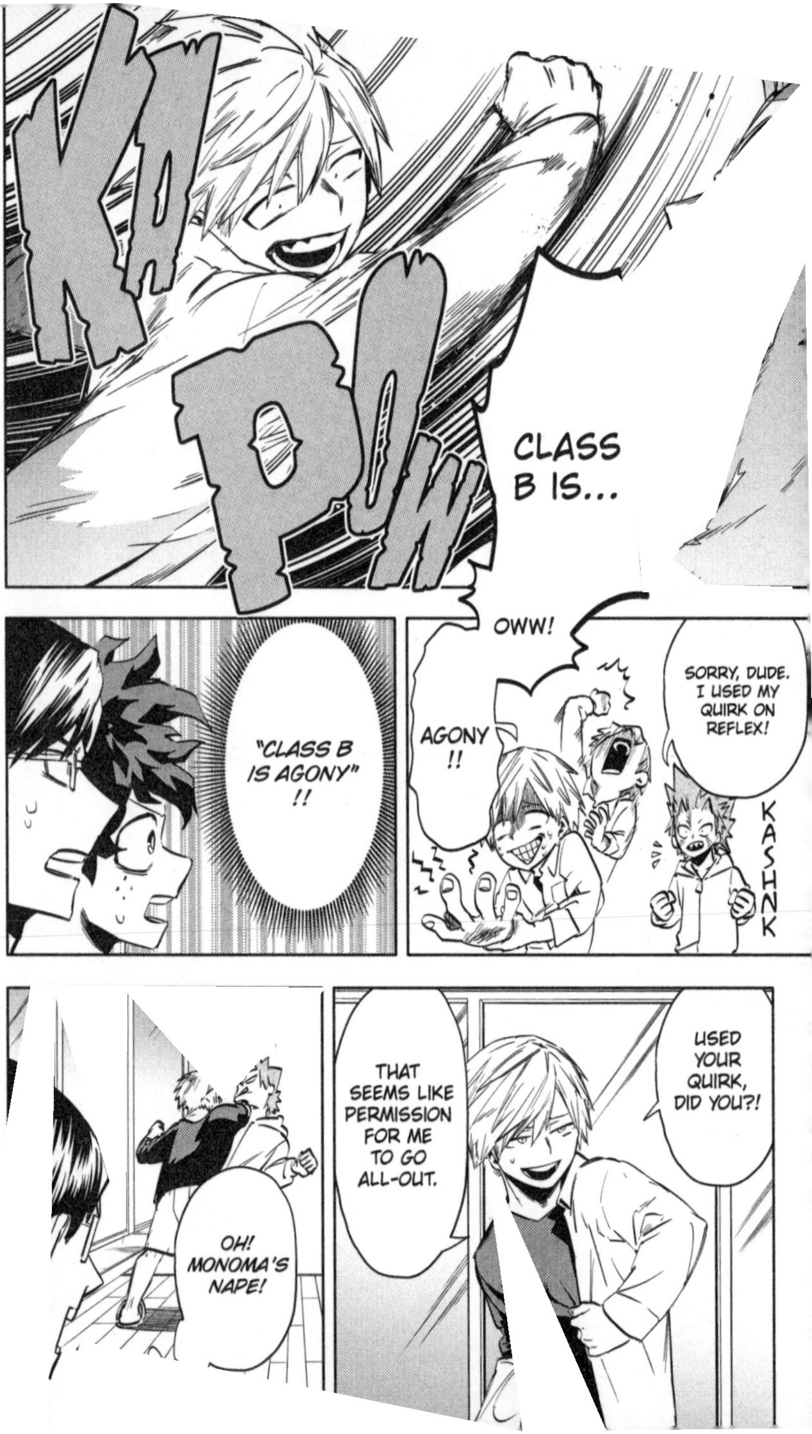
KA
POW
CLASS B IS...
OWW!
SORRY, DUDE. I USED MY QUIRK ON REFLEX!
AGONY !!
KASHNK
"CLASS B IS AGONY" !!
USED YOUR QUIRK, DID YOU?!
THAT SEEMS LIKE PERMISSION FOR ME TO GO ALL-OUT.
OH! MONOMA'S NAPE!

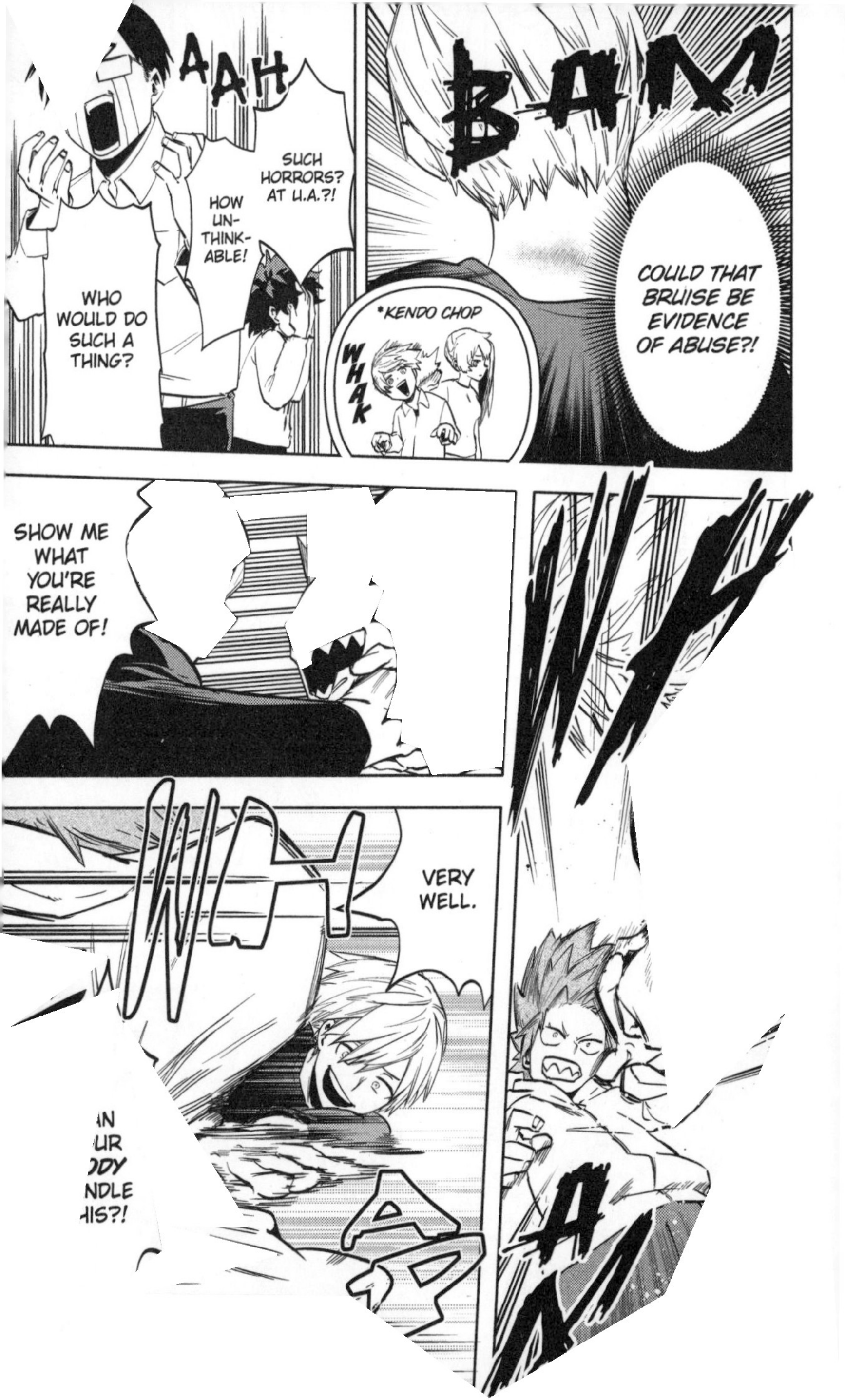
BAM
COULD THAT BRUISE BE EVIDENCE OF ABUSE?!
*KENDO CHOP
WHAK
AAH
SUCH HORRORS? AT U.A.?!
HOW UN-THINK-ABLE!
WHO WOULD DO SUCH A THING?
SHOW ME WHAT YOU'RE REALLY MADE OF!
VERY WELL.

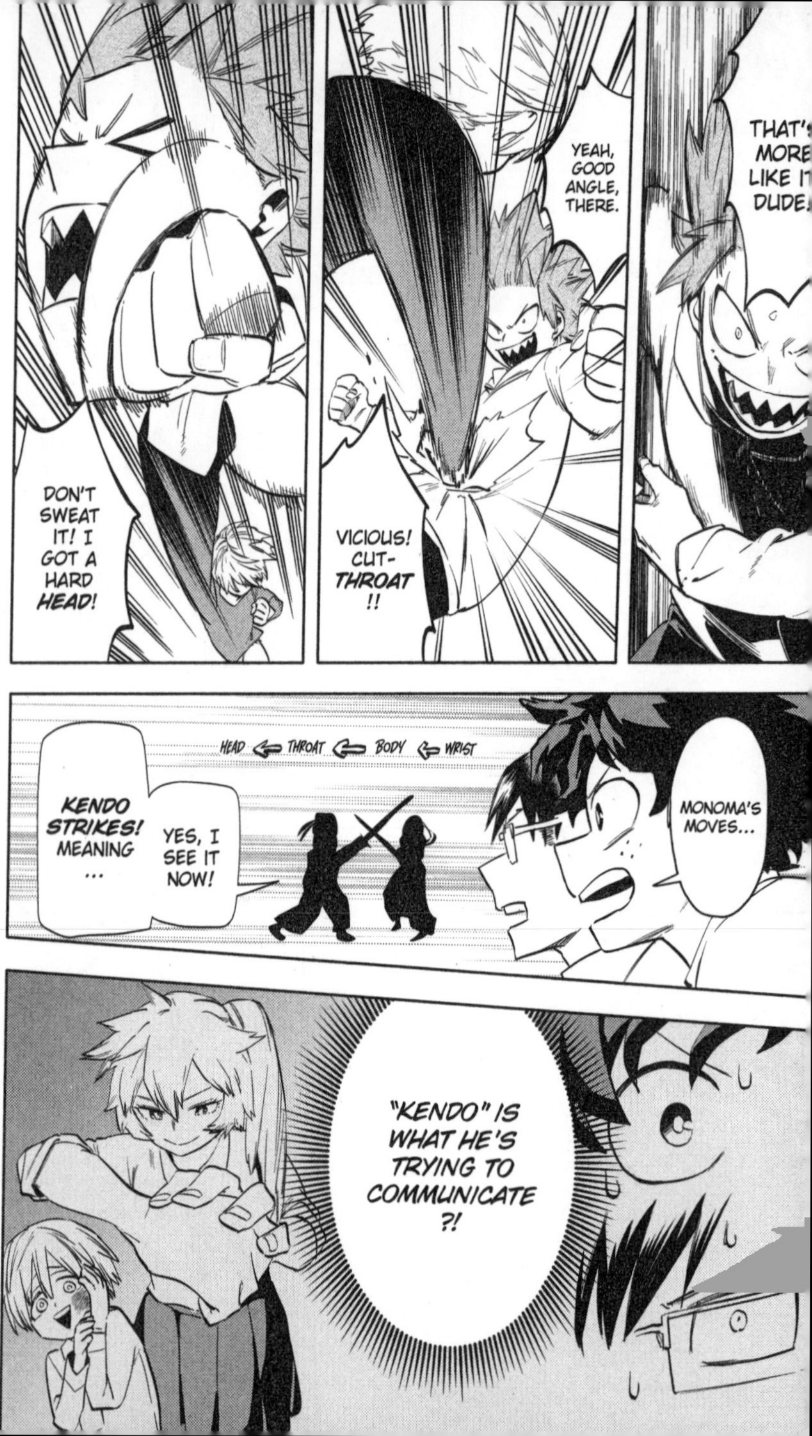
THAT'S MORE LIKE IT DUDE!
YEAH, GOOD ANGLE, THERE.
VICIOUS! CUT-THROAT!!
DON'T SWEAT IT! I GOT A HARD HEAD!
MONOMA'S MOVES...
HEAD ⇐ THROAT ⇐ BODY ⇐ WRIST
YES, I SEE IT NOW!
KENDO STRIKES! MEANING ...
"KENDO" IS WHAT HE'S TRYING TO COMMUNICATE?!

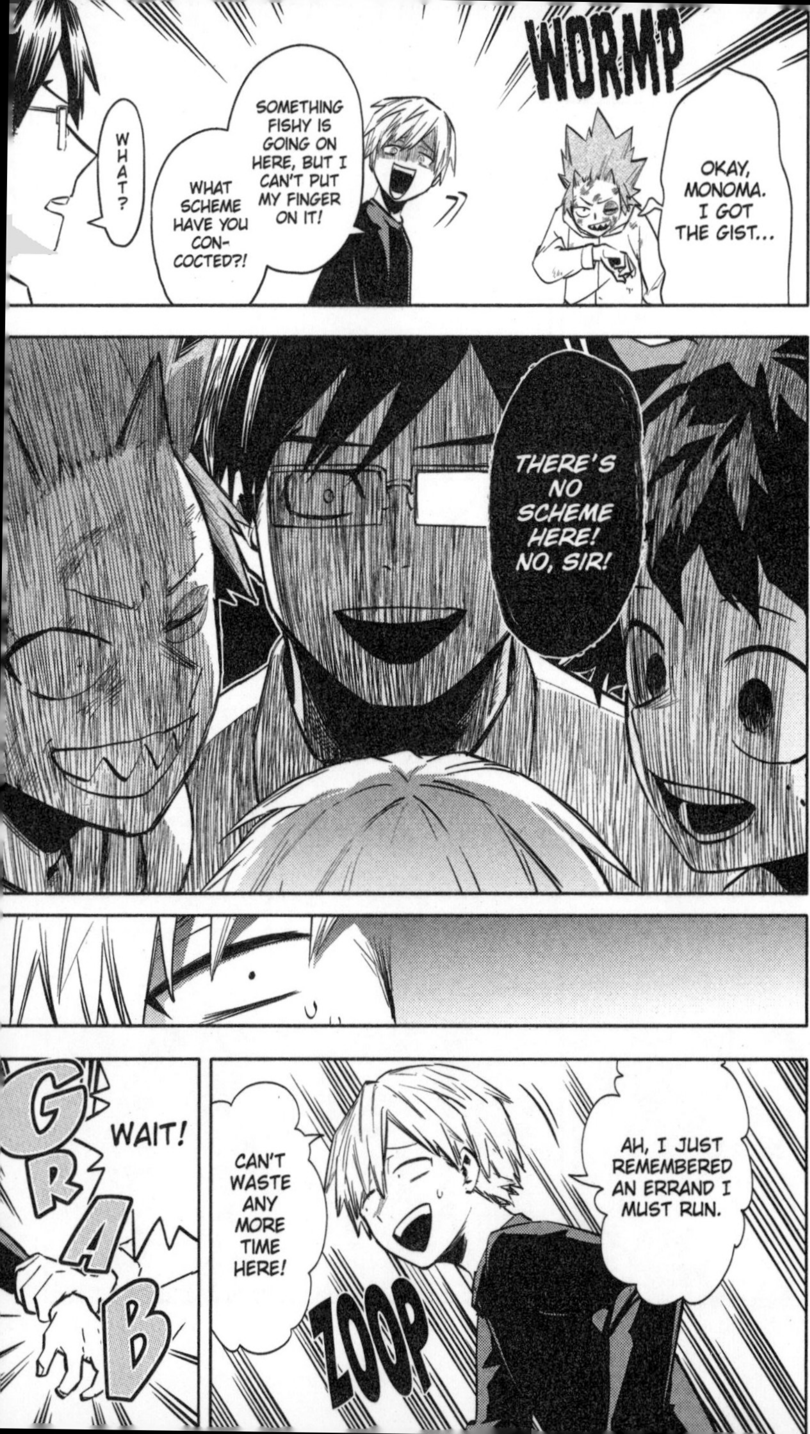
WORMP
OKAY, MONOMA. I GOT THE GIST...
SOMETHING FISHY IS GOING ON HERE, BUT I CAN'T PUT MY FINGER ON IT!
WHAT SCHEME HAVE YOU CON-COCTED?!
WHAT?
THERE'S NO SCHEME HERE! NO, SIR!
AH, I JUST REMEMBERED AN ERRAND I MUST RUN.
CAN'T WASTE ANY MORE TIME HERE!
ZOOP
GRAB
WAIT!

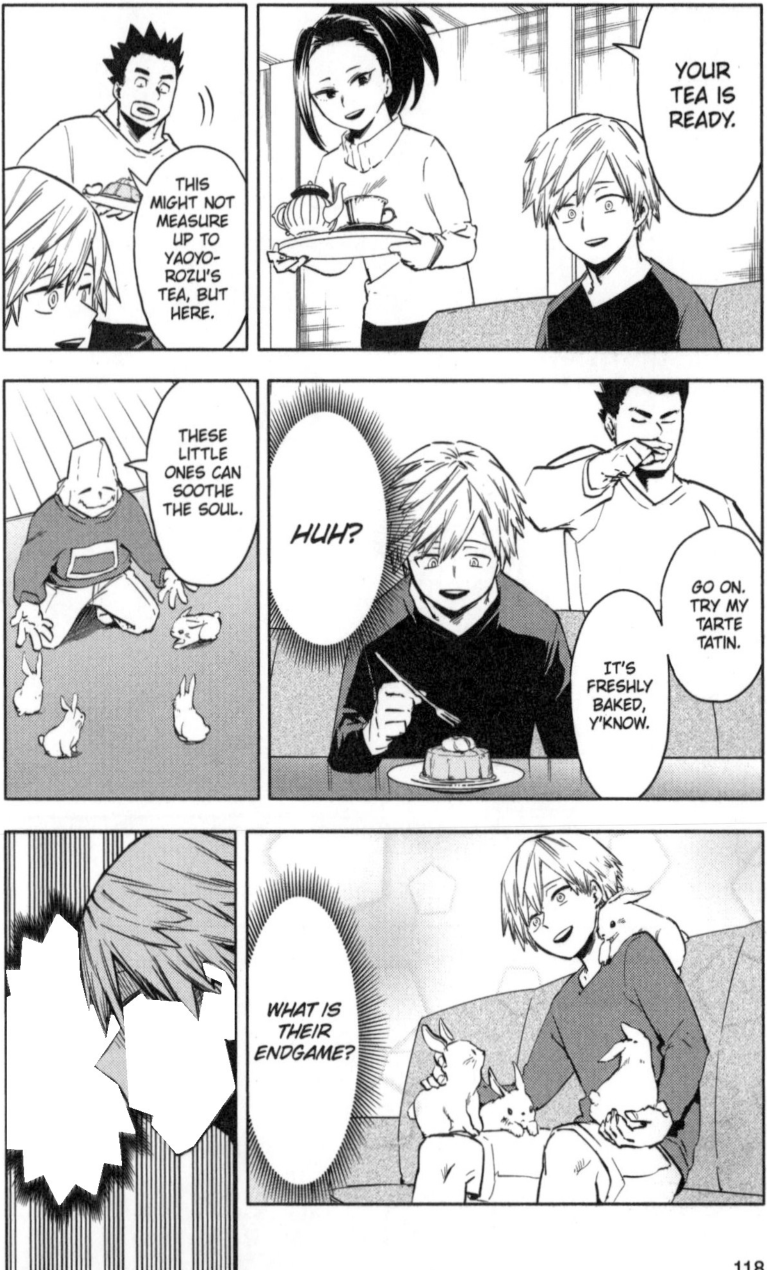
YOUR TEA IS READY.
THIS MIGHT NOT MEASURE UP TO YAOYO-ROZU'S TEA, BUT HERE.
GO ON. TRY MY TARTE TATIN.
IT'S FRESHLY BAKED, Y'KNOW.
HUH?
THESE LITTLE ONES CAN SOOTHE THE SOUL.
WHAT IS THEIR ENDGAME?

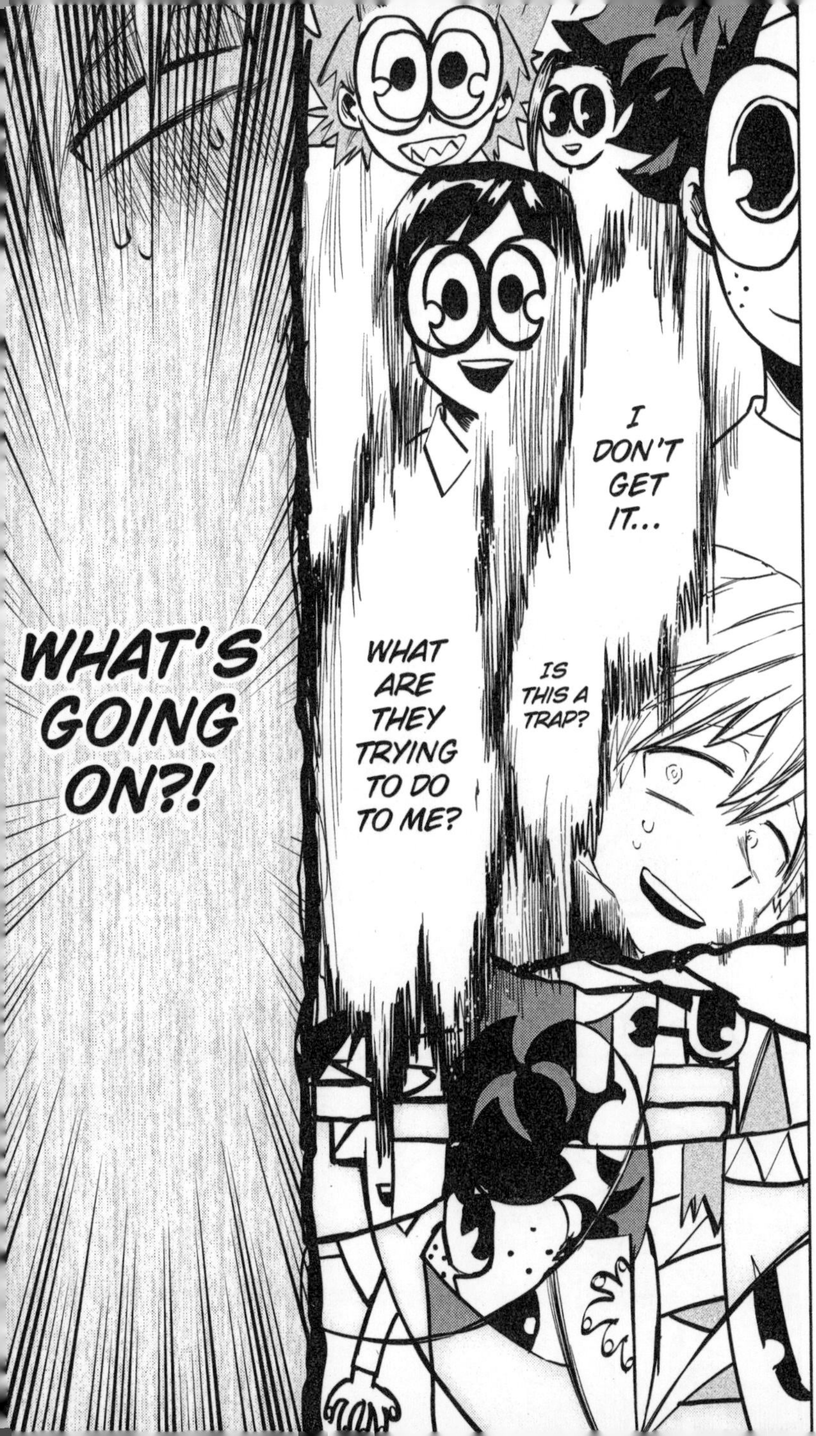
I DON'T GET IT...
IS THIS A TRAP?
WHAT ARE THEY TRYING TO DO TO ME?
WHAT'S GOING ON?!

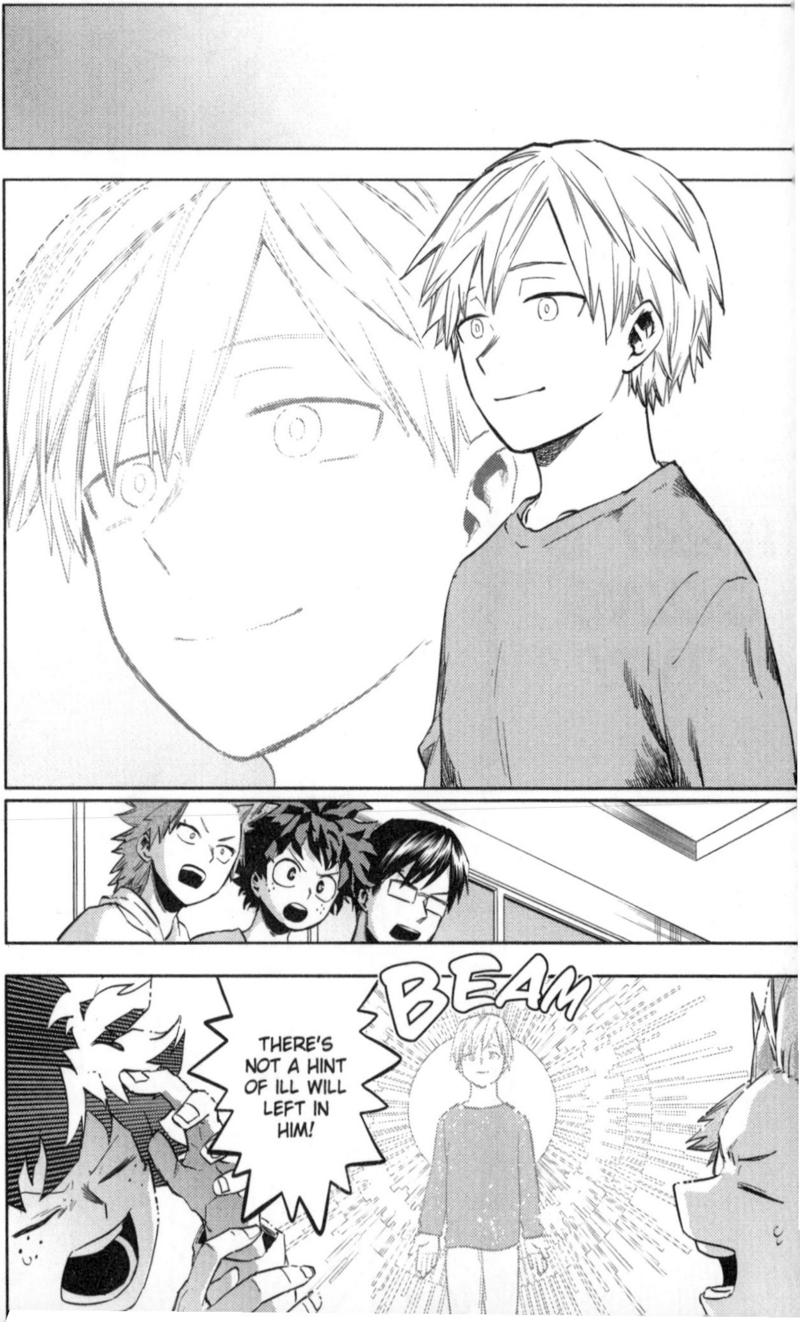
BEAM
THERE'S NOT A HINT OF ILL WILL LEFT IN HIM!

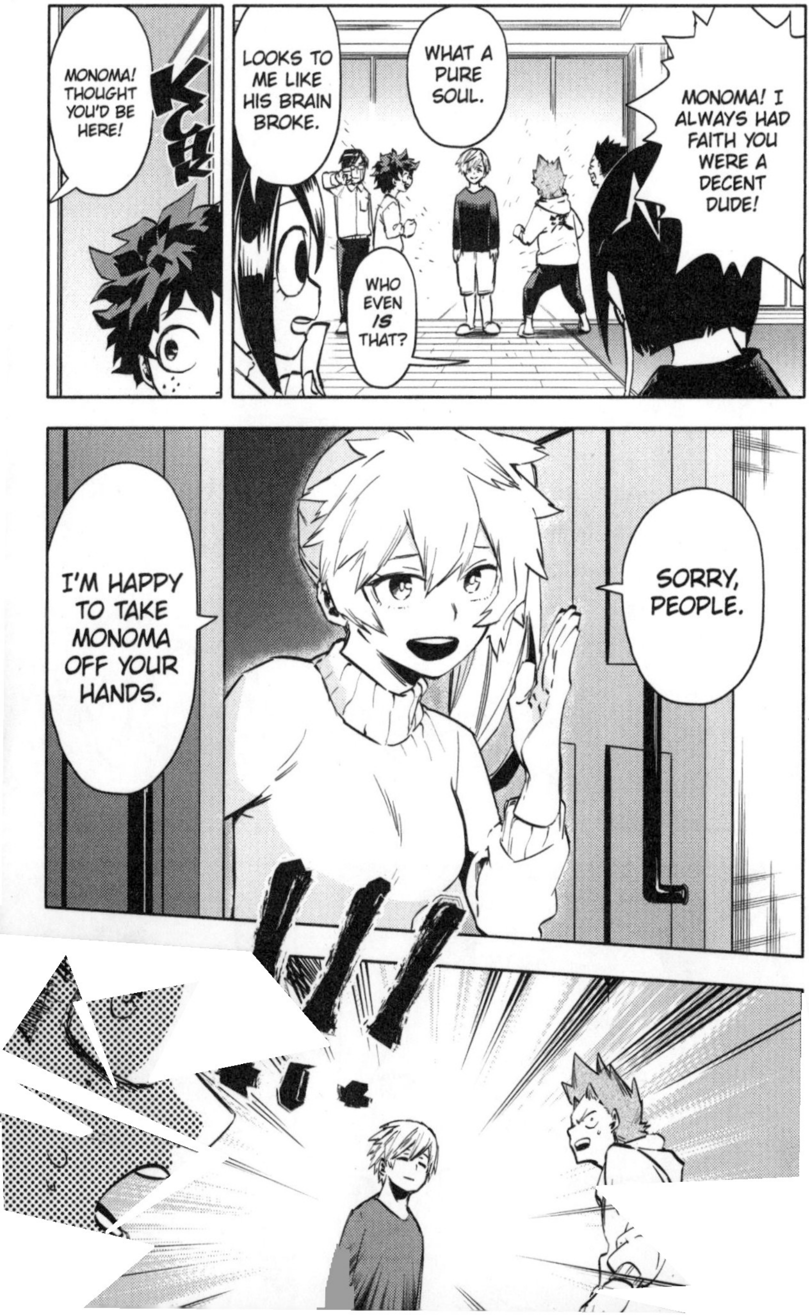
MONOMA! I ALWAYS HAD FAITH YOU WERE A DECENT DUDE!
WHAT A PURE SOUL.
LOOKS TO ME LIKE HIS BRAIN BROKE.
WHO EVEN *IS* THAT?
MONOMA! THOUGHT YOU'D BE HERE!
SORRY, PEOPLE.
I'M HAPPY TO TAKE MONOMA OFF YOUR HANDS.

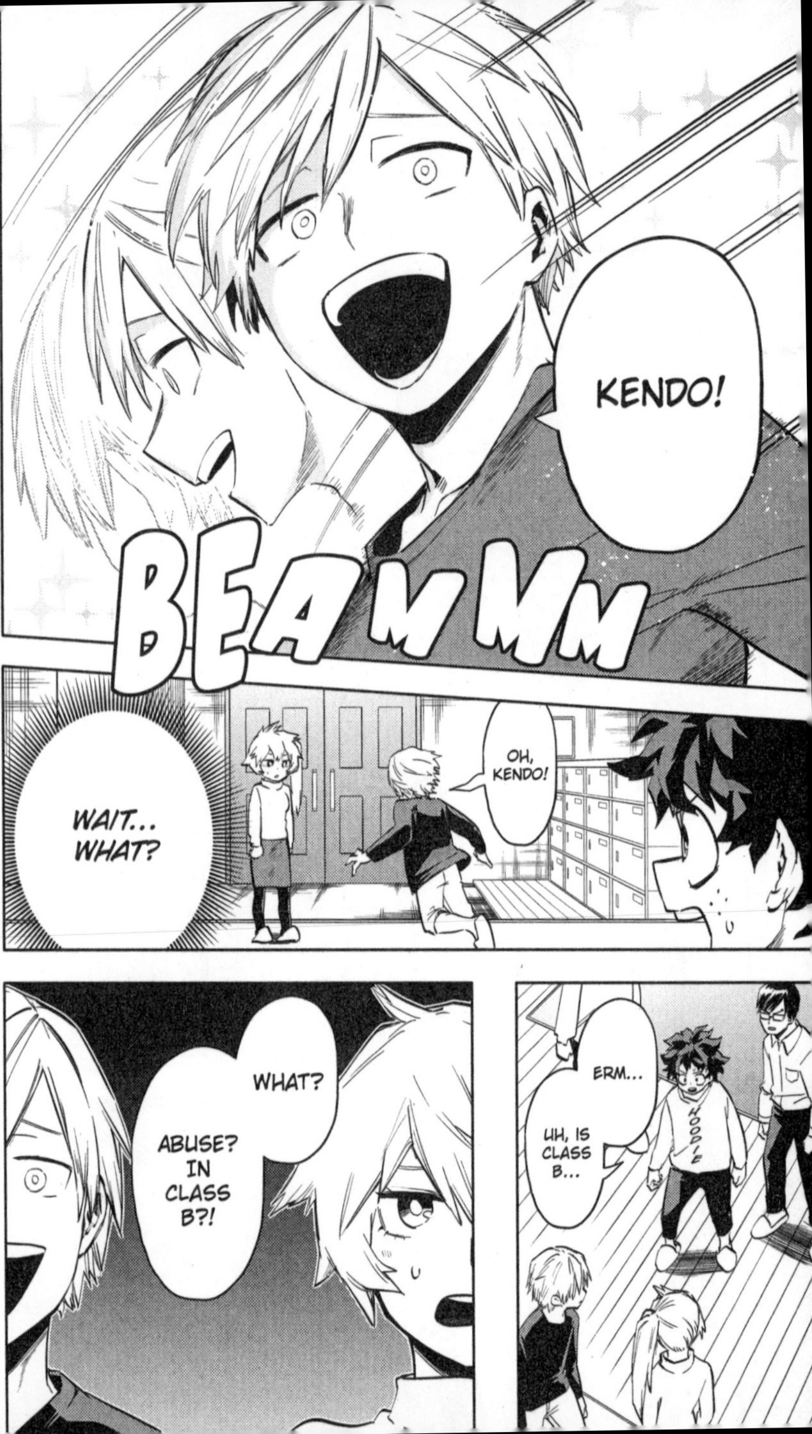
KENDO!
BEAMMM
OH, KENDO!
WAIT... WHAT?
ERM...
UH, IS CLASS B...
HOODIE
WHAT?
ABUSE? IN CLASS B?!

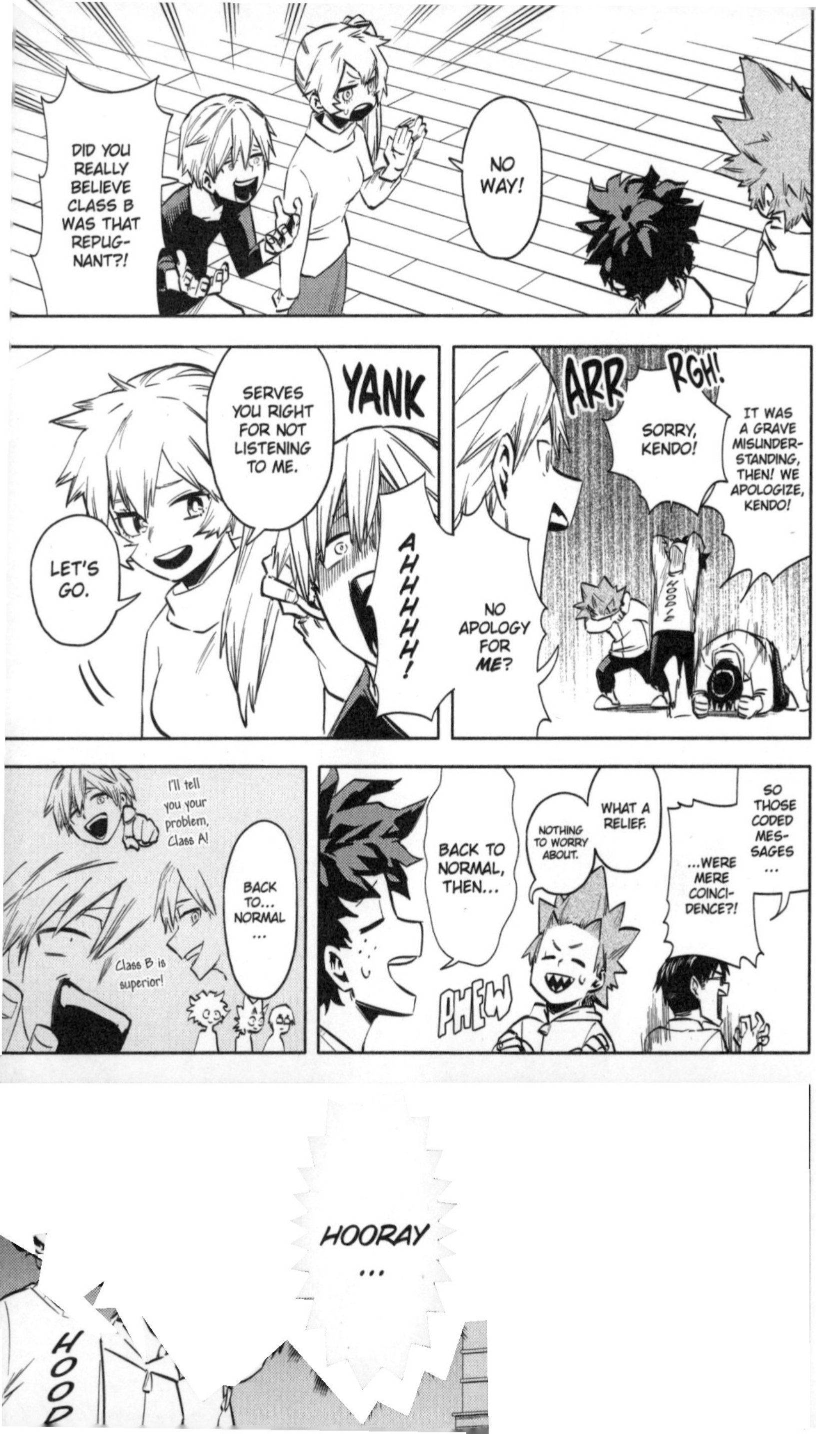
NO WAY!
DID YOU REALLY BELIEVE CLASS B WAS THAT REPUGNANT?!
ARRRGH!
IT WAS A GRAVE MISUNDERSTANDING, THEN! WE APOLOGIZE, KENDO!
SORRY, KENDO!
HOODIE
NO APOLOGY FOR ME?
YANK
SERVES YOU RIGHT FOR NOT LISTENING TO ME.
AHHHHHH!
LET'S GO.
SO THOSE CODED MESSAGES...
...WERE MERE COINCIDENCE?!
WHAT A RELIEF.
NOTHING TO WORRY ABOUT.
BACK TO NORMAL, THEN...
PHEW
I'll tell you your problem, Class A!
BACK TO... NORMAL...
Class B is superior!
HOORAY...
HOOD

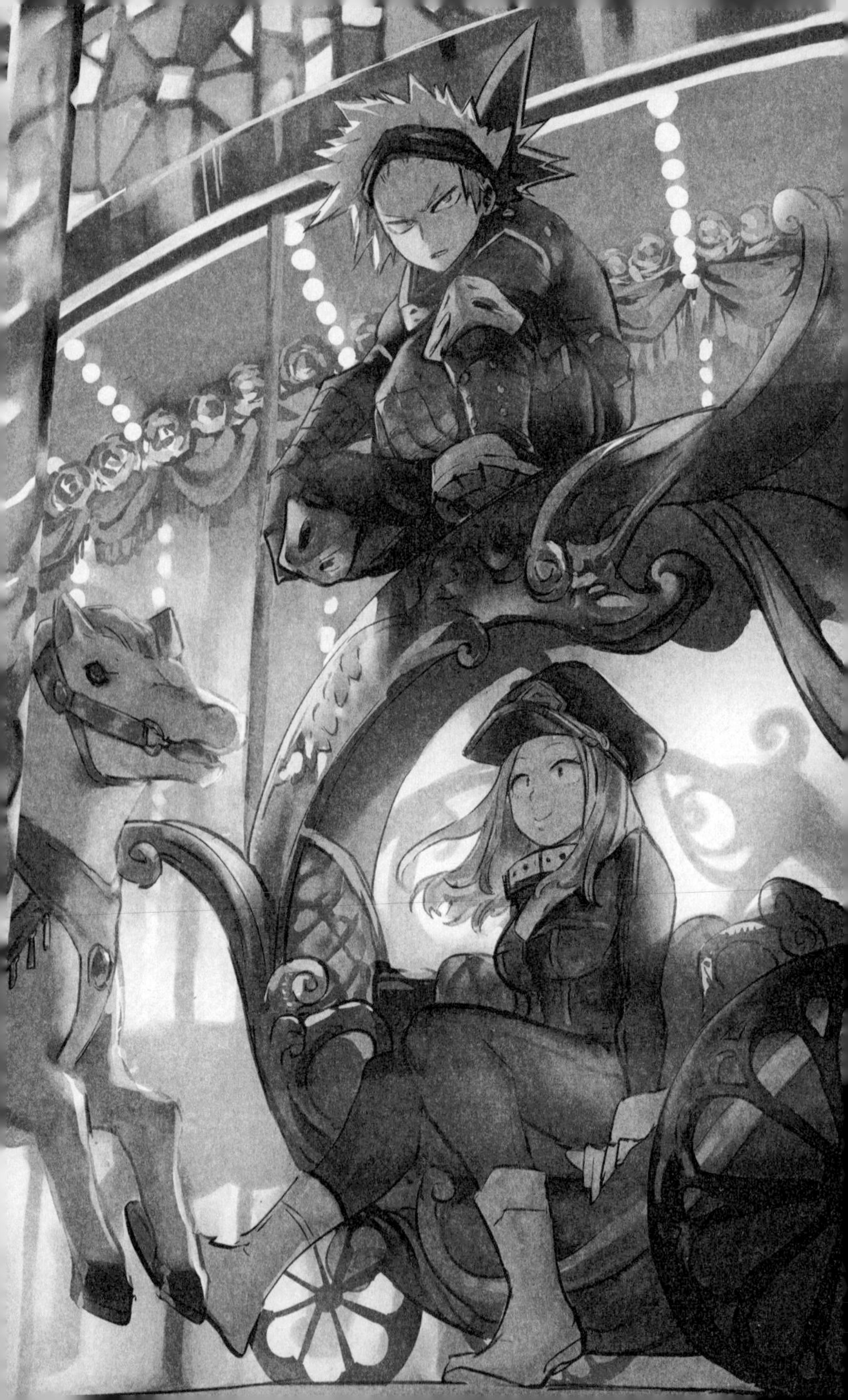

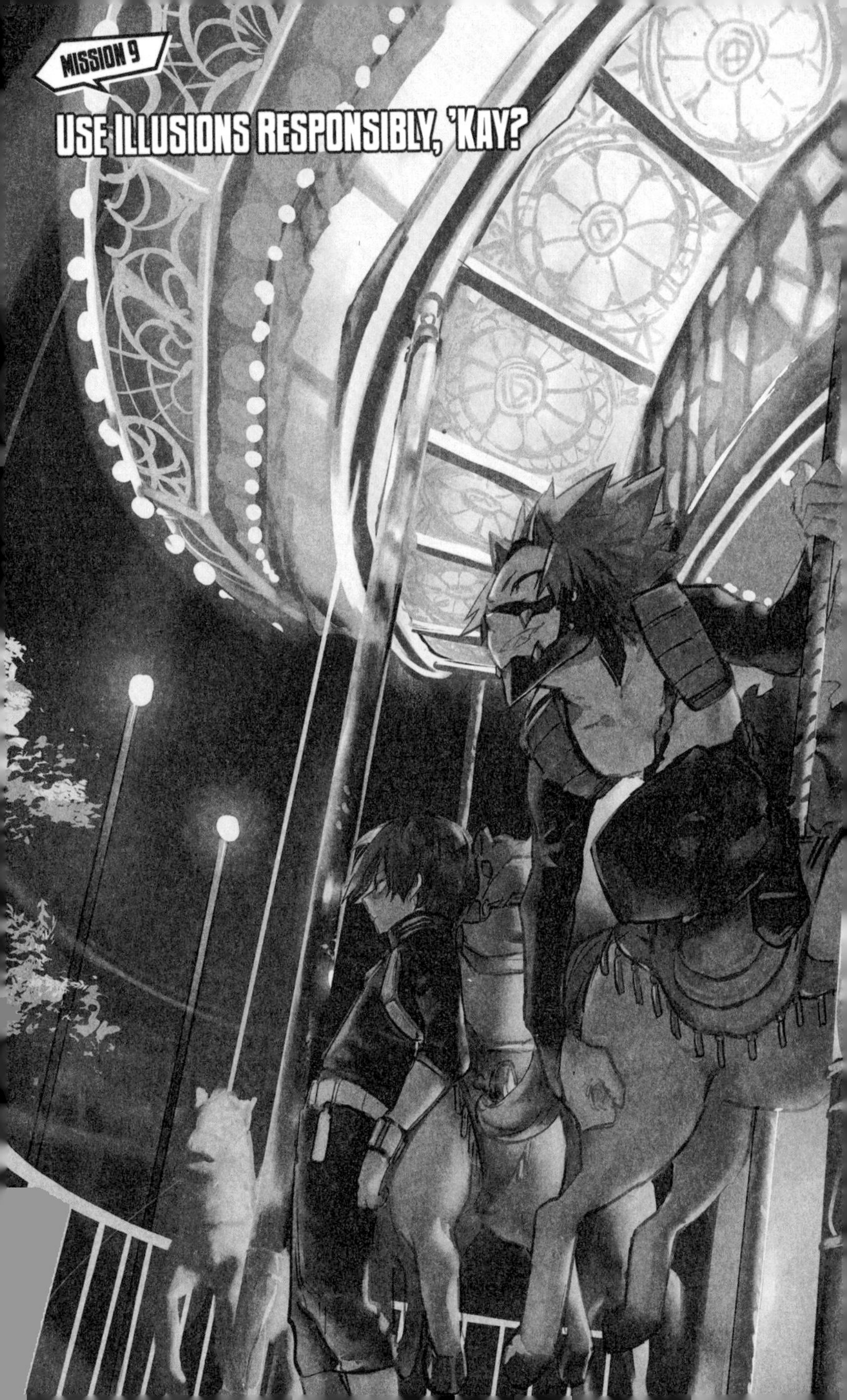
MISSION 9
USE ILLUSIONS RESPONSIBLY, 'KAY?

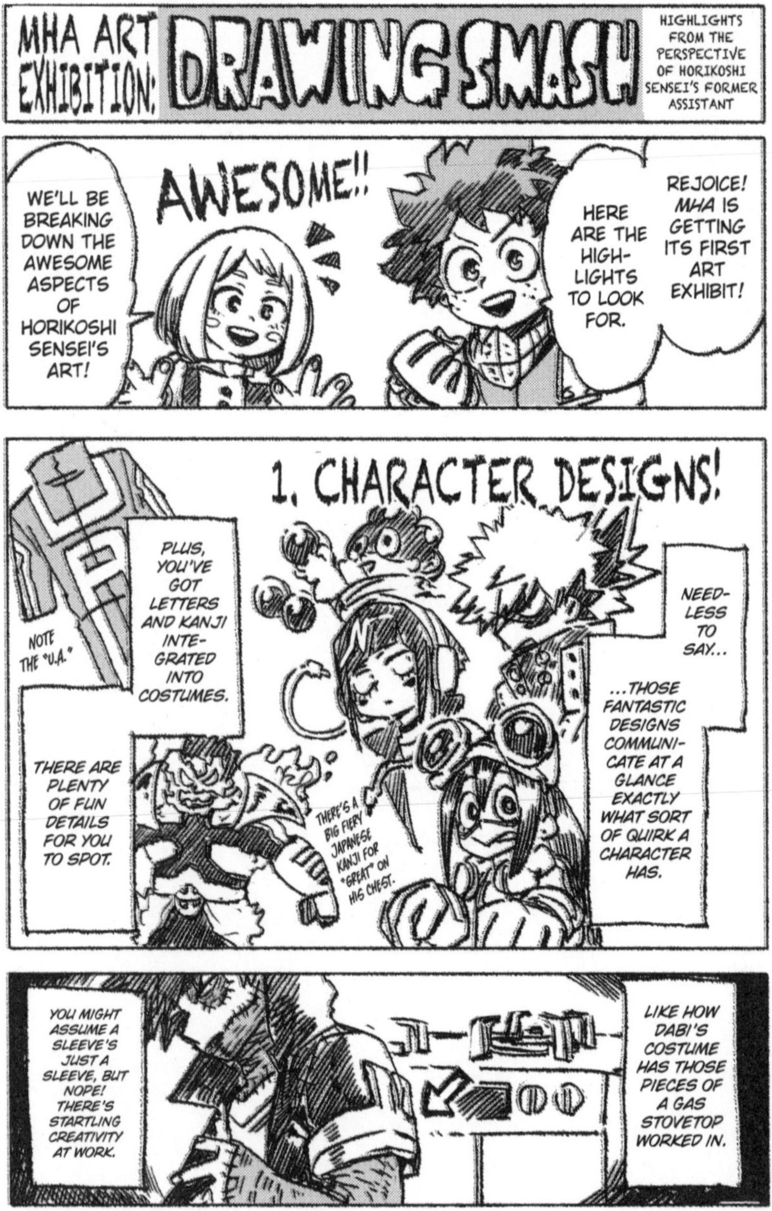
MHA ART EXHIBITION: DRAWING SMASH
HIGHLIGHTS FROM THE PERSPECTIVE OF HORIKOSHI SENSEI'S FORMER ASSISTANT
REJOICE! MHA IS GETTING ITS FIRST ART EXHIBIT!
HERE ARE THE HIGHLIGHTS TO LOOK FOR.
AWESOME!!
WE'LL BE BREAKING DOWN THE AWESOME ASPECTS OF HORIKOSHI SENSEI'S ART!
1. CHARACTER DESIGNS!
NEEDLESS TO SAY...
...THOSE FANTASTIC DESIGNS COMMUNICATE AT A GLANCE EXACTLY WHAT SORT OF QUIRK A CHARACTER HAS.
THERE'S A BIG FIERY JAPANESE KANJI FOR "GREAT" ON HIS CHEST.
PLUS, YOU'VE GOT LETTERS AND KANJI INTEGRATED INTO COSTUMES.
NOTE THE "U.A."
THERE ARE PLENTY OF FUN DETAILS FOR YOU TO SPOT.
LIKE HOW DABI'S COSTUME HAS THOSE PIECES OF A GAS STOVETOP WORKED IN.
YOU MIGHT ASSUME A SLEEVE'S JUST A SLEEVE, BUT NOPE! THERE'S STARTLING CREATIVITY AT WORK.

CONTINUED ON PAGE 156!

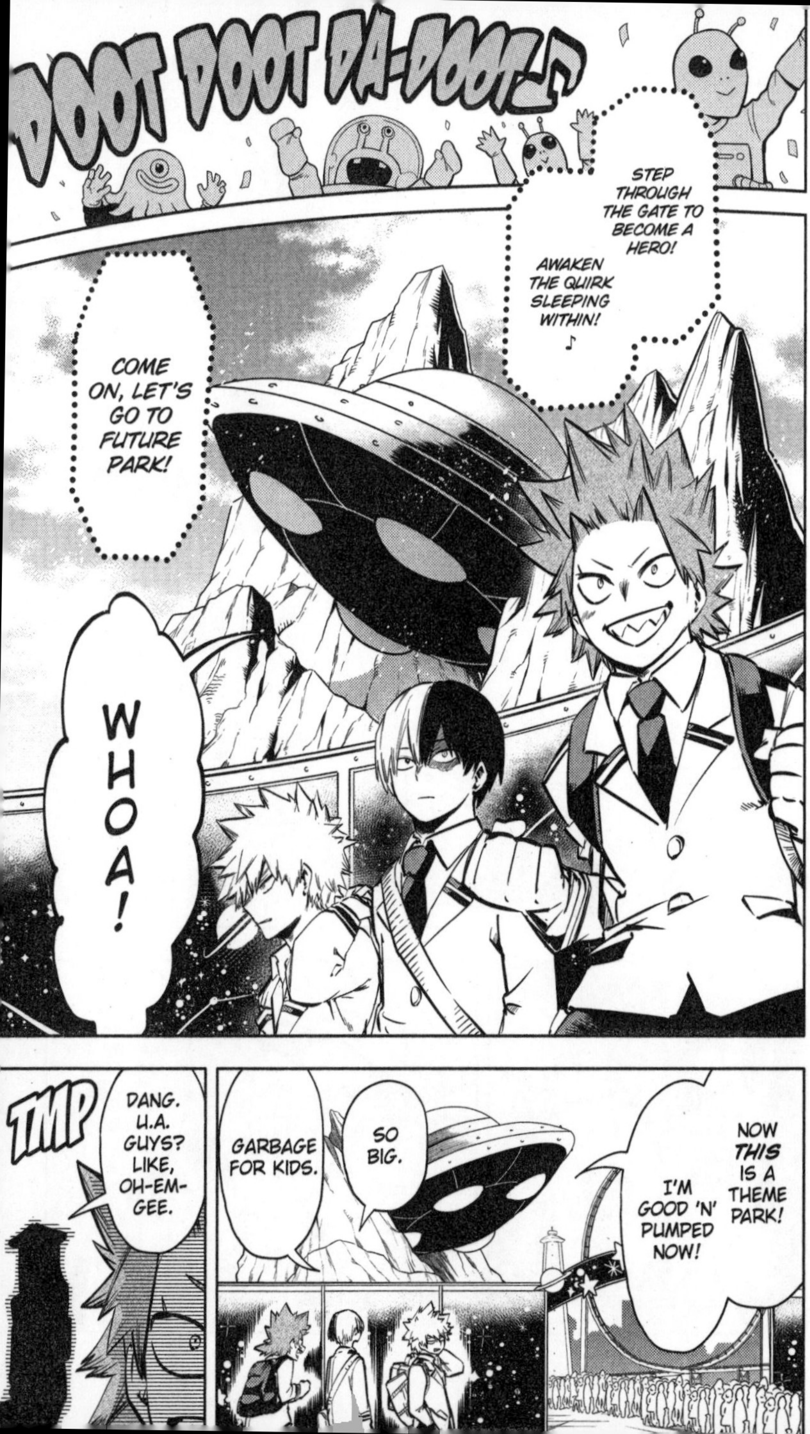
DOOT DOOT DA-DOOT♪
STEP THROUGH THE GATE TO BECOME A HERO!
AWAKEN THE QUIRK SLEEPING WITHIN! ♪
COME ON, LET'S GO TO FUTURE PARK!
WHOA!
NOW *THIS* IS A THEME PARK!
I'M GOOD 'N' PUMPED NOW!
SO BIG.
GARBAGE FOR KIDS.
TMP
DANG. U.A. GUYS? LIKE, OH-EM-GEE.

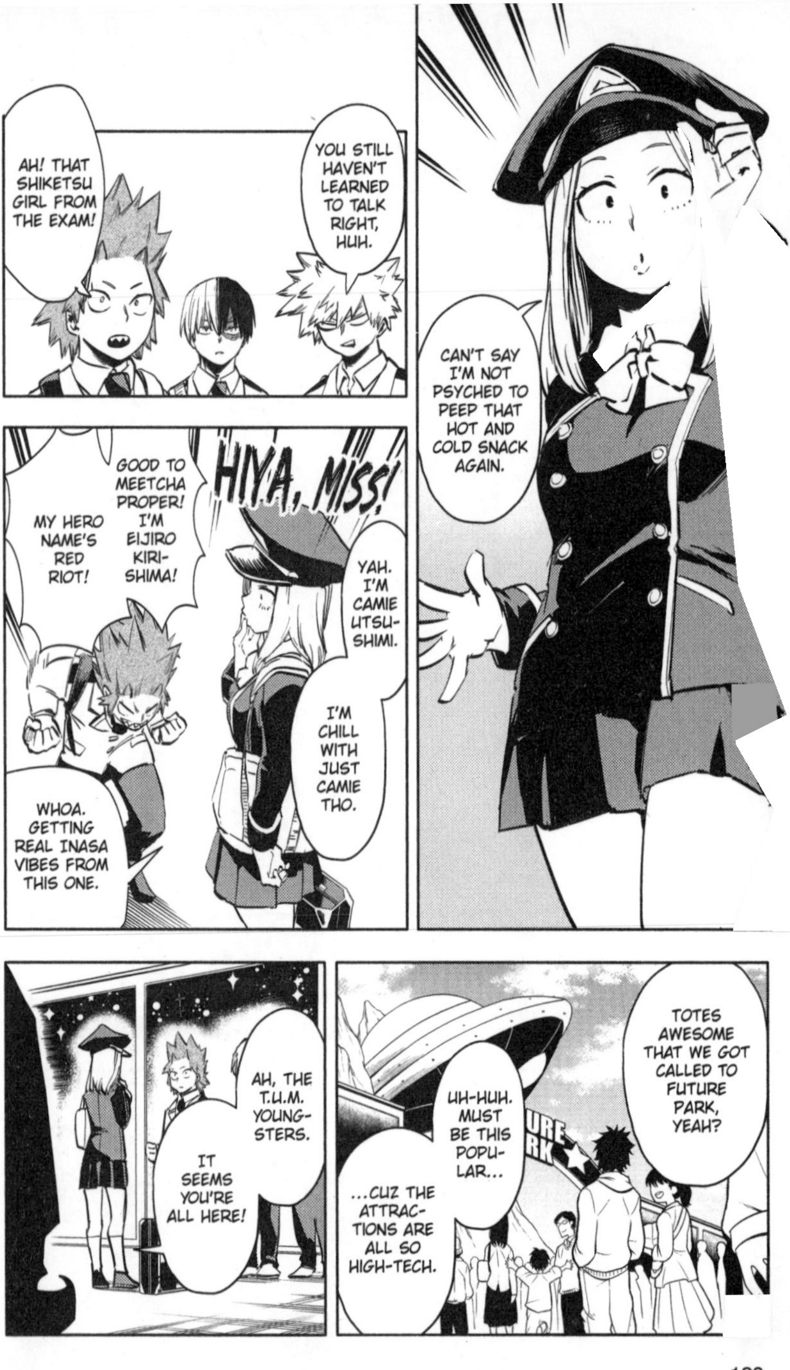
CAN'T SAY I'M NOT PSYCHED TO PEEP THAT HOT AND COLD SNACK AGAIN.
YOU STILL HAVEN'T LEARNED TO TALK RIGHT, HUH.
AH! THAT SHIKETSU GIRL FROM THE EXAM!
HIYA, MISS!
GOOD TO MEETCHA PROPER! I'M EIJIRO KIRI-SHIMA!
MY HERO NAME'S RED RIOT!
YAH. I'M CAMIE UTSU-SHIMI.
I'M CHILL WITH JUST CAMIE THO.
WHOA. GETTING REAL INASA VIBES FROM THIS ONE.
TOTES AWESOME THAT WE GOT CALLED TO FUTURE PARK, YEAH?
UH-HUH. MUST BE THIS POPU-LAR...
...CUZ THE ATTRAC-TIONS ARE ALL SO HIGH-TECH.
AH, THE T.U.M. YOUNG-STERS.
IT SEEMS YOU'RE ALL HERE!

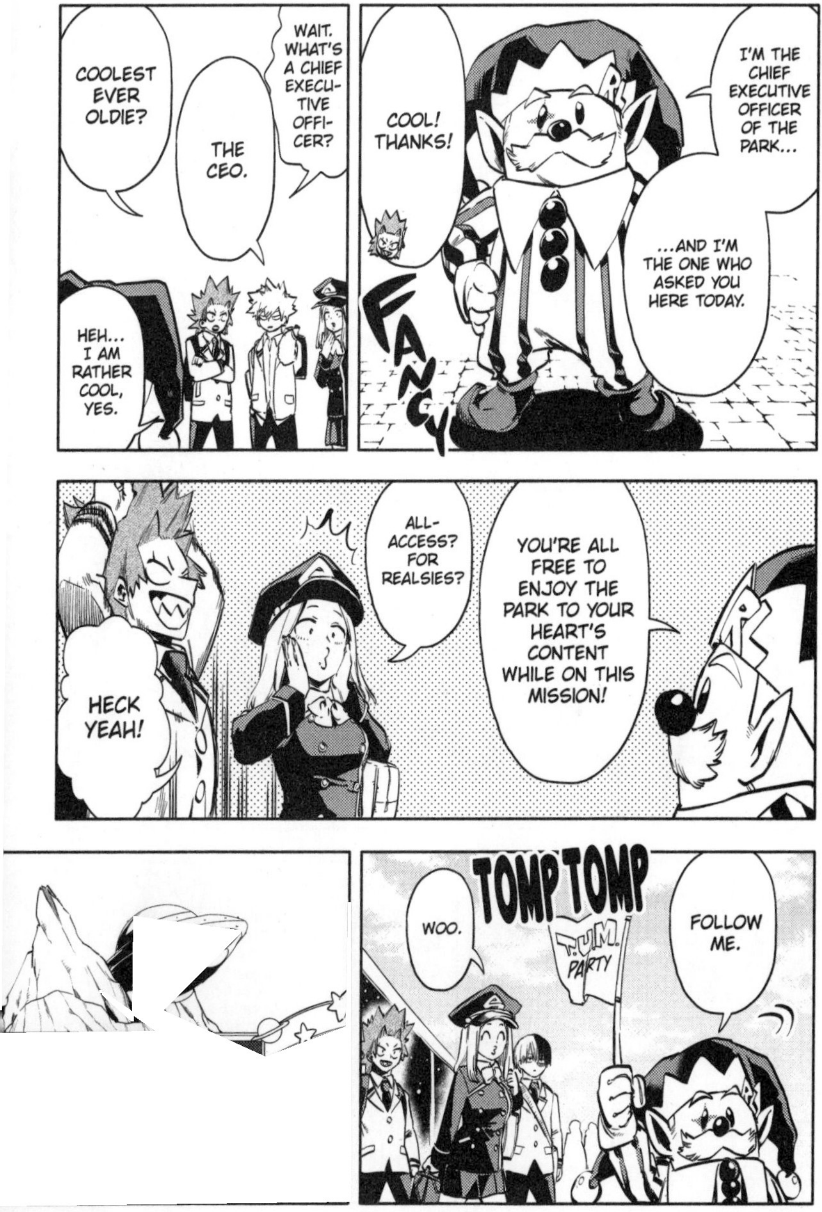
I'M THE CHIEF EXECUTIVE OFFICER OF THE PARK...
...AND I'M THE ONE WHO ASKED YOU HERE TODAY.
COOL! THANKS!
FANCY
WAIT. WHAT'S A CHIEF EXECU-TIVE OFFI-CER?
THE CEO.
COOLEST EVER OLDIE?
HEH... I AM RATHER COOL, YES.
YOU'RE ALL FREE TO ENJOY THE PARK TO YOUR HEART'S CONTENT WHILE ON THIS MISSION!
ALL-ACCESS? FOR REALSIES?
HECK YEAH!
TOMP TOMP
FOLLOW ME.
T.U.M. PARTY
WOO.

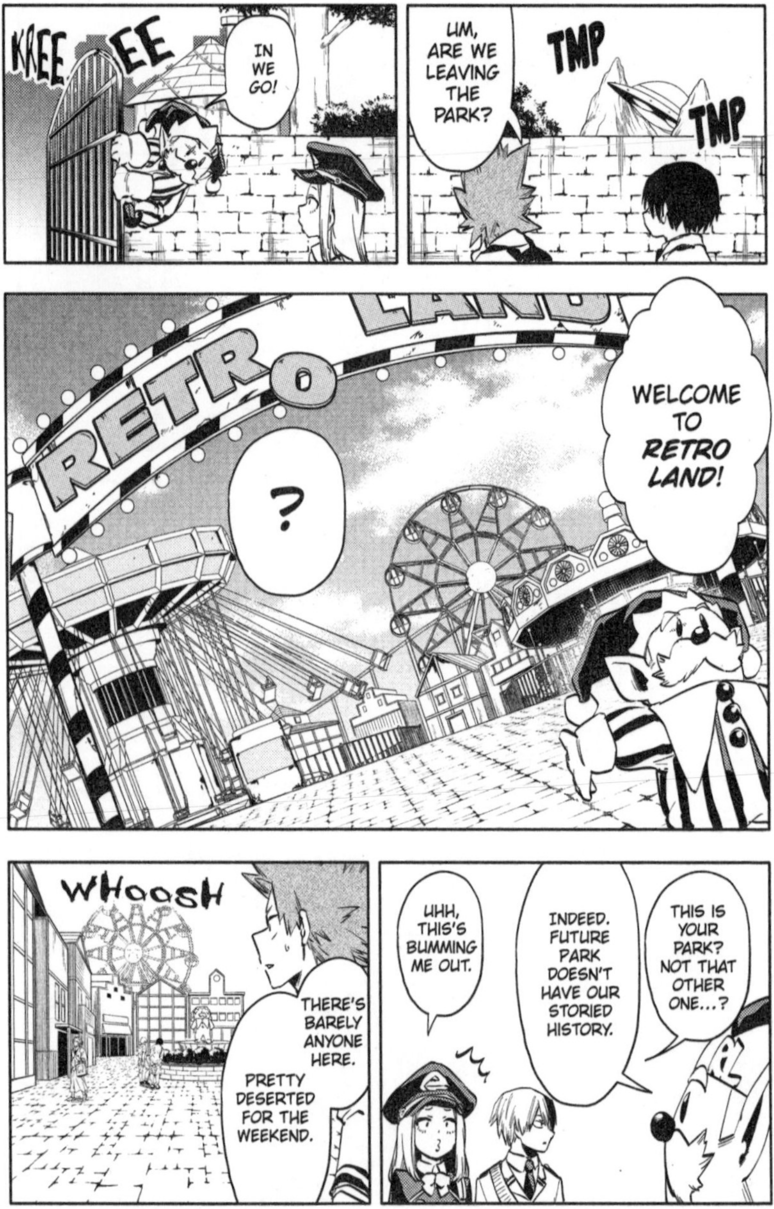
UM, ARE WE LEAVING THE PARK?
TMP
TMP
KREE EE
IN WE GO!
WELCOME TO RETRO LAND!
?
RETRO LAND
THIS IS YOUR PARK? NOT THAT OTHER ONE...?
INDEED. FUTURE PARK DOESN'T HAVE OUR STORIED HISTORY.
UHH, THIS'S BUMMING ME OUT.
THERE'S BARELY ANYONE HERE.
PRETTY DESERTED FOR THE WEEKEND.
WHOOSH

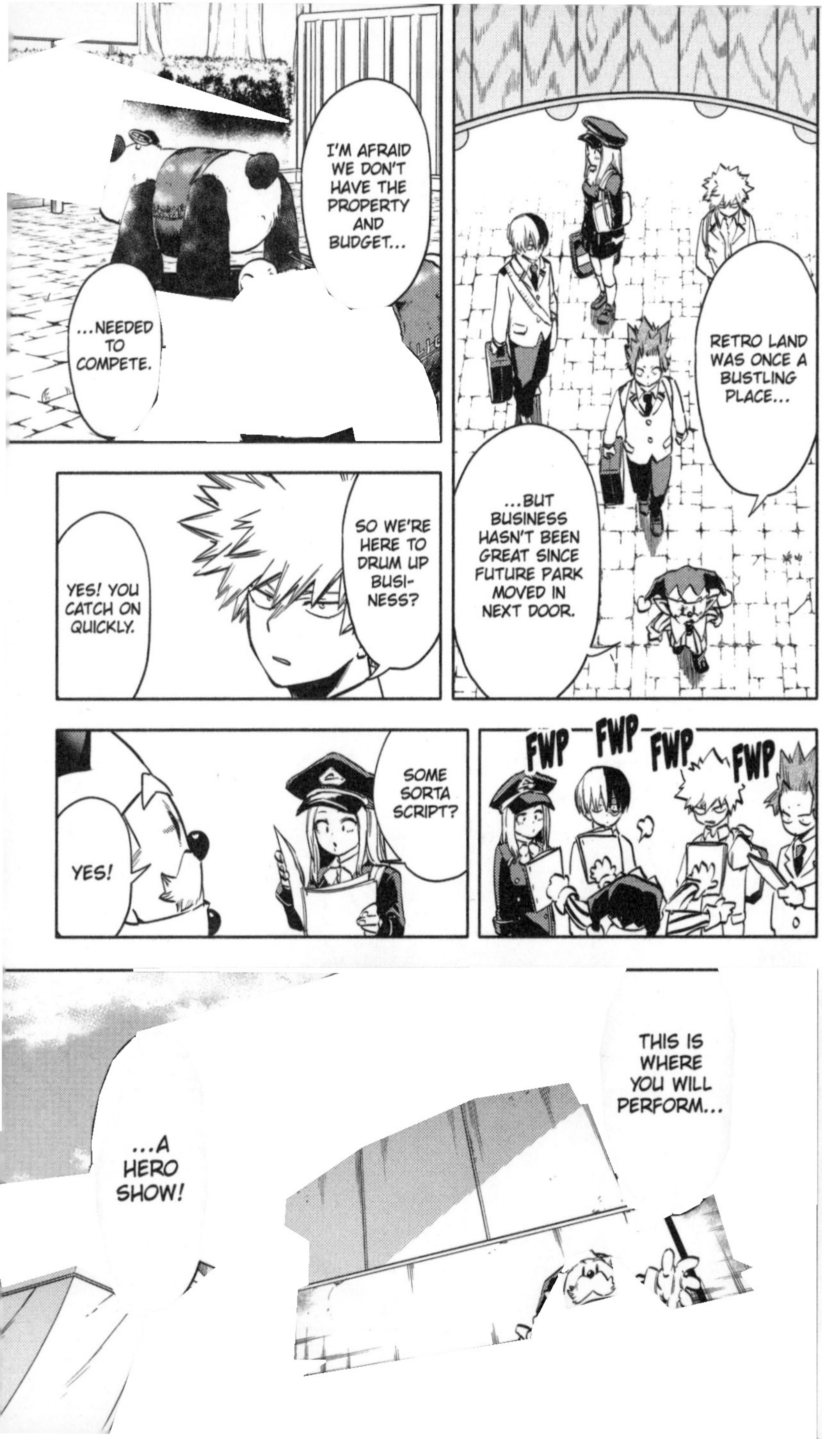
RETRO LAND WAS ONCE A BUSTLING PLACE...
...BUT BUSINESS HASN'T BEEN GREAT SINCE FUTURE PARK MOVED IN NEXT DOOR.
I'M AFRAID WE DON'T HAVE THE PROPERTY AND BUDGET...
...NEEDED TO COMPETE.
SO WE'RE HERE TO DRUM UP BUSI-NESS?
YES! YOU CATCH ON QUICKLY.
FWP FWP FWP FWP
SOME SORTA SCRIPT?
YES!
THIS IS WHERE YOU WILL PERFORM...
...A HERO SHOW!

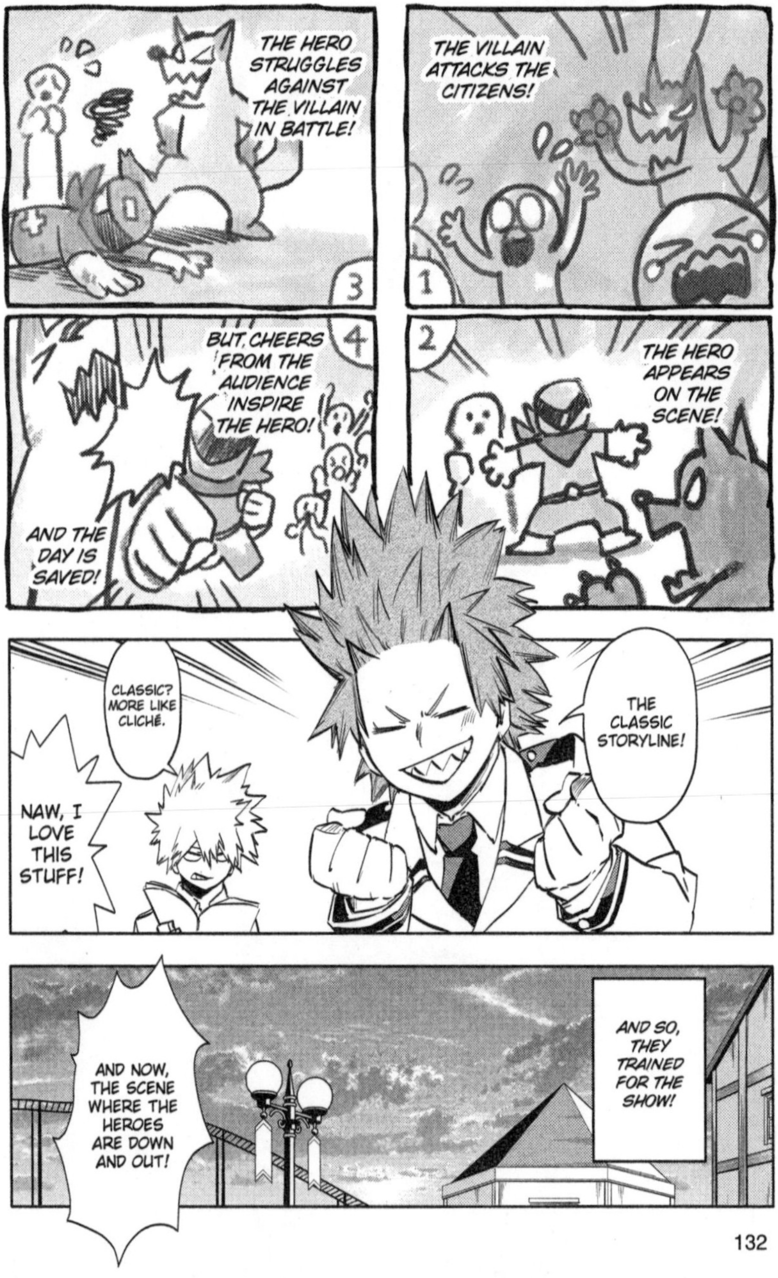
THE VILLAIN ATTACKS THE CITIZENS!
THE HERO APPEARS ON THE SCENE!
THE HERO STRUGGLES AGAINST THE VILLAIN IN BATTLE!
BUT, CHEERS FROM THE AUDIENCE INSPIRE THE HERO!
AND THE DAY IS SAVED!
THE CLASSIC STORYLINE!
CLASSIC? MORE LIKE CLICHÉ.
NAW, I LOVE THIS STUFF!
AND SO, THEY TRAINED FOR THE SHOW!
AND NOW, THE SCENE WHERE THE HEROES ARE DOWN AND OUT!

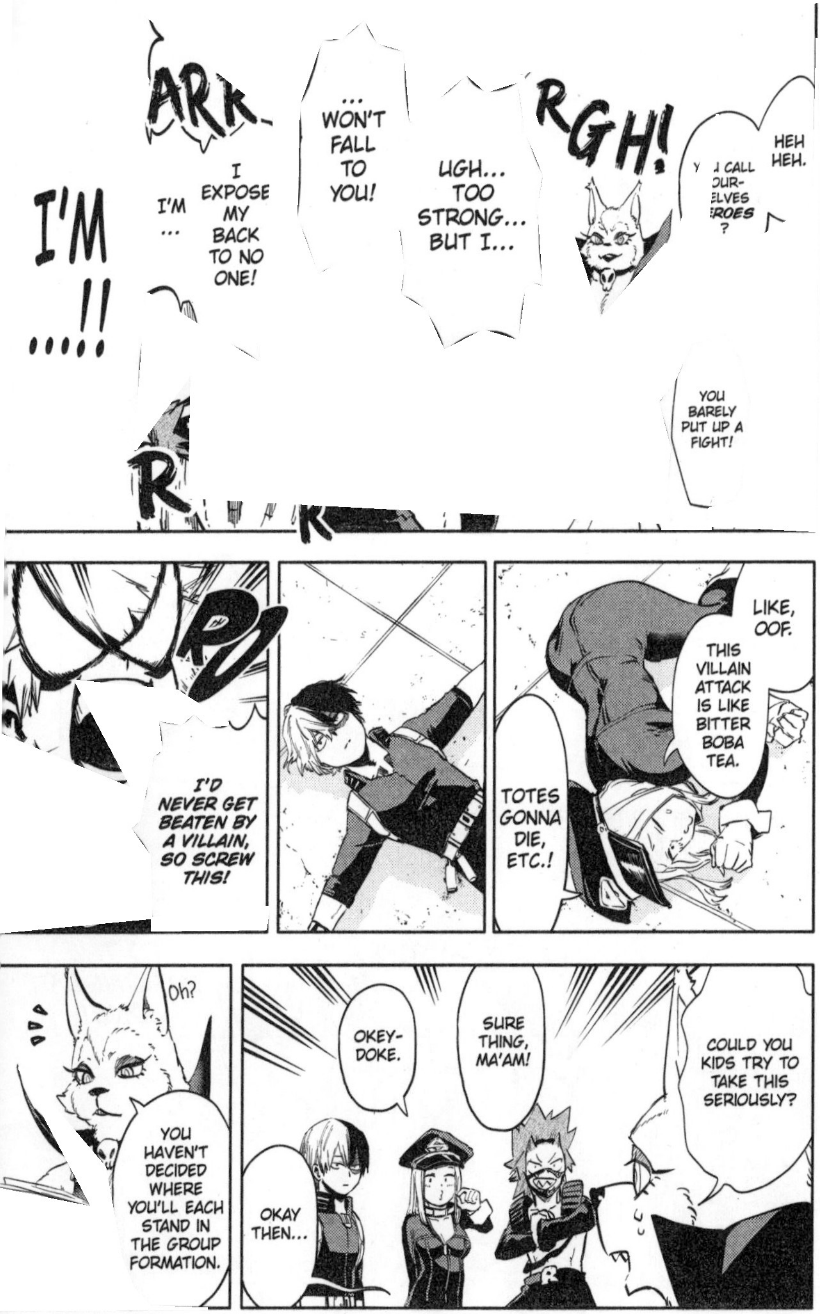
HEH HEH.
Y CALL OUR- ELVES EROES ?
YOU BARELY PUT UP A FIGHT!
RGH!
UGH... TOO STRONG... BUT I...
... WON'T FALL TO YOU!
ARK
I EXPOSE MY BACK TO NO ONE!
I'M ...
I'M .....!!
R
R
LIKE, OOF.
THIS VILLAIN ATTACK IS LIKE BITTER BOBA TEA.
TOTES GONNA DIE, ETC.!
I'D NEVER GET BEATEN BY A VILLAIN, SO SCREW THIS!
COULD YOU KIDS TRY TO TAKE THIS SERIOUSLY?
SURE THING, MA'AM!
OKEY-DOKE.
OKAY THEN...
Oh?
YOU HAVEN'T DECIDED WHERE YOU'LL EACH STAND IN THE GROUP FORMATION.

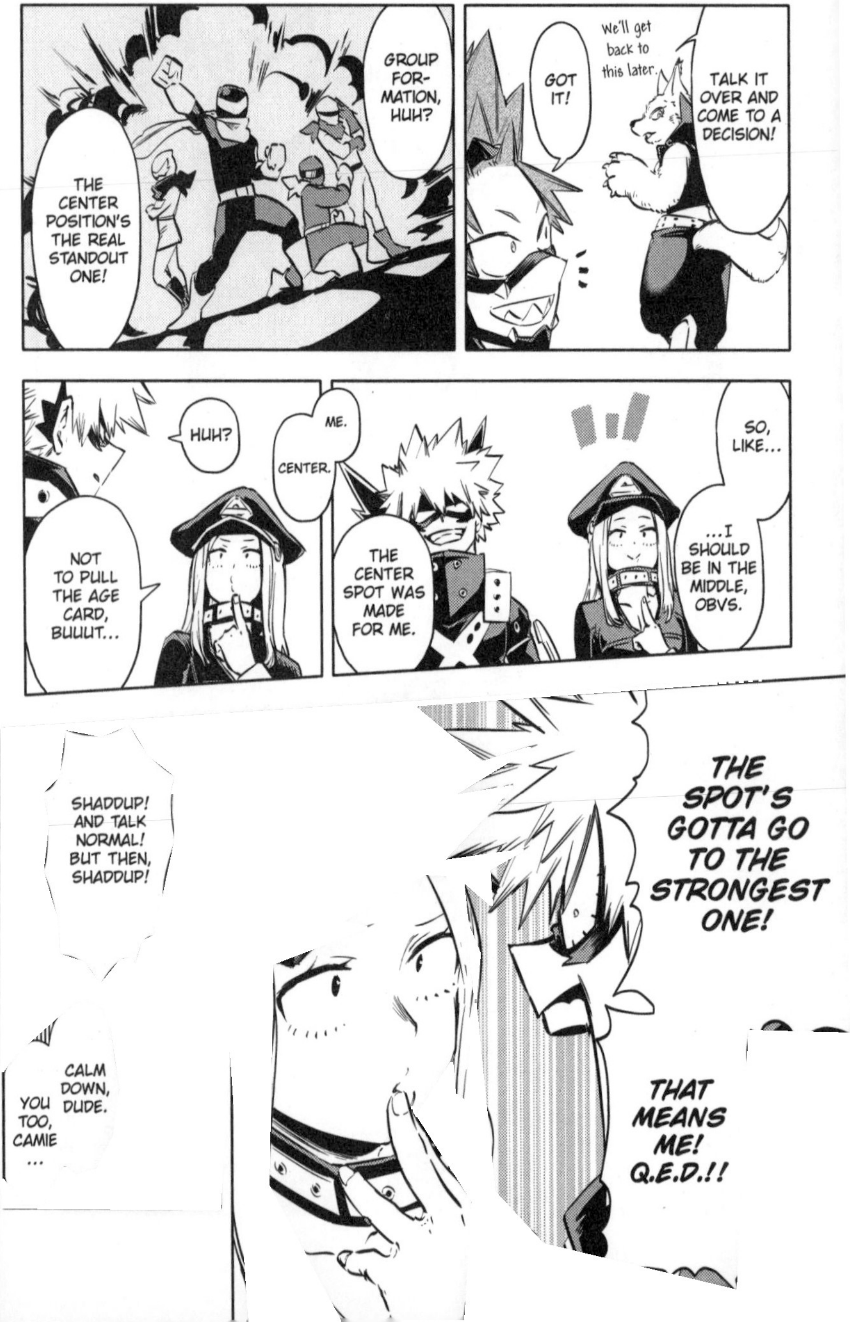
TALK IT OVER AND COME TO A DECISION!
We'll get back to this later.
GOT IT!
GROUP FORMATION, HUH?
THE CENTER POSITION'S THE REAL STANDOUT ONE!
SO, LIKE...
...I SHOULD BE IN THE MIDDLE, OBVS.
THE CENTER SPOT WAS MADE FOR ME.
ME.
CENTER.
HUH?
NOT TO PULL THE AGE CARD, BUUUT...
THE SPOT'S GOTTA GO TO THE STRONGEST ONE!
THAT MEANS ME! Q.E.D.!!
SHADDUP! AND TALK NORMAL! BUT THEN, SHADDUP!
CALM DOWN, DUDE.
YOU TOO, CAMIE...

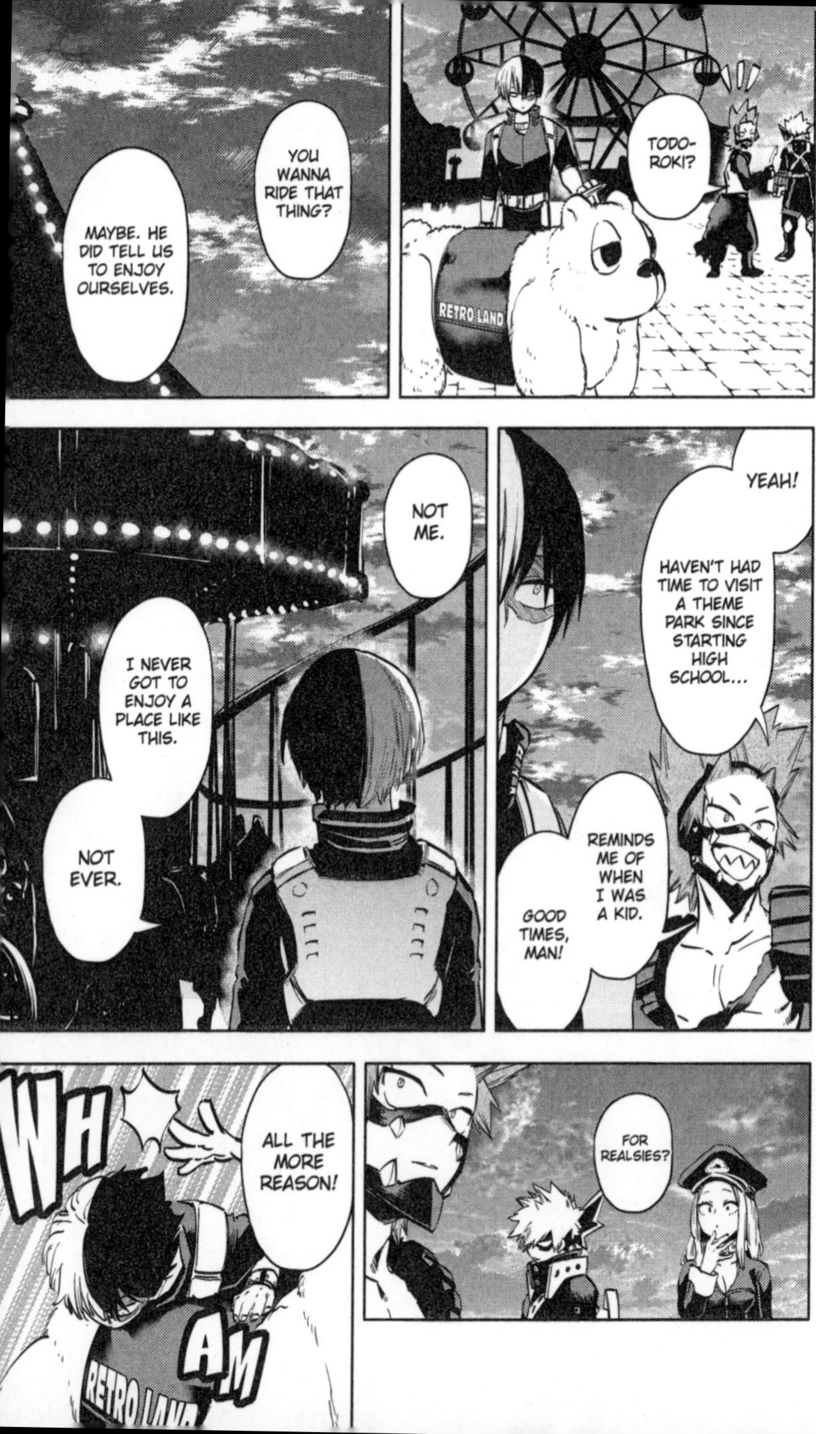
TODO-ROKI?
RETRO LAND
YOU WANNA RIDE THAT THING?
MAYBE. HE DID TELL US TO ENJOY OURSELVES.
YEAH!
HAVEN'T HAD TIME TO VISIT A THEME PARK SINCE STARTING HIGH SCHOOL...
REMINDS ME OF WHEN I WAS A KID.
GOOD TIMES, MAN!
NOT ME.
I NEVER GOT TO ENJOY A PLACE LIKE THIS.
NOT EVER.
FOR REALSIES?
ALL THE MORE REASON!
WHAM
RETRO LAND

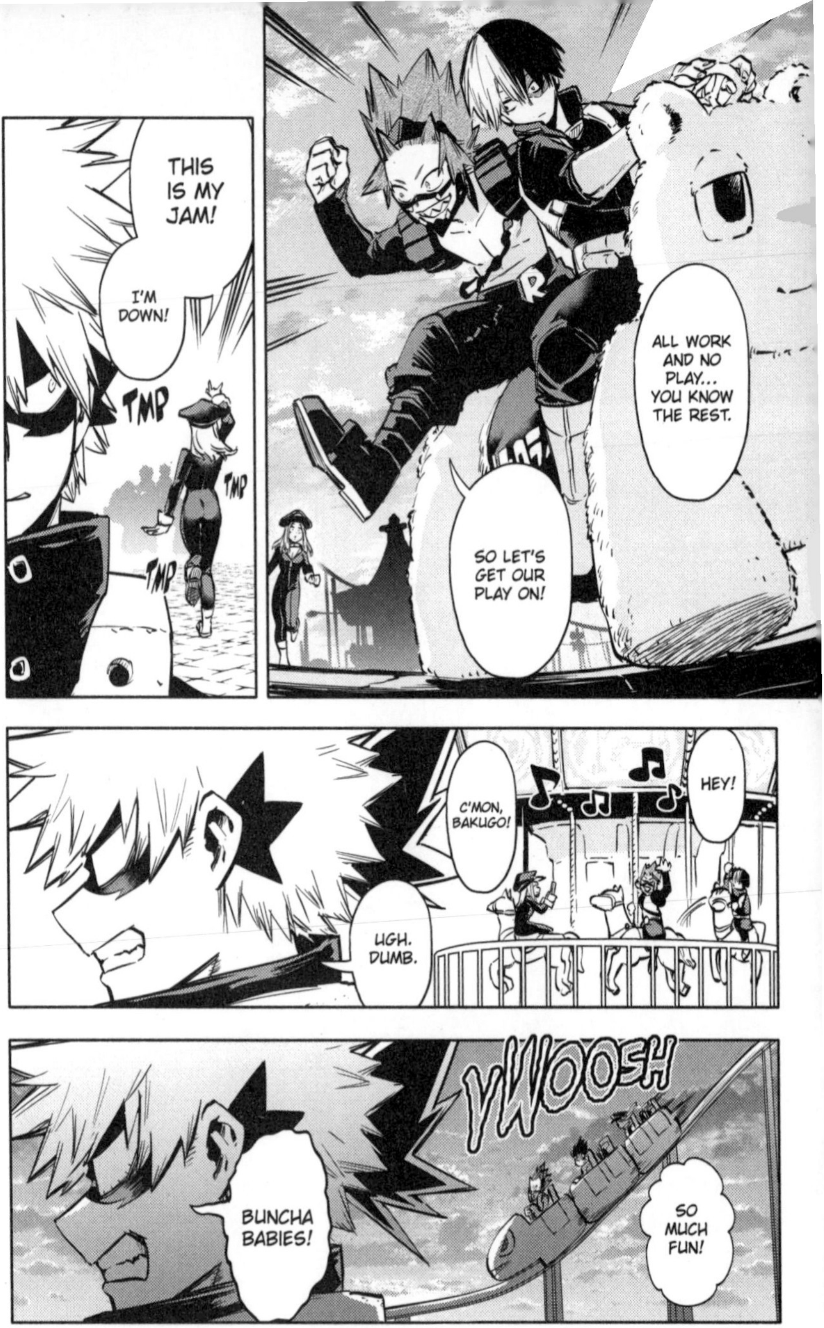
ALL WORK AND NO PLAY... YOU KNOW THE REST.
SO LET'S GET OUR PLAY ON!
THIS IS MY JAM!
I'M DOWN!
TMP
TMP
TMP
HEY!
C'MON, BAKUGO!
UGH. DUMB.
VWOOSH
SO MUCH FUN!
BUNCHA BABIES!

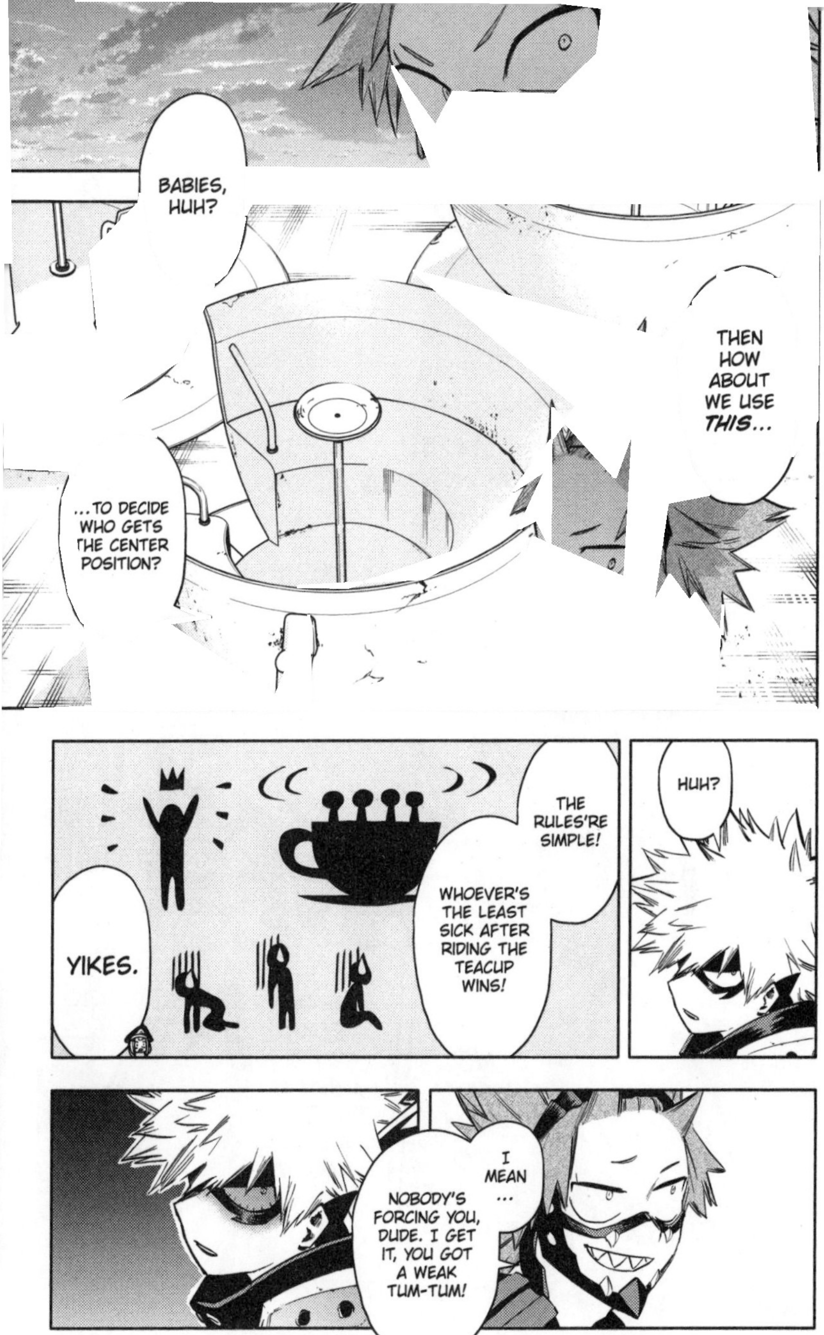
BABIES, HUH?
THEN HOW ABOUT WE USE *THIS*...
...TO DECIDE WHO GETS THE CENTER POSITION?
HUH?
THE RULES'RE SIMPLE!
WHOEVER'S THE LEAST SICK AFTER RIDING THE TEACUP WINS!
YIKES.
I MEAN ...
NOBODY'S FORCING YOU, DUDE. I GET IT, YOU GOT A WEAK TUM-TUM!

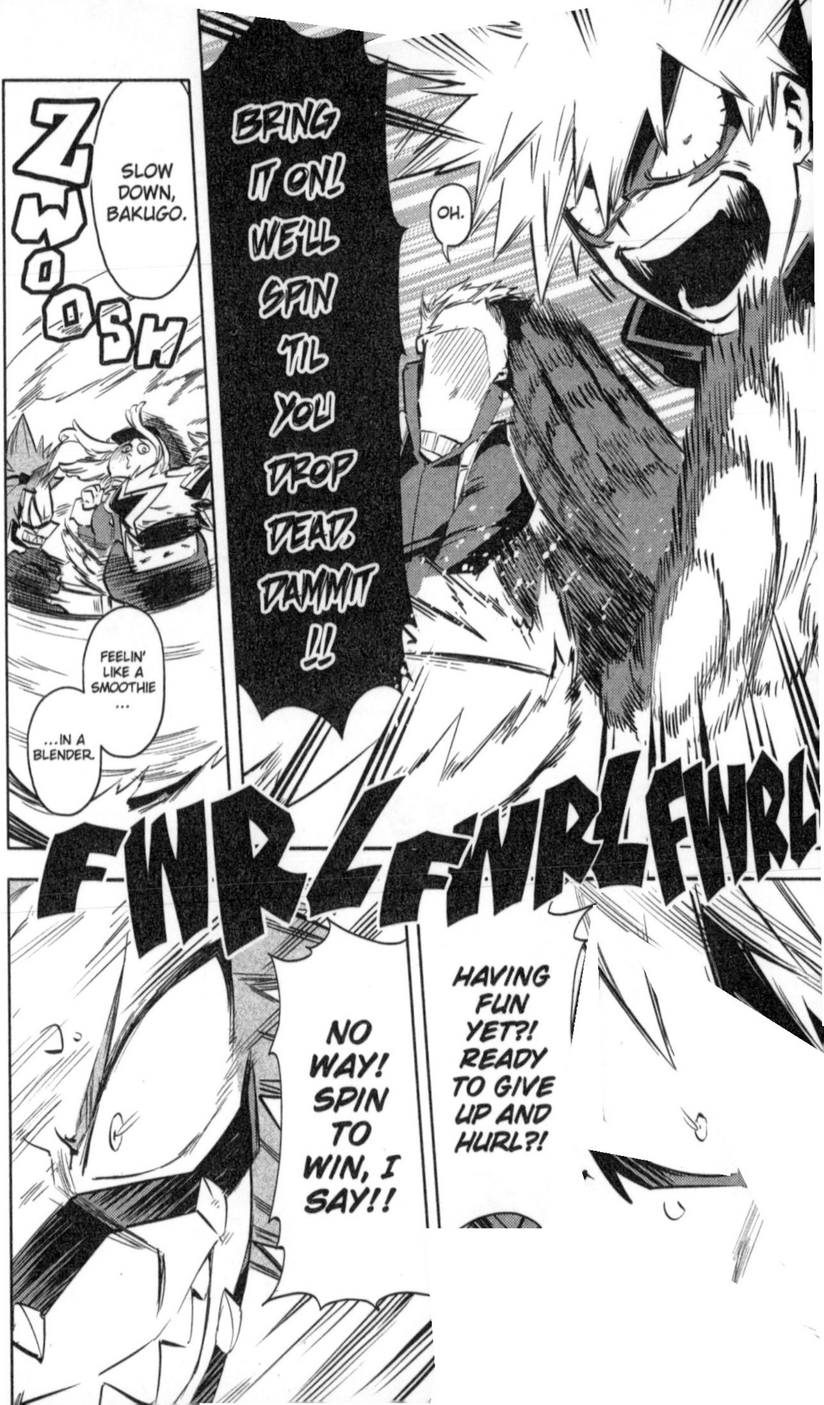
OH.
BRING IT ON! WE'LL SPIN 'TIL YOU DROP DEAD, DAMMIT!!
SLOW DOWN, BAKUGO.
ZWOOOSH
FEELIN' LIKE A SMOOTHIE...
...IN A BLENDER.
FWRL FWRL FWRL
HAVING FUN YET?! READY TO GIVE UP AND HURL?!
NO WAY! SPIN TO WIN, I SAY!!

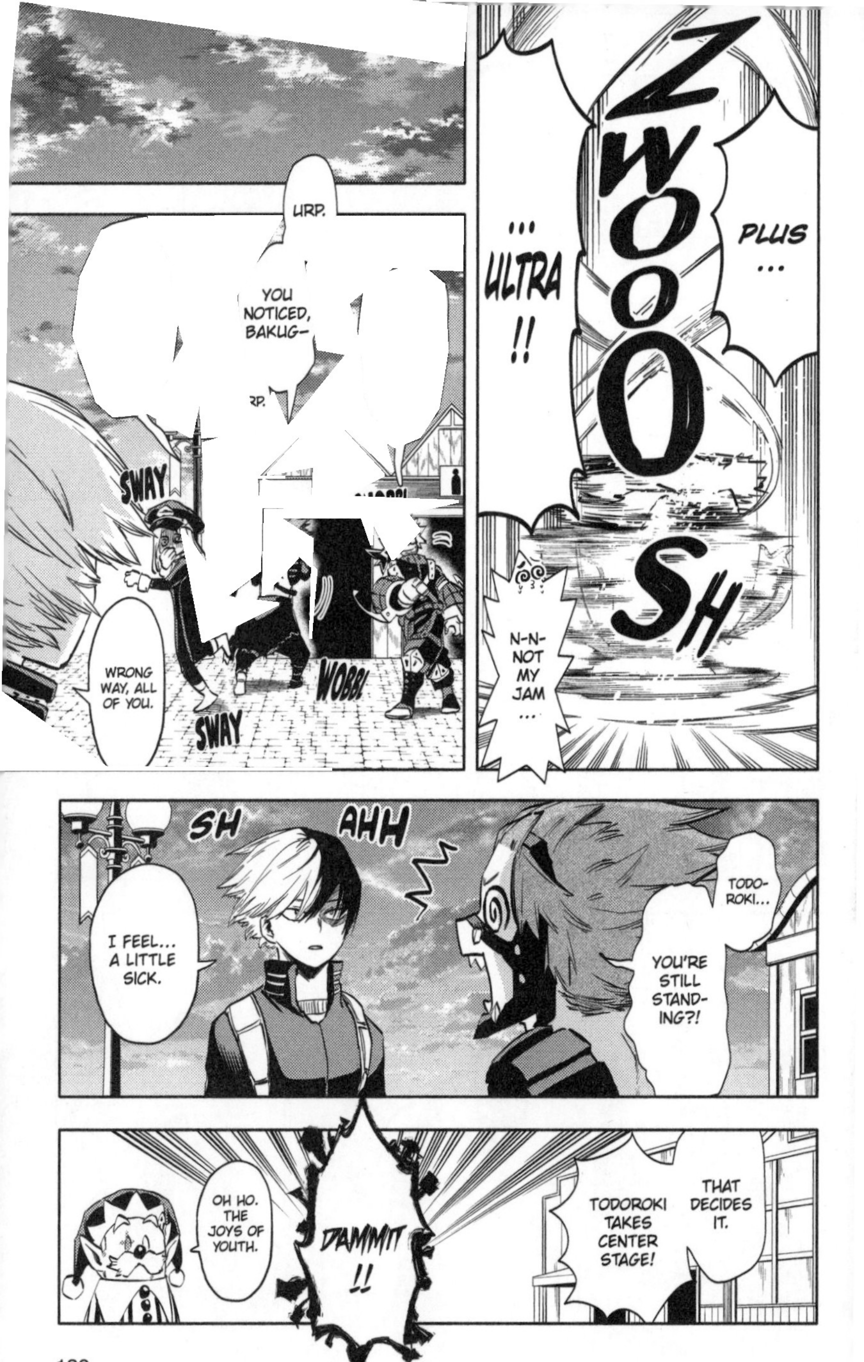
ZWOOOSH
PLUS ...
... ULTRA !!
N-N-NOT MY JAM ...
URP.
YOU NOTICED, BAKUG-
SWAY
WRONG WAY, ALL OF YOU.
WOBBL
SWAY
TODOROKI... YOU'RE STILL STANDING?!
SHAHH
I FEEL... A LITTLE SICK.
THAT DECIDES IT.
TODOROKI TAKES CENTER STAGE!
DAMMIT !!
OH HO. THE JOYS OF YOUTH.

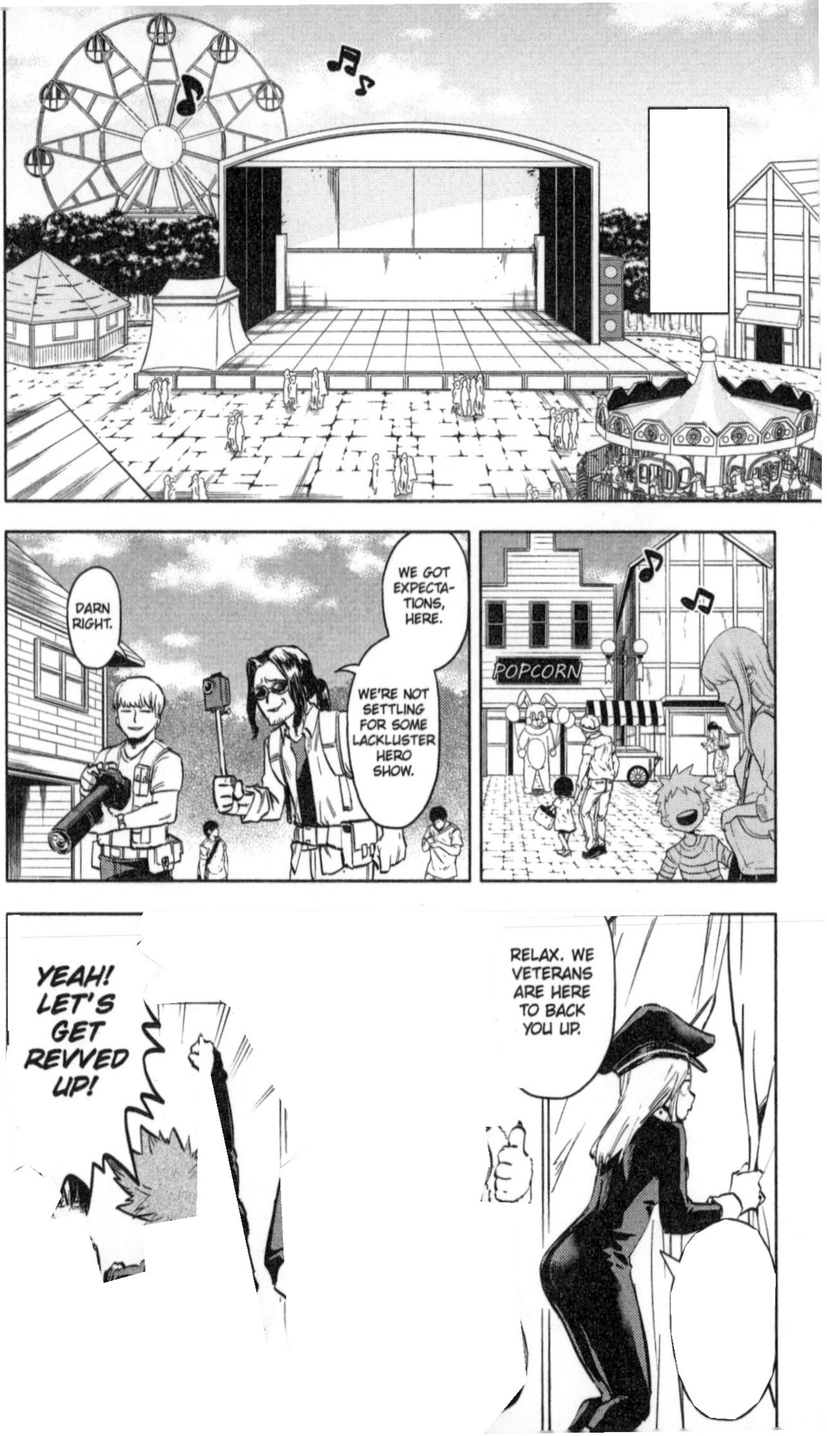
WE GOT EXPECTA-TIONS, HERE.
WE'RE NOT SETTLING FOR SOME LACKLUSTER HERO SHOW.
DARN RIGHT.
POPCORN
RELAX. WE VETERANS ARE HERE TO BACK YOU UP.
YEAH! LET'S GET REVVED UP!

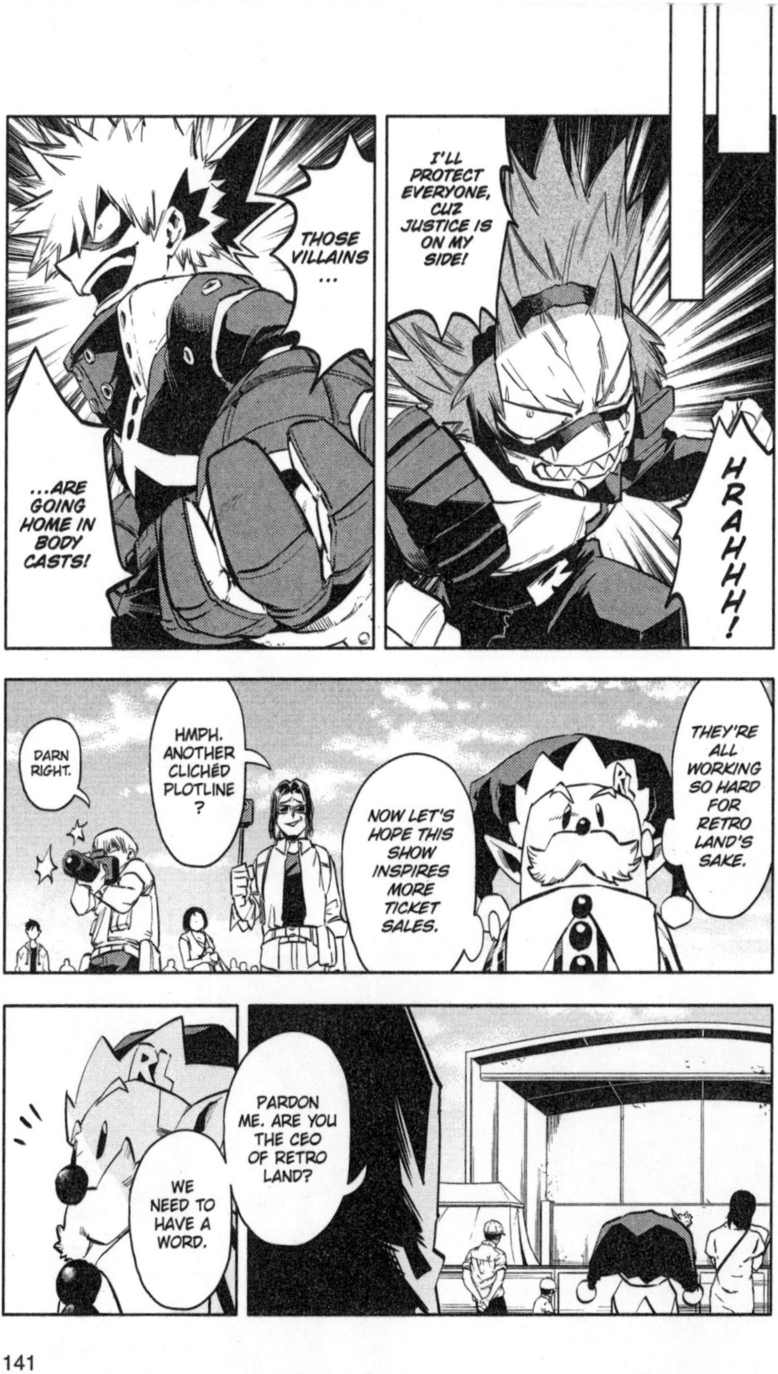
I'LL PROTECT EVERYONE, CUZ JUSTICE IS ON MY SIDE!
HRAHHH!
THOSE VILLAINS ...
...ARE GOING HOME IN BODY CASTS!
THEY'RE ALL WORKING SO HARD FOR RETRO LAND'S SAKE.
NOW LET'S HOPE THIS SHOW INSPIRES MORE TICKET SALES.
HMPH. ANOTHER CLICHÉD PLOTLINE?
DARN RIGHT.
PARDON ME. ARE YOU THE CEO OF RETRO LAND?
WE NEED TO HAVE A WORD.

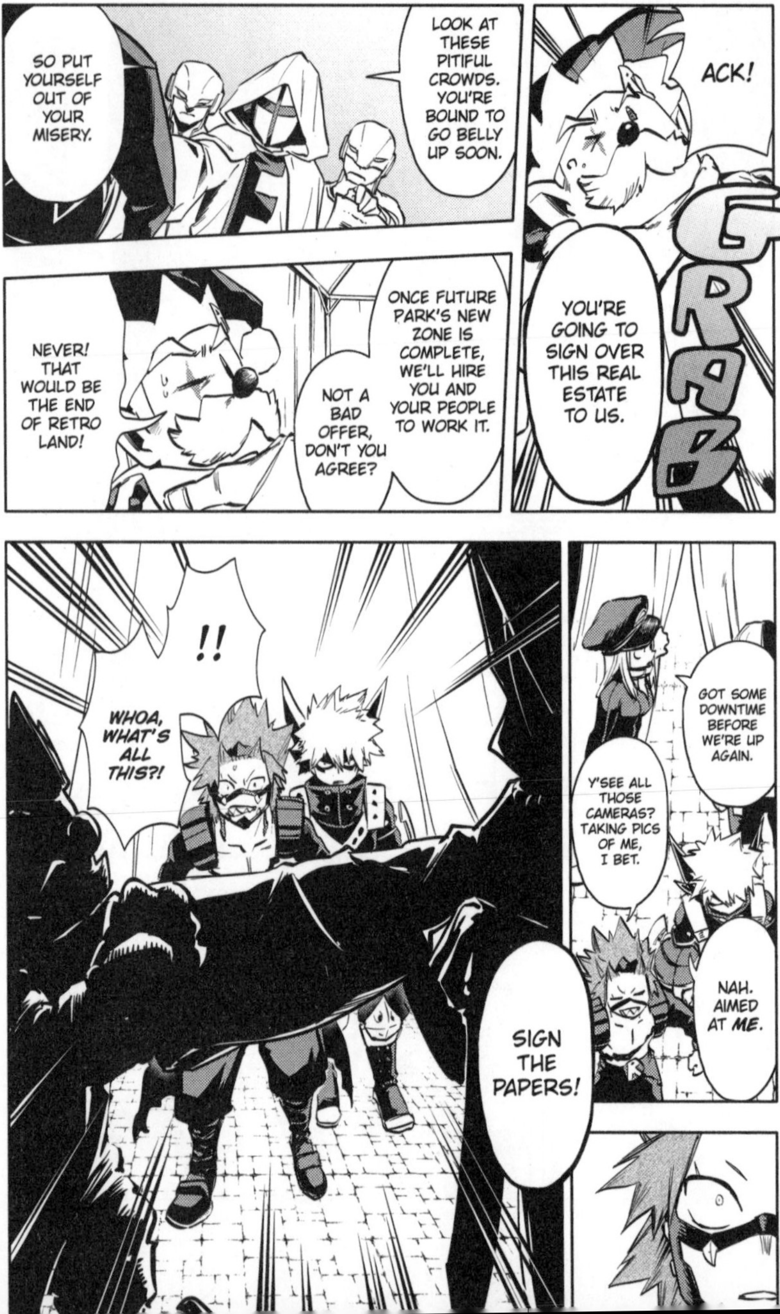
ACK!
GRAB
YOU'RE GOING TO SIGN OVER THIS REAL ESTATE TO US.
LOOK AT THESE PITIFUL CROWDS. YOU'RE BOUND TO GO BELLY UP SOON.
SO PUT YOURSELF OUT OF YOUR MISERY.
ONCE FUTURE PARK'S NEW ZONE IS COMPLETE, WE'LL HIRE YOU AND YOUR PEOPLE TO WORK IT.
NOT A BAD OFFER, DON'T YOU AGREE?
NEVER! THAT WOULD BE THE END OF RETRO LAND!
GOT SOME DOWNTIME BEFORE WE'RE UP AGAIN.
Y'SEE ALL THOSE CAMERAS? TAKING PICS OF ME, I BET.
NAH. AIMED AT *ME*.
SIGN THE PAPERS!
!!
WHOA, WHAT'S ALL THIS?!

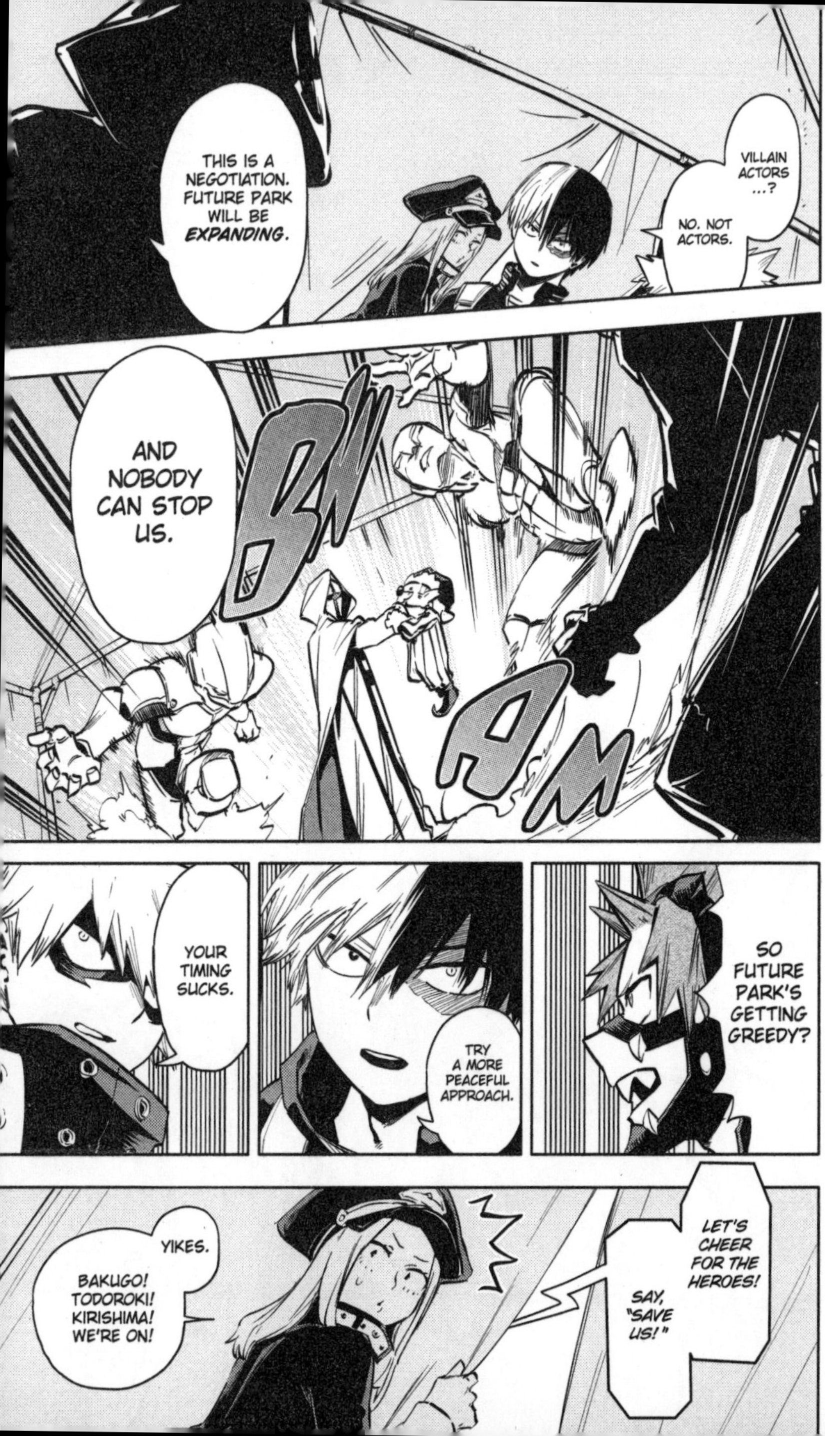
VILLAIN ACTORS ...?
NO. NOT ACTORS.
THIS IS A NEGOTIATION. FUTURE PARK WILL BE *EXPANDING*.
AND NOBODY CAN STOP US.
BAM
SO FUTURE PARK'S GETTING GREEDY?
TRY A MORE PEACEFUL APPROACH.
YOUR TIMING SUCKS.
LET'S CHEER FOR THE HEROES!
SAY, "SAVE US!"
YIKES.
BAKUGO! TODOROKI! KIRISHIMA! WE'RE ON!

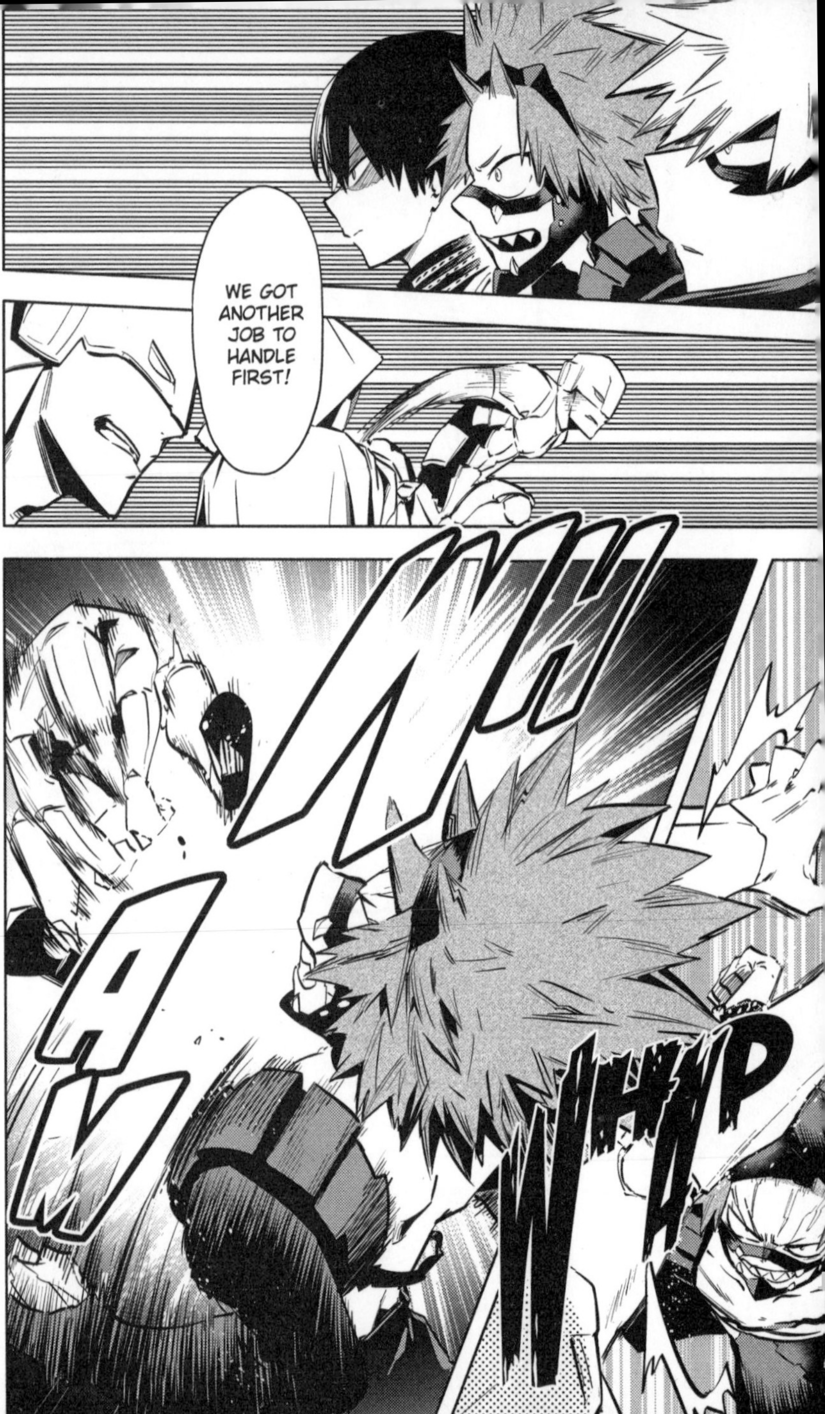
WE GOT ANOTHER JOB TO HANDLE FIRST!
WHAM
WHAP

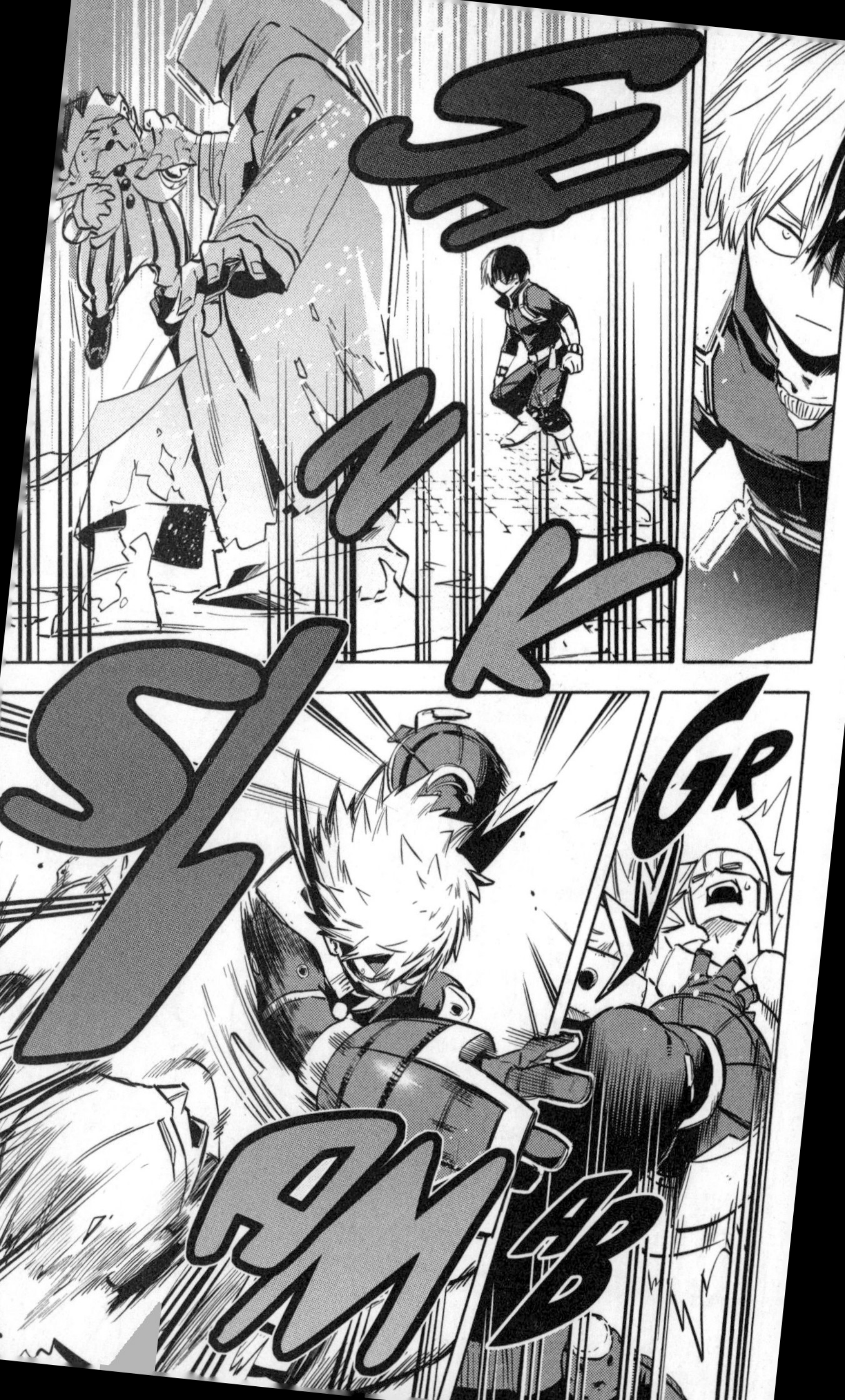
GRAB

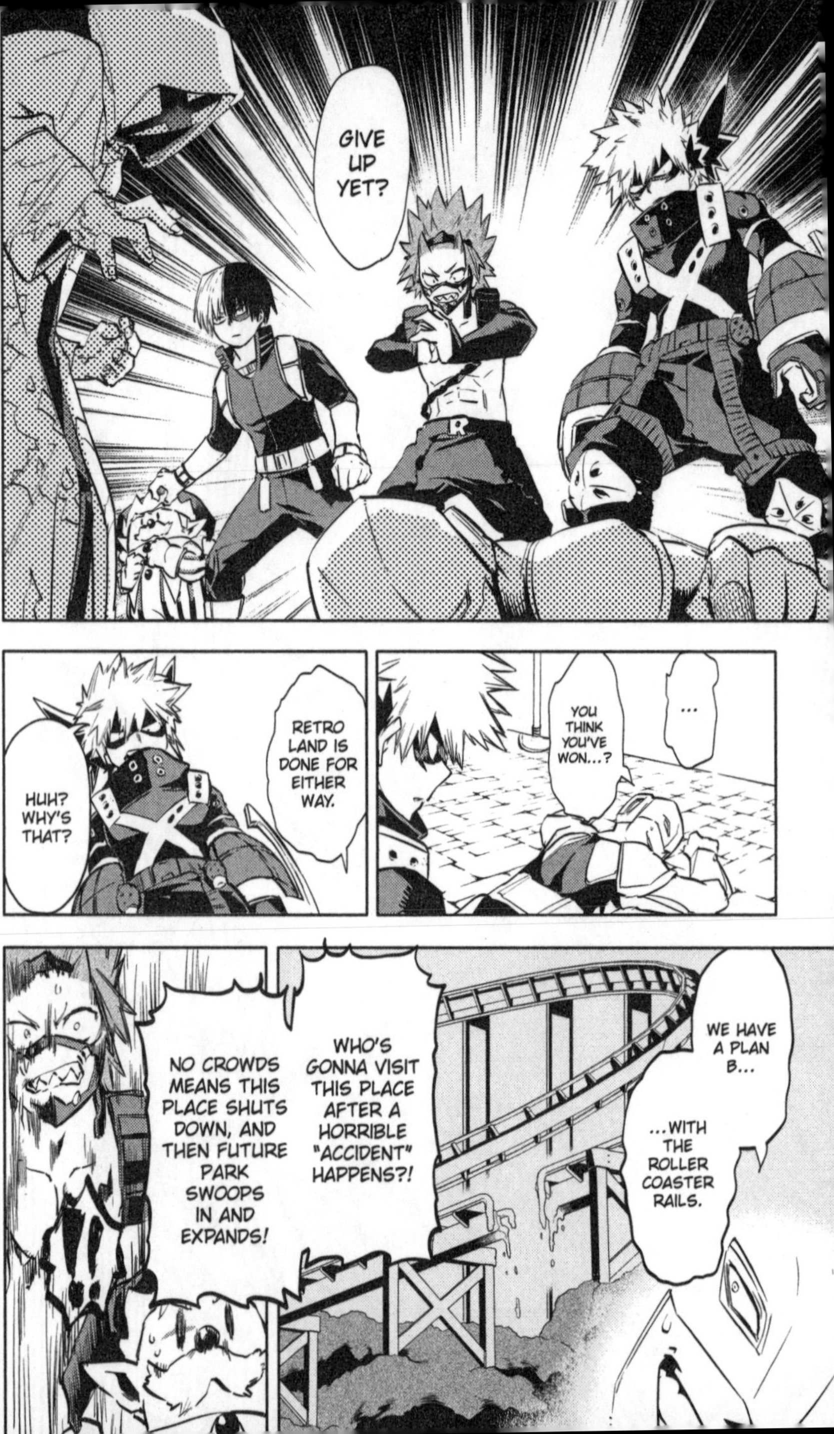
GIVE UP YET?
...
YOU THINK YOU'VE WON...?
RETRO LAND IS DONE FOR EITHER WAY.
HUH? WHY'S THAT?
WE HAVE A PLAN B...
...WITH THE ROLLER COASTER RAILS.
WHO'S GONNA VISIT THIS PLACE AFTER A HORRIBLE "ACCIDENT" HAPPENS?!
NO CROWDS MEANS THIS PLACE SHUTS DOWN, AND THEN FUTURE PARK SWOOPS IN AND EXPANDS!

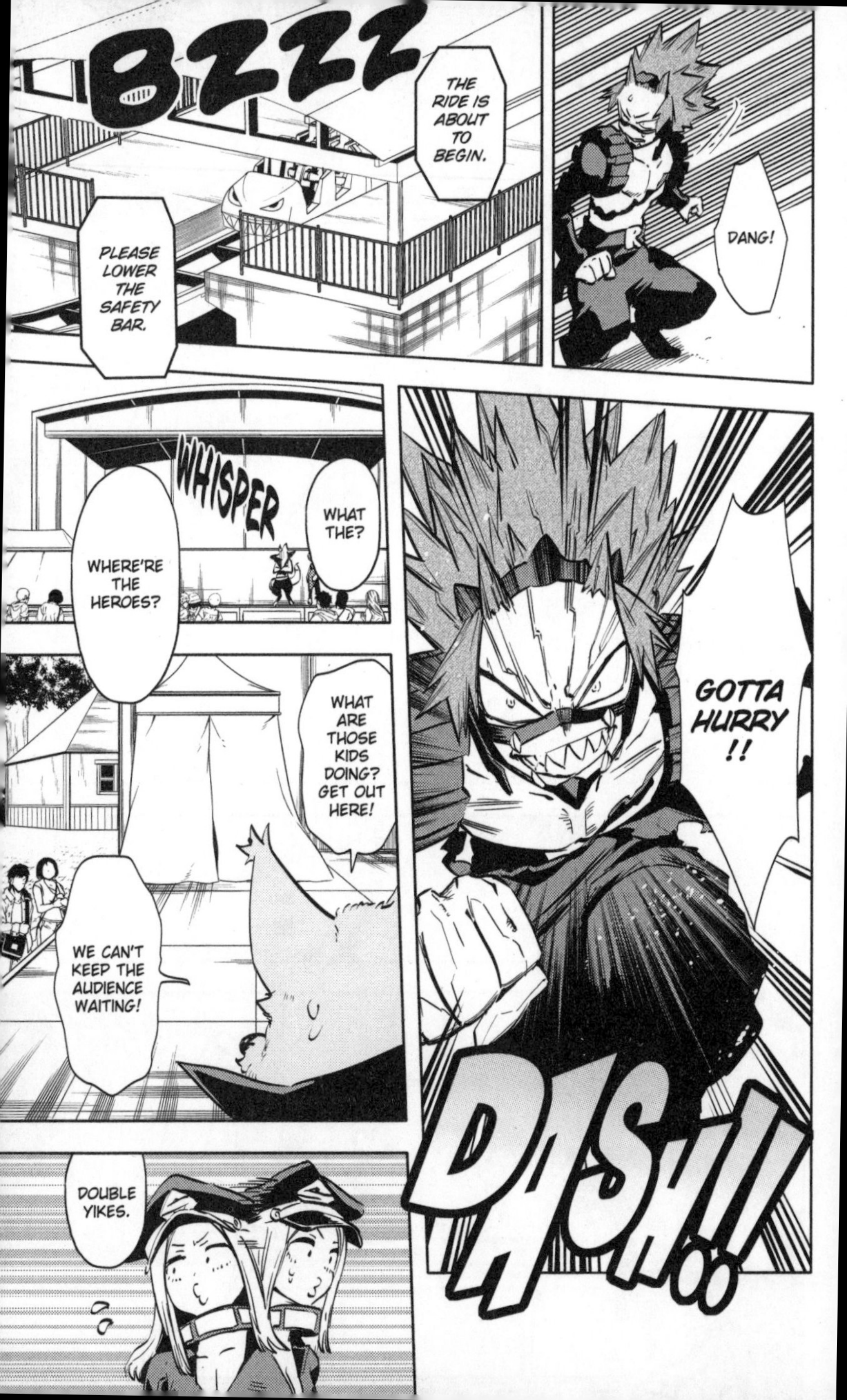
DANG!
BZZZ
THE RIDE IS ABOUT TO BEGIN.
PLEASE LOWER THE SAFETY BAR.
GOTTA HURRY!!
DASH!!
WHAT THE?
WHISPER
WHERE'RE THE HEROES?
WHAT ARE THOSE KIDS DOING? GET OUT HERE!
WE CAN'T KEEP THE AUDIENCE WAITING!
DOUBLE YIKES.

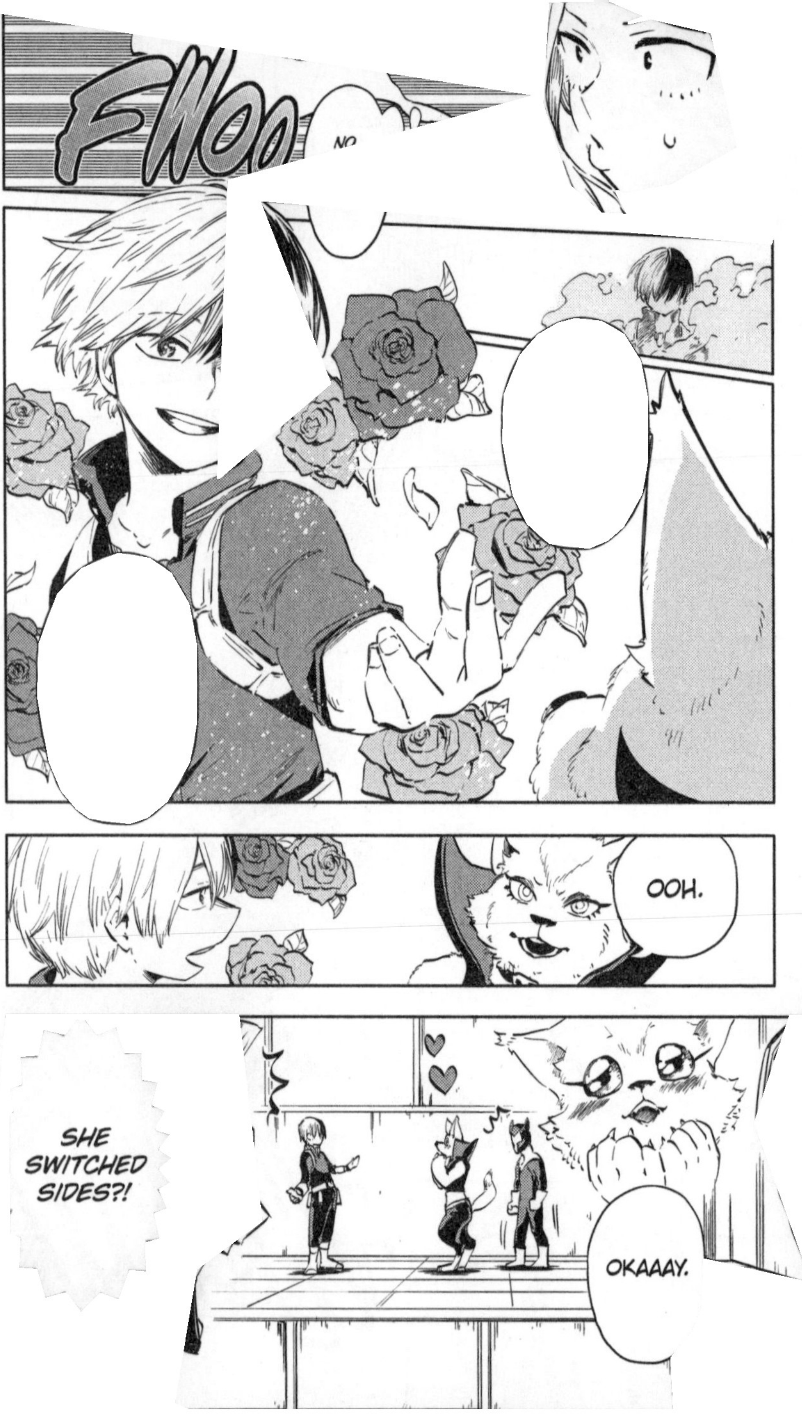
FWOO
NO
OOH.
OKAAAY.
SHE SWITCHED SIDES?!

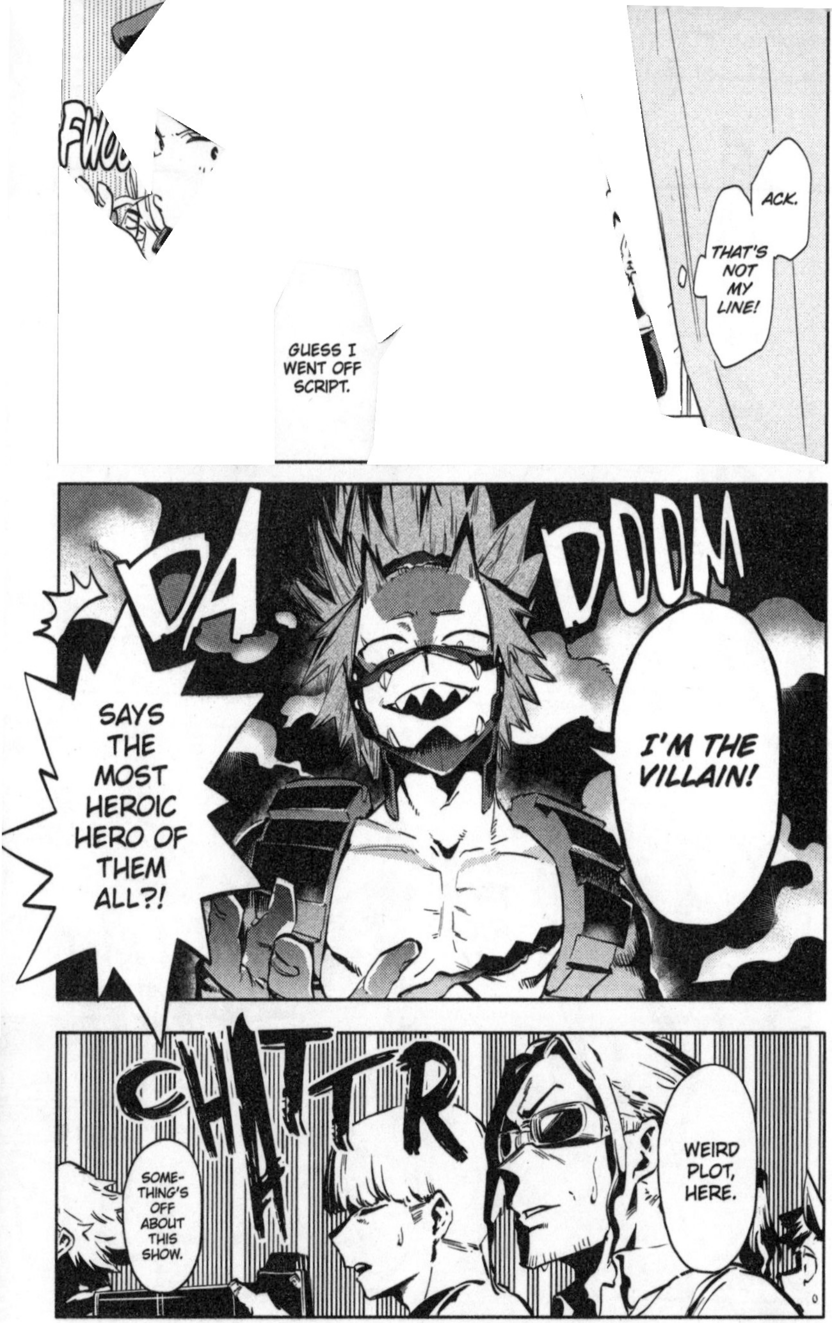
ACK.
THAT'S NOT MY LINE!
FWOO
GUESS I WENT OFF SCRIPT.
DA
DOOM
I'M THE VILLAIN!
SAYS THE MOST HEROIC HERO OF THEM ALL?!
CHATR
WEIRD PLOT, HERE.
SOME-THING'S OFF ABOUT THIS SHOW.

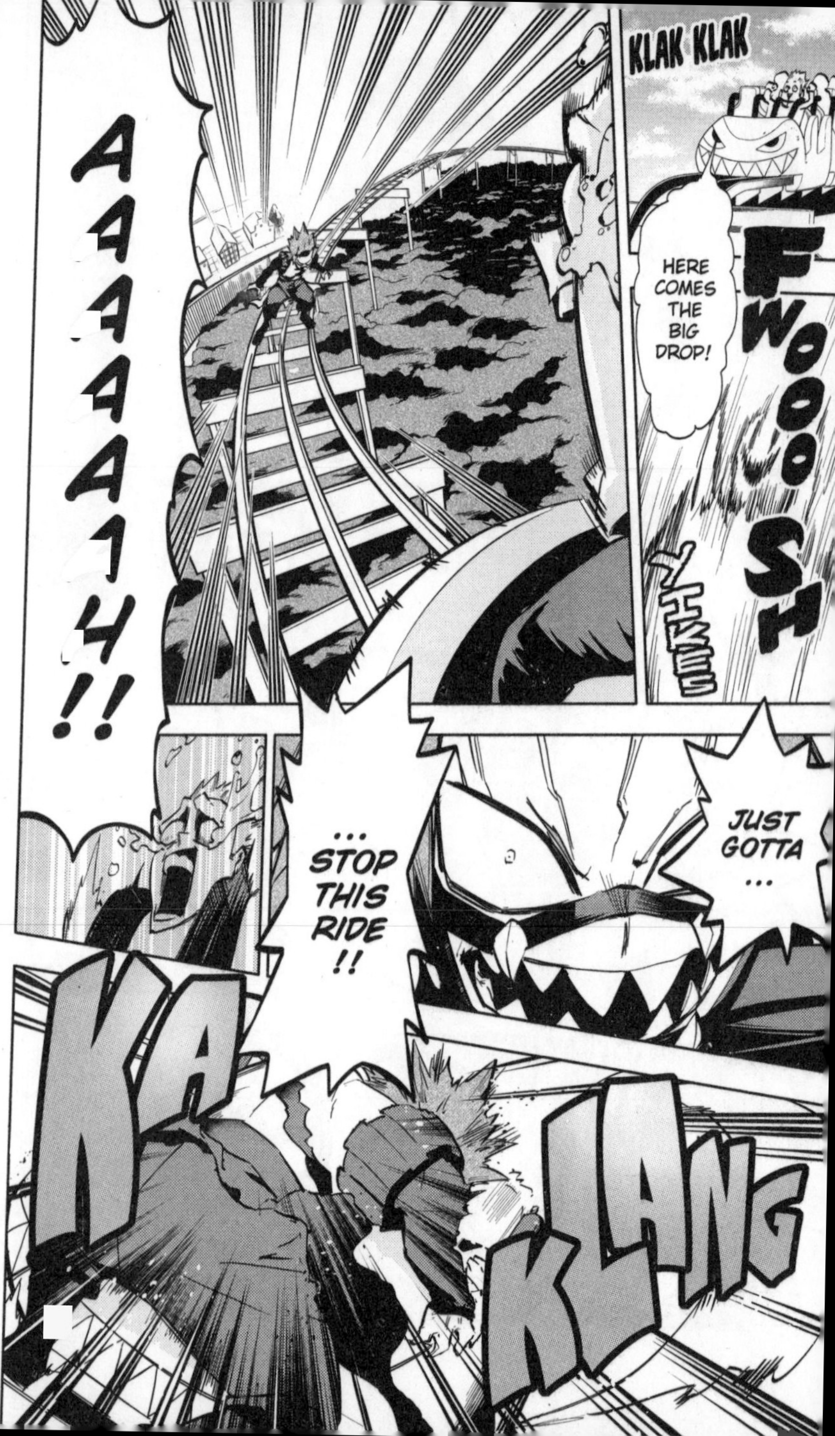
KLAK KLAK
HERE COMES THE BIG DROP!
FWOOOSH
YIKES
AAAAAAAH!!
JUST GOTTA ...
... STOP THIS RIDE!!
KA KLANG

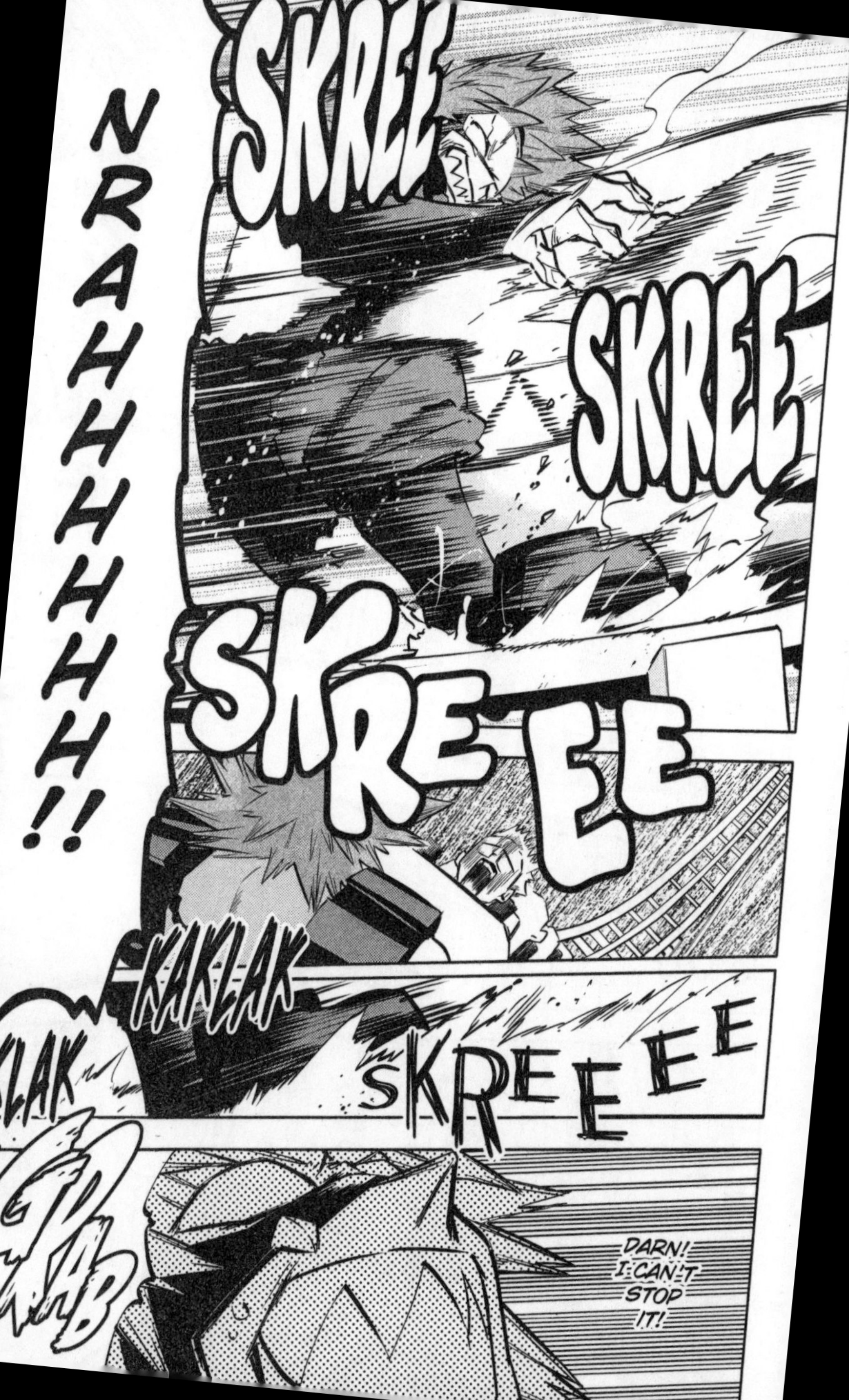
SKREE
SKREE
NRAHHHHHHH!!
SKREEE
KAKLAK
KLAK
SKREEEE
GRAB
DARN! I CAN'T STOP IT!

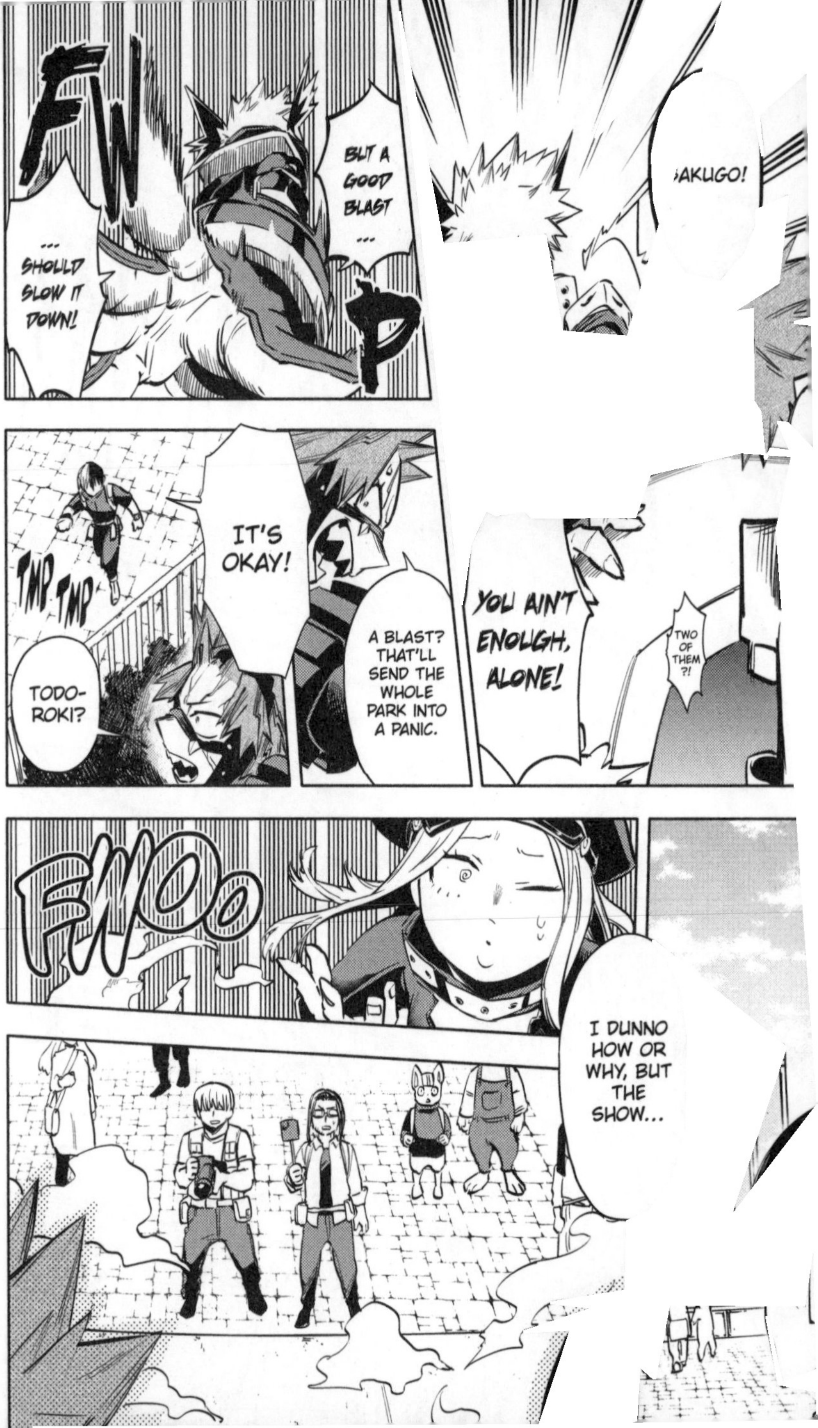
AKUGO!
BUT A GOOD BLAST ...
... SHOULD SLOW IT DOWN!
FW
P
TWO OF THEM ?!
YOU AIN'T ENOUGH, ALONE!
A BLAST? THAT'LL SEND THE WHOLE PARK INTO A PANIC.
IT'S OKAY!
TODO-ROKI?
TMP TMP
I DUNNO HOW OR WHY, BUT THE SHOW...
FWOO

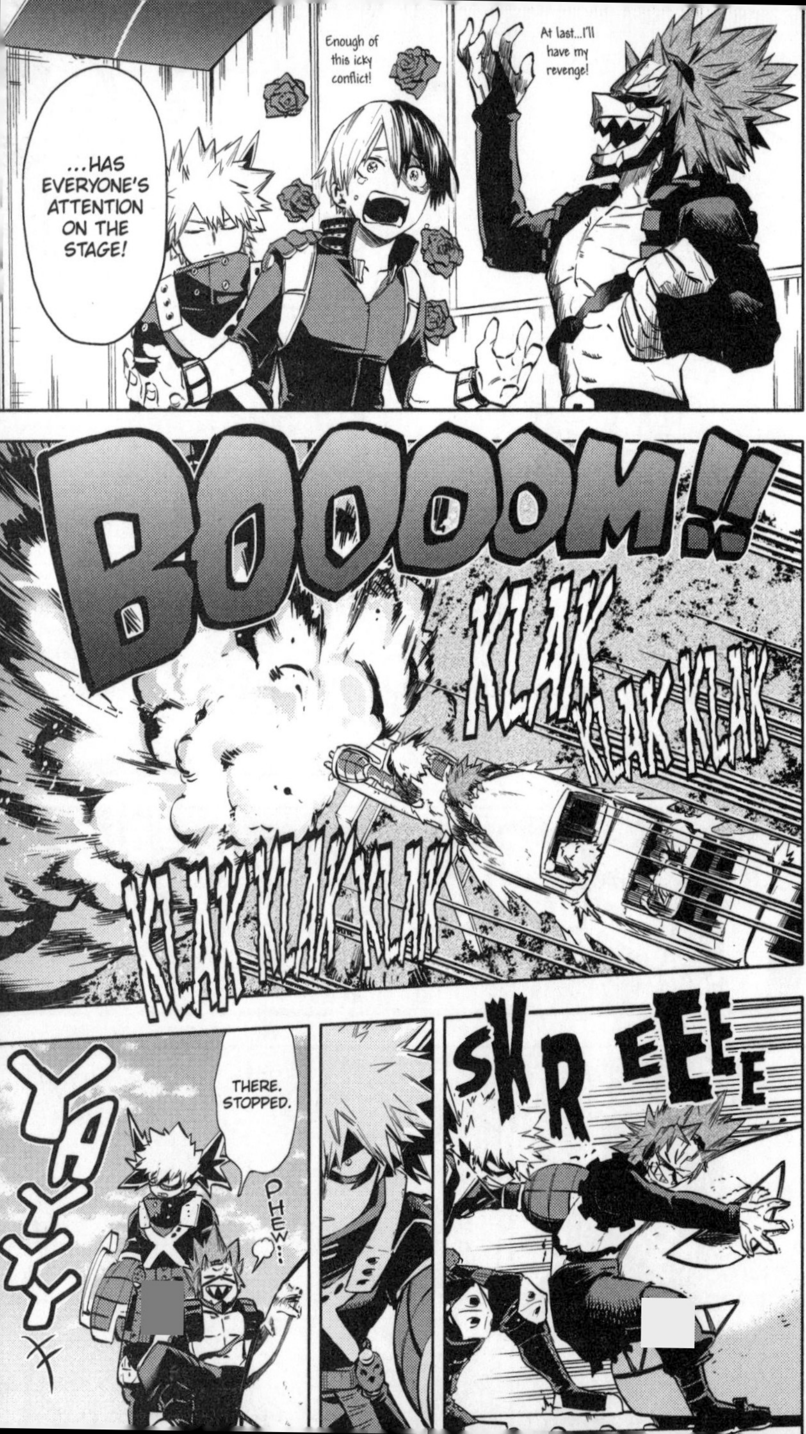
At last...I'll have my revenge!
Enough of this icky conflict!
...HAS EVERYONE'S ATTENTION ON THE STAGE!
BOOOOM!!
KLAK KLAK KLAK
KLAK KLAK KLAK
SKREEEE
THERE. STOPPED.
PHEW...
YAYYYY

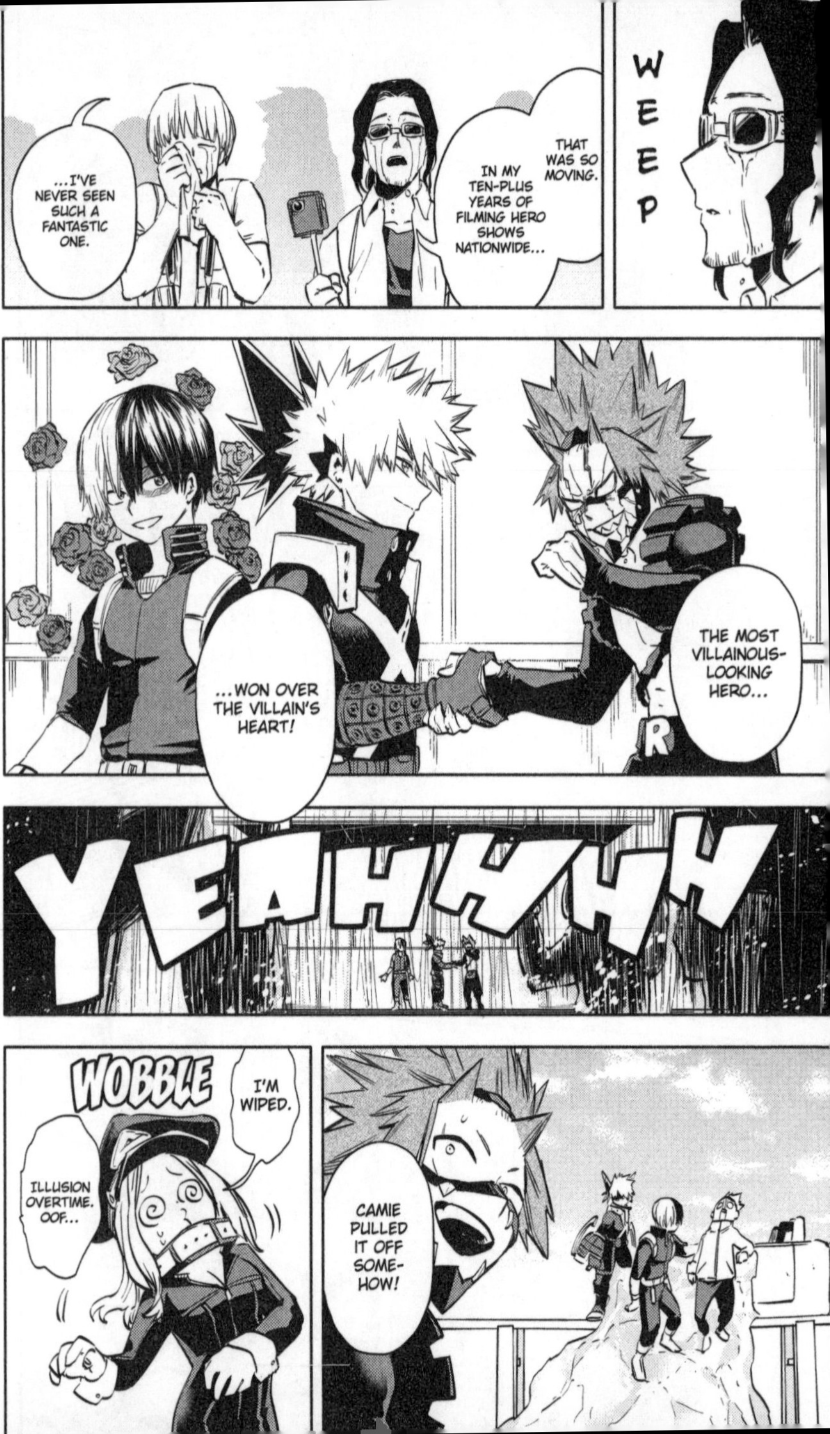
WEEP
THAT WAS SO MOVING.
IN MY TEN-PLUS YEARS OF FILMING HERO SHOWS NATIONWIDE...
...I'VE NEVER SEEN SUCH A FANTASTIC ONE.
THE MOST VILLAINOUS-LOOKING HERO...
...WON OVER THE VILLAIN'S HEART!
YEAHHHH
CAMIE PULLED IT OFF SOME-HOW!
WOBBLE
I'M WIPED.
ILLUSION OVERTIME. OOF...

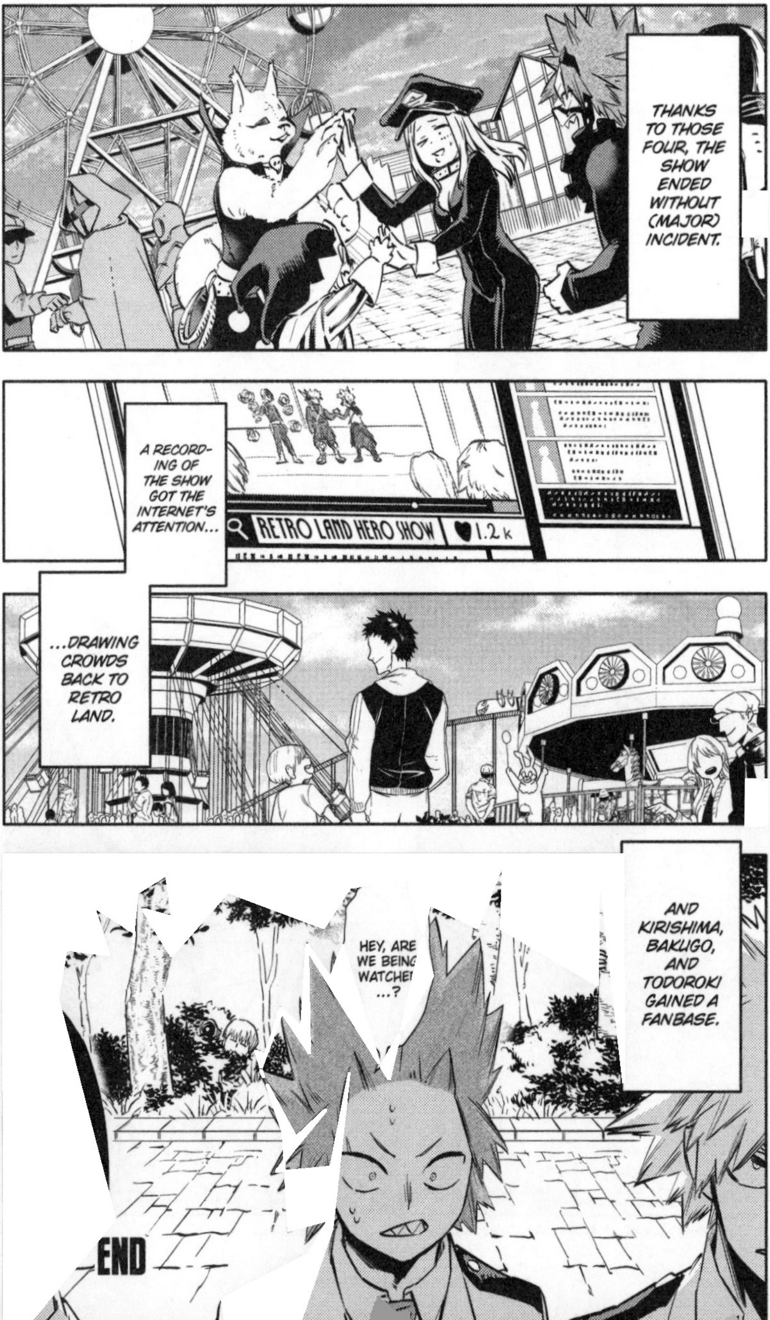
THANKS TO THOSE FOUR, THE SHOW ENDED WITHOUT (MAJOR) INCIDENT.
A RECORDING OF THE SHOW GOT THE INTERNET'S ATTENTION...
RETRO LAND HERO SHOW
1.2 k
...DRAWING CROWDS BACK TO RETRO LAND.
AND KIRISHIMA, BAKUGO, AND TODOROKI GAINED A FANBASE.
HEY, ARE WE BEING WATCHED ...?
END

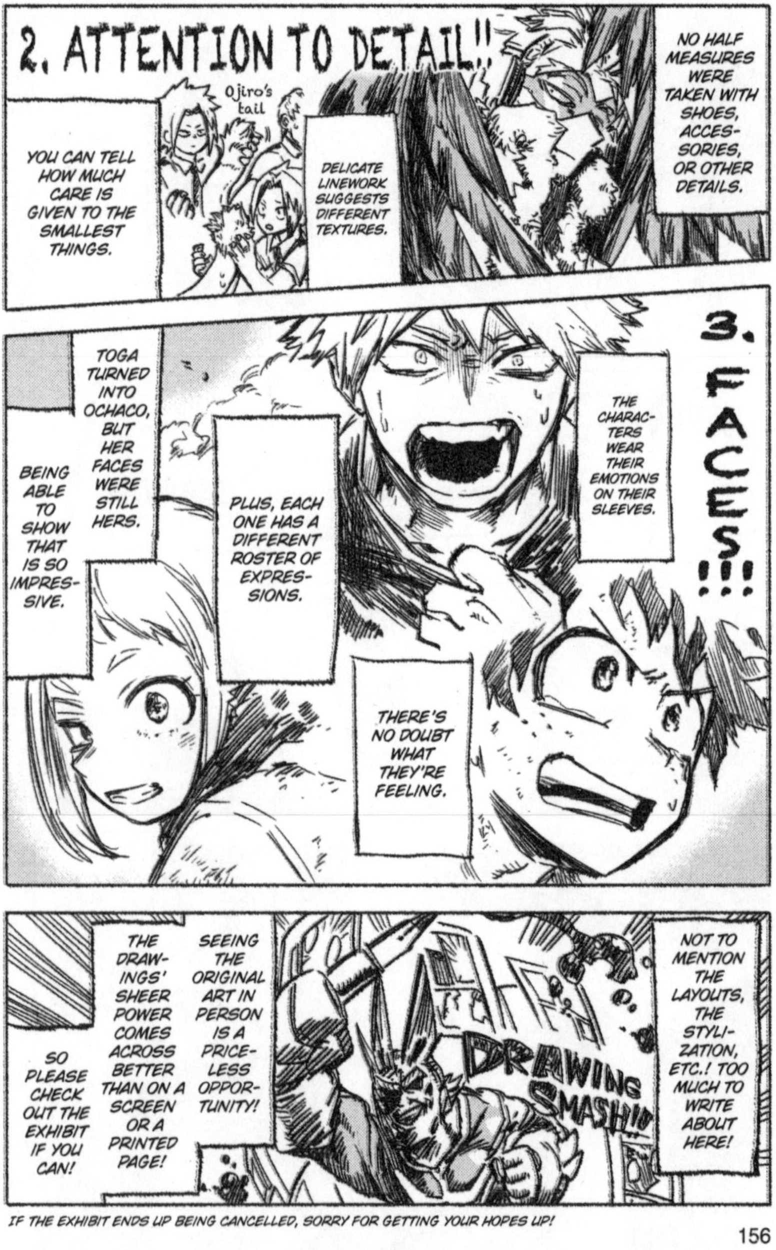
2. ATTENTION TO DETAIL!!
NO HALF MEASURES WERE TAKEN WITH SHOES, ACCES-SORIES, OR OTHER DETAILS.
DELICATE LINEWORK SUGGESTS DIFFERENT TEXTURES.
Ojiro's tail
YOU CAN TELL HOW MUCH CARE IS GIVEN TO THE SMALLEST THINGS.
3. FACES!!!
THE CHARAC-TERS WEAR THEIR EMOTIONS ON THEIR SLEEVES.
TOGA TURNED INTO OCHACO, BUT HER FACES WERE STILL HERS.
PLUS, EACH ONE HAS A DIFFERENT ROSTER OF EXPRES-SIONS.
BEING ABLE TO SHOW THAT IS SO IMPRES-SIVE.
THERE'S NO DOUBT WHAT THEY'RE FEELING.
NOT TO MENTION THE LAYOUTS, THE STYLI-ZATION, ETC.! TOO MUCH TO WRITE ABOUT HERE!
DRAWING SMASH!!
SEEING THE ORIGINAL ART IN PERSON IS A PRICE-LESS OPPOR-TUNITY!
THE DRAW-INGS' SHEER POWER COMES ACROSS BETTER THAN ON A SCREEN OR A PRINTED PAGE!
SO PLEASE CHECK OUT THE EXHIBIT IF YOU CAN!

IF THE EXHIBIT ENDS UP BEING CANCELLED, SORRY FOR GETTING YOUR HOPES UP!

ONE-SHOT

DEKU AND BAKUGO RISING, PART 1

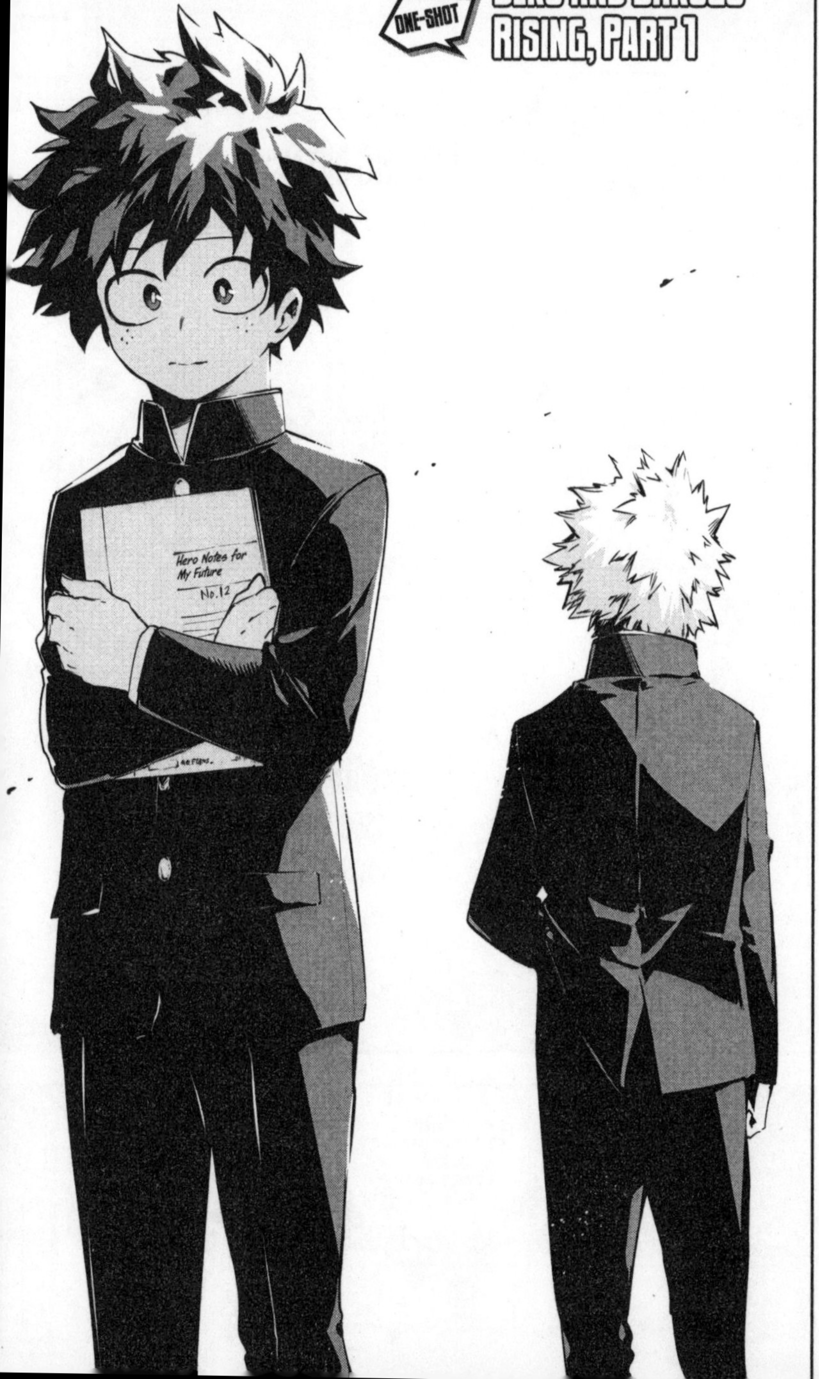
Hero Notes for My Future
No.12

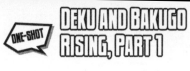

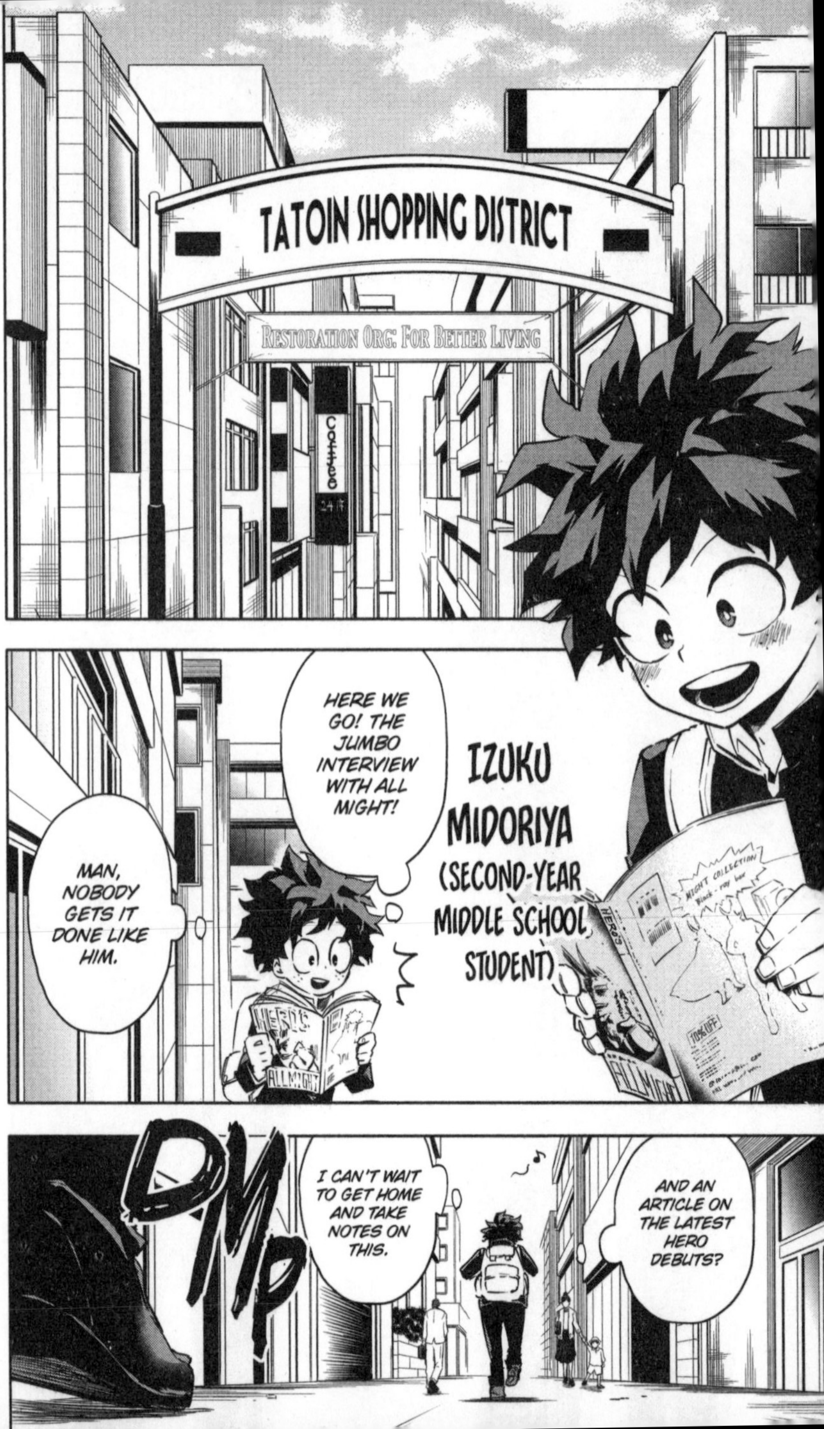
TATOIN SHOPPING DISTRICT
RESTORATION ORG: FOR BETTER LIVING
COFFEE
IZUKU MIDORIYA (SECOND-YEAR MIDDLE SCHOOL STUDENT)
HERE WE GO! THE JUMBO INTERVIEW WITH ALL MIGHT!
MAN, NOBODY GETS IT DONE LIKE HIM.
AND AN ARTICLE ON THE LATEST HERO DEBUTS?
I CAN'T WAIT TO GET HOME AND TAKE NOTES ON THIS.
DMP

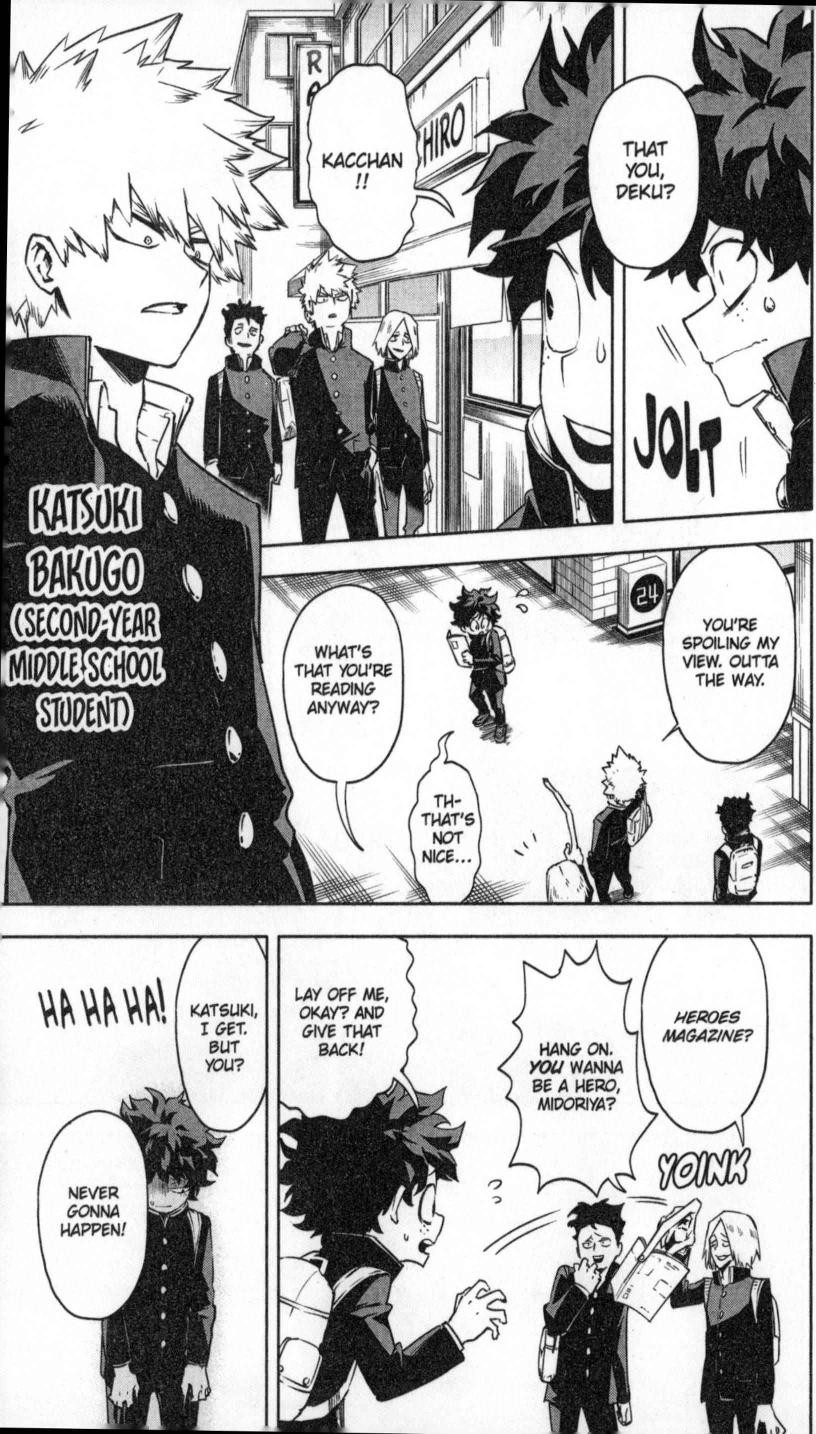
THAT YOU, DEKU?
JOLT
KACCHAN !!
KATSUKI BAKUGO (SECOND-YEAR MIDDLE SCHOOL STUDENT)
YOU'RE SPOILING MY VIEW. OUTTA THE WAY.
WHAT'S THAT YOU'RE READING ANYWAY?
TH- THAT'S NOT NICE...
HEROES MAGAZINE?
YOINK
HANG ON. YOU WANNA BE A HERO, MIDORIYA?
LAY OFF ME, OKAY? AND GIVE THAT BACK!
KATSUKI, I GET. BUT YOU?
HA HA HA!
NEVER GONNA HAPPEN!

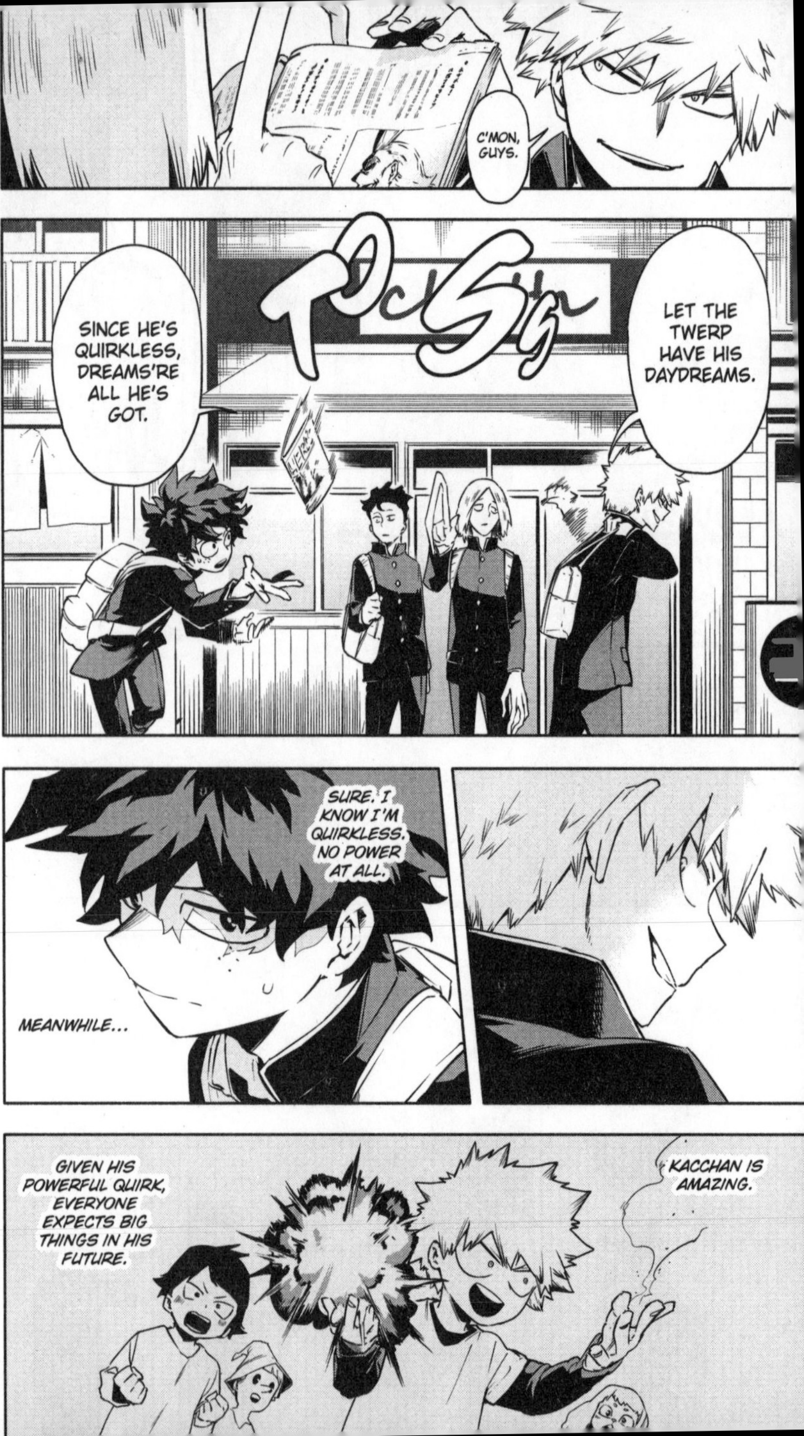
C'MON, GUYS.
LET THE TWERP HAVE HIS DAYDREAMS.
TOSS
SINCE HE'S QUIRKLESS, DREAMS'RE ALL HE'S GOT.
SURE. I KNOW I'M QUIRKLESS. NO POWER AT ALL.
MEANWHILE...
KACCHAN IS AMAZING.
GIVEN HIS POWERFUL QUIRK, EVERYONE EXPECTS BIG THINGS IN HIS FUTURE.

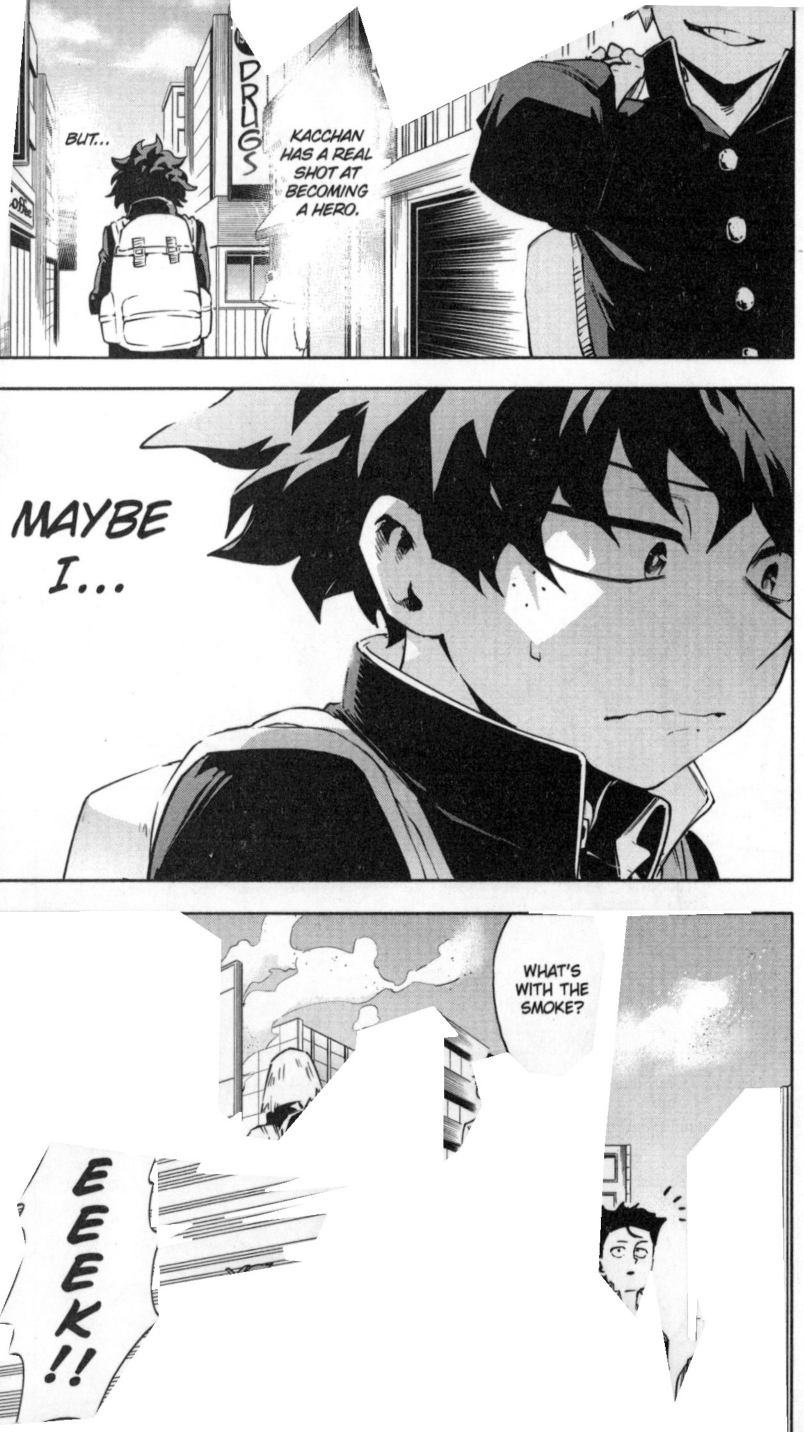
KACCHAN HAS A REAL SHOT AT BECOMING A HERO.
BUT...
DRUGS
MAYBE I...
WHAT'S WITH THE SMOKE?
EEEK!!

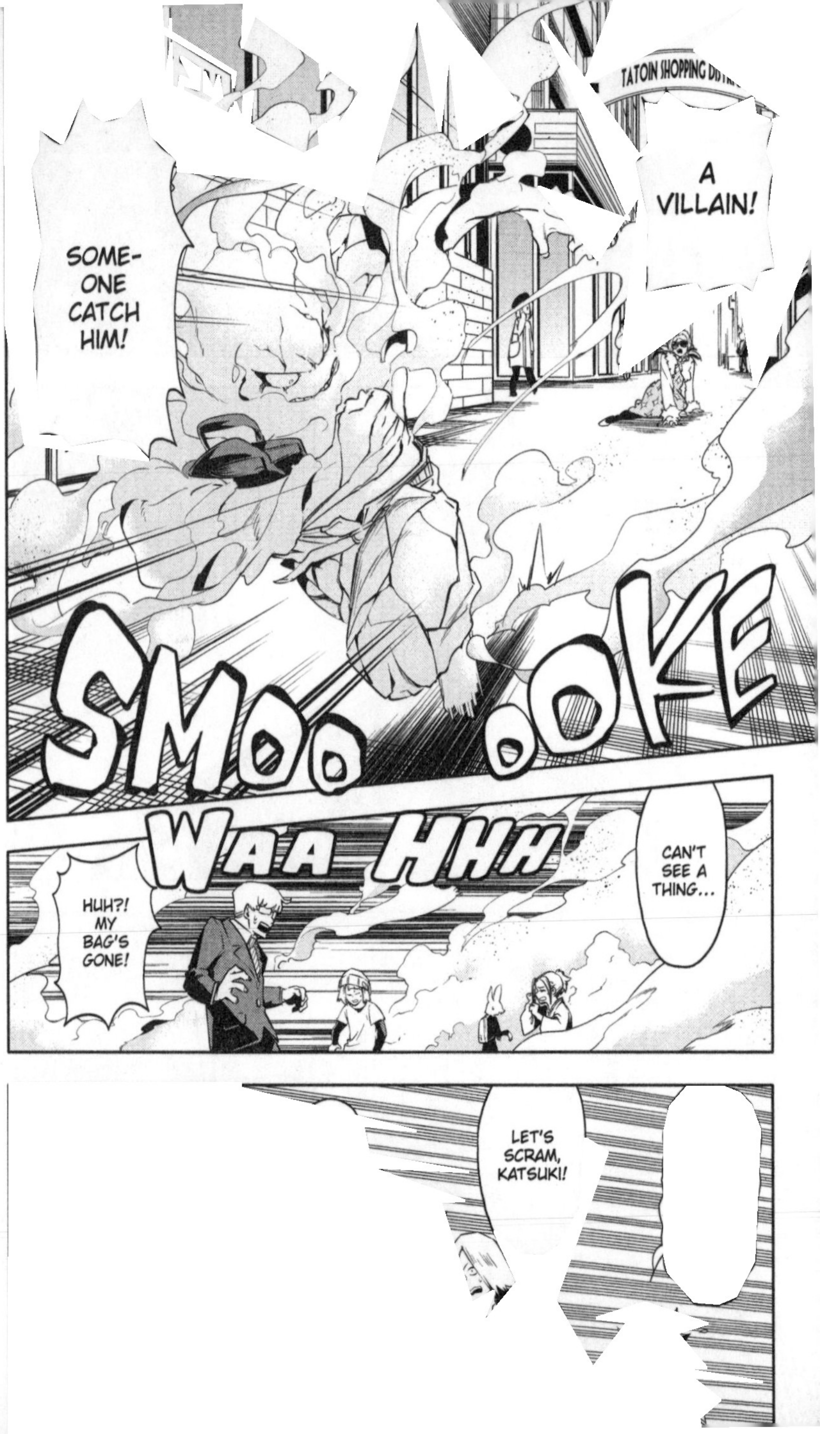
TATOIN SHOPPING
A VILLAIN!
SOME-ONE CATCH HIM!
SMOO OOKE
WAA HHH
CAN'T SEE A THING...
HUH?! MY BAG'S GONE!
LET'S SCRAM, KATSUKI!

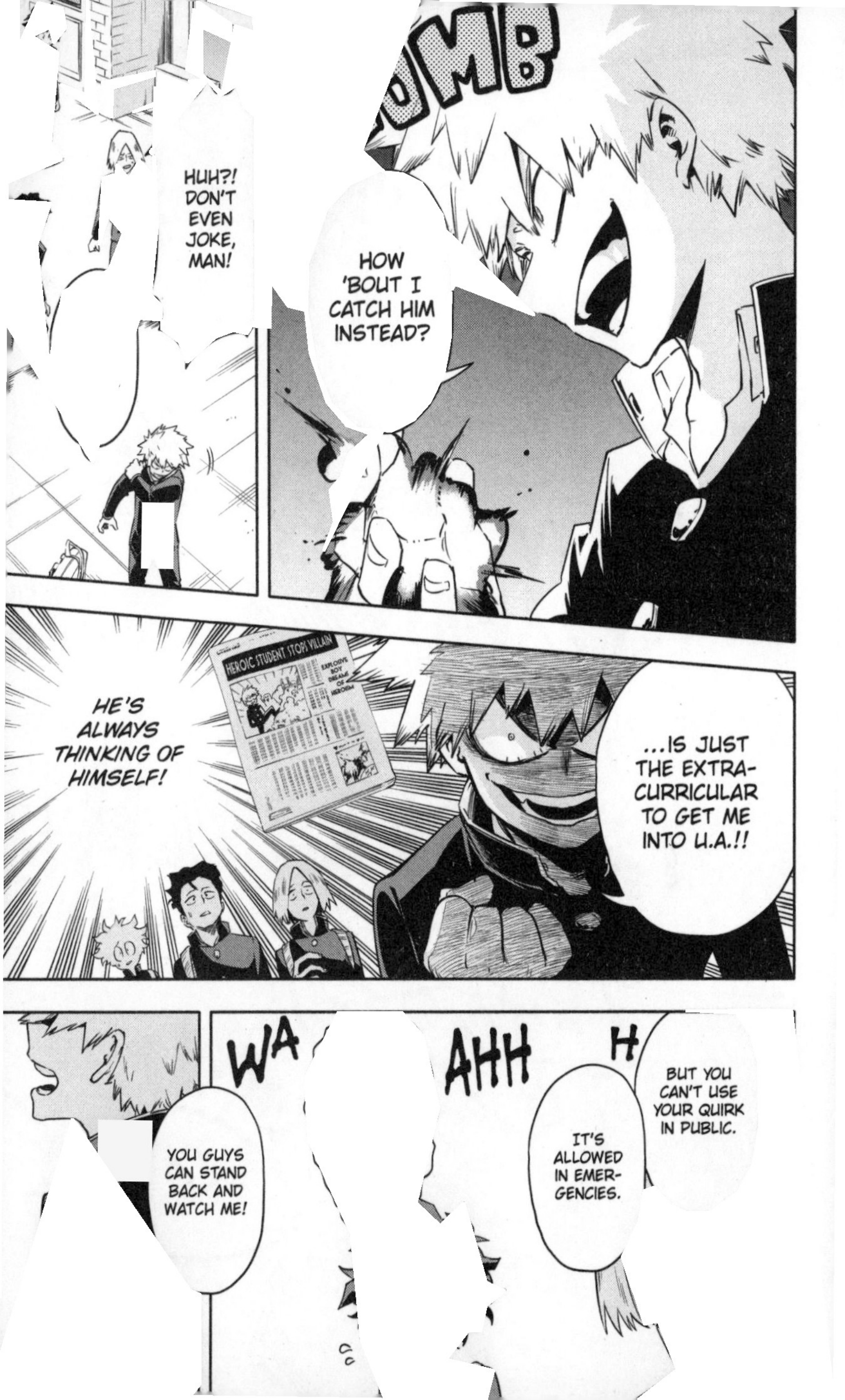
OMB
HOW 'BOUT I CATCH HIM INSTEAD?
HUH?! DON'T EVEN JOKE, MAN!
...IS JUST THE EXTRA-CURRICULAR TO GET ME INTO U.A.!!
HEROIC STUDENT STOPS VILLAIN
EXPLOSIVE BOY DREAMS OF HEROISM
HE'S ALWAYS THINKING OF HIMSELF!
BUT YOU CAN'T USE YOUR QUIRK IN PUBLIC.
H
IT'S ALLOWED IN EMERGENCIES.
WA AHH
YOU GUYS CAN STAND BACK AND WATCH ME!

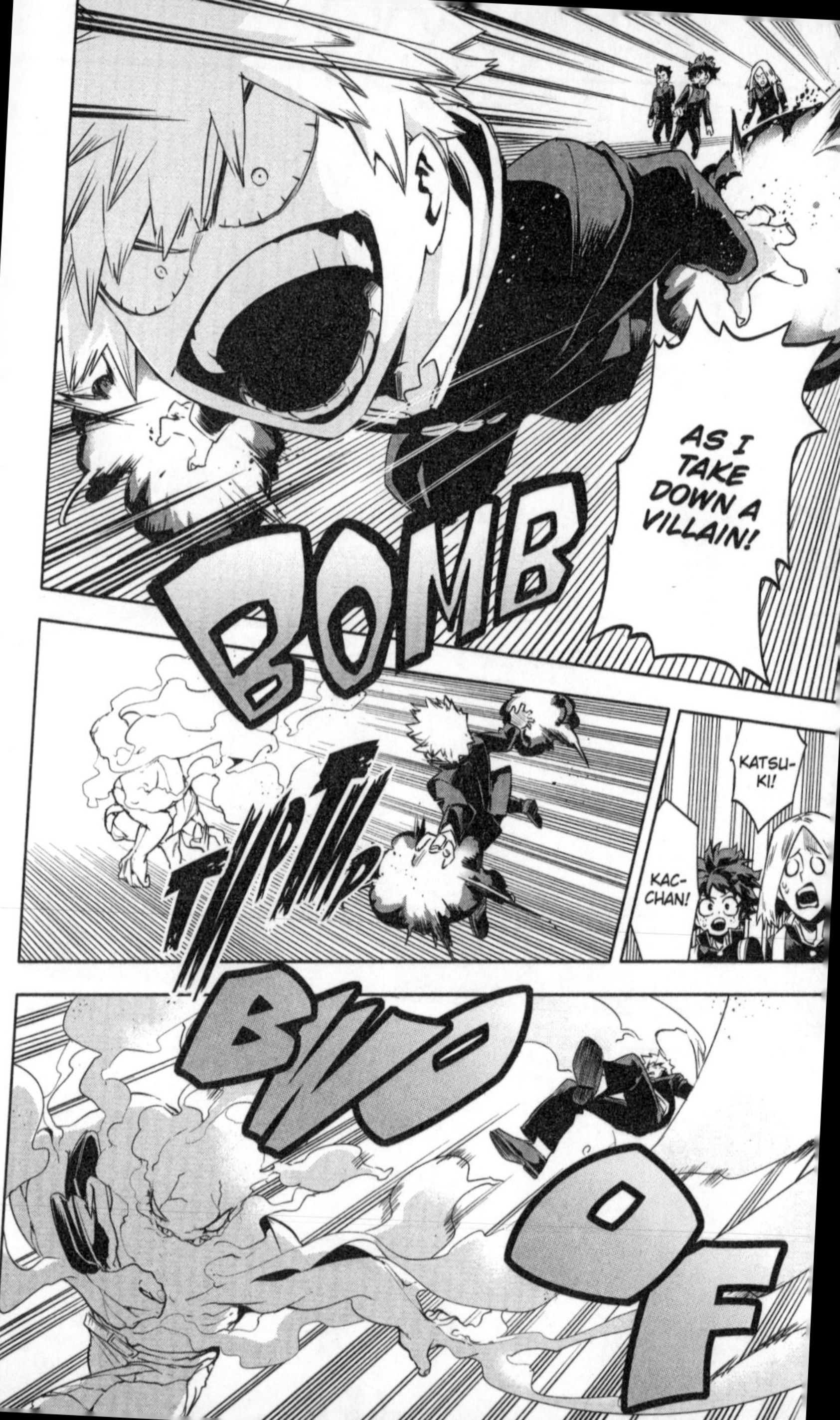
AS I TAKE DOWN A VILLAIN!
BOMB
KATSU-KI!
KAC-CHAN!
THWOMP
BWOOOF

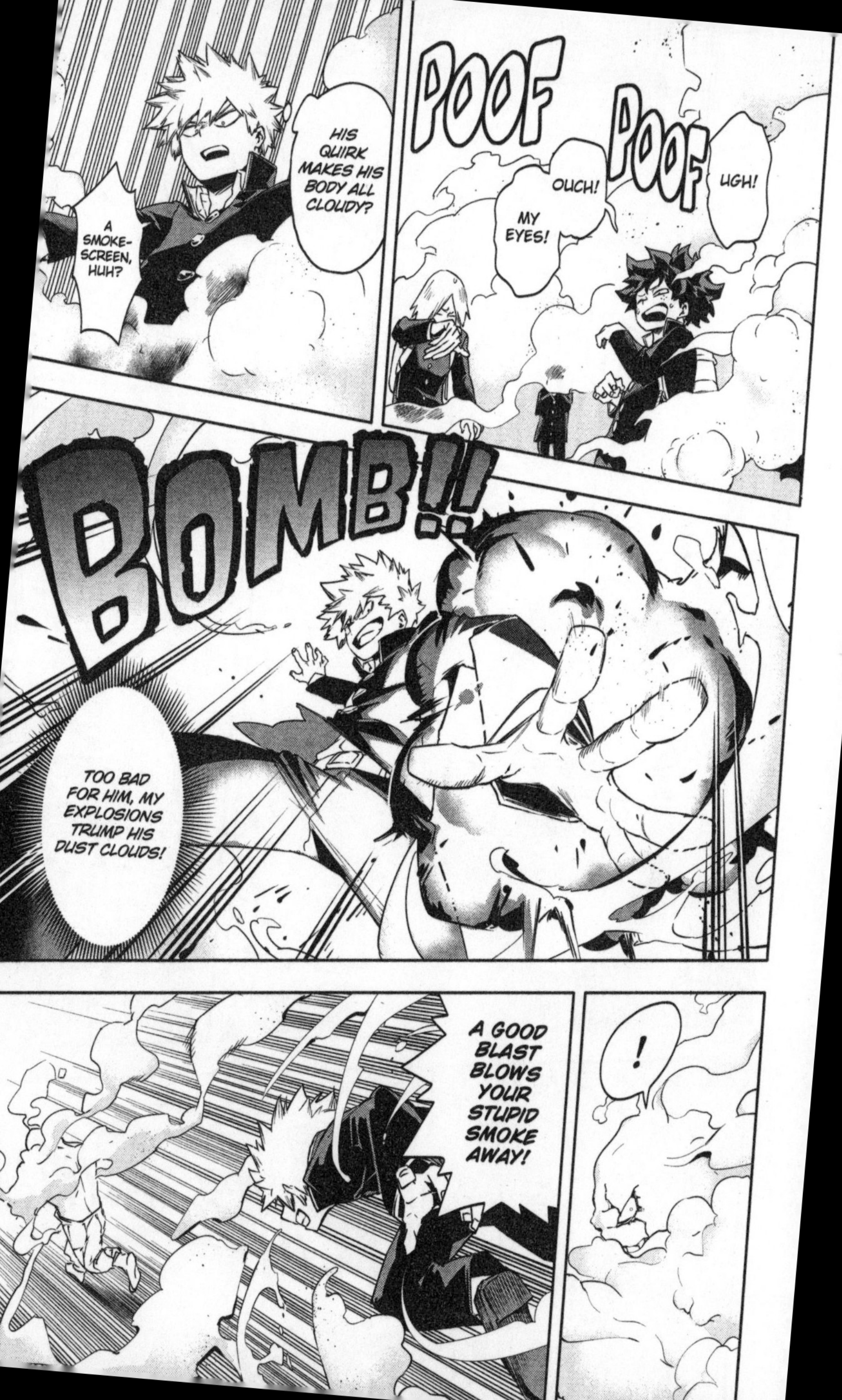
POOF
POOF
UGH!
OUCH!
MY EYES!
HIS QUIRK MAKES HIS BODY ALL CLOUDY?
A SMOKE-SCREEN, HUH?
BOMB!!
TOO BAD FOR HIM, MY EXPLOSIONS TRUMP HIS DUST CLOUDS!
!
A GOOD BLAST BLOWS YOUR STUPID SMOKE AWAY!

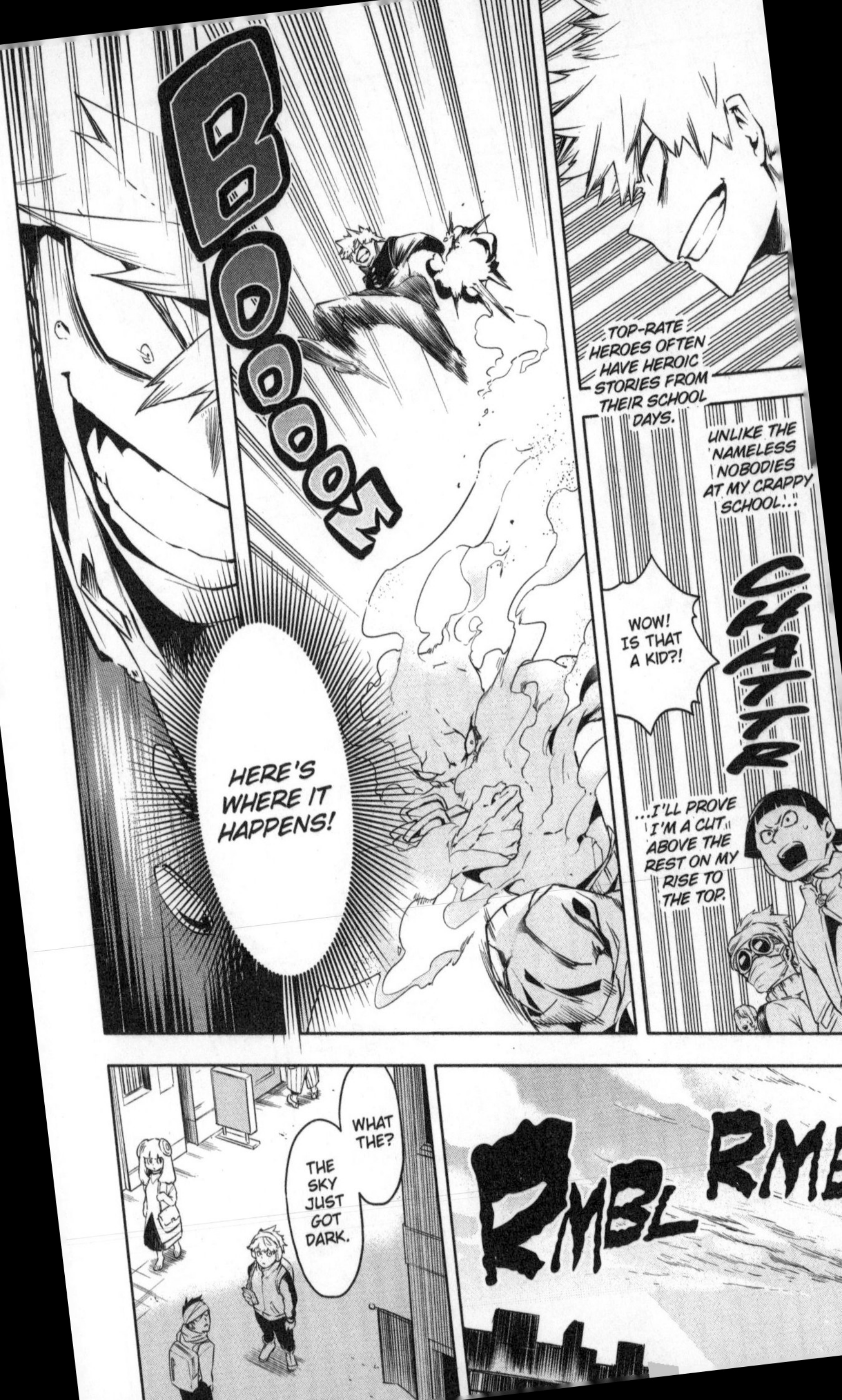
TOP-RATE HEROES OFTEN HAVE HEROIC STORIES FROM THEIR SCHOOL DAYS.
UNLIKE THE NAMELESS NOBODIES AT MY CRAPPY SCHOOL...
WOW! IS THAT A KID?!
CHATTR
...I'LL PROVE I'M A CUT ABOVE THE REST ON MY RISE TO THE TOP.
BOOOOOOM
HERE'S WHERE IT HAPPENS!
RMBL RMB
WHAT THE?
THE SKY JUST GOT DARK.

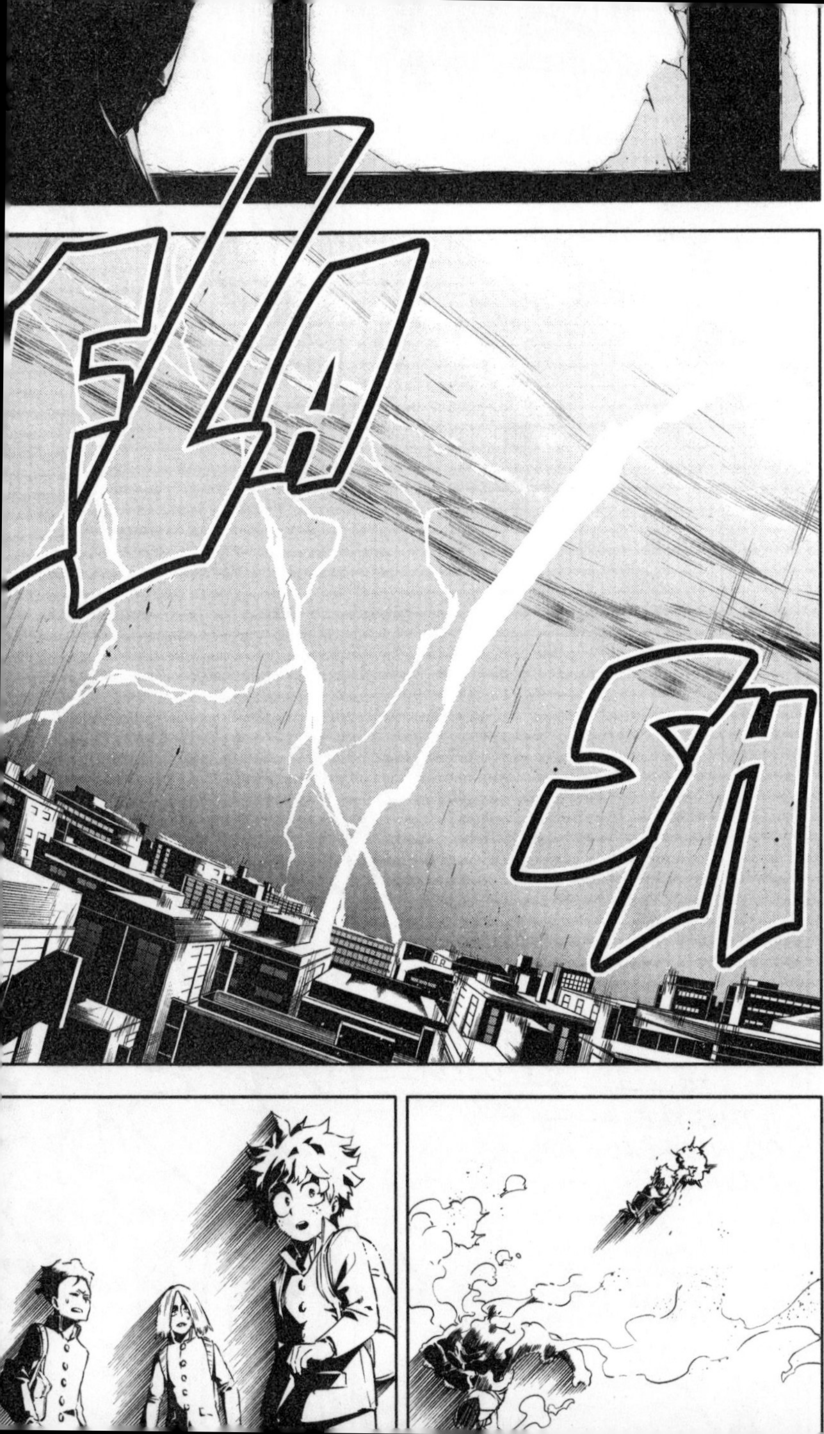
FLASH

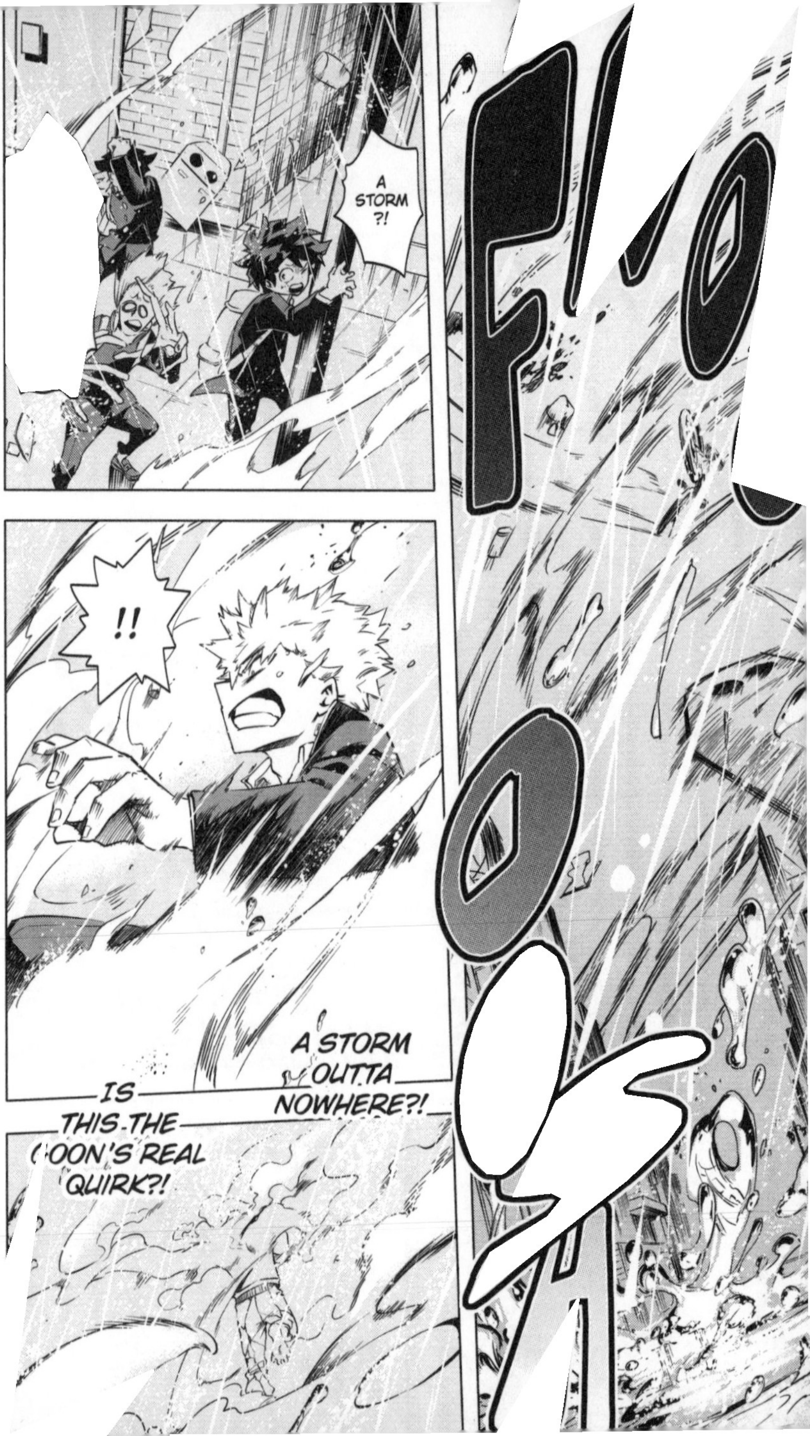
FWOOSH
A STORM ?!
!!
A STORM OUTTA NOWHERE?!
IS THIS THE GOON'S REAL QUIRK?!

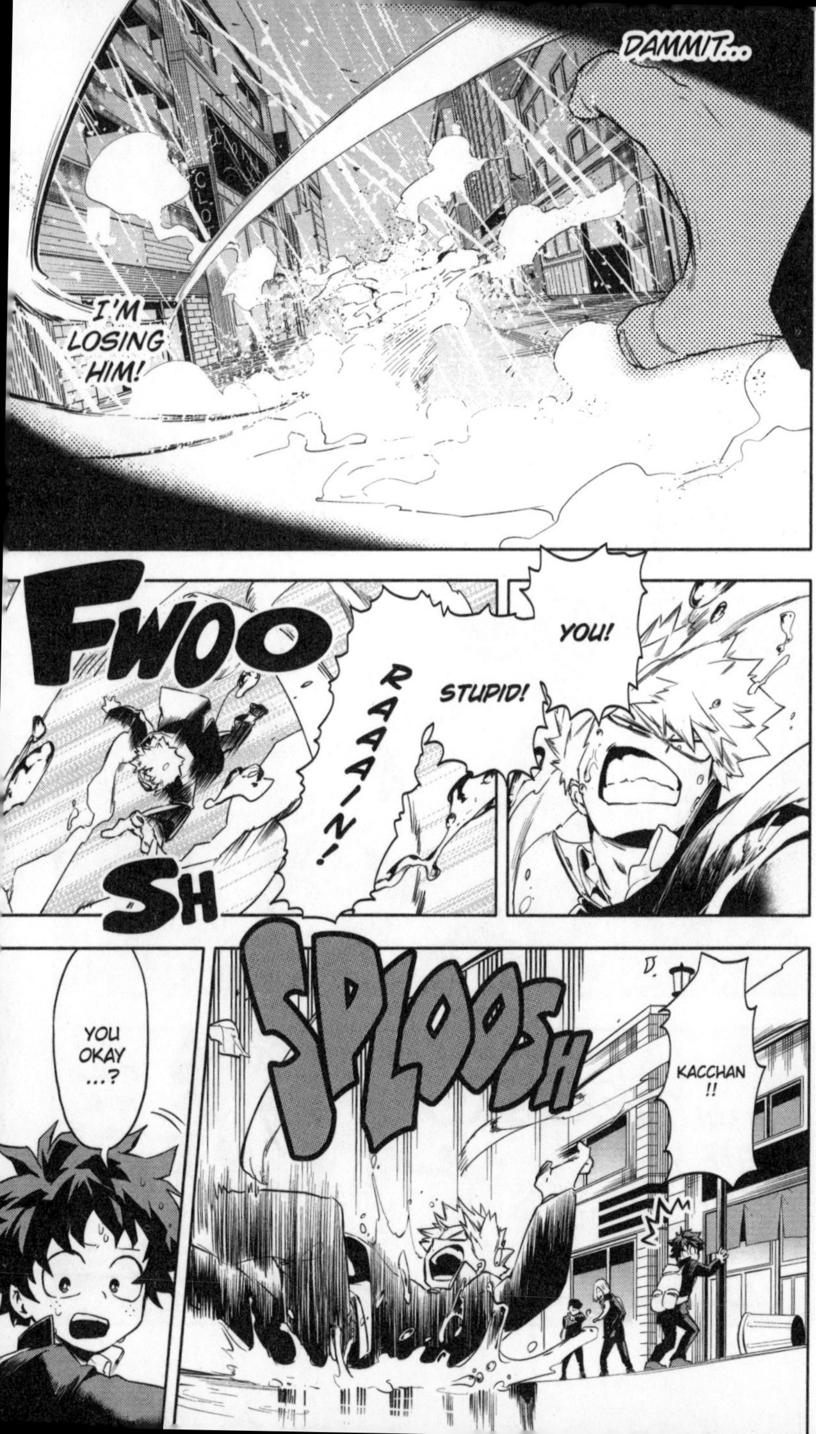
DAMMIT...
I'M LOSING HIM!
YOU!
STUPID!
RAAAAIN!
FWOOSH
KACCHAN!!
SPLOOSH
YOU OKAY ...?

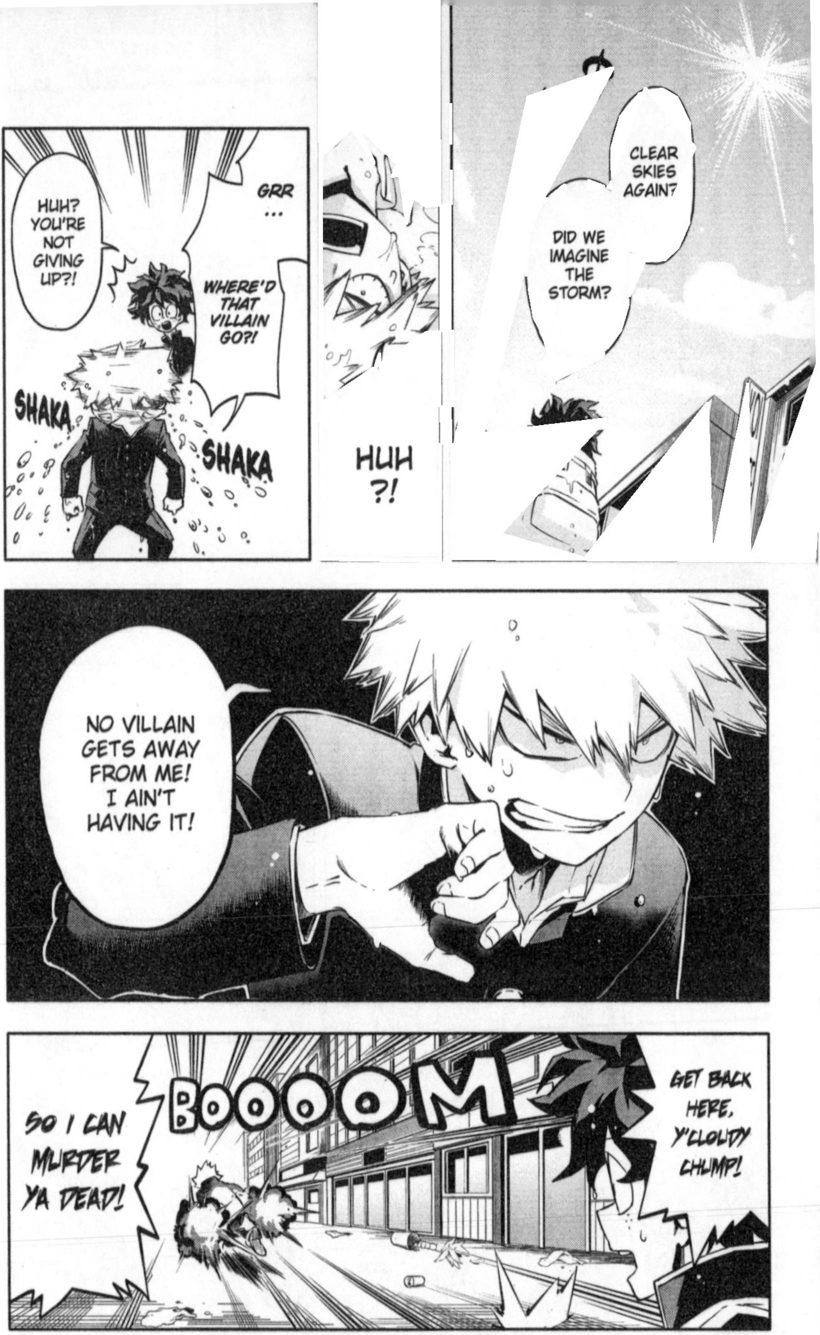
CLEAR SKIES AGAIN?
DID WE IMAGINE THE STORM?
HUH ?!
GRR ...
HUH? YOU'RE NOT GIVING UP?!
WHERE'D THAT VILLAIN GO?!
SHAKA
SHAKA
NO VILLAIN GETS AWAY FROM ME! I AIN'T HAVING IT!
GET BACK HERE, Y'CLOUDY CHUMP!
BOOOOM
SO I CAN MURDER YA DEAD!

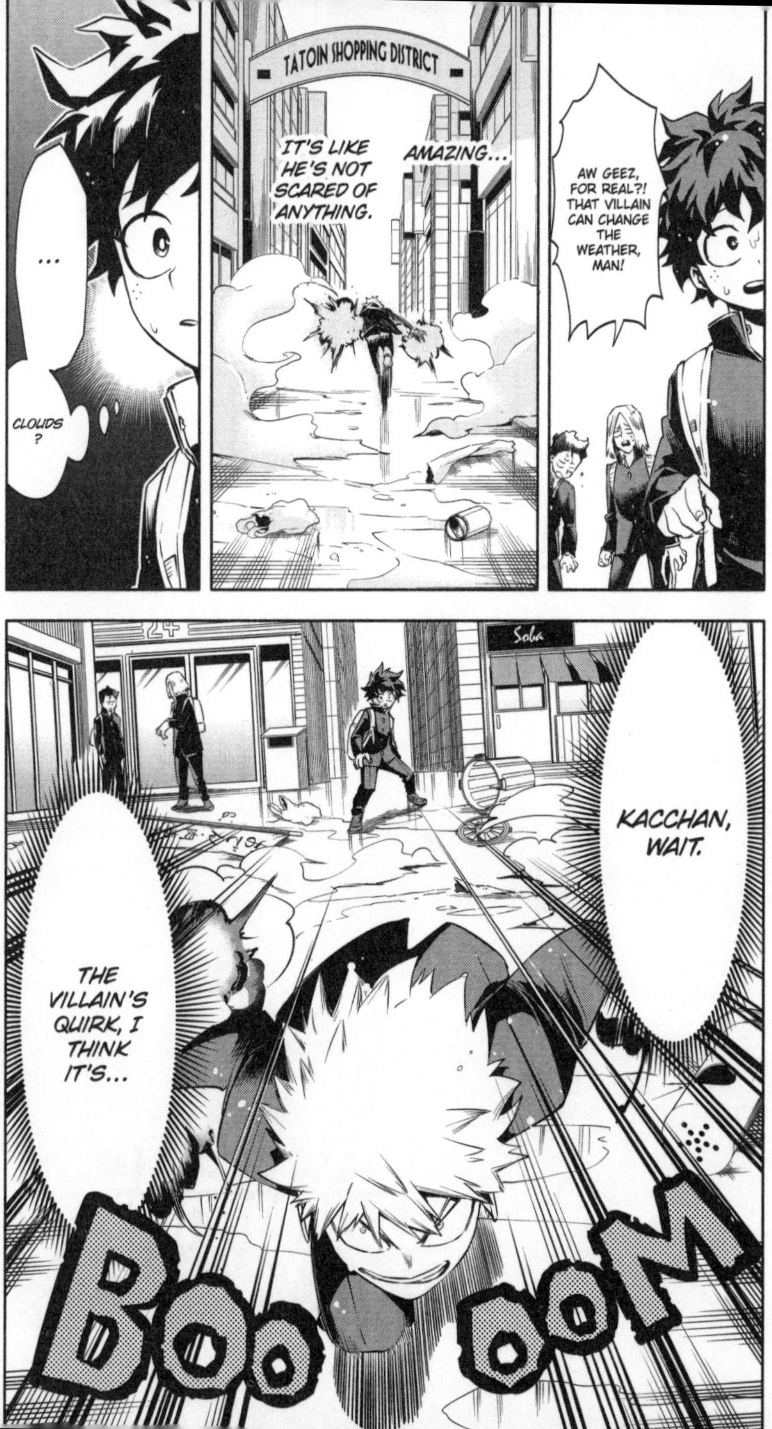
AW GEEZ, FOR REAL?! THAT VILLAIN CAN CHANGE THE WEATHER, MAN!
TATOIN SHOPPING DISTRICT
AMAZING...
IT'S LIKE HE'S NOT SCARED OF ANYTHING.
...
CLOUDS ?
24
Soba
KACCHAN, WAIT.
THE VILLAIN'S QUIRK, I THINK IT'S...
BOO OOM

MY HERO ACADEMIA

Team-Up Missions

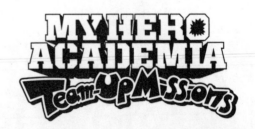

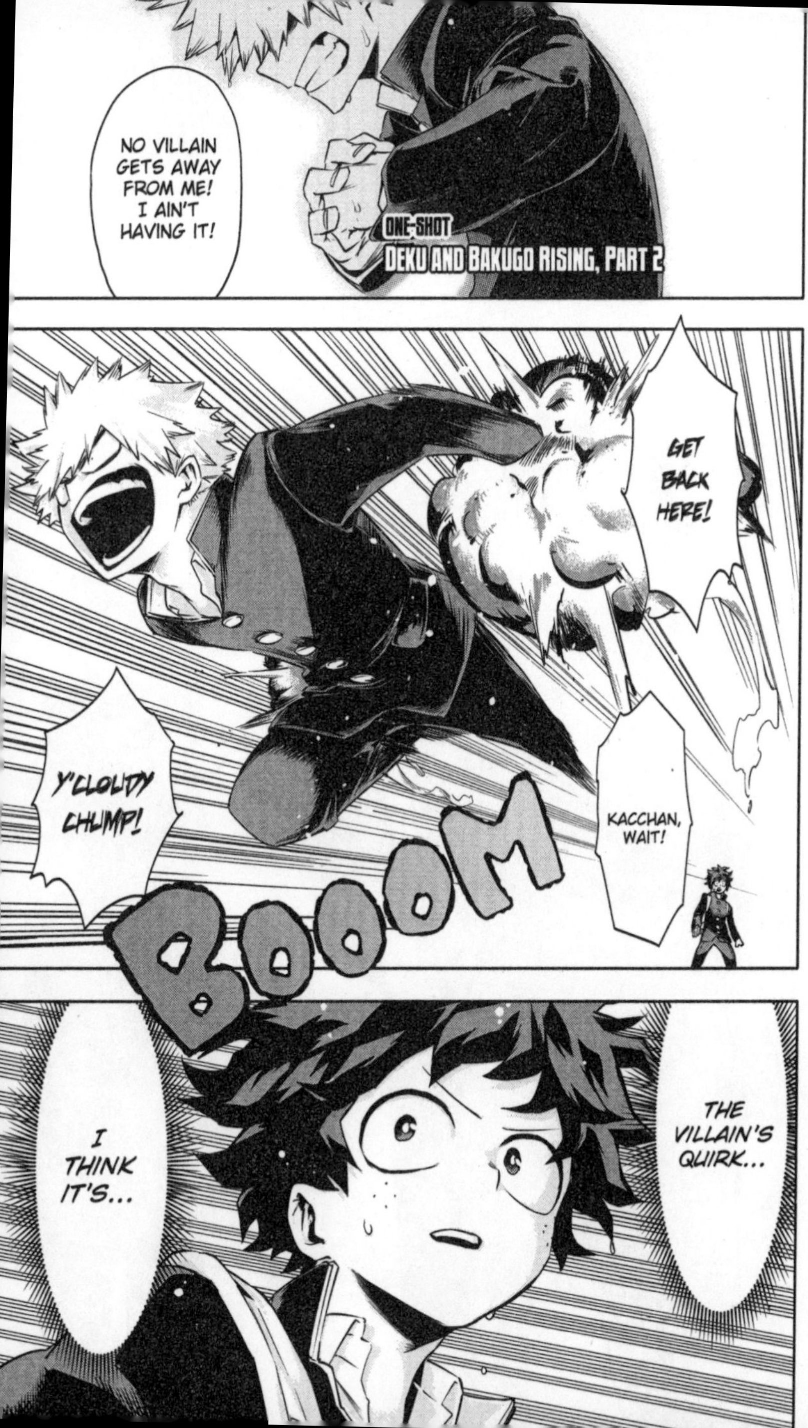
ONE-SHOT
Deku and Bakugo Rising, Part 2
NO VILLAIN GETS AWAY FROM ME! I AIN'T HAVING IT!
GET BACK HERE!
KACCHAN, WAIT!
Y'CLOUDY CHUMP!
BOOOOM
THE VILLAIN'S QUIRK...
I THINK IT'S...

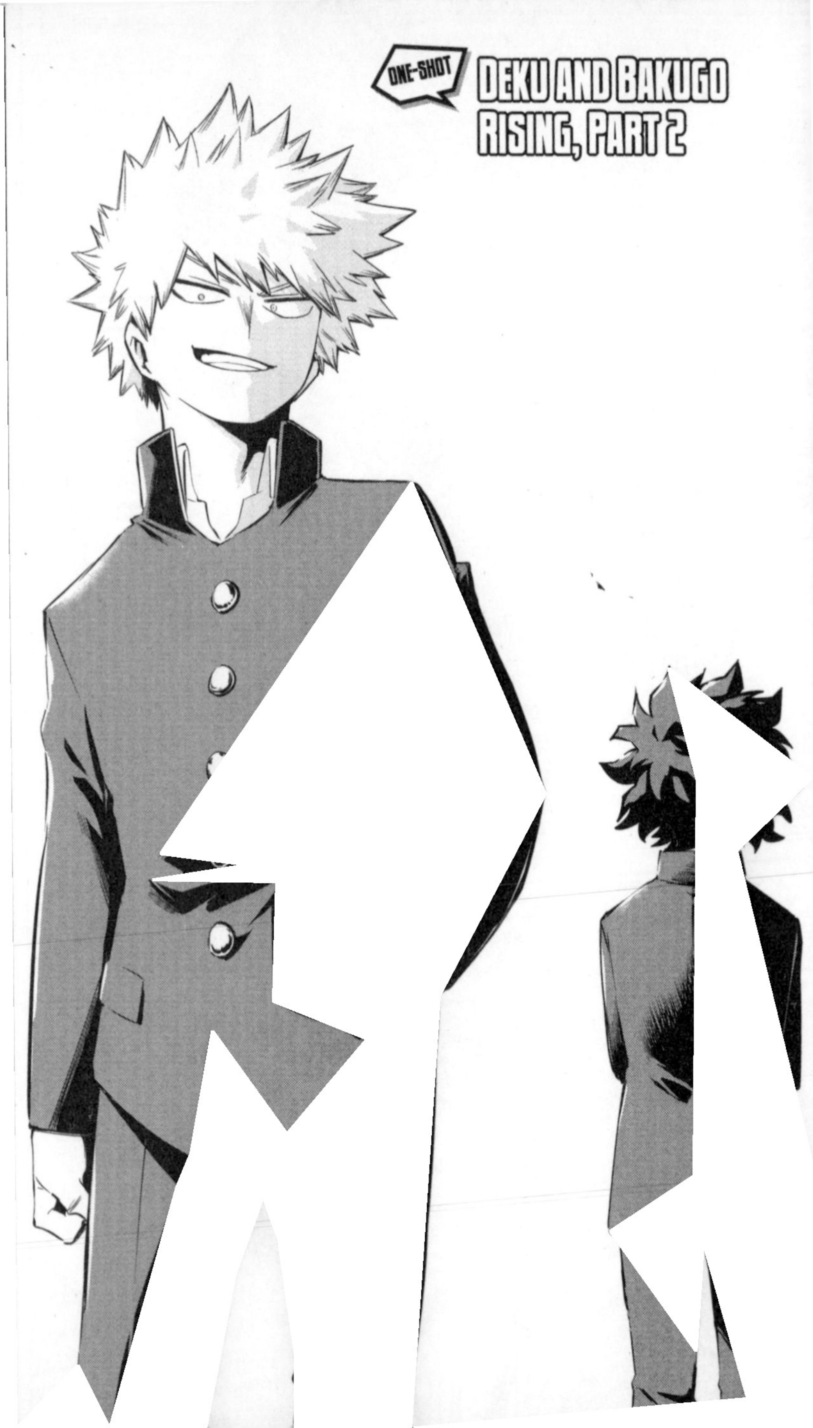
ONE-SHOT
DEKU AND BAKUGO RISING, PART 2

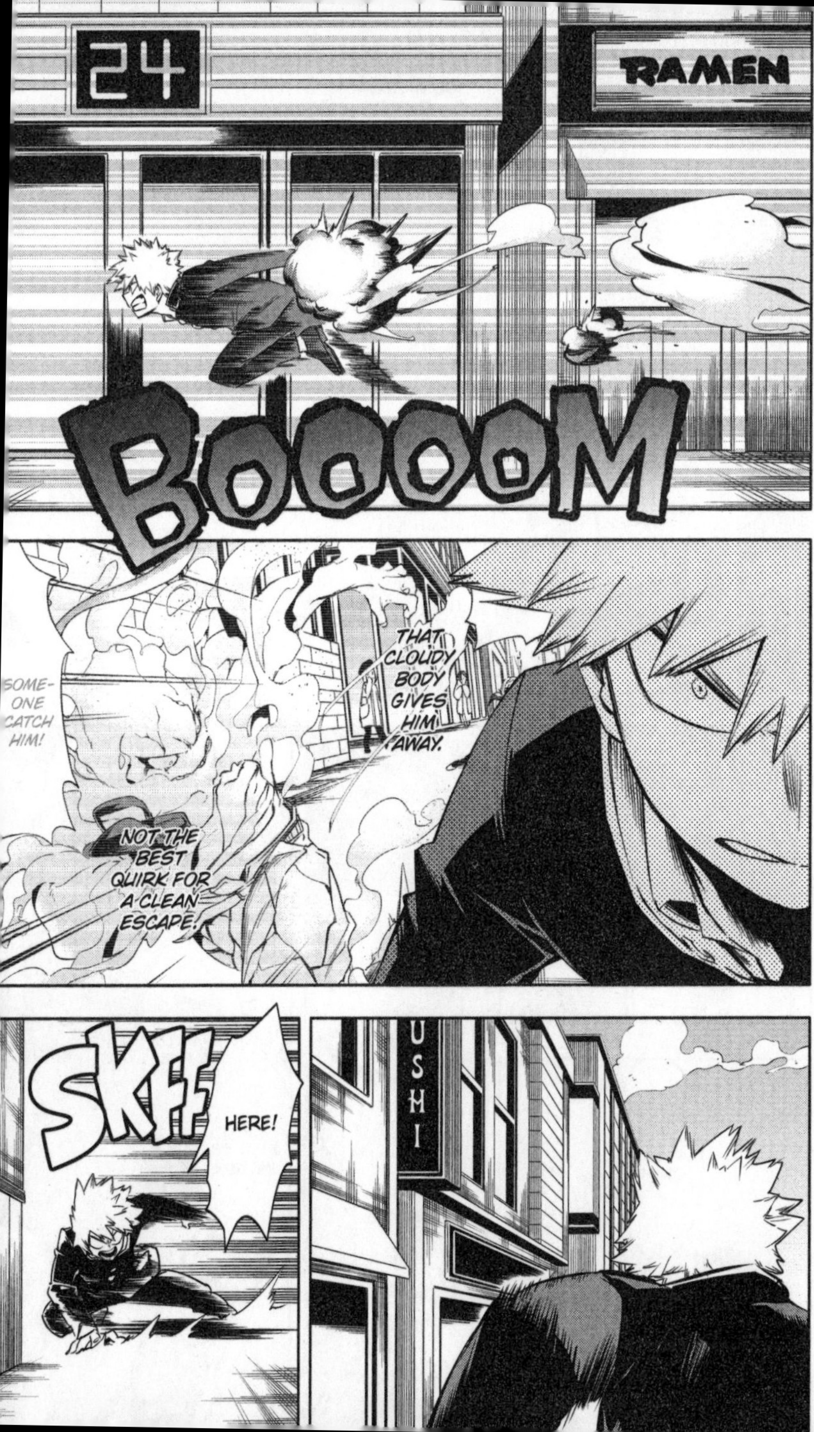
24
RAMEN
BOOOOOM
THAT CLOUDY BODY GIVES HIM AWAY.
SOME-ONE CATCH HIM!
NOT THE BEST QUIRK FOR A CLEAN ESCAPE!
USHI
SKFF
HERE!

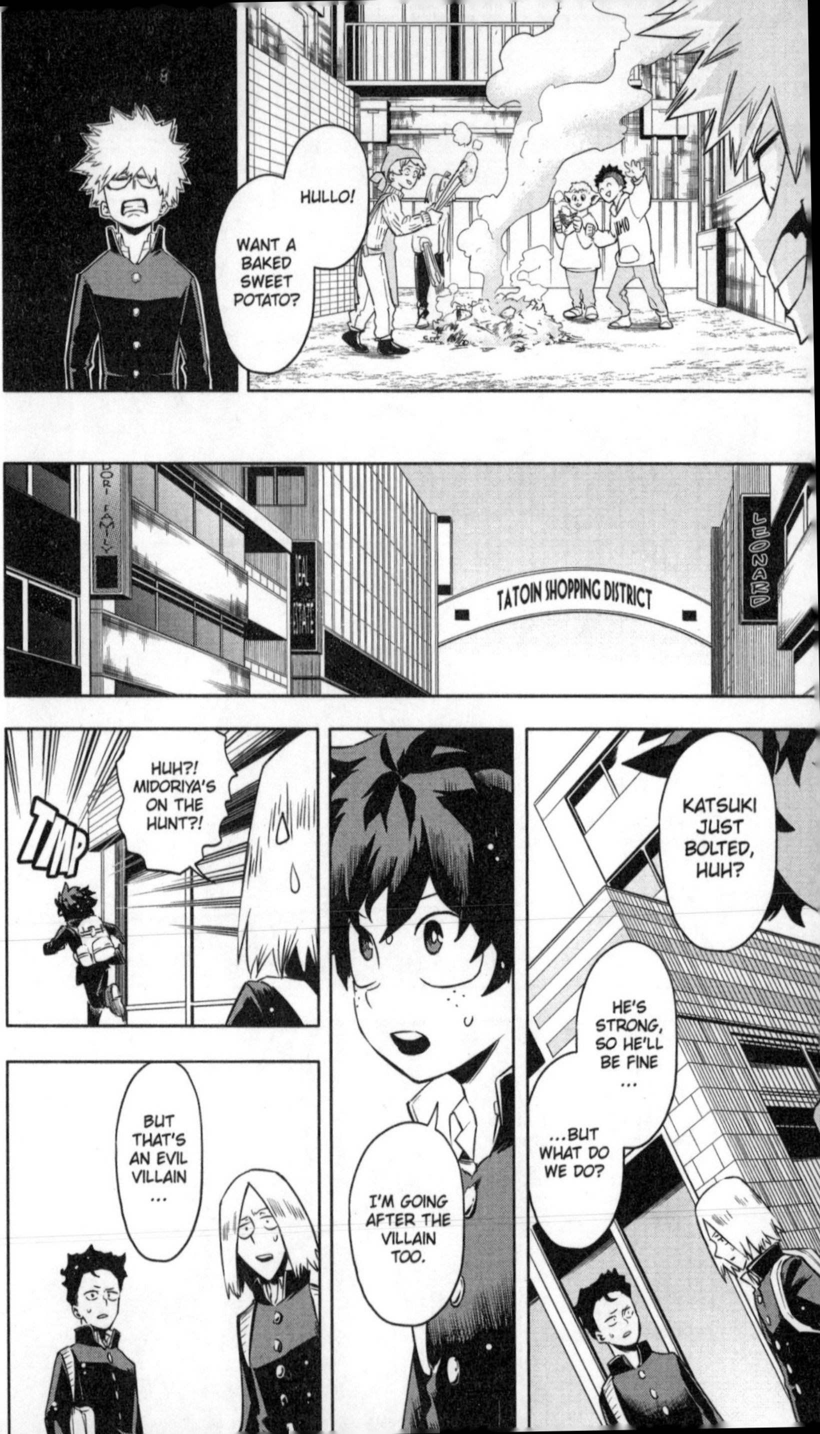
HULLO!
WANT A BAKED SWEET POTATO?
TATOIN SHOPPING DISTRICT
LEONARD
KATSUKI JUST BOLTED, HUH?
HE'S STRONG, SO HE'LL BE FINE ...
...BUT WHAT DO WE DO?
I'M GOING AFTER THE VILLAIN TOO.
HUH?! MIDORIYA'S ON THE HUNT?!
TMP
BUT THAT'S AN EVIL VILLAIN ...

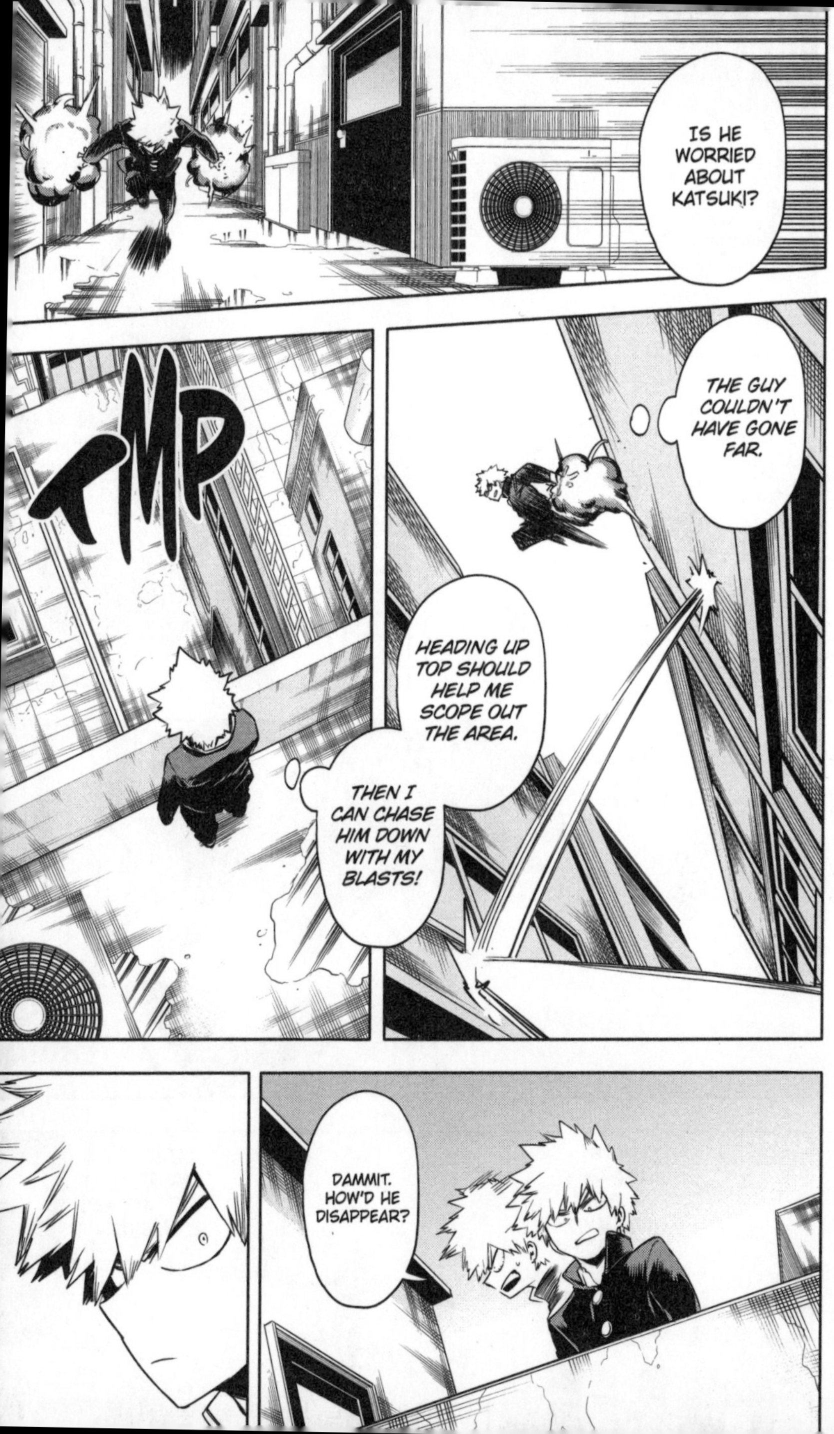
IS HE WORRIED ABOUT KATSUKI?
THE GUY COULDN'T HAVE GONE FAR.
HEADING UP TOP SHOULD HELP ME SCOPE OUT THE AREA.
THEN I CAN CHASE HIM DOWN WITH MY BLASTS!
TMP
DAMMIT. HOW'D HE DISAPPEAR?

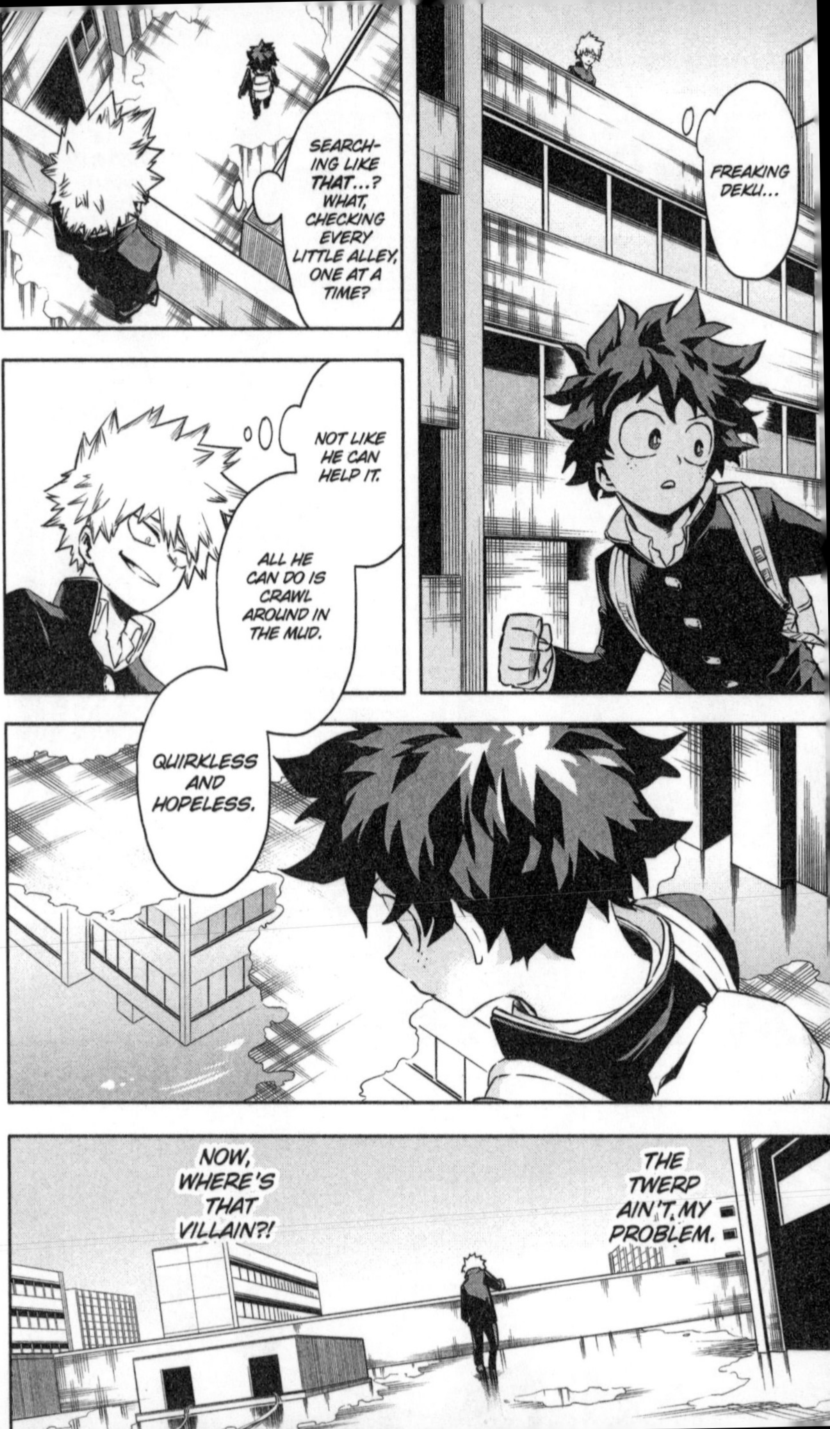
FREAKING DEKU...
SEARCHING LIKE THAT...? WHAT, CHECKING EVERY LITTLE ALLEY, ONE AT A TIME?
NOT LIKE HE CAN HELP IT.
ALL HE CAN DO IS CRAWL AROUND IN THE MUD.
QUIRKLESS AND HOPELESS.
THE TWERP AIN'T MY PROBLEM.
NOW, WHERE'S THAT VILLAIN?!

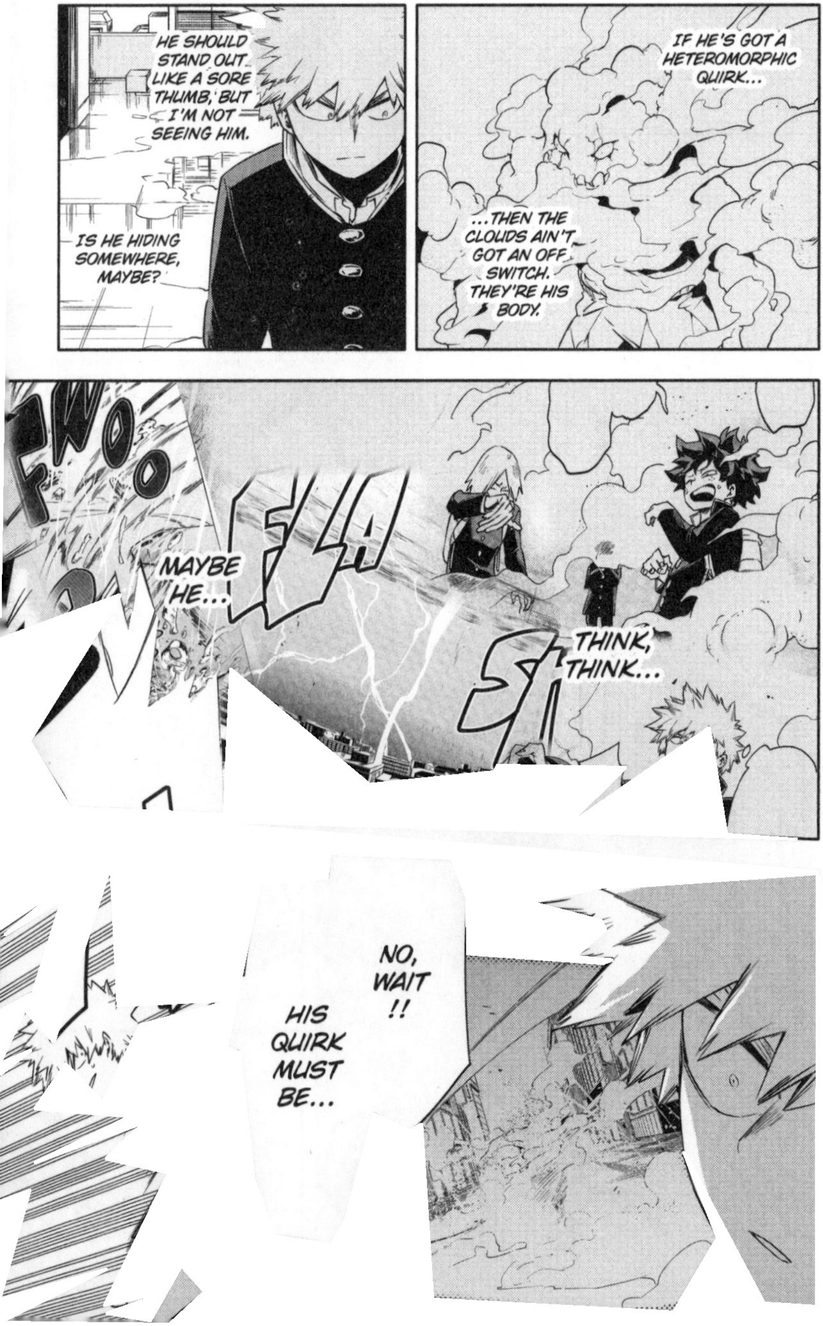
IF HE'S GOT A HETEROMORPHIC QUIRK...
...THEN THE CLOUDS AIN'T GOT AN OFF SWITCH. THEY'RE HIS BODY.
HE SHOULD STAND OUT LIKE A SORE THUMB, BUT I'M NOT SEEING HIM.
IS HE HIDING SOMEWHERE, MAYBE?
THINK, THINK...
MAYBE HE...
FWOO
NO, WAIT!!
HIS QUIRK MUST BE...

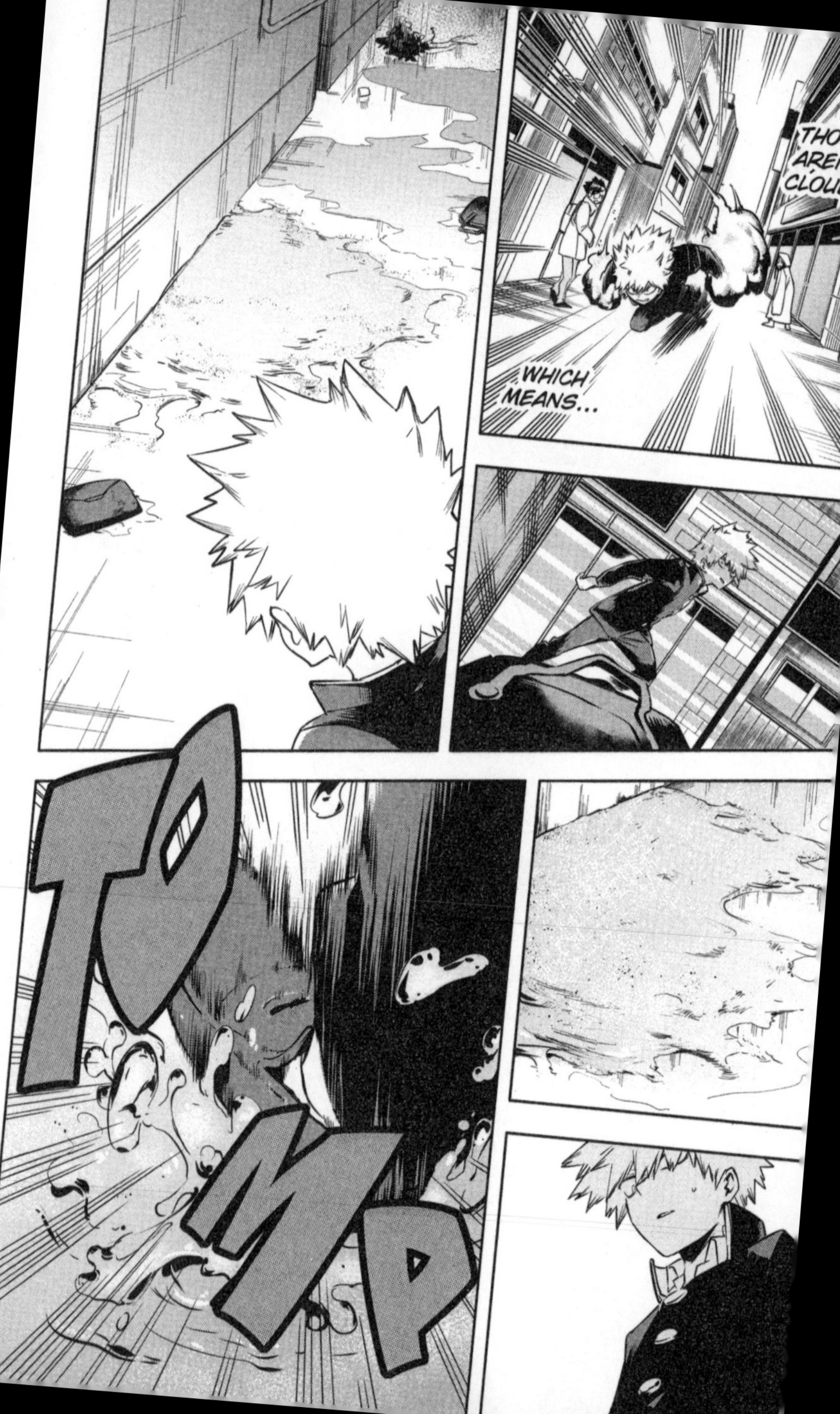
WHICH MEANS...
TOMP

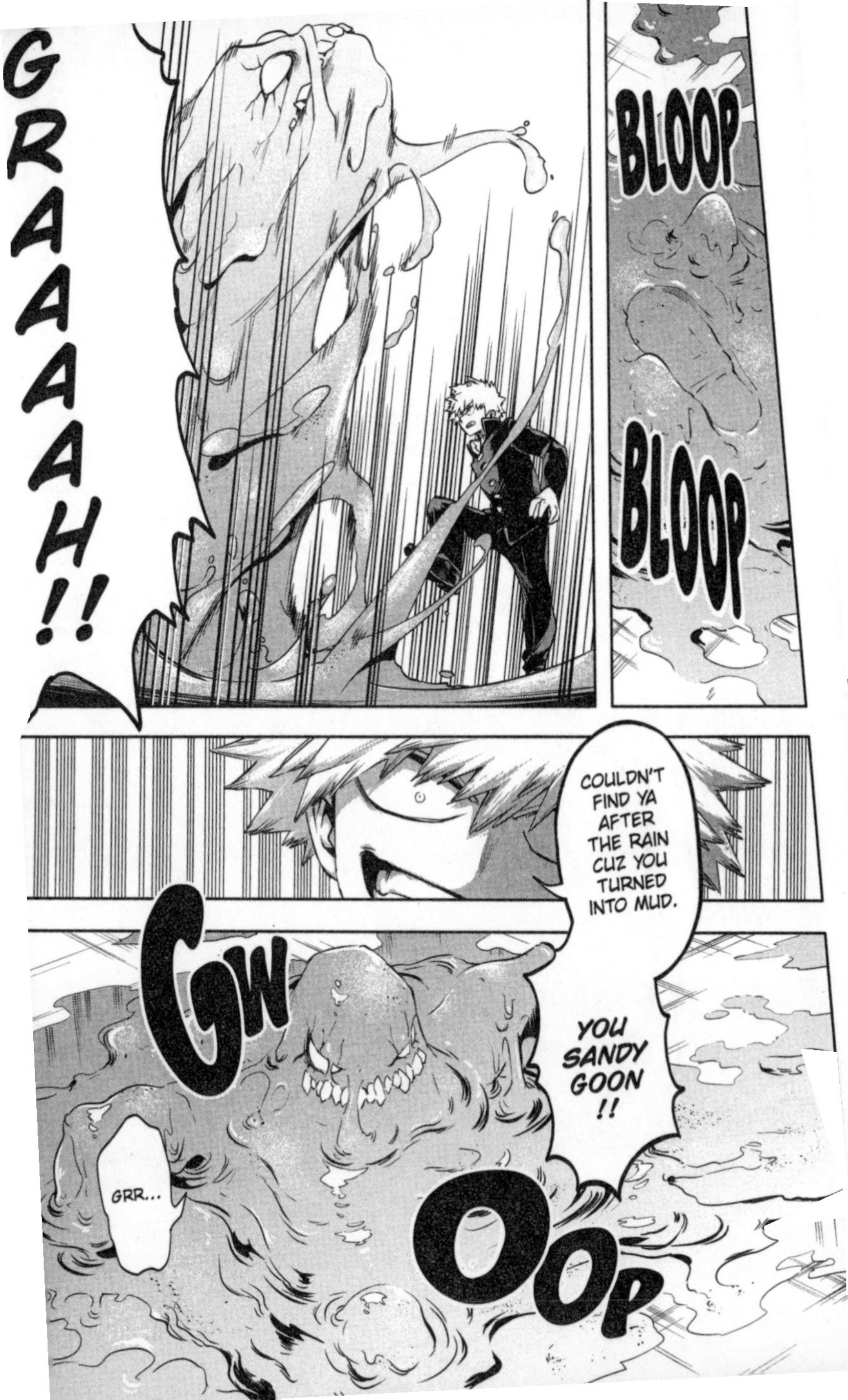
BLOOP
BLOOP
GRAAAAH!!
COULDN'T FIND YA AFTER THE RAIN CUZ YOU TURNED INTO MUD.
YOU SANDY GOON!!
GW
OOP
GRR...

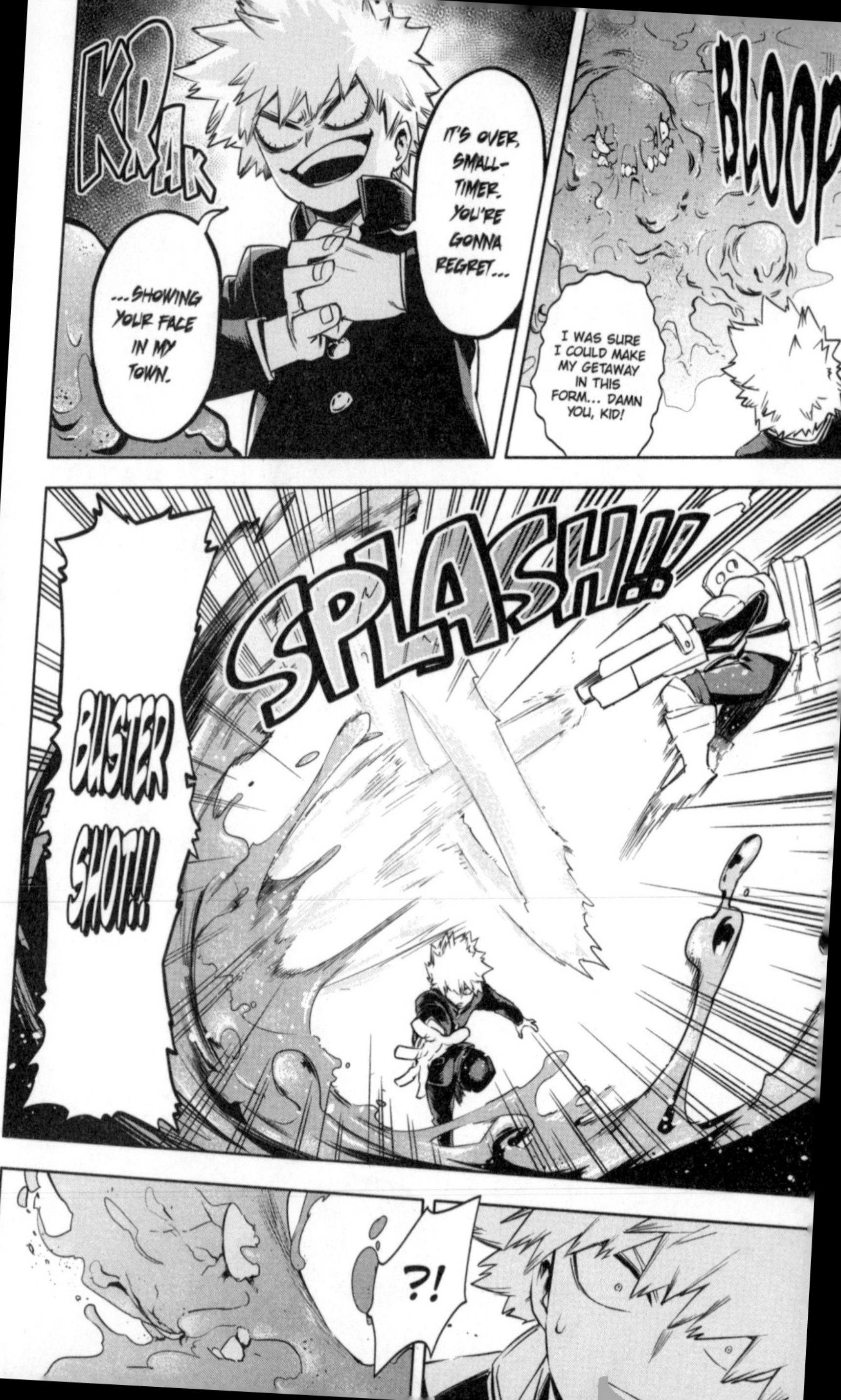
BLOOP
I WAS SURE I COULD MAKE MY GETAWAY IN THIS FORM... DAMN YOU, KID!
KRAK
IT'S OVER, SMALL-TIMER. YOU'RE GONNA REGRET...
...SHOWING YOUR FACE IN MY TOWN.
SPLASH!!
BUSTER SHOT!!
?!

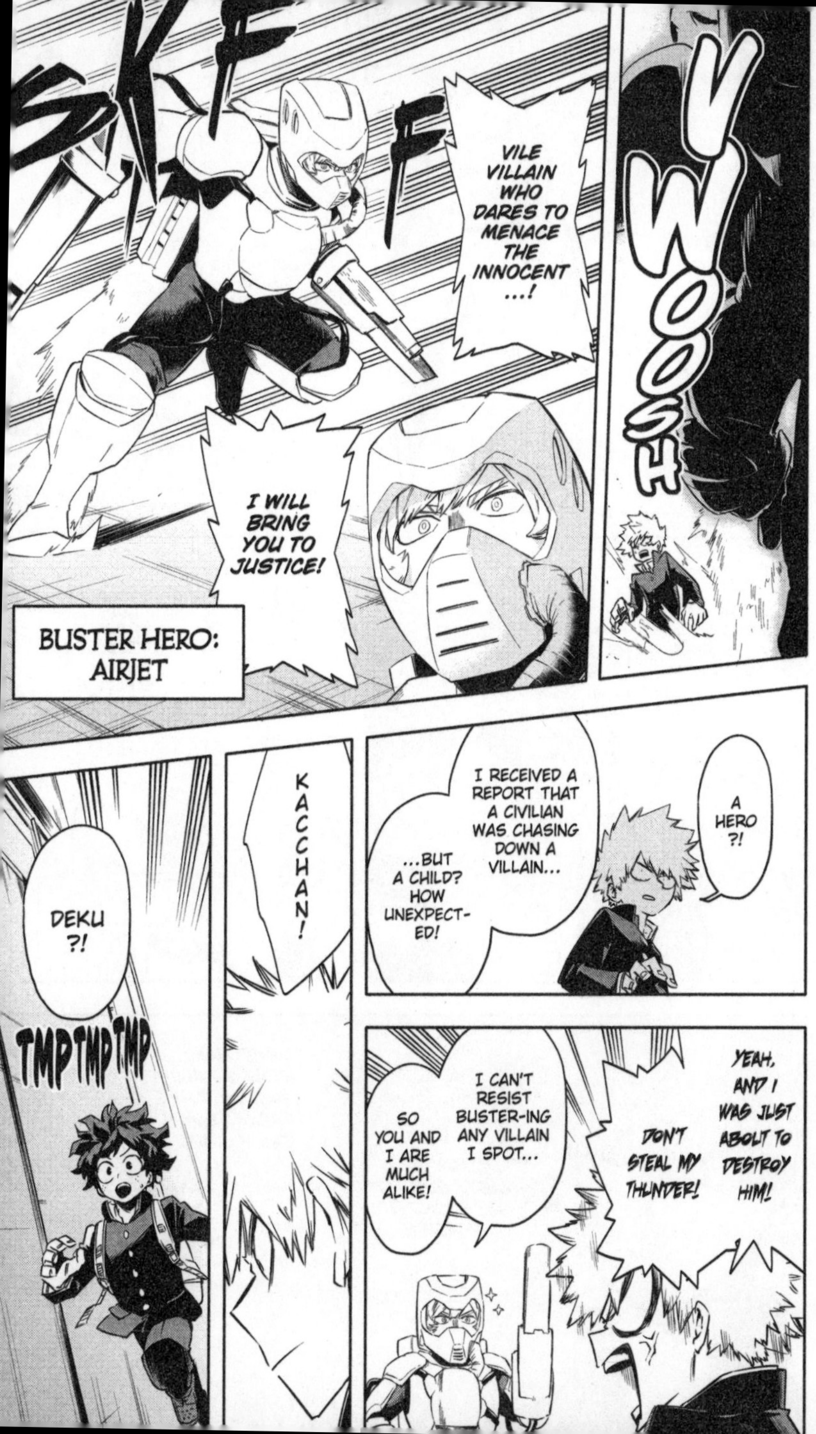
VWOOOSH
SKF F
VILE VILLAIN WHO DARES TO MENACE THE INNOCENT...!
I WILL BRING YOU TO JUSTICE!
BUSTER HERO: AIRJET
A HERO?!
I RECEIVED A REPORT THAT A CIVILIAN WAS CHASING DOWN A VILLAIN...
...BUT A CHILD? HOW UNEXPECT-ED!
YEAH, AND I WAS JUST ABOUT TO DESTROY HIM!
DON'T STEAL MY THUNDER!
I CAN'T RESIST BUSTER-ING ANY VILLAIN I SPOT...
SO YOU AND I ARE MUCH ALIKE!
KACCHAN!
DEKU?!
TMP TMP TMP

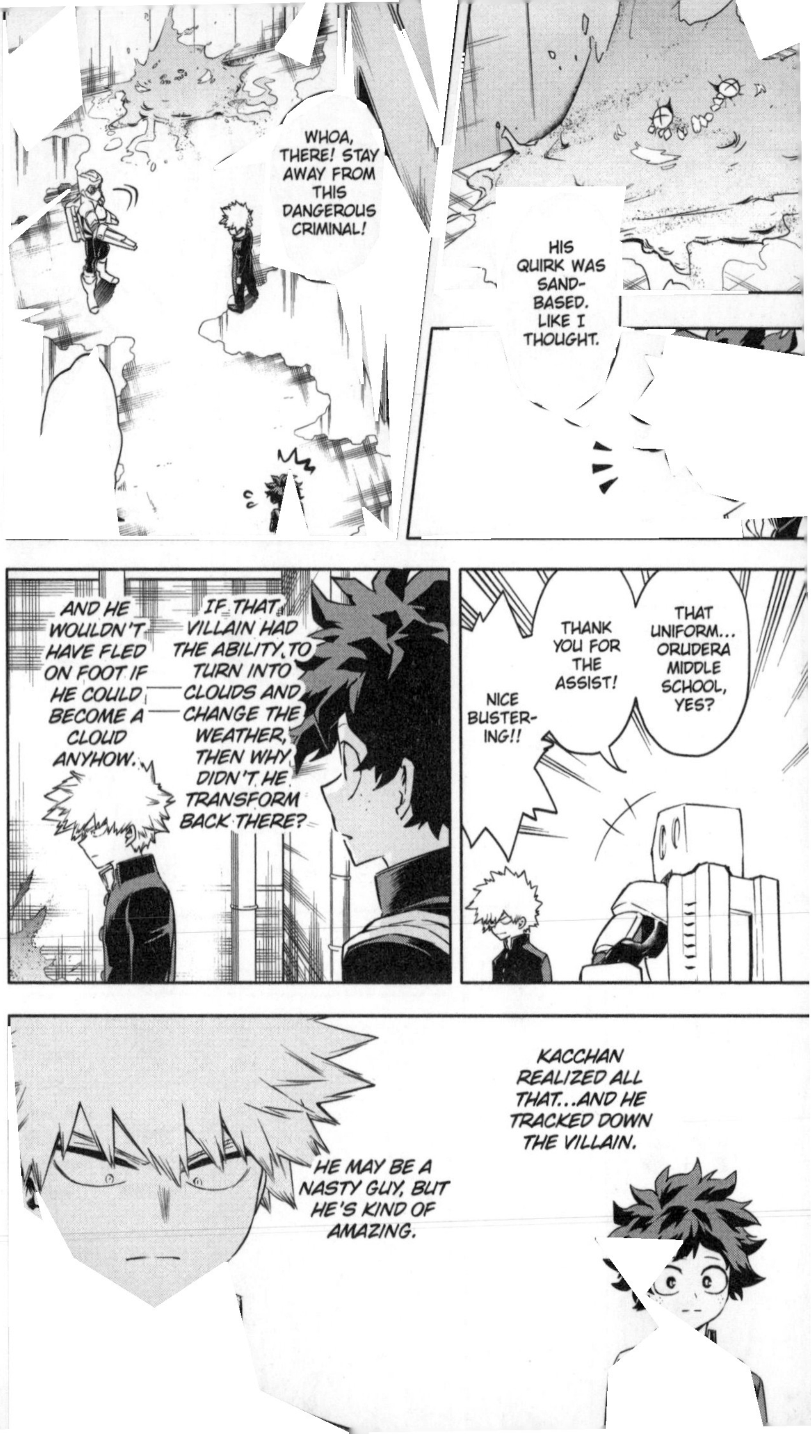
HIS QUIRK WAS SAND-BASED. LIKE I THOUGHT.
WHOA, THERE! STAY AWAY FROM THIS DANGEROUS CRIMINAL!
THAT UNIFORM... ORUDERA MIDDLE SCHOOL, YES?
THANK YOU FOR THE ASSIST!
NICE BUSTER-ING!!
IF THAT VILLAIN HAD THE ABILITY TO TURN INTO CLOUDS AND CHANGE THE WEATHER, THEN WHY DIDN'T HE TRANSFORM BACK THERE?
AND HE WOULDN'T HAVE FLED ON FOOT IF HE COULD BECOME A CLOUD ANYHOW.
KACCHAN REALIZED ALL THAT...AND HE TRACKED DOWN THE VILLAIN.
HE MAY BE A NASTY GUY, BUT HE'S KIND OF AMAZING.

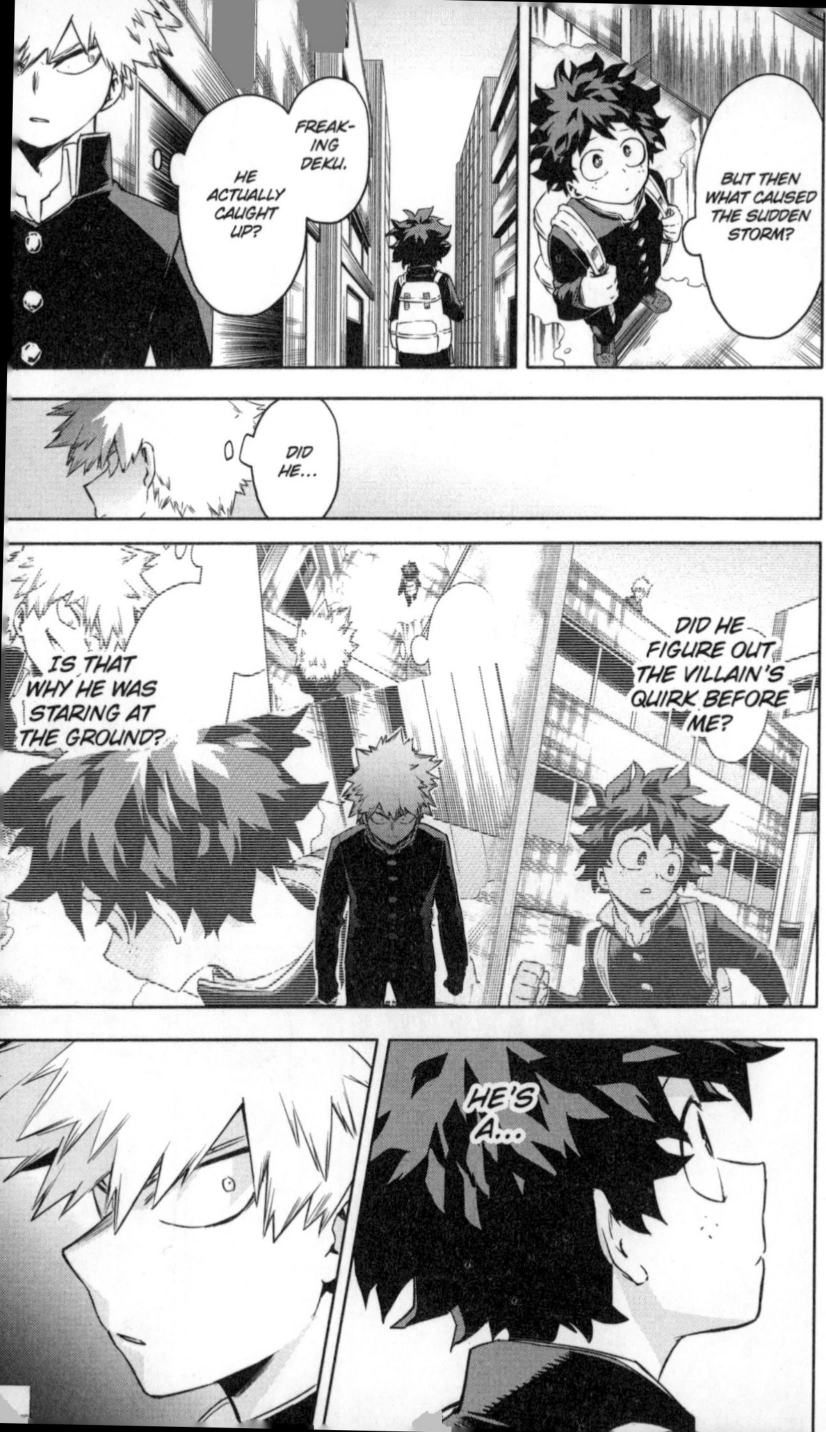
BUT THEN WHAT CAUSED THE SUDDEN STORM?
FREAKING DEKU.
HE ACTUALLY CAUGHT UP?
DID HE...
DID HE FIGURE OUT THE VILLAIN'S QUIRK BEFORE ME?
IS THAT WHY HE WAS STARING AT THE GROUND?
HE'S A...

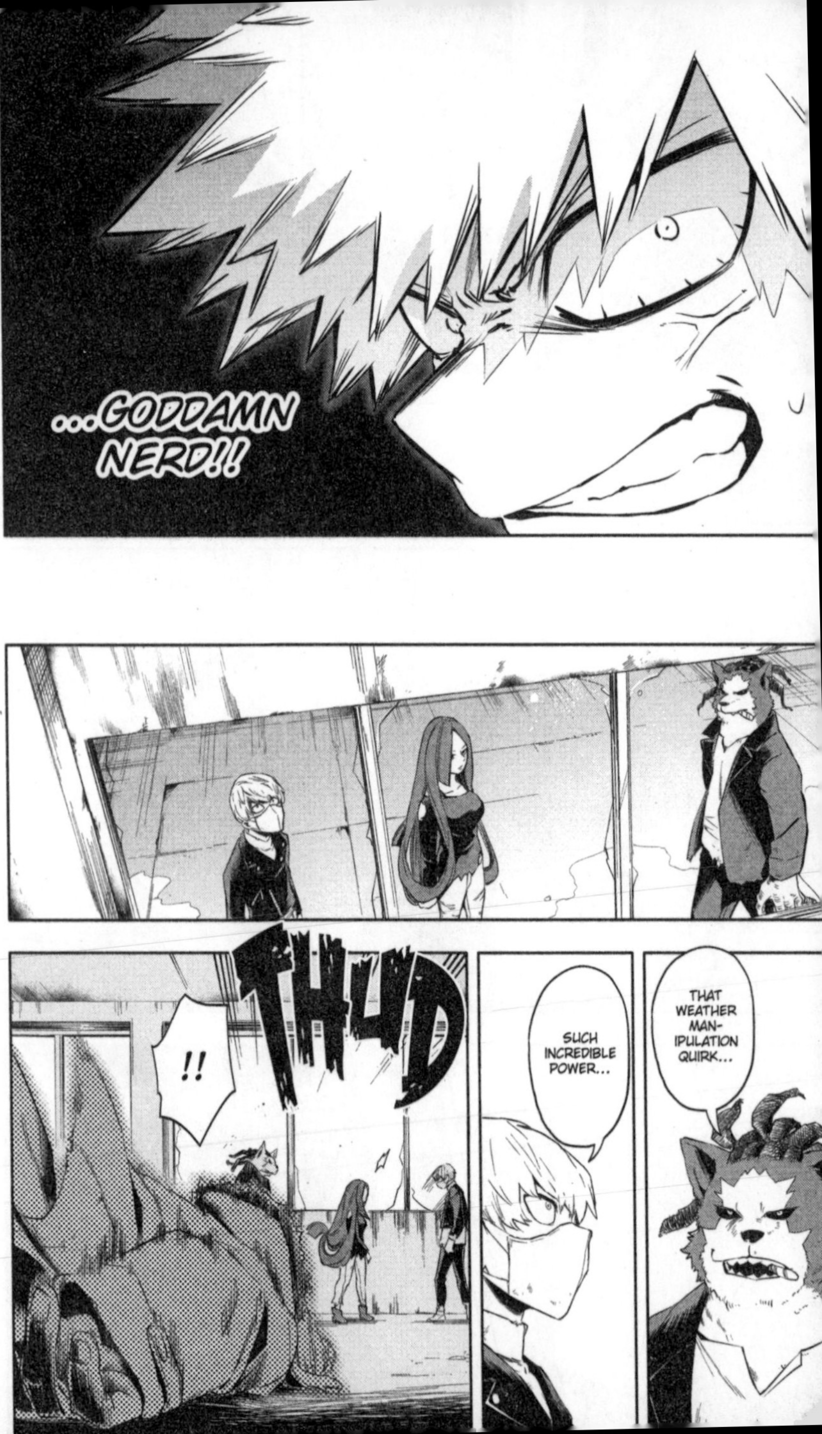
...GODDAMN NERD!!
THAT WEATHER MAN-IPULATION QUIRK...
SUCH INCREDIBLE POWER...
THUD
!!

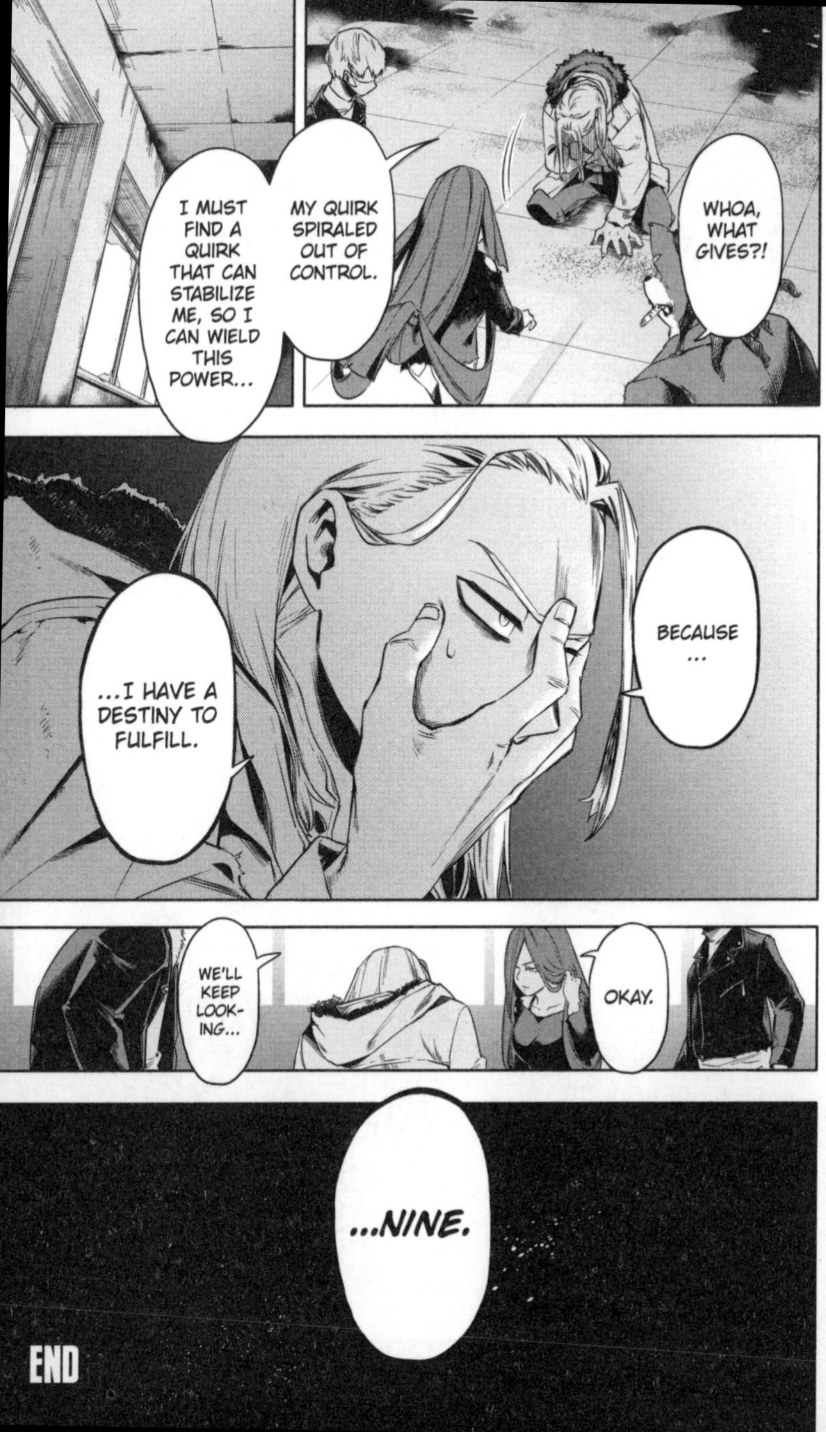
WHOA, WHAT GIVES?!
MY QUIRK SPIRALED OUT OF CONTROL.
I MUST FIND A QUIRK THAT CAN STABILIZE ME, SO I CAN WIELD THIS POWER...
BECAUSE ...
...I HAVE A DESTINY TO FULFILL.
OKAY.
WE'LL KEEP LOOKING...
...NINE.
END

THE SECOND MOVIE!!

"Deku and Bakugo Rising" ran as a two-part one-shot in *Weekly Shonen Jump* to celebrate the release of *My Hero Academia: Heroes Rising*.

Airjet, the Buster Hero, appears in the main story, so go look for him.

And I received another piece of art from Horikoshi Sensei! Thank you so much!

WOO-HOO!!

Message from Kohei Horikoshi

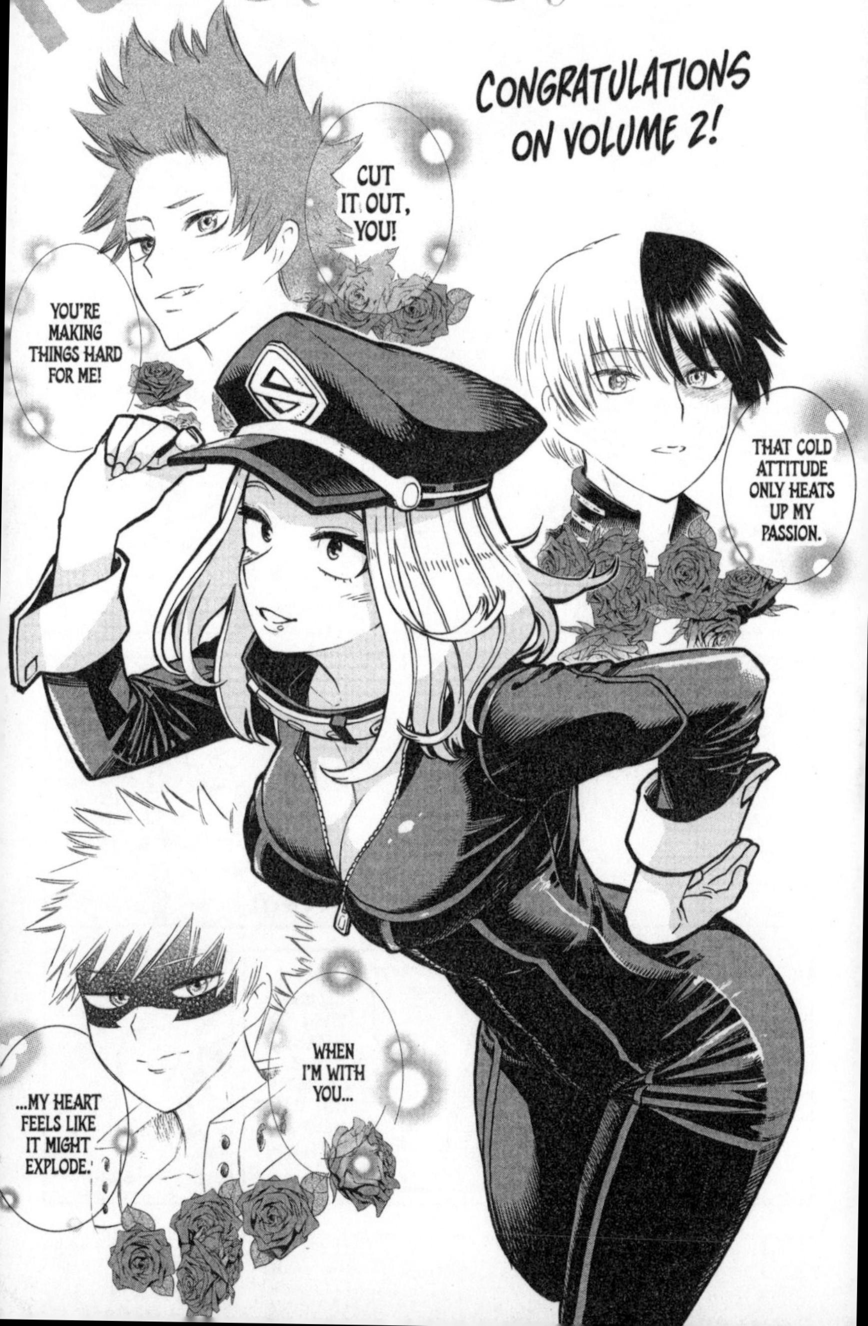
CONGRATULATIONS ON VOLUME 2!
CUT IT OUT, YOU!
YOU'RE MAKING THINGS HARD FOR ME!
THAT COLD ATTITUDE ONLY HEATS UP MY PASSION.
WHEN I'M WITH YOU...
...MY HEART FEELS LIKE IT MIGHT EXPLODE.

THE MAN WHO'S TOO FAST

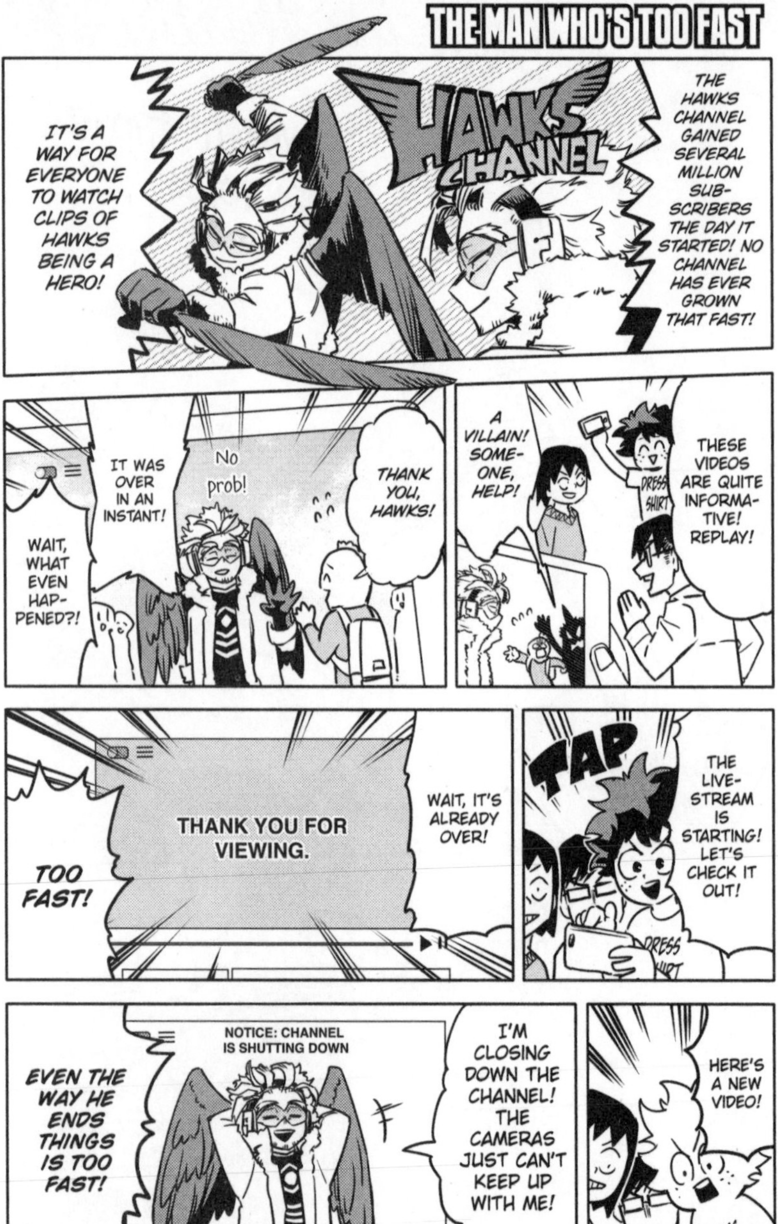
THE HAWKS CHANNEL GAINED SEVERAL MILLION SUBSCRIBERS THE DAY IT STARTED! NO CHANNEL HAS EVER GROWN THAT FAST!
HAWKS CHANNEL
IT'S A WAY FOR EVERYONE TO WATCH CLIPS OF HAWKS BEING A HERO!
THESE VIDEOS ARE QUITE INFORMATIVE! REPLAY!
DRESS SHIRT
A VILLAIN! SOME-ONE, HELP!
THANK YOU, HAWKS!
No prob!
IT WAS OVER IN AN INSTANT!
WAIT, WHAT EVEN HAPPENED?!
THE LIVE-STREAM IS STARTING! LET'S CHECK IT OUT!
TAP
DRESS SHIRT
WAIT, IT'S ALREADY OVER!
THANK YOU FOR VIEWING.
TOO FAST!
HERE'S A NEW VIDEO!
DRESS SHIRT
I'M CLOSING DOWN THE CHANNEL! THE CAMERAS JUST CAN'T KEEP UP WITH ME!
NOTICE: CHANNEL IS SHUTTING DOWN
EVEN THE WAY HE ENDS THINGS IS TOO FAST!

END

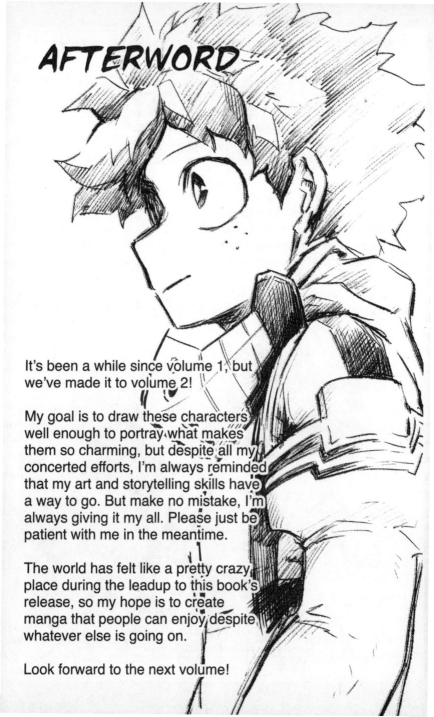

AFTERWORD

It's been a while since volume 1, but we've made it to volume 2!

My goal is to draw these characters well enough to portray what makes them so charming, but despite all my concerted efforts, I'm always reminded that my art and storytelling skills have a way to go. But make no mistake, I'm always giving it my all. Please just be patient with me in the meantime.

The world has felt like a pretty crazy place during the leadup to this book's release, so my hope is to create manga that people can enjoy despite whatever else is going on.

Look forward to the next volume!

YOU'RE READING THE WRONG WAY!

MY HERO ACADEMIA Team-Up Missions

My Hero Academia: Team-Up Missions reads from right to left, starting in the upper-right corner. Japanese is read from right to left, meaning that action, sound effects, and word-balloon order are completely reversed from English order.

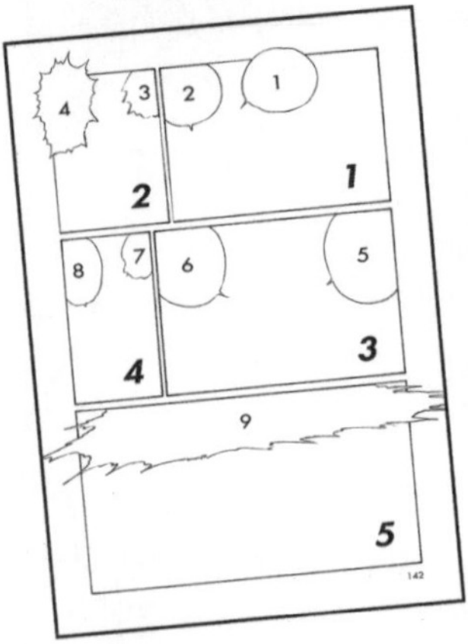
1
2
3
4
1
2
5
6
7
8
3
4
9
5
142

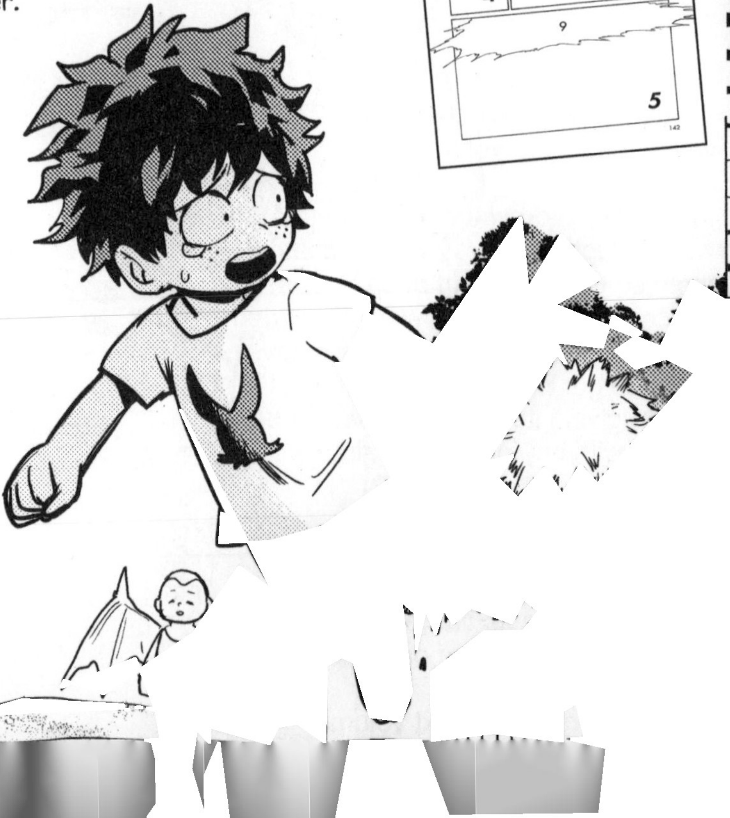